Movements in Chicano Poetry draws lines between three critical points: the poetic traditions of Chicano culture, the critical discourses of postcoloniality and postmodernism, and the production of contemporary Chicano poetry. The issues of cultural nationalism, subjectivity, history, origin, and resistance inform many of the critical and imaginative texts produced by both postcolonial and Chicano writers. As an integral part of the labor force that has driven North American production, Chicanos have expressed through writing the sense of decentered subjectivity and the violence that results from the pursuit of such master narratives as progress and expansion. Chicano texts act as a primary testament to the social and economic disparities made plain by the critical light of postmodernism. Consequently, individuals interested in postcoloniality and postmodernity can learn much from the study of Chicano cultural production.

In this study, Pérez-Torres engages these critical issues in analyses of poems by such writers as Sandra Cisneros, Gary Soto, Gloria Anzaldúa, Ana Castillo, Lorna Dee Cervantes, Corky Gonzales, Jimmy Santiago Baca, Alurista, José Montoya, and Lucha Corpi. He addresses a series of questions important to the study of resistant cultural practices: How do the critical issues raised in the early phase of Chicano poetry manifest themselves today? How do contemporary poets write themselves and their work against their immediate past? How do they write themselves against the disempowering positions offered by hegemonic cultural constructions of Chicano identity? How does the poetry write itself against the grain of history?

Pérez-Torres argues that Chicano poetry, rather than excluding or denying, incorporates and includes. This signals a movement toward a hybridization and crossbreeding on a cultural level that mirrors the racial mestizaje responsible for producing the Chicano people. This book represents part of new inquiry into notions of marginalization and assimilation, into processes of cultural identification and construction, and into the movements of a culture flourishing in a country which itself has been, from the very beginning, a nation consumed with enacting and denying its own hybrid identity.

CAMBRIDGE STUDIES IN AMERICAN LITERATURE AND CULTURE 88

Movements in Chicano Poetry

CAMBRIDGE STUDIES IN AMERICAN LITERATURE AND CULTURE

Books in the Series

87. Rita Barnard, *The Great Depression and the Culture of Abundance*
86. Kenneth Asher, *T. S. Eliot and Ideology*
85. Robert Milder, *Reimagining Thoreau*
84. Blanche H. Gelfant, *Literary Reckonings: A Cross-Cultural Triptych*
83. Robert Tilton, *The Pocahontas Narrative in Antebellum America*
82. Joan Burbick, *The Language of Health and the Culture of Nationalism in Nineteenth Century America*
81. Rena Fraden, *Blueprints for a Black Federal Theatre, 1935–1939*
80. Ed Folsom, *Walt Whitman's Native Representations*
79. Alan Filreis, *Modernism from Right to Left*
78. Michael E. Staub, *Voices of Persuasion: The Politics of Representation in 1930s America*
77. Katherine Kearns, *Robert Frost and a Poetics of Appetite*
76. Peter Halter, *The Revolution in the Visual Arts and the Poetry of William Carlos Williams*
75. Barry Ahearn, *William Carlos Williams and Alterity: The Early Poetry*
74. Linda A. Kinnahan, *Poetics of the Feminine: Authority and Literary Tradition in William Carlos Williams, Mina Loy, Denise Levertov, and Kathleen Fraser*
73. Bernard Rosenthal, *Salem Story: Reading the Witch Trials of 1692*
72. Jon Lance Bacon, *Flannery O'Connor and Cold War Culture*
71. Nathaniel Mackey, *Discrepant Engagement: Dissonance, Cross-Culturality and Experimental Writ*
70. David M. Robinson, *Emerson and the Conduct of Life*
69. Cary Wolfe, *The Limits of American Literary Ideology in Pound and Emerson*
68. Andrew Levy, *The Culture and Commerce of the American Short Story*
67. Stephen Fredman, *The Grounding of American Poetry: Charles Olson and the Emersonian Traditi*
66. David Wyatt, *Out of the Sixties: Storytelling and the Vietnam Generation*

Continued on pages following the Index

MOVEMENTS IN CHICANO POETRY

Against Myths, Against Margins

RAFAEL PÉREZ-TORRES
University of California, Santa Barbara

Published by the Press Syndicate of the University of Cambridge
The Pitt Building, Trumpington Street, Cambridge CB2 1RP
40 West 20th Street, New York, NY 10011–4211, USA
10 Stamford Road, Oakleigh, Melbourne 3166, Australia

First published 1995

Library of Congress Cataloging-in-Publication Data

Pérez-Torres, Rafael.

Movements in Chicano poetry / [Rafael Pérez-Torres].

p. cm. – (Cambridge studies in American literature and culture : 88)

Includes index.

ISBN 0–521–47019–6. – ISBN 0–521–47803–0 (pbk.)

1. American poetry – Mexican American authors – History and criticism. 2. Mexican Americans – Intellectual life. 3. Mexican Americans in literature. I. Title. II. Series
PS153.M4T67 1995
811.009′86872 – dc20 94–22380
CIP

A catalogue record for this book is available from the British Library.

ISBN 0-521-47019-6 hardback
ISBN 0-521-47803-0 paperback

Transferred to digital printing 2002

This book is dedicated
to Sergio and Arturo
and the 40 million more

Contents

Acknowledgments

OBVIOUSLY, THERE ARE MANY PEOPLE to whom I owe a great deal, and some to whom I owe everything. The following can do little but reveal how, in naming some, I leave absent so many.

My love and thanks go to long-time friends Deborah Haley and Tso-Yee Fan in whose home this project came to completion. Thanks as well are due my colleagues and friends in Madison, Wisconsin, whose emotional support has been generous and overwhelming. Ray Harris, Aline Fairweather, Cece Ford, Jane Zuengler, Severino Albequerque, Mary Layoun, and Kent Harris offered unselfishly their love and support and I am privileged to call them friends. Nellie Y. McKay agreed to act as my mentor when this project began. In that capacity, I thank her. For being, in addition, a friend of the heart on whom I know I can always rely, I count my blessings. Thanks also to all those other good friends and dear colleagues whose warmth and support got me through those very cold midwest winters. In particular, I am grateful to Larry Scanlon, Gordon Hutner, Ron Rodano, Rubén Medina, and Dale Bauer for being good and considerate friends as well as very astute critics. Their sound advice has benefited me numerous times. More importantly, their concern and kindness demonstrates to me what genuine collegiality is.

I am indebted to the University of Wisconsin System Institute on Race and Ethnicity which offered its very tangible support during the Spring semesters of 1991 and 1992. This allowed me to research and begin writing the present study.

My colleagues at the University of Pennsylvania deserve thanks for expanding my intellectual horizons and giving me the imaginative space to continue this project. Houston Baker, Herman Beavers, Peter Stallybrass, and Alan Filreis have been wonderful colleagues. Especially, I offer thanks to Inés Salazar, who has become a good and trusted friend. On the other coast, my colleagues in the Department of Chicano Studies at UC Santa Barbara have offered nothing but encouragement and support. I look forward to a long and productive relationship. My sincere appreciation goes as well to the anonymous reader at Cambridge University Press who offered such engaged and generous commentary. The final chapter owes much to the provocative suggestions made by my best reader.

I can only offer a wholly inadequate sense of gratitude and love to my families in both Northern and Southern California. I especially thank my beloved mother and father from whom, through it all, all love and encouragement flow. They, my sister, and my grandmother have shown me that to survive with grace is a form of triumph. This book in a small way indicates how proud I am of them.

Above all else: to the person who has borne it all, my companion, my heart, Beth Marchant, my love.

1

Introduction: Movements in a "Minority" Literature

The fifth Sun, its sign 4-Movement, is called the Sun of Movement because it moves and follows its path.

– Leyenda de los Soles

THE SHIFTS AND RUPTURES of cultural production inevitably make any schematic mapping of culture a quixotic venture. This book is no exception. Ours are times suspicious of metanarrative and totalization. So to undertake a project tracing movements in Chicano poetry might appear futile. To suggest that this sketch is an attempt to map a "minority" literature within an atlas of "American" culture – as opposed to situating it in its margins or appendices – could seem foolhardy. And to focus critical attention on a realm of literary production as implicated in history and politics as is Chicano poetry might, in a notoriously conservative American society, seem like plunging into a swiftly moving river headed for the falls.

The present project does not attempt anything as ambitious as sketching out the landscape of contemporary Chicano poetry. The motivation for this book comes simply from the enthusiasm (and occasional disappointment) I have felt in reading across various texts that comprise the body of Chicano creative and critical literature. Although the quality and interest of these various texts are perforce uneven (what discourse isn't?), their significance as a resistant "minority" critical practice is undeniable. What emerges most clearly from these texts is the knowledge that our cultural practices have consistently challenged and problematized other critical practices, be they the inscription of the literary canon or the projection of feminist criticism. They also reveal the truth behind the argument that those prophets of doom who so bewail the end of literature fail to look beyond mainstream Euramerican literary products.[1]

It may be true that there are no literary tricks yet to pull, that it has all been done before, that literature is a dying art, that our postliterate age has destroyed the vitality and viability of a literary project. Maybe all that remains for multicultural writers – as the last group to wander the ruins of the literary museum – is to go about picking up the shards and fragments scattered across a postmodern cultural junkyard, reusing and recycling discarded forms, genres, and styles. Or perhaps something more vital, more enriching, more empowering unfolds in the interstices and liminal spaces of multicultural literary production.

Through the Gaps, across a Bridge

Certainly the proponents and producers of Chicano literature understand it as something more than just another turn of the cultural commodity wheel. Sympathetic readers who have devoted attention to the literature find in it something urgent and pertinent to the communities about which and for which it is written. At times these readers have produced studies highlighting the diversity and deficiency of other critical terrains: feminism, canon construction, national definitions, political engagement. At other times, Chicano critical works highlight the uneven terrain of their own practices in addition to those of other critical projects. The struggle in the late 1960s and 1970s with the very term "Chicano" – the desire to trace a line of descent from pre-Cortesian indigenous cultures, the belief in a return to origins and a homeland, the reclamation of voice and subjectivity – came to write some of us in and others of us out of a name. Where do the concerns of Chicanas fit? How is sexuality to be a part of our cultural identity? Although many of us are bilingual, many of us are solely English speakers; does language remain a marker of the Chicano/a? Besides gravitating toward a single language, more and more of us – especially the college-educated – move toward financial privilege. What role can the economically prosperous play within the terrain we demarcate "Chicano"?

The power and dynamism of Chicano cultural creation manifests itself in the turns and shifts it takes in addressing these and other difficult issues. This book traces a few of these issues as they help propel the highly diverse movements of Chicano poetry. It also seeks to foreground those points at which Chicano cultural currents cross with global and national concerns.

This move mirrors the one undertaken by a number of critical studies involving Chicano literature.[2] For too long Chicano cultural products have been treated as excrescences on "American" culture, poorer and more primitive cousins only recently transplanted from the ranchos to the big city. Critics at times talk about Chicano culture as if it were a realm separate from the dominant (hegemonic if you will) concerns of U.S. culture. The present study joins with others in writing across borders.

The primary assumption undergirding this study is that Chicano culture – particularly poetry – moves both through the gaps and across the bridges between numerous cultural sites: the United States, Mexico, Texas, California, the rural, the urban, the folkloric, the postmodern, the popular, the elite, the traditional, the tendentious, the avant-garde. Chicano culture moves against and with these diverse sites. It variously participates in the practices inherent to those sites while positing a critique of those selfsame practices. This complicitous critique (to lift Linda Hutcheon's phrase) emerges from cultural practices adept at transformation and adaptation, from a self-identity that knows itself as simultaneously self and other. This double consciousness (to lift another phrase) allows for a migratory sensibility, the ability to move through numerous realms, becoming a part of without fully submitting to them.

Roger Rouse provides a concrete example of this migratory sensibility. His essay "Mexican Migration and the Social Space of Postmodernism" addresses the practices of a migrant community from Aguililla, Michoacán, taking up residence in Redwood City, California. The Aguilillans, he writes, "see their current lives and future possibilities as involving simultaneous engagements in places associated with markedly different forms of experience. Moreover, the way in which at least some people are preparing their children to operate within a dichotomized setting spanning national borders suggests that current contradictions will not be resolved through a simple process of generational succession" (1990: 14).[3] This type of transnational social organization and personal identification – one based on the simultaneous occupation of two distinct geocultural sites – disrupts received notions of nationalism and cultural identity. The practice Rouse sketches suggests a liminality that may move Chicanos into a different future. Contemporary Chicano poetry responds to this future. Developing in the borderlands of our contemporary postmodern migratory society, this cultural production represents a new means of engagement and understanding, one that suggests the formation of new and more fluid epistemologies.

This is all to say that contemporary critical interest in postcoloniality and postmodernity has much to learn from the study of Chicano cultural production. Not simply trendy theoretical positions grafted onto the Chicano, postmodernism and postcolonialism stake out critical realms that Chicano cultures traverse. Angie Chabram has noted that the function of Chicano literary criticism can no longer be considered in isolation from the problematics of general critical discourse:

> The heightened development of Chicano criticism, together with our growing awareness of its linkages with other critical sectors, requires that this function be dialectically articulated from within the very critical traditions and institutional contexts that are mediating its symbolic readings or interpretations of reality under the impact of determinate social and historical conditions. (1991: 138)

Without apology, postmodernism and postcolonialism thus form the two main critical foci by which this book views Chicano poetry. The issues of cultural nationalism, subjectivity, tradition, self-identity, history, origin, and resistance so pertinent to the concerns of the postcolonial inform a great deal of critical and imaginative Chicano texts. Indeed, El Movimiento Chicano of the 1960s and 1970s was clearly influenced by the great nationalist movements that spurred the articulation of postcolonial discourses following World War II. Chicano culture has also developed through and against the various economic and cultural transformations undergone by the United States since the Mexican–American War. As an integral part of the labor force that has driven North American production, Chicanos, as *los de abajo,* know all too intimately the reality of decentered subjectivity and the violence that results from the pursuit of master narratives – progress, expansion, Manifest Destiny. This is not to say that Chicanos have formed a postmodern culture *avant la lettre*. It is to say that Chicanos have lived and survived (which is a form of triumph over) the disparities made plain by the critical light of postmodernism. U.S. society has much to learn from the discredited forms of knowledge Chicano culture exemplifies. The issues of tradition and heritage – and the role they play in constructing a sense of self – assume within a developing migratory consciousness new and dynamic functions.

Grounding

The present study is not a survey of Chicano poetry or a critical introduction to the literature. It intentionally does not provide an overview of the vast field of Chicano literary production; several books on the market function as excellent introductions for those as yet unfamiliar with this literary terrain.[4] Although it does schematize and sketch several powerful trajectories in Chicano literary discourse – colonialism, nativism, politics, myth, history, language – this book does not attempt to document the various traditions from which contemporary Chicano literature emerges. Nor does it trace the different historical phases of the poetry and their characteristics. That type of periodization has already been undertaken quite successfully by a number of other critics.[5]

Readers seeking a more clearly defined critical project rather than an introduction should turn to the excellent work undertaken by Ramón Saldívar (*Chicano Narrative: The Dialectics of Difference,* 1990) and José David Saldívar (*The Dialectics of Our America*, 1991). Their studies analyze the resistant function of Chicano narrative and its intersection with other world cultures in a postcolonial articulation of non-Eurocentric identity. In this respect, they form nodes with which the present discussion seeks to form a dialogue.[6] Of equal relevance to the present study is Juan Bruce-Novoa's *Chicano Poetry: A Response to Chaos* (1982). Bruce-Novoa's work presents a sustained argument that the "deep-structure" of Chicano poetry works to evoke and counter the chaos of human existence: "The *axis mundi,* threatened by disappearance in the world's real order, is named as Other, as a word whose represented object, its signified, is absent. The Other takes on the poem's body, the language, until its presence is the poem itself as an image" (1982: 6). Therefore both the *axis mundi* as the ontological "center" of human existence and its disappearance are present in the poem.

Although Bruce-Novoa's work represents a type of structural and archetypical analysis from which the present study distances itself, it too seeks to engage Chicano poetry with a clearly defined critical project in sight. Notwithstanding the similarities and differences between that study and this, the terrain of Chicano poetry has so changed in the decade since Bruce-Novoa's work appeared that, for example, the last poet Bruce-Novoa studies, Gary Soto, has published over ten collections of poetry and prose since the publication of *Chicano Poetry.* And whereas Bruce-Novoa's book treats the work of one Chicana poet – Bernice Zamora's *Restless Serpents,* published in 1976 – the flourishing of Chicana poetic expression leads me to examine the work of, among others, Gloria Anzaldúa, Ana Castillo, Lorna Dee Cervantes, Sandra Cisneros, Lucha Corpi, Pat Mora, and Evangelina Vigil-Piñon. All these women have published extensively since 1982. Another book-length critical study worth mentioning here is José Limón's *Mexican Ballads, Chicano Poems* (1992), which argues that the corrido represents the master-poem for Chicano poetics. His text thus works to trace the way contemporary poetry has dealt with its "anxiety of influence" in the face of the heroic corrido. His study focuses on a type of historical continuity. The present text, by contrast, seeks to concentrate on historical rupture.

What follows, then, is a critical interrogation of the contemporary situation of Chicano poetry. Working within the realm of generalization that makes intellectual analysis possible means that I will overlook deserving poets, be blind to certain critical positions, remain oblivious of some perspectives. This is inevitable. I do not claim to present a totalizing vision of the poetic scene in Chicano culture. The poems held up for scrutiny by this study should be considered manifestations of particular strains and tensions within Chicano culture, responding to themes, tones, techniques that for various reasons have come to form part of a specific literary repertoire. In this way, the poems I study form a dialogue with specific issues and texts that comprise a classic Chicano poetics.

By "classic" I mean poetry that evinces a strong narrative or dramatic line – thus suggesting, as Limón points out, connection to the tradition of the corrido that has so strongly influenced the course of Chicano poetic expression; poetry that deals overtly with issues of repression, discrimination, exploitation undertaken by the dominant society against Chicanos; poetry that critiques the effects of racist and ethnocentric ideologies; poetry whose mode of expression often assumes the hitherto silenced voice of Chicano communities. This means that, by and large, the poetry derives from a socioeconomic position of disempowerment (though as recent work by Pat Mora, Gary Soto, Alberto Ríos, and others demonstrates, the thematics of Chicano poetry can also move out of the barrio and into the middle class). Because they seek to give voice to historically silenced voices, the texts often employ bilingual or interlingual modes of expression. Because they emerge from a population whose forms of knowledge and culture have historically been discredited by Euramerican (the term often used is "Anglo") society, the texts foreground issues of identity formation. They valorize forms of Mexican and Chicano cultural expression as a way of advancing a unique sense of identity distinct from other ethnic or racial groups, most especially from the dominant Euramerican.

Classic Chicano poetry thus responds to a literary heritage it both draws upon and constructs, it employs and deploys a variety of vernacular expressions, and it affirms indigenous cultural elements as a residual culture that helps form an emergent culture. In this study, I examine the dialogue between specific Chicano poetic texts and these classic characteristics under four general areas: Aztlán as an icon that manifests the relationship between Chicano cultural identity and land; figures of dispossession who help form loci around which the strong political interests of Chicano poetry center; a mythic "memory" that connects Chicanos to pre-Cortesian cultures, thus manifesting a form of cultural reconstruction and identity formation; and the code-switching or interlingualism by which Chicano poetry seeks to articulate a third language neither Spanish nor English but other.

The poems I have selected – written primarily in the 1980s but going back to the inception of contemporary Chicano poetry in the 1960s and coming up to the early 1990s – help establish and engage with classic Chicano poetry. The multiplicitous expressions of Chicano poetry are not limited to the various forms and themes I explore in this study. The love poetry, the lyric poems, the experimental texts, the vast and various forms of Chicano poetic expression inevitably and fruitfully exceed the scope of this limited study.

By using the term classic I mean to avoid entirely the issue of "authenticity" – a bankrupt notion when it comes to defining a people and a culture. Notions of authenticity are misguided. There are no poems that are more or less Chicano, none that manifest a truer Chicano expression than others. For a poem to be studied in the pages that follow, it need only form a dialogue with issues pertinent to Chicano cultural identity. In part, this criterion implies that the poetry is best read through a historical lens. The development of a classic poetry, the rejection of authenticity, leads to questions that focus most sharply on the politics of interpretation. Whom has the poetry sought to empower? To which audiences does it speak? With which forms of sociohistorical and cultural discourses does it engage?

The marvelous Chicano scholarship undertaken since the 1950s has sought to answer these questions. It has brought to light the varying influences and trajectories helping to shape our conceptions of Chicano poetry. As a critic, I owe a great debt to this body of work. Rather than seek to supercede this knowledge, the present study is undertaken in the spirit of collaboration. The goal ultimately is to help construct a genealogy of Chicano poetry. In so doing, I seek to answer a series of questions: How do the critical issues raised in the early phase of Chicano poetry manifest themselves today? How do contemporary poets write themselves and their work against their immediate past? How do they write themselves against the disempowering and victimizing positions offered by hegemonic cultural constructions of Chicano identity? How does the poetry write itself against the grain of history?

By using the term "against" I mean not simply a counterposition but a juxtaposition as well. As I examine the dialogue among the poems that follow, I seek to avoid a discourse of progress or teleology. Chicano poetry has not been following a trajectory, an endless revolution against itself in order to modernize and advance. The ideology behind such assumptions of endless progress contradicts the engagement with tradition and history with which so many Chicano poems deal. This poetry does not turn away from its past. On the contrary – and this will become clearer as the discussion proceeds – it reentrenches itself in history, scrutinizes history, reenvisions, and – finally – rewrites history. So the subtitle of this study, *Against Myths, Against Margins,* does not mean to imply that Chicano poetry turns against or renounces the role of myth or the role of marginalization in the production of culture. Rather than excluding or denying, I argue, Chicano poetry incorporates and includes. This signals a movement toward mestizaje, toward a hybridization and crossbreeding on a cultural level that reflects the racial mestizaje which has produced the Chicano people.

Postcoloniality

Counterpoised and juxtaposed, Chicano poetry emerges from historical conditions that continually inflect its production. The consciousness of dispossession and the fact of displacement inform the construction of a cultural identity. Be it a result of the dispossessions marked by "1848" and the expansionist practices of an imperial United States during the Mexican–American War, or of the displacements caused by continued immigration and economic exploitation, Chicano cultural identity emerges from a keen historical consciousness.

Chicano literary criticism forms part of a contemporary strategy toward self-definition and self-determination – sparked first and foremost by the Delano grape strike of 1965 – that has sought dialogue with other affirmations of a Chicano self on political, economic, and social levels. El Movimiento – the activism in the sixties and seventies calling for self-determination and self-identification – was marked by a sense of purpose that stood behind the intellectual, political, cultural, and social endeavors of Chicanos. This struggle for self-articulation forms a legacy to which anyone currently writing about Chicano literature owes a great deal. At the same time, acknowledging a debt, it is imperative that contemporary critics examine the movements of El Movimiento as they reveal the discontinuities, tensions, and disjunctures evident in the construction of cultural identity. These ruptures reveal the difficult position marked by the term "Chicano." The term, after all, emerges from an extraordinarily violent and exploitative history.

In part, the difficulties encountered by Chicano cultural articulation center on the impossible "minority" position Chicanos are forced to assume. The model of internal colonialism is sometimes used to discuss the nature of this position. Like postcolonial peoples throughout the (Third) world, the development of cultural identity involves a number of conflicting desires.

At one point, there exists the need to distinguish oneself from the colonizing society. This involves a reevaluation of traditional cultural forms, a reclamation of a discredited heritage, an affirmation of the unique character of the colonized culture. This can, when productive, empower an entire constituency. At worst, it can result in an unexamined nativism that values without scrutiny those things it takes to be precolonial.[7] Within Chicano cultural formations, the reflexive validation of pre-Cortesian culture and indigenous thought represents a certain type of nativism. At moments, the uncritical (and often reified) reclamation of the Aztec comes dangerously close to being a blithe and uninformed celebration of anything non-Western. At other moments (as with more recent critical and literary production), the deployment of indigenous cultural elements serves as a part of a larger strategy I characterize as counterdiscursive.

The tension between the precolonial and the colonial forms the postcolonial space that affords a critical lens by which to understand the production of Chicano cultural identity. Chapter 2 thus examines the mapping of literary critical practices overlayed by a grid of postcolonial theory, tracing several strong currents that run through Chicano literary discourse. Although the move to define the literature represents an empowering act of agency and self-identification, it also leads to an inadvertent erasure of difference within the term Chicano. The discontinuities and dislocations from which Chicano culture emerges become reinscribed in the very term. Thus develops a type of cultural and literary naming that leaves some nameless. In short, the desire to establish a Chicano identity at its most destructive can delimit the word, create borders, erase differences, and replicate some of the discursive violence against which the establishment of a Chicano cultural discourse speaks.

The movements toward an affirmation of identity – especially during the heady days of the Movement – are inflected by a perception of culture as a privileged site where universal or archetypical configurations emerge. Thus some early literary criticism forms an essentializing discourse that must be reexamined and critiqued. This universalization can also be understood in light of the violence committed against Chicano cultural identity. Even now, in times that celebrate multicultural difference, the specificity of Chicano identity as a "minority" identity washes away difference in the uncritical and ultimately reified affirmation of alterity. Otherness – vilified or embraced by academic institutional practices – becomes a concept that reinscribes the marginalization of all that is non-Western, non-European, noncanonical.

The move toward essentialization – internally by Chicano literary critics affirming the universal, externally by institutional practices that either denounce or reify cultural difference – stands in contradistinction to those spaces that allow for the greatest critical insight into cultural construction: the historical. As with many postcolonial literatures, Chicano poetry entrenches itself in the significances of history. The interaction between Chicano art and social action forms the horizon against which its literary production can be understood. The art serves to articulate an identity forged from the very discontinuities and tensions – economic, social, political, cultural – that run throughout the terrain of Chicano culture. The poetry thus forges a connection with historical reality. The multiplicity of Chicano poetic creation, the use of linguistic code-switching, the incorporation and transformation of various genres and forms of expression, all indicate the fluidity and variety of that history. It has led to a highly textured and diverse cultural landscape.

Although literary criticism champions "classic" Chicano poetry as a resistant practice, the specificity of this resistance is multiplicitous. From one perspective, the poetry promises a form of teleology that allows insight into the "heart" of a living eternal reality. The spirituality of the Indio forms an opposition to the sterility and violence of the Euramerican alienated present. From a slightly different perspective, the poetry forms a healing or salving remedy to the alienation and fragmentation of Chicano subjectivity by offering affirmative images of an identity descended from indigenous ancestors. The poetry also serves an instrumental function, attacking ideological positions in order to enable political criticism and action. The motivation in all these cases is to work toward spiritual and political agency.

The ruptures inherent in the term Chicano make themselves manifest in the relationship between that term and the uses of land. The dispossession that informs Chicano cultural identity crystallizes in the notion of "Aztlán" as the name of the legendary Mexica homeland. The displacements evinced by "1848" and immigration are counteracted by a claim to possession and entitlement made by "El Plan Espiritual de Aztlán" in 1969. Chapter 3 opens by scrutinizing the development and uses of the term Aztlán, from its inception as a nationalistic strategy of reclamation to its reification by Chicano literary production. In this respect, the articulation of cultural identity resonates with the postcolonial interest in national identity. However, the singular contrast between postcolonial strategies and Chicano cultural identification centers on the uses of land. Although there have been movements within Chicano projects of affirmation that reflect a quintessential nationalism – Reies Tijerina and the Alianza Federal de Mercedes primary among them – the more recent movements toward cultural identification seldom include a claim of national sovereignty.[8]

Land nevertheless proves a compelling issue around which Chicano cultural identity centers. The poetry studied in this chapter affirms past claims to land as a means of concretizing a condemnation of repressive living conditions in the present. Rodolfo Gonzales's *Yo Soy Joaquín* represents a classic example of a turn toward cultural empowerment through an examination of the Chicano's relationship to and reclamation of land. At the time of *Joaquín's* composition in 1967, "Aztlán" had not yet entered our cultural vocabularies. Nevertheless the central tensions that led to Aztlán present themselves in the poem: issues of self-determination, the desire for cultural empowerment, a call to popular political action, an insistence upon geographic reclamation. These claims for land within the United States are informed by the poetic evocation of a link to land in Mexico. The Mexican Revolution once resolved the issue of land for the Mexican laborer – he who works the land already stakes some claim to it. Mexico and its history thus forms a matrix of cultural identification. Consequently, within the poem, the United States is never home, only a menace from which Joaquín recoils in a reaffirmation of his real home – Mexico.

The grandeur and sweeping vision offered by *Joaquín* implies a type of heroism and larger-than-life quality that the political movements of the 1960s seemed to feed. By the mid-eighties, Chicano poetry configures the significance of land in a very different way. Although still making claims to the land as a part of the Chicano heritage, the emphasis is no longer on mass empowerment. The process of affirmation enacted by Rodolfo Gonzales's poem occurs, for example, in Jimmy Santiago Baca's poetry on a personal level. This in part represents a retreat from mass political movement, a reflection of the political situation during the Age of Reagan. It also represents a recognition of heritage and history more complex than that offered by *Joaquín*. Rather than a singular trajectory leading directly from pre-Cortesian civilization through Mexican nationalism to contemporary struggle, history in Baca's poetry is a varied terrain marked by a heterogeneity, a mosaic of violence and beauty that crystallizes in the New Mexican land of the Black Mesa. The Black Mesa forms a contemporary geography evocative of Aztlán. Lorna Dee Cervantes and Ana Castillo offer equally complex visions of home and land characterized by instability. Aztlán becomes, in opposition to the portrait suggested by Gonzales's poem, a site fully marked by a history that is not fully empowering. These later poets, including Gloria Anzaldúa, create an image of Aztlán that is no longer homeland. Instead, it becomes the borderlands between various terrains. And it is this notion of the borderlands that has captured the contemporary Chicano imagination.

Like the land surrounding the border between the United States and

Mexico, the borderlands are a terrain in which the ramifications of history make themselves plainly and painfully manifest. The borderlands make history present. This history is one in which power proliferates unequally, in which people must flee economic oppression, in which military power wielded by a powerful industrial giant is used to keep out economically desperate workers. The border as a naked manifestation of power stimulates an imaginative response in which the borderlands emblematize the condition of Chicano existence. The discontinuities of history and power – the tensions, contradictions, hatred, and violence as well as resistance and affirmation of self in the face of that violence – mark the borderlands.

Not a homeland, not a perpetuation of origin, the borderlands allude to an illimitable terrain marked by dreams and disruptions, marked by history and the hope of what history can be. The borderlands represent the multiplicity and dynamism of Chicano experiences and cultures. They form a terrain in which Mexicans, Chicanos, and mestizos live among the various worlds comprising their cultural and political landscapes: Euramerican, Mexican, pre-Cortesian, indigenous, barrio, suburb, city, country, field, kitchen, boardroom, and stockroom. Viewing the borderlands as an interstitial site suggests a type of liminality. The betweenness leads to a becoming, a sense of cultural and personal identity that highlights flux and fluidity while connected by a strong memory of (a discredited) history and (a devalued) heritage. The articulation of Chicano poetry is one embodiment of this becoming. Drawing on the various heritages and histories that comprise the Chicano space, the poetry points toward what can and should be. The borderlands become a region in which possibilities and potentialities abound for new subject formations, new cultural formations, new political formations.

From the beginning, Chicano poetry has been intimately linked to the political struggles of the Chicano people. The corridos and other forms of folk poetry (as Américo Paredes has so brilliantly shown) represent a type of political engagement, a response by the imagination to the repression and injustice felt on the sociopolitical level. During the Chicano Movement of the 1960s and 1970s, poetry articulated discontent, expressed a desire for solidarity, argued that a revolutionary project was underway. The poetry – like *Yo Soy Joaquín,* which was written, after all, as an organizing tool – signaled that change was imminent. The conditions of marginality and exploitation were being transformed into something powerful and emancipating, and the poetry stood as a clarion call, a prophecy, a catalyst of change. Other Movement poetry served to celebrate the events and accomplishments of El Movimiento. These early poems – some no more than aggressive propaganda, others much more interesting as the expression of genuine longing – inform, celebrate, exhort national and global political change.

This sense of fervor and political engagement subsides as the Movimiento dissolves through the late 1970s into the 1980s. Later poetry privileges a type of local or molecular political change that shifts from the momentous clarion calls of the 1960s. Delimited by repressive, exploitative, and discriminatory social forces, segments of the Chicano population employ strategies for empowerment and resistance at personal and interpersonal levels. A section of Chapter 4 examines how Chicano politics – politics along the borderlands – function at a local rather than global level. In part, influenced by the activist work of Saul Alinsky, local Chicano politics express a need for coalitional politics. The grassroots populism of one strain of Euramerican labor movements crosses with currents of liberation theology and peasant resistance deriving from Mexican and other Latin American influences. Thus the neighborhood activist groups, the labor organizers in the maquiladoras, the church-based community groups all represent a type of micropolitical activity quite distinct from the revolutionary rhetoric of the Movement.

On a poetic level, Chicano imaginative response has been to examine the ways fragmented political practices influence specific localities: communities, families, individuals. In this respect, recent Chicano poetry engaged with social issues revives the cliché that the personal is political. This insight of course resonates with the political positions of the feminist movements (both in the United States and Latin America) that influenced the course of Chicana self-identification. The political plays itself out in localities that help form a configuration of micropolitics, often crystallizing around sexual and gender issues, worker's rights and environmental issues, worker safety and immigration laws. The poetry evokes political discourses crossed at the site of the individual. Subjectivity becomes the locus at which numerous discourses of power meet. Gone are the sweeping tableaux of history and politics evoked by much Movement poetry. The later poetic work articulates on a personal level the disenfranchisement of and potential hope available to members of a dispossessed margin.

Specifically, Chapter 4 explores the development of three figures of dispossession whose presence in the various movements of Chicano poetry has marked a transforming political landscape. The migrant, the pinto, and the pachuco represent the nexus between political discourse and identity formation. These three figures – the economic nomad as marginal laborer, the prisoner as unwilling ward of the state, the cultural rebel as social misfit –

crystallize the issues surrounding the effects of dominant political discourses. Recent Chicano poetry evokes these figures less as stock characters used to draw quick critiques of dominant society than as complex and varied subjects whose positions in society reveal tensions and ruptures in Chicano culture itself. They become nodes at which the divergent, contradictory, and contesting discourses of power – institutional, subversive, counterdiscursive, rebellious, resourceful – running through the Chicano landscape come together. In this respect, these figures stand as embodiments of an identity, imagined through the poetic, that draw together the various strands comprising the postcolonial condition of U.S. minority populations.

Postmodernity

The second half of this book crosses the study of Chicano cultural and poetic practices with discussions of the postmodern as a characterization of the contemporary cultural scene. Chapter 5 scrutinizes the relationship between Chicano literary criticism as a manifestation of multiculturalism and current debates about postmodernism. Postmodernism names the cultural condition that forms a dialogic relationship with postmodernity, analogous to the interaction between modernism and modernity. I argue that postmodernism marks the end of teleological thinking in the secular sphere. The ideas of Project and Progress give way to positions of locality and negotiation, issues we have seen inform the discussion of contemporary Chicano politics. The equalizing and flattening effect described as "collapse" within postmodern discourses reflects a dehierarchizing impulse. But this impulse cannot be celebrated as a fully liberating political practice.

Postmodernism, as the cultural condition in and against which we in the United States act, moves in two ways. Following the models of Hal Foster and Andreas Huyssen, I argue that there are two forms of postmodernism: one of reaction and one of resistance. A reactionary postmodernism is characterized by an antimodern position that reifies traditions as an antidote to the alienation wrought by the modern era. This reactionary position can be exploited by politicians and political movements seeking to reinscribe social control; Ronald Reagan's "Morning in America," Dan Quayle's "Family Values," and George Bush's "Thousand Points of Light" provide recent examples. A resistant postmodernism, by contrast, "seeks to question rather than exploit cultural codes, to explore rather than conceal social and political affiliations" (Foster 1983: xii).

As there are two divergent postmodernisms, I argue that there are two forms of multiculturalism. One replicates the ideology of the melting pot, foregrounding the equal position of all racial/ethnic groups in the United States. This neotraditional vision of the multicultural erases the unequal distribution of power among diverse constituencies. A resistant multiculturalism – the kind embodied by Chicano literary criticism – foregrounds a basic inequality within the mosaic of multicultural America. From this perspective, the game is to illuminate the discontinuous and contradictory terrain negotiated by those groups who function within different and dissimilar cultures: Euramerican, indigenous, Mexican, colonial Spanish, peasant class, working class, ruling class, native, and others.

The point finally is to highlight "the difference within" postmodernism, to shed light on its discontinuities by focusing on Chicano literary criticism as a part of a larger multicultural field. Discussing the multicultural in relation to the postmodern is not some disingenuous or calculated effort to discuss multicultural concerns in a fashionable register. The concerns of the multicultural and the postmodern are integrally related and, ultimately, mutually dependent. Within the contemporary construction of cultural sites, multiculturalism must strategize against being posited as a civilizational Other or as a margin to dominant U.S. culture and its institutions. For its part, postmodernism and its celebration of alterity must come under scrutiny by "minority" discourses if a historically accurate, accountable, and constructive space is ever to be cleared for this country's cultural margins.

Chapter 6 takes up the uses of mythic memory within Chicano poetic creation as an issue that helps clear marginal space. Mythic memory forms that realm in which myths, legends, folktales resurface in Chicano poetry. "Memory" is a problematic term. I question the acceptance of an unconscious or archetypical memory that, particularly in the 1960s and 1970s, served as a highly influential discourse in the articulation of Chicano cultural identity. Work by Carl Jung – along with Mircea Eliade, Octavio Paz, Carlos Castaneda – set the agenda. The uses of mythic "memory" have been various: as a way of distinguishing Chicano literary production from other forms of literature, as a way of marking the "authentic" identity of particular cultural products, as an evocation of universal "truths." In every case, the use of pre-Cortesian and other indigenous symbology, myths, and legends forms the material of which cultural objects are constructed.

This issue presents a great impediment in grasping the significance of Chicano poetry. An emphasis upon the mythic propels Chicano culture beyond history. If one is to argue – as several critics have done – that its strength is its universality, one runs dangerously close to a type of essentialization that for years has excluded Chicano and other multicultural literature for not meeting a standard of greatness. Nevertheless, several critics of Chicano literature celebrate the use of archetypical elements as central to the moral dynamism and validation of a universal Chicano literature. It is seen as forming one last matrix in which the "truth" of myth can speak. Ironically, this position runs counter to the very strength of Chicano cultural production – its intimate and overt links to history. The entrenchment in history leads to a vexing question: How is a reader – postmodern, alienated, critical, suspicious of mystification, grounded in history – to understand the relationship between contemporary literary production and myth? Can the recuperation of myth, the revivification of spirituality within the space of Chicano literature be taken at face value? Do faith and belief enter into the processes of reception? Although there is no doubt that the use of mythic elements associated with pre-Cortesian cultures has stimulated a great deal of interest in the function of myth, in archetypical criticism, and in mysticism, it is also equally clear that Chicano poetry is involved in a much more complex relationship with myth and legend than simple invocation or recuperation.

This is not to discount the significance of mythic memory. Its presence in Chicano poetry serves to articulate a genuine longing, a movement toward a reclamation of the spirituality missing in the alienated and alienating world of Euramerican society. The evocation of mythic figures manifests a desire to reconnect to a spiritual relationship with the land, with the world, with humankind.

The use of mythic memory in Chicano poetry can also be understood as a tool that helps to construct cultural identity. In this respect, the reclamation of myth proves sympathetic with the strategies of postmodern cultural construction. The use of mythic figures, legends, and so forth, forms a connection to discredited forms of knowledge. This connection is assembled rather than remembered, constructed rather than resurrected. The evocation of pre-Cortesian cultural elements proclaims a pre-European relationship to the New World. Pre-Cortesian elements are thus a strategy of empowerment and entitlement. The claim of entitlement appeared in the 1960s and 1970s from Chicano artists and activists who sought to separate Chicano identity from Euramerican categorization. The process of self-definition differentiates us from the other. In naming the self, Chicano activists and artists reclaim and reform autochthonous cultural elements. The naming of the self leads, however, to an erasure of difference. Consequently, we see such Chicana writers as Ana Castillo and Gloria Anzaldúa reclaiming again, this time from androcentric critics, the right to name. They reformulate pre-Cortesian mythology as a strategy of Chicana affirmation and empowerment. In these respects, the citation of indigenous cultural identities moves Chicano literary production away from the universe of the archetype and back into a world historical arena.

The citation of pre-Cortesian symbology and mythology becomes a strategy implicated in a process of self-identification. This involves the articulation of a subjectivity based upon discredited forms of knowledge, a knowledge drawn from the stories of non-Euramerican culture, which is to say that Chicano identity is forged in sympathy with other postcolonial and antiimperialist projects. The inscription of the premodern into the postmodern also signals a strategy of incorporation akin to a process of pastiche. Chapter 7 explores how this process of incorporation, of mestizaje, makes itself most evident in the linguistic elasticity of poetic expression. Code-switching among Spanish, English, and the vernacular is a common means of expression used by multilingual speakers, a verbal strategy for conveying such information as sociopolitical identity and economic position. This particular speech-act establishes or reinforces social roles, and aids or precludes the construction of bonds and relations. Within the discourse of Chicano aesthetics, it becomes involved in a complex strategy of formal experimentation, political commentary, and empowering representations.

Code-switching within poetic texts is at one level an attempt to represent accurately the culture and economics of specific communities. This writing against the margin is certainly part of a powerful counterdiscourse, an assertion of agency and subjectivity. Beyond this, an aestheticized code-switching forms an interlingualism (as Juan Bruce-Novoa terms it) that points toward a language suspended between English and Spanish. Interlingualism allows for the possibility of a third, "minor" language, which breaks down false binaries like that represented by the choice between English or Spanish. As a mestizaje of linguistic forms, interlingualism resonates on a formal level with some of the dichotomous social conditions through and against which Chicano poetry writes. The poetry employs elements of the premodern and the postmodern, emerges from a community voice yet speaks through the alienated medium of print poetry, and seeks to rewrite history while being fully inscribed by history.

The tensions and complexity of the Chicano poetic field make any breakdown of the issues somewhat artificial. Though some may balk at the attempt to overlay this discussion with the theoretical grids of postcoloniality and postmodernity, these perspectives allow a critical and ultimately fruitful interaction between these theoretical realms and the field of Chicano culture. For readers who may be more interested in textual analyses than in theoretical considerations, it would be fair to note that the book can be read without having to dwell upon Chapter 2 or Chapter 5. For others, who are more drawn to fields of cultural studies, these two chapters represent concerns central to the contemporary development of Chicano culture. Although it maintains its own integrity and emerges from a unique heritage and history, Chicano culture does not exist in isolation. Its terrain, its resources, its methods of expression and articulation are numerous, shifting and changing with vitality. The structure of the present study is but a small attempt to map temporarily the fluidity of Chicano poetic expression.

Literary and critical works that claim the term Chicano set themselves into a field of play whereby "tradition" and "identity" become disputed notions. Critics sympathetic with Chicano causes have used these words as a form of counterdiscourse. They seek to redress decades of imposed silence and marginalization by dominant Euramerican society, which employs terms like "identity" and "tradition" to define Chicano experiences out of existence. Chicano critics, writers, and thinkers respond by valorizing other traditions, identities, languages, aesthetic forms, histories, perceptions. And they call these others "Chicano." This inevitably political act can lead to the formation of a discourse that essentializes the term Chicano, reproduces the discursive violence already perpetrated by Euramerican culture, and reifies Chicano "identity" and "tradition."

What I explore here are ways of situating this process of reification historically, methods for counteracting the reification, and analyses of cultural products that seek to make essentialization impossible. This book owes a great deal to work undertaken by other Others in addition to Chicano scholars, especially Latin American, feminist, postcolonial, and African American critics. Their various projects and theoretical positions are not identical, indeed are different within themselves. None of us is attempting to speak the same language. I believe, however, that we are translating across gaps, speaking to each other. In times that seek to mute differences, the drone of these voices forms a constant – and one hopes nettling – reminder that those on whose back wealth is accumulated will one day have their say.

Notes on Terms and Methods

An indication of the complexity of Chicano expression has to do with the very term Chicano itself. Within a North American context the word implicitly subsumes all identity within the masculine. One attempt to draw attention to the linguistic privileging of gender in the term is to inscribe the dichotomy of exclusion/inclusion into the very phrase, hence the use of "Chicano/a" or "Chicana/o." Throughout the body of this study I alternate between using "Chicano" and "Chicana," "Chicanos" and "Chicanas" as inclusive terms of identity. I use this strategy in order to address the problems of erasure and identification. When I mean to inflect the discussion with gender-specific issues – masculine machismo, feminist self-identification – the context of the discussion should make clear how "Chicano" or "Chicana" is used.

Another problem with terminology: "Mexican-American" and "Chicano" are sometimes taken to be interchangeable. This is true if one ignores the political charge each carries. "Mexican-American" can be taken as either a purely descriptive or fully assimilationist term. The connotations of its use depend on the social situation and geographic location in which the term is used. "Chicano" carries with it both its original pejorative connotations and its politicized reclamation. By and large, within academic institutions, the term "Chicano/a" represents a type of cultural affirmation and critical stance toward dominant Euramerican society. "Chicano" and "Chicana" appear repeatedly in my discussion for precisely this reason.[9] "Mexican-American" appears for rhetorical purposes. The term "Latino/a" indicates all those groups of Spanish-speaking descent who for various economic and political reasons now reside in North rather than Latin America. The term "Hispanic" is a bureaucratic word that has gained currency during the past decade but which many Latinos with a political consciousness reject.

There are a few more terms that bear explaining before proceeding. I use the word "pre-Cortesian" instead of pre-Columbian to describe the native cultures extant in the "New World" before the arrival of European adventurers. The term "pre-Columbian," although more popularly used, seems to me to erase the differences between the varied experiences of European contact among the original nations. Moreover, Columbus was a minor exploiter of the indigenous people when compared to the scale of enslavement, oppression, and genocide initiated by the more bloodthirsty and goldhungry Hernán Cortés.[10]

Cortés and his compatriots encountered a highly complex economic and military empire ruled by the twin city-states Tlatelolco and Tenochtitlan. The inhabitants of these cities – the Tlatelolca and the Tenocha – maintained their own separate identities. Together, they called themselves the Mexica (or more properly the Culhua Mexica). Through political alliance and military subjugation, the Mexica ruled what came to be known throughout the world as the Aztec empire.[11] The language the Mexica employed was Nahuatl, and the culture they enjoyed (to which they owed the Toltecs a good deal) was called Nahua. Throughout the present study, I avoid using the term "Aztec," referring instead to the Nahuatl language, the Nahua culture, or the Mexica people.

Finally, a word or two on methodology. As I have indicated, this study provides a critical theoretical framework upon which to hang some examples of Chicano poetic expression. The text thus oscillates between discussions of theoretical, historical, and social issues and formal, textual explication. This constant oscillation between theory and practice, so to speak, works to articulate one type of critical framework by which contemporary Chicano poetry can be discussed.

The movement among a variety of poems means that much of the biographical material about particular poets that is so interesting can – unfortunately – only occasionally be sketched out in the interest of explication. This study examines the author-function behind these particular poems only insofar as it crosses with other functions under scrutiny: political, institutional, sexual, social. The private lives of the poets are left to themselves. And whatever authorial intentionality may lie behind any of these poems is likewise left alone.

My interest here is how these various poems can be read as parts of a dialogue, a tradition, an ongoing discussion about what the terms Chicano and Chicano poetry can mean. This realm of literary creation – as part of a larger project of cultural identification – is undergoing a continual creation and re-creation that marks it as a highly volatile and energetic realm of aesthetic expression. Whereas a good deal of the contemporary poetic scene in North America has become so enervated that its audience continually becomes smaller and smaller, within the "marginal" realms of Chicana and other multicultural literatures, the import and effect of poetry cannot be easily dismissed. The Chicano and Chicana who take time to think about identity, heritage, and culture soon realize that the stakes are great in the continued process of cultural expression. The words that comprise the poetry of the Chicano are the same words that mark our flesh and our lives. These are also words that separate us, for better and worse, from the systems of exchange enjoyed through entitlement by the dominant socioeconomic and racial/ethnic groups of this country. Whatever gains and losses Chicanas, Latinos, and other multicultural groups in the United States enjoy or suffer, the voices of poets calling for understanding and justice, for the hand of friendship and the coin of compensation will sound and sound.

I

The Postcolonial

2

Four or Five Worlds: Chicano/a Literary Criticism as Postcolonial Discourse

> [We] have in the Negro the embodiment of a past tragic enough to appease the spiritual hunger of even a James; and we have in the oppression of the Negro a shadow athwart our national life dense and heavy enough to satisfy even the gloomy broodings of a Hawthorne. And if Poe were alive, he would not have to invent horror; horror would invent him.
>
> – Richard Wright

BECAUSE "-" IN "MEXICAN-AMERICAN" suggests both a (linguistic) bridge and a (mathematical) absence, it serves as an apt marker for the condition of Chicano literary criticism. This criticism attempts to bridge the discontinuities of its position at "the borderland," to construct – out of a terrain that both is and is not either fully Mexican or fully American – some sense of place and belonging. Chicano literary criticism as a cultural project attempts to forge identity out of rupture. This identity rests on bridges between the Mexican and the American, between Spanish and English, First World and Third World, insider and outsider. Chicano literary criticism bridges the numerous borders placed around the Chicano by dominant discursive practices that separate and erase a continued history of resistance to repression.

It also maps the contours of a culture traced by a history of aggressive expansionism and inner-colonialism (forming a part of a larger and more inclusive atlas with other "Third World" and postcolonial positions). In so doing, it negotiates through a critical process that both replicates and refuses the same segregation, violence, and erasure it has endured. In deciding what is Chicano, the literary criticism (and the project of cultural identification as a whole) delimits and determines while affirming and including. The term Chicano (as opposed to, for example, the term Chicana) attempts to become an all-encompassing word that seeks to contain an identity. Thus the hyphen in "Mexican-American" as a link and a gap is appropriate not just because it marks the absences and ruptures of our history, but because the progress of Chicano literary criticism can lead to a simultaneous sketching and erasing of a cultural terrain. Against these dynamics, Chicano/a literary discourse stands as a form of postcolonial identity formation.

At the Interstices

The concern with tracing and erasing, demarcating "space" in relation to Chicana/o literature, forms a significant strain in Chicano literary criticism. Juan Bruce-Novoa in "The Space of Chicano Literature" argues that Chicano/a literature occupies "the space (not the hyphen) between the two [terms Mexican and American], the intercultural nothing of that space" (1975: 27). Suspended between worlds, Chicana literature forms out of these interstices a cultural practice that expands the interstitial. Bruce-Novoa goes on to footnote the observation, "This space is not a 'gap' as someone has suggested, for a gap suggests that the two elements should come together. I call it a space that should expand and grow, not disappear. We are that space. No gap; not at all" (1975: 41). "Gap" in Bruce-Novoa's conceptualization implies a lack; "space" points toward potential. The "space" of Chicano literature that is not "gap" proves, however, to be indeed marked by gaps just as it is marked by connections. Rupture and connection comprise the two primary characteristics of Chicana literary criticism, a condition resonant with discourses negotiating the colonial (rupture) and pre-colonial (connection) toward an articulation of postcoloniality.

Bruce-Novoa goes on to suggest quite explicitly that Chicano literary criticism (and Chicano cultural production in general) relies on discontinuity and dissimilarity:

> The critic must make every effort to expand the total space of our literature. He can point out fields of experience ignored by the writers, such as the middle class one, long avoided for fear of the vendido label; or the oppression of Chicanos by other Chicanos in the name of cultural, social or political goals; or the Chicana as seen by her [self. . . .] Lastly, he can help create a space of Chicano criticism in which all the theories act as interrelated tensions to in turn create the central sum of Chicano perspectives. The center will be where the opinions can contrast and compare themselves. (1975: 40)

The various constituencies Bruce-Novoa evokes – the middle class, marginal Chicanos, Chicanas – form realms that have begun to find their own space within contemporary Chicano literary configurations. These realms, often overlooked in the initial construction of "the Chicano," find their theoretical correlative in the interrelated tensions that form "the central sum of Chicano perspectives," where opinions contrast and compare themselves. Implicit in Bruce-Novoa's argument: Chicano experiences are formed out of difference. His work thus opens the space of Chicano literature by emphasizing not a return to origin or authenticity as a dominant trope, but difference. This opening to difference, however, serves primarily to position Chicana literature in a universal relation to all world literature. The rule by which one measures Chicano cultural production must be the same, Bruce-Novoa's argument implies, for all world literatures.[1]

Ramón Saldívar attempts to spin out a theoretical matrix that weaves together the seeming paradox of gap and connection begun by Bruce-Novoa.[2] Although Bruce-Novoa does not directly appropriate poststructural thought in order to articulate his critical position on Chicano literature, Ramón Saldívar's overt use of Derridian terminology allows him to apply notions of *differance* to historically bound cultural production. Focusing specifically on the novel, Saldívar argues that the "Chicano novel's ideology of difference emerges from a more complex unity of at least two formal elements: its paradoxical impulse toward revolutionary deconstruction and toward the production of meaning. A unified theory of the Chicano novel must be able to handle this duality" (1979: 88). The Chicano novel (and one could add Chicano poetry, especially in its most narrative forms) stands at the point of tension between two actions: resistance toward, and construction of, meaning. The first involves a "revolutionary deconstruction" traversing ossified and repressive discourses that erase or delimit Chicano subjectivity. The second involves "the production of meaning," which seeks to articulate discredited or residual forms of knowledge – the folk-based literature and wisdom accumulated within Chicano families and communities. Saldívar goes on to note that "The general notion of 'difference' I have proposed allows us to consider this dual tendency of the Chicano novel faithfully, for it uses a dialectical concept that determines the *semantic* 'space of Chicano literature' as that intersection of cultural–historical reality appropriated by the text to produce itself, and of the esthetic reality produced by the text" (1975: 88).[3] The "space" here becomes the site where historical and aesthetic realities meet. Chicano literature thus brings together the real and the imaginative in a process that opts "for conflict rather than resolution, for difference over similarity." At the site of these tensions stands, for Saldívar, the space of Chicano literature.

The space of Chicano literary criticism amplifies the tensions evoked by Saldívar's theorizing. As a body of work, Chicano literary critical texts resound with the discontinuities of cultural identification. These tensions radiate from the histories of political and economic disenfranchisement that Chicano communities have endured; from the forms of self-empowerment Chicanos have employed to carve out some resistant cultural space; from the gender stratification that has haunted Chicano communities; from the ideology of sexual orientation and machismo that can define and delimit Chicano identity; from the conflicted trajectories of racial identification. All these make up what is all too blithely called "the Chicano." Chicano literary criticism as a process of cultural definition and identification strikes these dissonances in its analysis of the literature.

Chicano literary criticism also insists that its subject cannot be placed in some "separate but equal" cultural or institutional class. It thus occupies a space in which such metaphorical grids used to define its culture as "ethnic" versus "mainstream" or "Third World" as distinct from "First World" prove woefully antiquated. It highlights those processes of discursive violence in which identity and agency have been historically circumscribed and denied. The criticism thus insists upon the right of agency, the right to name and construct a self-identity whose premise rests on devalued forms of knowledge and history.

Obvious examples of devalued forms of knowledge evident in Chicano letters include the use of Spanish or Caló as language systems, critical or affirmative invocations of religious faith, belief in folk medicine, repetition of legends and folk tales, folk songs, proverbs, folk drama, and poetry.[4] These all embody discredited knowledge and articulate a history in the margins.

The reclamation of these various bodies of knowledge arises from a historical discontinuity in the valuation of Chicana culture. However, this reclamation is itself not free of its own discontinuities. Raymund Paredes, in "The Evolution of Chicano Literature," enumerates its various discursive and literary influences. His essay traces a Chicana literary heritage from the moment of Spanish incursion into North America to the reflowering of Chicana literary expression. This comprehensive survey traces the descent and legitimacy of Chicana literature, but nevertheless commits the type of erasure against which it ostensibly works. Paredes's study concludes by characterizing Chicana literature as "that body of work produced by United States citizens and residents of Mexican descent for whom a sense of ethnicity is a critical part of their literary sensibilities and for whom the portrayal of their ethnic experience is a major concern" (1982: 74). It thus includes as part of Chicano literature John Rechy's essay "El Paso del

Norte," but not his novel *City of Night,* "which is virtually devoid of ethnic content." In delimiting the terrain of Chicano literature, Paredes's argument stands judgment over who should be in and who outside the Chicano cultural world. The absence of "ethnic content" in Rechy's work could, one might argue, in its silence evoke a most interesting relationship between sexual and ethnic self-identity. Most dangerously, in the case of John Rechy – one of our most prolific Chicano novelists – Paredes's argument excludes an already too marginal constituency: gay Chicanos.

As Juan Bruce-Novoa observes in "Homosexuality and the Chicano Novel": "Homosexuals are absent from the Chicano Movement's self image, and their attempts to gain recognition have had little success. Homophobia may not be more prevalent among Chicanos – though some would aver it – but as products of Mexico and the United States, neither of which tolerates gays, Chicanos reflect norms of their wider socio-cultural context" (1988: 98). Unintentionally, no doubt, Paredes's argument circumscribes the "space" of Chicano literature by opposing homosexuality to ethnicity, suggesting that the literary representation of one realm precludes – or at least takes precedence over – the other. Paredes's essay replicates forms of discursive erasure that Chicanos cannot afford to commit.[5] In its struggle to note the distinguishing generic, linguistic, rhetorical and thematic marks of Chicano literature, the literary criticism serves to found cultural identity and yet disenfranchise at the same time. The tensions evident in the literary critical articulation of self make manifest the problem encountered by any discourse seeking to erase marginality. While advocating and celebrating a sense of self, Chicano literary criticism effects a disenfranchisement felt strongly among gay and lesbian Chicanas/os, among monolingual speakers of English, among the many Chicana writers who were not included among the founding "fathers" of the Chicano Renaissance.[6]

Chicano literature and literary criticism undertake a number of contradictory projects: delimiting the "Chicano" literary space and yet proclaiming its liberation and freedom; defining a uniquely national culture and yet connecting it to universal cultural qualities; negotiating the treacherous cultural terrain where strategies of resistance move against and with hegemonic constructions like "quality," "universality," "self," "art." These contradictions emerge from a culture confronting a difficult history. Through it all, Chicano literary criticism has sought to discuss processes of empowerment, of subject positionality, of cultural identity, in terms that highlight a history of disempowerment and claims to agency. It articulates how Chicano literature – distinct from, resistant to, complicitous with Euramerican dominant culture – creates and expresses a "minority" relationship to power.[7]

Although Chicano literary criticism has not as yet been widely discussed as a postcolonial discourse, similar tensions and discontinuities are at work in both forms of discourse. Those arguments in postcolonialism that seek to establish a national culture independent of colonial domination are not too distinct from those offered by Francisco Lomelí as recently as 1988. Lomelí discusses Chicano experiences as a form of internal exile. Socially, linguistically, and culturally marginalized, Chicanos "choose an independent and autonomous – some would emphasize unattached – posture toward the act of creating literature" (1988: 108). Chicano literary creation, Lomelí implies, involves a cultural formation independent of dominant norms. Beyond this cultural separatism, Lomelí's comments indicate that some critics view Chicano cultural production as independent from and counterpoised to dominant ideological positions. Raymund Paredes suggests in "Mexican American Authors and the American Dream," for example, that the Chicano condition of internal exile manifests itself in a rejection of the American dream: "Mexican American writers have been disinclined to subscribe to a myth that regards success as lying within everyone's reach and that deems those who fail to achieve it as themselves somehow culpable" (1981: 71).

It seems that both Lomelí and Paredes overemphasize the separation of the Chicano from the Euramerican. Rather than enforce the circumscription of borders, we might shift our critical focus away from the distinctions that demarcate the cultural terrains of Euramerica and Chicano America and toward points of interrelationship and interpenetration between these cultural spaces. Gloria Anzaldúa, for one, has been key in arguing for a Chicano identity based on a radical mestizaje. As early as 1981 in her essay "La Prieta" she writes:

> Think of me as Shiva, a many-armed and legged body with one foot on brown soil, one on white, one in straight society, one in the gay world, the man's world, the women's, one limb in the literary world, another in the working class, the socialist, and the occult worlds. A sort of spider woman hanging by one thin strand of web. Who, me confused? Ambivalent? Not so. Only your labels split me. (1981: 205)

This interpenetrative and deterritorializing position, moving against labels and categories, reveals a more fluid and dynamic sense of Chicano/a identity than that allowed by a critical discourse dead set on defining "the" Chicano cultural and personal identity. This is not to argue that early Chicano criticism was all about ossification through classification, as the discussions by Juan Bruce-Novoa and Ramón Saldívar have shown. And Francisco Jiménez's 1979 collection *The Identification and Analysis of Chicano Literature* opens with three essays – by Luís Leal, Rolando Hinojosa, and Tomás Rivera – that problematize the notion of Chicano cultural and personal identity.

In varying degrees, the work of all these critics expresses a sense that Chicano culture perpetually negotiates two worlds: the (colonizing) North American and the (colonized) Mexican-American. In actuality, one could argue that Chicano culture bridges three worlds, taking into account the mestizaje of Mexican culture, comprised of the (colonizing) Spanish and (colonized) indigenous identities. One might expand this to four worlds by acknowledging the Spanish colonial age, the historical bridge to European culture and a residual living presence in the language and lifestyle of various regions of the contemporary American Southwest. Five worlds, if one recognizes the North American indigenous cultures that, along with pre-Cortesian cultures, form something of a touchstone for the Chicano imagination.[8]

Bridging Other Worlds

The blank and bridge – the construction and rupture – marked by "-" in Mexican-American suggests a simultaneous erasure and connection to all these worlds. The positions articulated by Bruce-Novoa and Ramón Saldívar represent a type of deconstructive project as regards dominant social organizations, which suggests that the "-" in Mexican-American resonates with the (unseen) "-" in postcolonial. In both cases, the hyphen separates and connects in a complex double-movement revealing "the difference within" identity. This notion of difference within highlights the contradictory position of all postcolonials whose identity arises from histories of oppression, exploitation, violence, erasure. Without negating the reality of these histories, postcolonials engage with their disempowered pasts, and reinvoke strategies of resistance, survival, and empowerment in that past. Their identities incorporate the other, become the other, transform the other. Chicano culture as one that occupies the borderlands between and within Mexico and the United States manifests such an identity.

Of particular use here is Elizabeth Meese's and Alice Parker's note that in articulating "the difference within," "we must abandon the dream of an outside or an inside that would provide firm footing, whether we call it 'reality,' 'experience,' or 'consciousness'" (1989: 2). This giving up of firm footing is analogous to that step so many citizens of the Americas take when they cross oceans or rivers to breach the borders at the Center of Empire. Within Chicana literary production, the abandonment of terra firma forms a homologously transgressive strategy. It is true that much of Chicana literary production rests on the claims that it emerges from experiences erased by dominant Euramerican society. The affirmation of a Chicana "reality" or "experience" certainly has formed a crux in cultural production and critique.

Rather than think of it in terms of "origin" or "authenticity" (as a good deal of its literary criticism has done for specific political and institutional reasons), Chicano literature challenges its readers to consider the processes of identity construction. Decentering Euramerican claims of authority and identity, Chicano literature cannot in good conscience turn around and posit another alternate but equally prohibitive claim to authority. Indeed, constituents whose identities were overlooked in the early proclamation of identity – primary among them Chicanas, lesbians, and gays – rail against the essentialist myths surrounding claims to "experience" and "reality." These serve to underscore the fact that claims to identity do not become illegitimate. On the contrary, they are based on genuine discontent, on actual exploitation, and upon a history that has been "disappeared" by dominant society. Recent claims to other identities not included in the early articulations of the Chicano reveal precisely how important these claims are. In this continuing project, the space of Chicano cultural production reveals its own contradictions as well as those of hegemonic society. The claim by literary criticism to identity and agency – claimed as well by the huddled masses coming to the shores of the Rio Bravo – becomes a radical critique of hegemonic structures. Not that these claims to identity ever manifest a singularly fixed, original, authentic configuration. They reveal themselves, instead, to be finally involved in an endless project of becoming, rather than being, Chicana/o.

In this respect, Chicana literary criticism posits another way which is not one whose opposition to dominant social order mirrors dominant structures.[9] Chicana cultural production posits a condition not like that offered by Euramerican society. While projecting this antiimperial stance, Chicana literary production simultaneously rushes to empire. Juan Rodríguez, for example, tries to articulate the interconnection between the colonizers and the colonized. Chicana writers (and one should add critics) must come to see that "whether we like it or not, we have incorporated – some more than others – a vision of the world belonging to the dominant classes, and that consequently our actions – including literary creation – will be mediated by these circumstances" (1979: 175).[10] The Chicana writer and critic, even while articulating the composition of a Chicana subject, is still subject to the ideological power of dominant society. Hence recent critical attention paid to shortcomings in Chicana cultural criticism focuses on identity construction as a strategy of resistance inexorably connected to systems of oppression.

Rosa Linda Fregoso and Angie Chabram in "Chicana/o Cultural Representations" argue that although the term "Chicano was a strategic relation and a strategy of struggle that thematized the Chicano community and called for social struggle and reform," the notion of Chicano cultural identity became problematic when it "failed to acknowledge our historical differences in addition to the multiplicity of our cultural identities as a people" (1990: 205). In a similar vein, José David Saldívar in "Towards a Chicano Poetics" indicates that Chicano literary criticism must find solutions to "the failure in earlier formalist, archetypal, and also structuralist theories to include in any integrated way the contexts of the literary work in relation to the negating and uplifting existence of dialectics in general, and to sexual, cultural, linguistic–semiotic, and formal differences in particular" (1986: 10). Saldívar, Chabram, and Fregoso all note the lack of differentiation manifested by earlier Chicano criticism. Their emphasis upon articulating the differences within Chicano cultural formation resonates with the scrutiny of identity formation undertaken by postcolonial theory.

To designate Chicano culture as postcolonial, however, is to glide all too easily from one framework of reference – Third World, multicultural, ethnic, or whatever – to another. Although resonances between Chicano cultural production and postcolonial projects can be heard, sharp distinctions must be drawn. The discussion of Chicano culture as postcolonial presupposes that the socioeconomic reality of Chicano peoples in the United States was, until "liberation" in the 1960s, colonial or neocolonial. Mario Barrera, for one, makes this argument, stating that "the manner in which the original Chicanos came about links Chicano history firmly with the history of other Third World people who have been subjected to the colonial experience in one or another of its forms" (1979: 218). The economic penetration of the United States into the Southwest drew all parts of the area into the new order and Chicanos had their land expropriated, often under the cover of the law: "It is perhaps in this expropriation that we can most clearly see the role the American state has played in creating and perpetuating the colonial status of Chicanos."[11] Although Barrera's statement proves true as a general description of nineteenth-century relations, the highly dynamic processes of migration and immigration in the twentieth century suggest that the internal colonial model goes only so far in accounting for the contemporary conditions of Chicanos and other people of color in the United States.[12] Alan Wald, for example, argues that an integrated critical approach toward racial and ethnic issues that takes into account the internal colonial theory as well as contemporary class and gender analysis "would bring a perspective with superior explanatory potential to the study of the cultural practice of people of color and U.S. literature in general" (1987: 24).[13]

As Wald's argument suggests, the situation of people of color in the United States arises from a colonial experience compounded by the complexities of a social order based on gender, race, and class differentiation. This much is true: The historical conditions of Chicanos have been dominated by the economic exploitation of U.S. industries and businesses; the memory of the Anglo-American incursion into Mexico's northern territories is still painful and informing; and the relationship between Mexico and its northern neighbor has been one of tension, intervention, and exploitation. But to equate these conditions with an internal colonialism in order to explain the contemporary position of Chicanos in the United States is to rely upon a vision of the sociocultural that is not fully accurate.

Chris García and Rudolph de la Garza, for example, argue that internal colonialism is marked by the forced entry of the colonized into the colonizing society, the genocide of the colonized culture, the imposition of external administration, and the perpetuation of racist practices by the colonizing group (1977: 8).[14] These conditions form to a greater or lesser degree the historical and current experience of Chicanos. However, it must also be said that these conditions are experienced in a number of widely variant and mediated ways. Most Chicanos, for example, trace their connection to Mexico to a date much more recent than 1848. Yet many Chicanos are second- or third- or fourth-generation citizens of the United States. The Chicano population is primarily an immigrant rather than a colonized population. Moreover, the interest in the exotic and multicultural as a marketing tool problematizes the actuality of a current cultural genocide. One might argue that "ethnic chic" forms a marketing ploy that, although not championing Chicano culture as a critical source of devalued knowledge, serves at least to resonate with the power of a collective memory. The success of Victor Villaseñor's *Rain of Gold*, for example, marketed as a Chicano *Roots*, marks yet again the appropriative power of the market economy. The works by the late Alex Haley and Villaseñor do of course speak a new and important truth to the racial/ethnic communities they address. Simultaneously, the successes of these books indicate the flexibility of a marketplace able to use the articulation of a historically discredited cultural identity in order to sell a product. Finally, the growing politicization of Chicano and other Latino communities serves to dismantle somewhat the processes of gerrymandering and other political manipulation that have long disempowered Chicano communities.[15]

Moreover, the distinctions between the colonized and colonizers – between the "First World" and the "Third World" within the United States – are not as clear-cut as a model of internal colonization would suggest. Mario García, for one, argues that the internal colonial theory fails to recognize the historical development of a Chicano working class and its integration into the working class of the United States: "We do not have a separate white America, a separate black America, and a separate Mexican America, but rather a society characterized by a relatively small number of capitalists dominating the wealth of the country and a vast and complex working population composed of men and women and a variety of ethnic and racial backgrounds" (1978: 38). Thus, rather than conceptualize the space of the Chicano as a postcolonial region within a colonizing nation – which would suggest the possession of "a national structure whose project for the future implies a national liberation, its independence as a country" (Epple 1983: 151 n. 2) – we need to be aware of the specificity of the Chicano as a racialized, colonized, migrant, and immigrant experience. This experience is highly textured and highly diverse.[16]

Strategically, however, to consider Chicana literary criticism a postcolonial discourse serves two primary functions. It bridges the domestic projects of Chicana, African American, and other "minority" cultural producers with an international agenda of empowerment and identity construction. As José David Saldívar proposes in *The Dialectics of Our America,* Chicana literary criticism can be fruitfully employed in focusing on the relationship between global history and local knowledge. In addition, viewing Chicana criticism as a postcolonial discourse helps crystallize some of its most pressing problems: how to conceptualize a cultural practice while simultaneously acknowledging and resisting delimiting dominant forms of thought; how to think and reconstruct notions like subjectivity and agency without willfully projecting their existence at some essentialist level; how to comprehend cultural objects produced within a contradictory and discontinuous postcolonial condition.

One strain in the articulation of postcolonial projects has formed along the faultline that runs between the postcolonial as an isolationist national culture and the postcolonial as a hybridized borderlands culture: an amalgamation of various cultures. Within the various movements of Chicana cultural production, this tension becomes evident. Statements made in 1980 by the perennial spokesman for Chicana cultural nationalism, Alurista, reveal something of this tension. Of his writing, Alurista observes: "Some people say my poetry is protest poetry. No. It's also about reconstructing. To reconstruct ourselves, because being colonized people, the self that we possess, the view that we have, is colored by the colonization that we have suffered, by the schooling that we have been subjected to. We have to expel the Yankees from our heart" (Bruce-Novoa 1980: 276). Alurista's comments reveal a double process, one of reconstruction and another of expulsion. The reconstruction implies a type of re/formation based on empowerment and resistance. The expulsion posits the Chicana as a space of pure alterity, a move that proves to be more problematic than Alurista's position would imply.

Chicano literary practices function as a form of counterdiscourse. This is an important point, worth emphasizing. They write through and against, not in place of, dominant and dominating discourses. This does not imply simply finding an authentic or original voice of complete alterity, an expulsion of the Yankee from the heart. Rather, counterdiscursive practices incorporate and deconstruct dominant discourses, incorporating "marginal" or devalued forms of knowledge and discourse in the process. Thus some third form of knowledge is produced, one condition of postcoloniality with which Chicano cultural production can be productively allied.[17]

Chicano literature lives in the interstices between worlds (historical, geographic, cultural, racial, sexual) themselves comprised of a story concerned with conquest, colonialism, and confrontation. Out of a tightly woven history of conflict between Mexico and the United States, Chicanos "continually expand a space between the two, claiming from both sides a larger area for our own reality" (Bruce-Novoa 1982: 12). This larger area has in the past been named "Aztlán," a new cultural and geographic homeland that – as the mythic homeland of the Mexica – connects Chicano identity to its pre-Cortesian past and that – as the geographic region of the Southwest – evokes the history of U.S. conquest embodied by the Mexican–American War. "Aztlán" serves to conceptualize a reclamation that is spiritual, cultural, nationalistic, separatist, seminal.[18]

Although it may have been a necessary and constructive step at both a political and cultural level twenty years ago, the attempt to fix a space delimiting and bounding Chicana identity has disenfranchised those whose concerns and needs were not met by nationalist movements. Following the heady days of El Movimiento, Chicana cultural discourse has seemed to move away from trying to recapture a "homeland." Instead, the discourse tends to conceptualize the "borderlands," a discontinuous and fluid region where national borders form a part of the repressive and exploitative conditions against which Chicanas have struggled. As Gloria Anzaldúa notes: "A border is a dividing line, a narrow strip along a steep edge. The borderlands are a vague and undetermined place created by the emotional residue of an unnatural boundary. It is in a constant state of transition" (1987: 3). The "border" divides, separates, categorizes, dispossesses.[19] The "borderlands" by contrast form a metaphorical and literal space where worlds blend and cross. Recent work by Chicana and Chicano writers and thinkers has come to conceptualize a more complex and fluid map marking the discontinuities, disjunctures, and ruptures of Chicana history, culture, and subjectivity.

Rather than fixing on the dissociated and irremediably rent terms "home" and "land," Chicana critics and poets are now able to focus on the fact of rupture and, rather than negate, negotiate constructively with it. One means is to gaze on the placement of borders: the how and why of their creation. In the wake of their assembly, what can one do to construct and maintain identities that will not collapse into positions of victim or guerilla? When economic, political, racial, and military trajectories converge, it is hard to ignore what the force of their payload topples and what the logic of their deployment erects (witness Kuwait and southern Iraq in 1991). As similar trajectories converged in northern Mexico of 1846, it is evident why those who feel kinship and connection with either the old or new Mexicos would ascribe to "1848" a set of aesthetic and moral values, historical and economic facts, and emotionally charged resentments that cannot be let go.[20] The moment for Chicana cultural critique is formed, then, by "1848" when the borderlands – that terrain comprised of the bridge between four or five worlds and which replicates itself wherever the discontinuities and dislocations of Chicana experience are made manifest – bloomed.

Blocs, Parties, and La Raza Cósmica

One region of this borderland exists within the institutional halls of academia. Whether through the introduction of a few books or poems within a particular class, through the addition of an "ethnic" component to a course or a curriculum, or through the hiring of a person blessed with an education in (or simply a name evoking) "the Chicano," most academic departments, it seems, are aware that they cannot remain inert in the face of a changing intellectual terrain.[21]

Despite the growth of institutional Chicano literary studies, one readily hears the grumbling about tendentiousness, about the growing politicization of the academy and the culture it serves and protects, about the degeneracy of the academy as it slavishly rushes to embrace whatever latest trend – multiculturalism, gay and lesbian studies, cultural studies – comes down the pike. At the same time, one hears in this critique a sense of the inevitability of incorporating more literature by "minority groups" who have – let's be fair – some claim to changes in higher education as a "token of legitimation," "a sign of respectability," or "a symbol of success."[22] Change can occur, just so long as the change remains a "token," a "sign," a "symbol." The issue here is one that cannot be avoided when discussing the position of Chicano literary criticism within the terrain of contemporary academic institutions. The specter of curricular reformation (or counter-reformation, as the case may be) rises yet again like a tortured spirit from the grave. From Allan Bloom to Dinesh D'Souza to Roger Kimball, the tearing of hair and rending of clothes over the demise of academic integrity and rigor is by now a common enough sight. The demand for a curriculum less vested in celebrating the supremacy or centrality of Western culture has come under attack by these three (and others), who imply that curricular changes over the past two decades are part of an irrational, hysterical, and political ploy for power within the hallowed halls of academia. (It cannot be pointed out enough that their arguments are themselves often irrational, hysterical, and consummately political.) This neoconservative reaction to enemies perceived and real forms one bloc greeting Chicano culture within academia.

On the other side, there exists a tendency within academic communities not to relegate but rather to celebrate Chicano culture as a component of a much needed cultural pluralism or an academic diversity. The reception of Chicano issues to the curriculum comes to resemble a blockparty. This liberal position – welcoming, accommodating – is not overtly antagonistic toward a sociohistorical understanding of the literature. It does, however, severely skew the significance of that understanding. Angie Chabram notes, "Diversity, as defined in university sectors, goes hand in hand with cultural pluralism, a construct that erases inequality and the cultural specificity of the Chicano. Diversity is tantamount to assimilation. When we speak in these terms we are defining ourselves through the predominant academic discourse to our own detriment" (1990: 231 n. 6).[23] There are factions within academic institutions ready to embrace a multiculturalism devoid of historical and cultural specificity in favor of a celebration of difference and alterity. The rush to embrace Chicano literature is, then, from certain quarters, the result of a desire for correctness.[24] A response of active neglect comes to be replaced by one of almost blind or reverential acceptance. And in fact, the response is often a mixture of both at once – a distracted (and insincere) embrace. For though many academic departments desire the presence of a brown face among their faculty, how many members of those departments actually research the object of their desire?

This ghettoization, marginalization, snub under the aegis of a defense of the canon or of quality or of literary (as opposed to sociological) study on the one hand, and the inclusion, celebration, and commodification of diversity in the name of academic growth on the other, ultimately serve the same purpose. The specificity of Chicano culture is systematically erased, distorted, or rewritten. Moreover, the critical perspective afforded by a "minority" perspective drowns in the culturally plural flood of hyphenated American self-identity (Italian-American, Irish-American, Norwegian-American, German-American). Chandra Mohanty astutely points out about cultural pluralism: "The central issue . . . is not one of merely *acknowledging* difference; rather, the more difficult question concerns the kind of difference that is acknowledged and engaged. Difference seen as benign variation (diversity), for instance, rather than as conflict, struggle, or the threat of disruption, bypasses power as well as history to suggest a harmonious, empty pluralism" (1989/90: 181). Chicano criticism explicitly and implicitly engages with issues of empowerment, of agency, of asymmetrical power relations. The history of the Chicano/a as subject to economic and political disempowerment at the hands of Euramerican institutional practices, the development of the Chicana/o as a subject within a history of counterstrategic empowerment, the tracing of Chicano literary and cultural traditions, all form part of the Chicano literary critical scene. As such, the criticism refuses to bypass issues of power, refuses to ignore history. Yet this confrontation with history manifests itself in multiple ways within the terrain of Chicano literary criticism itself.

This criticism, especially in its earliest form, focuses on the issues we have seen Paredes, Lomelí, and Leal address: autonomy of Chicana culture, resistance to and critique of dominant ideologies, the insistence upon agency and self-empowerment in naming and validating Chicana experience. As such, it is possible to trace a strong thread of desire. Desire drives those producers and disseminators of Chicana culture who want (even demand) that its literature be taken on its own terms as a form of artistic expression speaking to the heart of all peoples. A number of producers and critics of Chicana literature want their object of study to stand alone among other more readily institutionalized products of Euramerican culture.

Strong political and cultural reasons underpin this desire. A prolific and influential critic, Francisco Lomelí articulates a position where the "universality" of Chicana literary production becomes a standard by which the critic must judge its worth: "Our literature needs to be judged according to universal literary criteria, but its own particular modes of expression and motifs should not be sacrificed in the process. Its origin already implies distinctive features, such as the motif of the barrio, codes of meaning through interlingualism, and the relationship between Anglo and Mexican histories" (1984: 106–7). Although Chicana literature is distinct in the particularities of expression, cultural codification, and the history it evokes, Lomelí posits a situation in which the deep structures of all literatures somehow signify in similar ways. In this instance, we might question Lomelí's critical judgment.

In a move sympathetic with Lomelí's observations, Salvador Rodríguez del Pino terms postmovement Chicana poets members of "The New Trajectory" who "consciously search, within traditional poetic forms, new models, new personal metaphors using a Chicano expression to create images within a Chicano artistic reality that locates our sensibility within the universal artistic mosaic."[25] These poets "are those who attempt to achieve a universality without leaving their roots" (1979a: 79).[26]

In a similar vein, Sylvia Gonzales writes that "the artist must be true to her own soul and her own personal experiences, and in so doing, the message will be universal and eternal" (1975: 15). "Chicano literature is a cumulative experience," Felipe de Ortego y Gasca states in an argument echoing the universalist line, "embodying literary values from the universal store of artistic expression which gives and has given rise to literary works in all times in the civilizations of mankind" (1981: 3). And Luís Leal notes that "the eagle, Aztlán, the Quinto Sol, and other Chicano symbols of Mexican origin form a part of a mythic system, a characteristic often attributed to the symbol" (1981: 17). Lomelí, Rodríguez del Pino, Gonzáles, Ortego y Gasca, and Leal all attempt to valorize Chicano literature by claiming for it the status of the "universal," insisting for it a place in the pantheon of timeless literature. (It is but one small step to Saul Bellow's demand for a Hottentot Tolstoy.)

Clearly, this emphasis upon eternal verities reflects an anxiety about how others will perceive the quality of Chicano poetry. The pernicious question of aesthetic judgment is a perpetually vexing one for critics of multicultural literature. The tired dichotomy between "color" and "quality" that is trotted out every now and again as a defense against incorporating multicultural perspectives in the classroom has been adequately answered by the wealth of anthologies and pedagogical aids published to date.[27] Yet as we have seen with Leal, Pino, and Lomelí, early critics of Chicano literature ponder directly or indirectly the question of its quality, worth, and place. The issue raises some questions that, like other restless ghosts, haunt Chicano criticism. How should one value the literary production of the subaltern? Does one maintain systematic criteria for the products of the dominant culture and posit alternate (and not as rigorous) criteria for those products from the margin? When the subaltern speaks with the voice and in the manner of the master, is that an indication of some kind of "arrival" to world class status or a blind and quite literal slavish imitation of the master?

These questions, though left unspoken, are ultimately misdirected. Under erasure for decades, the notion of some universal and comprehensible rule by which to measure the value of aesthetic texts remains the *bête noire* of contemporary literary study. Simply put, who is to judge quality? We know that the way literature signifies within specific cultural economies is circumscribed by the function of those economies. Its worth or value can be gauged only by understanding the system of exchange in which it moves. This clearly is the challenge posed by multicultural literatures of the world: One must understand a different history in order to understand the modes of exchange within different cultural communities. Cordelia Candelaria, for example, notes: "to teach Arthur Miller's *Death of a Salesman* (1949) to high school and college students usually does not require an in-depth introduction to U.S. history and culture, for students at that level can be expected to either know the sociohistorical context or to learn about it through easily available resources. To teach Zora Neal Hurston's *Their Eyes Were Watching God* (1937) is another matter entirely" (1989: vi). More to the point, I would argue, the teaching of Miller's play reinscribes the centrality of the history that produces it. Over again, our educational institutions underscore that the historical knowledge associated with Hurston's book is not central to U.S. society. The problem is finally one of pedagogical, critical, and discursive frameworks. Which communities are worth looking at? Which are central and which marginal? As bell hooks seeks to do, I would argue that a reclamation of the "marginal" is a critical strategy multicultural critics should seek to undertake, and one that Chicano literary critics have in their diverse ways sought to accomplish. Specifying this margin, hooks argues that marginality is much more than a site of deprivation; "it is also the site of radical possibility, a space of resistance . . . a central location for the production of a counter-hegemonic discourse that is not just found in words but in habits of being and the way one lives" (1990: 149). The marginal should be conceptualized as a potentially resistant space.

Because of their exploited position in the development of the modern world, communities historically dispossessed form a critical realm of privilege, the repository of historical knowledge so valued by Walter Benjamin. They see the world from top and bottom, so to speak, and offer a vision of endurance and strength in adversity that must be counted upon as an invaluable source of knowledge. Benjamin notes that in class struggle the refined and spiritual things manifest themselves "as courage, humor, cunning, and fortitude" (1940: 255). This spiritual dimension is evident in, for example, the testimony by Rigoberta Menchú about the struggle of her people the Quiché. One could argue that the experience and perspective of Chicanos, because of a history of exclusion and exploitation, forms a similarly coherent critical focal point, one made manifest in the literature. As José David Saldívar says of José Montoya's early poetry, they give "the impression of a new, Chicano sensibility: namely, its power to dramatize otherness and to bring readers into electrifying contact with social forms wholly different from Anglo-American ones" (1986: 10). For these reasons, reasons that focus on difference and distance, Chicano literature has become of world interest, with international symposia and conferences occurring annually in the United States and elsewhere. This condition is due, in a very large part, to the persistent efforts by talented and dedicated scholars and writers like Lomelí, Rodríguez del Pino, Gonzáles, Ortego y Gasca, and Leal, who have spoken with and for the voice of the subaltern.

In the rush to affirm the critical potential of Chicana literary production, however, we cannot lose sight of the differences within difference.[28] Although Chicana literary products often rely upon devalued forms of knowledge and expression as resources upon which to draw, these forms of knowledge cannot, in counteracting the silence imposed by dominant master narratives in the United States, replicate the violence of those master narratives. Differences among Chicanas – racial, economic, sexual, cultural, linguistic – preclude the understanding of *a* Chicana experience. The move toward essentializing Chicana cultural expression results, however, from the historical conditions that necessitated a critical expression to comprehend and affirm that culture.

That Chicana literature has not always been of world – nor even of national or of passing – interest is a point not to be overlooked. The study of Chicana culture was ignored or relegated to the most distant university outposts as it first gained grudging recognition by academic circles in the 1960s (a recognition that, unfortunately, is often still offered begrudgingly). As a result, it is possible to find in early critical works a tone that betrays a certain sense of anxiety about their object of study. "The central question which faced us when we began to formulate plans and ideas for this book was, 'Is it valid to speak of Chicano literature?'" ask the editors of *Literatura Chicana/ Chicano Literature* (Shular, Ybarra-Frausto, Sommers 1972: xxiii). The answer they come to, as one might expect, is indeed yes. But given that the very existence of its literature could be at question, it should not surprise us that one segment of early Chicana literary criticism underscores the need for universality, connection, and relevance beyond a racially, ethnically, or culturally delimited audience.

Early in the 1970s, these desires coalesced in the conceptualization of Chicano identity as – to use José Vasconcelos's well-known term – La Raza Cósmica. The discourse of a cosmic race was an attempt to convey a pride in the mestizo heritage of Chicano identity: "a pluralistic man, a universal man, combining the racial strains and cultures of the entire world in his own person" (Vasconcelos 1972: 284).[29] Beyond the obvious hyperbole, one cannot help but note the marked linguistic absence of woman in this articulation of the universality of La Raza. As Jean Franco points out, though Vasconcelos himself was a proponent of women's liberation and resisted traditional restrictions of family life, his attitude toward women was conflicted. As Minister of Education, he drew women into his campaign for literacy in postrevolutionary Mexico to "not only create a new social space for themselves but . . . alter education itself by giving it a more maternal image" (Franco 1989: 103). Franco's analysis of Vasconcelos indicates that despite his progressive policies, he was chained to the hero myth by which he understood his life and mission.[30] This is but an indication of the limitations that essentializing and universalizing notions can bear with them. And indeed this is an issue that Chicana literary critics will focus on when they add their voices to the discourse on literature. Early on, nevertheless, words like "mythic," "the unconscious" and "the universal" dot the Chicano critical literary terrain.

An example can be found in the autobiographical notes of one of the founding fathers (I use the term advisedly) of the Chicano novel, Rudolfo Anaya. He characterizes his works – *Bless Me, Ultima; The Heart of Aztlán;* and *Tortuga* – as arising from "the heart of the lake, the deep pool of my subconscious, the collective memory and history of my people" (1990: 377). Anaya's thought exemplifies a belief in the mythic and archetypical dimensions of literary creation, one that informs the intellectual life of several Chicano writers and thinkers. He argues for the relevancy and timeliness (perhaps more accurately, timelessness) of this strain of thought: "The step into the unconscious to discover symbology is not retrogressive. It is a step forward, because what you bring from the unconscious will serve you in the step that you are going to take in your profane reality" (Monleón 1990: 445). The desire to escape history (especially one of oppression and exploitation) is understandable and, to a certain degree, a laudable though deeply conflicted venture.[31] In addressing the critical role of certain archetypical

Chicano literature, we may want to shift our gaze from the authenticity or impossibility of a mythic vision to the aesthetic embodiment of that vision as a resistant and critical art form.

The appeal to some deeper space within the collective unconscious is, after all, itself marked by contradiction. The work on the archetypical and mythic undertaken by European thinkers like Carl Jung, Mircea Eliade, and Claude Lévi-Strauss – and appropriated by such Chicano critics as César González, Juan Bruce-Novoa and Enrique Lamadrid – is itself a project firmly planted in a historically bound (and, one might add, Eurocentric) structuralist framework.

Juan Bruce-Novoa, for example, in his study *Chicano Poetry: A Response to Chaos* (1982), relies upon a Chomskian-based "deep-structure" model and the archetypical criticism of Mircea Eliade to explain Chicano poetry. In the introduction, he argues that the *axis mundi,* conceptualized as a pillar that connects and supports the heavens and the earth and around which the universe is constructed, is threatened by disappearance in the world's real order. Within Chicano poetry, the *axis mundi* "is named as Other, as a word whose represented object, its signified, is absent. The Other takes on the poem's body, the language, until its presence is the poem itself as an image" (1982: 6). Both the *axis mundi* and its disappearance are present in the poem. Chicano literature, therefore,

> does not simply posit escapist panaceas. The threat remains present, though checked, in the literature. Moreover, if the reader does not activate the process – an action often demanding commitment and involvement much beyond casual reading – the disappearance will dominate the poem's surface image, resulting in misreading. An active reading that eventually reaches the last element of the deep structure can be compared to the pilgrimage to the sacred center. Like the journey from profane space to sacred space, it is difficult, and for those directly involved in the life-and-death venture it is a rite of passage. The reward is renewed cultural life. (1982: 6–7)

Bruce-Novoa ultimately argues that this paradigm springs from the literature and that it is revealed by close textual analysis. The body of his book undertakes precisely this type of close textual analysis, looking at the work of such poets as Rodolfo Gonzales, Alurista, Sergio Elizondo, Tino Villanueva, Bernice Zamora, and Gary Soto.

The dichotomous tension between order and chaos forms a traditional concern of European poetry in general, and this tension becomes evident in any close reading of the text. From Marvell to Shakespeare to Eliot,

Bruce-Novoa's model of poetic significance may very well apply. Moreover, Bruce-Novoa's argument has as its premise some sense of a unified and ordered culture made whole. Despite its shortcomings, Bruce-Novoa's archetypical reading can be understood as a response to destructive cultural institutional and academic practices.

At our present historical juncture, the question should no longer be whether a mythic reading of Chicana literature would be productive. Rather, the emphasis should fall upon the critical potentialities of evoking mythic elements and appropriating oral narrative techniques within such modern aesthetic forms as the novel, the short story, the modern long or short poem. The recovery of a devalued popular culture through a reexamination and revivification of archaic aesthetic codes is a strategy often employed by a number of Chicana writers – Alurista, Anaya, Anzaldúa, to begin alphabetically. The critics of these writers might want to examine the function played by a strategy of aesthetic appropriation beyond simply being a means of probing the psychic memory and subconscious myth-structures of Chicana culture.

The mythic quality evident in Chicana literature need not require one to embrace the mythoreligious underpinnings it evokes. This would suggest a simple mimetic model whereby the invocation of the Quetzalcoatl myth somehow makes present the universal truths, deep structures, or archetypical models that myth represents. Nor does it demonstrate the "universal" quality of Chicana literature, much as that validating claim was sought out as a strategy of cultural empowerment. Rather, the crossing of communal and ancient forms of communication with alienated and modern forms of expression presents a point at which genres, cultures, histories, and epistemes cross. The privileging of a mythic and universal quality (as politically important a move as that may have been) should give way to a criticism that focuses on the ruptures made manifest in the aesthetic forms of Chicana literature that cross the discontinuous concerns of a premodern world and a postmodern society.

Identidad, Movimiento, Resistencia

It has been pointed out many times, and so a complete elaboration is not necessary here, that for many critics, one of the first manifestations of Chicano cultural identity in which political resistance and aesthetic production cross remains the corrido.[32] The corrido and other forms of folk poetry remain as culturally resistant objects created around, out of, and against "1848."[33] These corridos, as Américo Paredes and others have shown, form part of a culture of resistance that confronts sociohistorical oppression and exploitation with poetic narratives – like the one celebrating the exploits of Gregorio Cortez – lionizing valiant individuals who stand up to the repressive forces of Anglo-American conquerors. These songs not only give voice to discontent, but they serve as articulations of outrage and (more importantly) pride that can galvanize the Chicano community.

The production of other late-nineteenth and early-twentieth century Chicano writing, as the archival works of Tey Rebolledo and Genaro Padilla serve to illustrate, is similarly marked by a resistance to the vectors of unjust social, political, cultural, and economic systems. Where an individual may have actually acquiesced to dominant forms of power – as, for instance, Padilla tells us one Jesse Pérez did by joining the violently oppressive Texas Rangers (the much hated *Rinches*) – the writing of his memoirs complicates, perhaps subverts, the intent of his autobiography. Padilla notes that his writing is "one of the most striking representations of thickly accented *mexicano* English" and that his language betrays the very cultural and racial associations his joining the Texas Rangers served to deny (Padilla 1988: 51). Rebolledo similarly argues that the writing of New Mexican women writers – disparaged as genteel, romantic or sentimental – reveals a subversion of "official" texts. These women chose to write in the language of the dominant culture – English – as they chronicled the life and culture threatened by that very dominance.[34] Employing a language of dominance, New Mexican women writers describe and name their colonized identity by detailing the cultural signs imbedded in that identity; they express a nostalgic longing for a lost past and a lost community; they blend and blur various forms of literary expression – the oral with the written, the historical and the autobiographical, the prosaic with the romantic – to form an account that avoids the logic of narrative "movement" (Rebolledo 1990: 136). The complex interaction between identity formation and cultural resistance – increasingly the subject of much-needed Chicana scholarly work – underscores the weight the term "history" carries within Chicano postcolonial discourse.

Where "1848" has served as the strongly evocative emblem of a conflicted Chicana cultural terrain, "the more contemporary date of 1965 is significant as a *symbolic spiritual rebirth* or resurgence. That year the Teatro Campesino joined the social struggle of La Causa with César Chávez. Literature and social reality converged in an inseparable entity" (Lomelí 1984: 105). This convergence of the social and aesthetic led to the explosion of Chicana literary production that has formed the body of work one might study in any garden-variety Chicana literature course. In this respect, "1965" represents an opportunity to address and redress the decades of rancor, injustice, and discontent evoked by "1848." Rafael Jesús González echoes Lomelí's observation:

> It would appear that 1965 was the year in which Chicanismo and consequently Chicano poetry . . . was born. This was the year of two extremely important events for the Chicano Movement. During 1965, U.S. intervention in Vietnam unmasked itself as an atrocious war in which the Chicano saw reflections of the United States invasion of Mexico. Also in that year, the workers in the vineyards of Delano declared themselves on strike under the leadership of César Chávez and the banner of Our Lady of Guadalupe. These two historical events were sufficiently strong enough to congeal the political and cultural disquiet and hopes of the people of Mexican descent into a movement with a sense of its uniqueness – it called itself Chicano. (1977: 132)

Thus "1965" forms an empowered double to the processes of dispossession signaled by the figure "1848." It marks a historical moment during which a radicalized Chicano literature was tied to a process seeking to synthesize aesthetics with political organization, communication with cultural recuperation, performance with activist instruction. Tomás Ybarra-Frausto's germinal essay "The Chicano Movement and the Emergence of a Chicano Poetic Consciousness" documents how the founding of such publications as *El Malcriado, El Grito, Aztlán, Con Safos,* and *El Grito del Norte,* the establishment of publishing houses like Quinto Sol and, later, Arte Público, the development of theater groups such as El Teatro Campesino, El Teatro Triste, and El Teatro Pachuco, resulted from this culminating moment in which Chicano political and literary interests met. And, as Ybarra-Frausto points out, this connection ultimately led to the changes that have inexorably altered the terrain of Chicano literature. There was "a basic contradiction which faced Chicano artists within the movement: how to remain true to the demands of their art while responding to the political exigencies of the moment" (1977: 87). One response was, as we have seen, to work toward an aesthetic "no longer focused on social ills" but rather "used to probe the psychic memory and sub-conscious myth structures of Chicanos" (1977: 88). This universalist path, as necessary as it may have been, led to a number of blindnesses and impasses, as any essentializing project is bound to do. Most significantly, this emphasis upon the mythic or universalist served to remove Chicana cultural concerns from the important political and historical matrices that had so long demarcated the space of Chicano productivity and fulfillment.

One project undertaken by a number of Chicano thinkers and writers moves about this region, in which concerns with the aesthetic and with the sociohistorical cross. Whereas we have seen one stratum of aesthetic and critical work in the Chicano cultural terrain foreground the essential and universal, another fixes its gaze on the political efficacy of cultural production. These two concerns form the central dichotomy of Chicano cultural criticism. As Carmen Parr notes, "Chicano critics have been polarized into two groups: those who see Chicano literature as reflecting the sociohistorical and cultural reality of the Chicano and those who defend it in terms of its universal, transcendental values" (1979: 134). Similarly César A. González-T. argues that the literary criticism surrounding the work of Rudolfo Anaya falls into two camps: those interested in "the mythico-mystical heartland of Anaya's writing" and those who "question the relevance of myth and cosmic purposefulness in the world" (1990: xvii). This tension between the historical and the mythical, to abbreviate the debate, emerges from a resistant positionality informing the courses of El Movimiento. The desire to articulate a realm of Chicano cultural production separate from dominant Euramerican culture leads to the affirmation of those elements most distinctive of the Chicano community: a spiritual strength that arises from a history of struggle, a link to autochthonous cultures, a vision of archetypical primordiality. On the other hand, the recognition of a history of struggle also leads critics to a critical scrutiny of that history. The political engagement of the 1960s and 1970s formed an influential context in which culture served the political and social expediency of Chicano liberation. The overtly political impetus behind the "renaissance" of Chicano cultural production lent an immediacy and urgency to the literary critical process.

The aesthetic and the intellectual serve not only or not primarily to delve into the universal or mythic soul of the Chicana people. Rather, these realms are meant to galvanize and empower the Chicana community, the production of culture a forging of plowshares into swords. Rudolph de la Garza and Rowena Rivera, for example, argue that the creative explosion accompanying early Chicana political militancy "negates the assumptions made by Anglo writers that Chicanos have not made, and will not or cannot make, significant contributions to American social, cultural, and intellectual life" (1977: 43). Political and cultural movements form "part of the Chicanos' efforts to define their own reality," integrally involved in "the Chicanos' movement toward intellectual and cultural self-determination" (1977: 43). At times, Chicana intellectuals (often political scientists) argue that the instrumentality of Chicana culture becomes an essential salve to heal the pain of historical dispossession. As Eugene García argues, "Literature, then, provided the road to recovery, as a type of spiritual reconquest of our ethos from which a fuller appreciation of our cultural heritage was regained. The first issue at hand was to establish an operational identity of personal dignity to serve as a rallying point" (García, Lomelí, Ortiz 1984: 99). García's position exemplifies the "historical" rather than the "mythical" strain of criticism running through the critical reception of Chicana literature. From this perspective, Chicana literature serves as an antidote to the disease of cultural (and spiritual) conquest. This medicinal healing of the Chicana ethos is crossed with the need to establish a mechanical or systemic "operational identity" that can function as an icon around which to rally the community.[35]

An excellent example of the socializing poem is Rodolfo Gonzales's *Yo Soy Joaquín/I am Joaquín*. The poem (of which Bruce-Novoa provides an exhaustive textual analysis in *Chicano Poetry*) traces Chicano struggle through a historical overview of Mexican/Chicano history. Gonzales employed the poem (treated more fully in Chapter 3) as an organizing tool. Written in 1967 for the Crusade for Justice, distributed by mimeographed copy, recited at rallies and strikes, the poem functions within a system of economic and political resistance. The preface (written by Gonzales) states that *I am Joaquín* "was the first work of poetry to be published by Chicanos for Chicanos and is the forerunner of the Chicano cultural renaissance. The poem was written first and foremost for the Chicano Movement" (1972: 3). Gonzales's text functions as the type of icon that Eugene García champions as a road to cultural–social–political recovery.

Although García argues that the main objective is to "establish an operational identity of personal dignity to serve as a rallying point," the move toward unity, dignity, and political action becomes associated for a writer–critic like Alurista with a metaphor for the land itself – "Aztlán":

> There was a real need for all of us to find a way, a metaphor, let me put it that way – and at this level I think I'm equating metaphor with myth – a metaphor that would serve as a unifying tool to look at each other as brothers and sisters. . . . The myth of Aztlán, as I saw it, in the '60s was just a way to identify a people, a land, and a consciousness that said, "Struggle, do not be afraid." (Monleón 1981: 442)

The desire to organize a community for political action shapes the role, function, and form of the art created within El Movimiento. The mythic quality – which was to become so suggestive and rich in archetypical imagery for a number of other artists and critics – becomes an organizing tool for Alurista and the critical stratum within the Chicano Movement for which political efficacy was the end point. This does not in any way denigrate the beauty and vitality of pre-Cortesian myths or cultures. On the contrary, the incorporation of these icons within literary and political tomes awakened an interest among Chicanos that led to an investigation and affirmation of a mestizo heritage comprised of European and indigenous cultures.

However, the manipulation of myth for political purposes – as J. Jorge Klor de Alva has noted in "California Chicano Literature and Pre-Columbian Motifs" – leads to a fetishization of pre-Cortesian icons. Thus an emphasis upon the historical diminishes the specificity and particularity of cultural production. In the interest of protecting Chicano culture, "Chicanos have used the symbols and ideas of the past civilizations of Mexico not only as a foil by which to attack the dominant Anglo society, but also as a fetish by which to protect themselves from its malice" (1986: 25). Klor de Alva's analysis of the historical and cultural inaccuracies in the use of pre-Cortesian motifs by Chicano writers thus takes into account the politico-cultural instrumentality of appropriation.[36] In this respect, Chicanos have sought to activate and articulate an identity through an appeal to the glories of past indigenous civilizations. Cultural pride is meant to serve as a nexus by which Chicanos can unite behind a common indigenous ancestry. Ultimately, a homogenization erases the ethnic and cultural differences of the disparate Chicano communities this strategy seeks to unite. Consequently, the transformation of the pre-Cortesian into fetish reinforces a type of cultural erasure at the same time that it seeks to articulate a vision of self-identity liberated from the models of Euramerican dominance.

Ironically, the emphasis upon political exigency at the expense of cultural specificity itself erases the particularity of the historical situations in which Chicana activism seeks to intervene. A small example: Chicana culture is often most valued when it manifests the quality of most resistance. One thinks of Americo Paredes's work on the corrido as a cultural product of antagonism. Indeed, resistance to European and Euramerican ideas has been manifested at a variety of levels throughout the history of Chicana culture. One cannot presume, however, that the entire history of Chicanas has been one of opposition and resistance. This presumption simply re-creates the subject-position of the Chicana as a perpetual saintly victim, long-suffering but ultimately short on agency.

David Weber's work on the history of the Southwest notes: "The reaction of the Mexican community in the Southwest – including much of the upper class – to the coming of the gringos was a mixed one, just as during the Texas revolt. Some collaborated with the enemy, some resisted, and others remained indifferent" (1973: 99). From another perspective and about another time period, Chris García and Rudolph de la Garza trace the history of Chicana political activism that grew out of assimilationist and accomodationist organizations like the League of United Latin American Citizens (LULAC), comprised mainly of an aspiring Mexican-American middle class.

The political and cultural histories of Chicanas form a complex and textured terrain. The interaction historically between Chicana art and social action – songs, autobiographies, chronicles as manifestations of political resistance and collaboration – indicates the need for yet more archival work, for more translations of texts into English, and for the greater circulation of these texts among a wider Euramerican and Chicana audience. This interaction also indicates that the historical and cultural specificity of Chicana cultural practices must be recognized if the true texture and diversity of Chicana art and history, the full nature of American art and history, are to be productively understood.

Writing Chicana/o

Chicano literary criticism moves in a number of divergent directions. It promises some (mythological/archetypical) teleology that allows insight into the "heart" of a living eternal reality; the spiritual vitality of indigenous thought is brought to the fore and positioned against the sterility and violence of the dissociated, dispossessed, and disenchanted present. It forms a healing or salving remedy to the alienation and fragmentation of Chicano subjectivity by presenting an image of cultural, social, and ultimately personal identity.[37] It serves an instrumental form, revealing and positing ideological positions that enable political criticism and action. The impetus for these different movements generally emerges from either a nationalist agenda or a fully universalizing myth. In either case, the motivation is to establish a Chicano identity that enables a spiritual and political agency. As García and de la Garza explain from a political scientific perspective: "Only after Chicanos develop a group identity and group consciousness will they be able to combat America's colonial structures" (1977: 9). This emphasis on the interrelationship between group identity and political action exemplifies the pressing need to articulate a Chicano identity, culture, and community. Such a need has led to the type of discursive erasure and violence Chicanos have endured in the United States. Exigency elided various constituencies within that multiplicitous term "Chicano," as the racial, sexual, historical, and cultural differences among Chicanos were subordinated to the nationalist need for unity. In the process, that defined as "the

Chicano" excluded many whose interests were not addressed by a postcolonialist national discourse.

Primary among the excluded were Chicanas, whose identities were bound to tradition within bedroom and kitchen walls. The insistence that their concerns and needs were not only important but central to the establishment of Chicano identity challenged the (ultimately) simplistic assertions for nation and culture. Chicana intervention in claiming Chicano identity highlights the problems inherent in processes of cultural self-identification. The recovery of pre-Cortesian culture as the origin of contemporary culture, for example, failed to perceive the historical androcentrism of the Mexica. Revolutionary change based on images that glorified the male–warrior erased potentially empowering identities for Chicanas by sanctifying images of the shrouded and passive mother waiting for her sons to return from war.[38] The reification of Mexican and indigenous cultures, in other words, bolstered those elements that delimited and reinscribed powerlessness for Chicanas. The rise of a Chicana movement formed a powerful response to the failures of El Movimiento: "For years the Chicana worked side by side with her man with the hope of bettering conditions for *la raza*, subordinating her own personal needs and wants to the good of the whole. As the Chicano movement unfolded in the late 1960s, it became increasingly clear that these needs and concerns were not being recognized or met" (Mirandé and Enríquez 1979: 234). Chicana writers, responding to the limitations and restrictions as well as to the erasure that they experienced within nationalist discourses, took to articulating other configurations of identity.

The issue of locality rather than nationalism – the notion that community can be found within the homes and kitchens as well as the streets and fields – crystallizes a number of issues pertinent to naming a Chicana cultural space. It is at the local level that Chicanas deal with the circumscription of a culture bound by notions of delimited gender-roles. These delimitations are evoked in the name of "tradition," that ontological bastion of identity which forms the one thin string of cultural continuity. This continuity, however, comes at a high price. Especially during nationalist movements, as a number of critics have observed, women become the guardians of tradition and the protectors of culture.[39] "Traditions," celebrated in a strategy serving to counteract the colonialist, racist attitudes that desecrate Chicano culture, become frozen idols representing processes of patriarchal control. Thus Chicanas note how they are silenced both by the society at large as racial and ethnic others and by their society at home, which imposes upon them, as gendered others, the charge of tradition. Notions of double silencing, double marginalization, and double oppression become the central tropes motivating Chicanas toward greater involvement in cultural and political worlds.

Since the mid–1980s, a burgeoning Chicana literary and historical criticism has accompanied the work of such writers as Sandra Cisneros, Alma Villanueva, Bernice Zamora, Ana Castillo, Denise Chávez, Lorna Dee Cervantes, and Evangelina Vigil. This criticism has helped nurture and disseminate Chicana literature, just as it has spurred other Chicanas to engage in the creation of more fictional, poetic, and critical work.[40] This work has also, however, been marked by a series of contradictions all its own. Largely disavowing an interest in nationalist projects or the establishment of a cosmic identity, Chicana critics have been split between searching in their mother's gardens for emblems and stories that articulate their own conflicted identities, and looking in other yards for discourses and strategies by which to posit a more powerful and resistant sense of agency.

One strategy has sought to articulate a "native" theory that faithfully emerges from and reveals the particularities of Chicana texts. Tey Diana Rebolledo, for example, discusses Chicano literature in terms of a longing for traditions and histories as a locus of unity, community, and safety: "One common theme in Chicano writing in general has been the nostalgia for a world lost, a world that signified spontaneity and comfort. The mythology of the past takes place spatially and emotionally: the past acquires enhanced meaning. These images contrast sharply with the stresses and ambiguity of today" (1987: 153). The past, Rebolledo argues, is embodied by the presence of grandmothers in a number of the works by Chicana writers. The abuelita comes to represent the myth of "determination, of integration, of finding one's own space: it is the fireplace passionately put together stone by stone" (1987: 158). Domestic space provides an alternate cultural space by which to define self and from which to assume strategies of survival. Thus Rebolledo argues: "I personally find it difficult to have theory (male oriented, French feminist, post-structural or whatever is the current fad) be what dictates what we find in our literature. I prefer to have the literature speak for itself and as a critic try to organize and understand it" (1988: 134). Rebolledo's critical project favors the "indigenous" or "domestic" text over the faddishness of an imperializing theory. It relegates the literary critic to the position of hermeneutic "organizer" (however that role may be understood as divorced from some theoretical position). As understandable as her suspicion of theory may be, Rebolledo's position involves a return to critical ground similar to that cultivated by a number of male critics before her. The emphasis upon and valorization of the Chicano text embodying the

Chicano place (put together stone by stone) implies a project of separation, isolation, nationalism. She valorizes the unique and essential Chicanismo of the text that distinguishes it and allows it to be read and understood.

Another critical strategy, embodied in the work of Norma Alarcón, relies quite heavily on "foreign" literary and critical theories by which to approach Chicana texts. Appropriating the discourses of Bakhtin, Jameson, Irigaray, and Kristeva, Alarcón reads the work of Cherríe Moraga, Helena María Viramontes, and Ana Castillo as an exploration of Chicana subjectivity that "takes as its point of departure 'woman's' over-determined signification as future wives/mothers in relation to the 'symbolic contract' within which women may have a voice on the condition that they speak as mothers'" (Alarcón 1988: 148).[41] This reading of Chicana literature at the intersection of political, racial and gendered trajectories marks a critical literary project circumscribed by institutional practices. These primarily European and heavily academic discourses are employed to analyze a literature historically positioned without the canon of academic Western literature. Although Alarcón's critical practice carefully balances the theoretical with the practical in a creative and constructive way, her approach raises the possibility that Chicana literature may at some basic level function in the same way, psychologically and politically, as other (more European, more canonical) literary texts. A Chicana text may therefore scrutinize and reveal particular Chicana themes and problems, but as a cultural object it can be observed and understood through a critical–theoretical lens in a manner identical with any Eurocentric literary text.

Yet another critical strategy foregrounds the political significance of literary criticism. Yvonne Yarbro-Bejarano, for example, argues that the project of the Chicana feminist critic is an engaged and practical one: "The exclusion of Chicanas from literary authority is intimately linked to the exclusion of Chicanas from other kinds of power monopolized by privileged white males. Their struggle to appropriate the 'I' of literary discourse relates to their struggle for empowerment in the economic, social and political spheres" (1988: 139). Thus, though the literature may not necessarily be tendentious (as it was sometimes called upon to be during the heat of the nationalist movements of "Aztlán"), its critical study certainly bears with it a political charge. Its purpose is yet again to draw together a community of the exploited and oppressed. Now, however, this creation of community involves a more encompassing scope, calling for "the development of a Chicana feminism in coalition with other women of color dedicated to the definition of a feminism which would address the specific situation of working-class women of color who do not belong to the dominant culture" (1988: 140). This feminist project, emerging from the twin dissatisfactions with white feminism and with Chicano nationalism, marks a new phase of coalition. This movement focuses Chicana criticism on forms of intervention and cultural critique that draw together the concerns of diverse and distinct constituencies, allowing for a practice and theory based upon difference and discontinuity. It thus points in a direction to which postcolonial literary discourses may move as they more fully scrutinize the tenacious problems involved in articulating postcolonial identities.

The project of alliance-building as proposed by such figures as Gloria Anzaldúa, Cherríe Moraga, and Yvonne Yarbro-Bejarano marks both a break and a continuity evident in the movements of Chicano literature: the clear interrelationship between historical reality and cultural production. As we have seen, this interrelationship is not uncomplicated. On several fronts there is the desire for art to intervene in life: "Our writers as image-makers are creators of a new sort who propose to document artistically the Chicano experience in all its facets" (E. García et al. 1984: 100). At the same time, this intervention of Chicano cultural identity into sociopolitical reality can be very contradictory. At its most essentializing – especially in its early phases – Chicano cultural production elides historical differences and cultural multiplicities, it presumes a static instrumentality about literature, it makes the cultural transparent. As Rosa Linda Fregoso and Angie Chabram argue, the main problem is that the basis of Chicano identity "as formulated by Chicano cultural nationalism postulated that collective identity was simultaneity and continuity between the object and its representation" (1990: 205–6). An example of this can be found in the introduction to one of the first collections of Chicano literature, *Literatura Chicana: Texto y Contexto,* published in 1972. The editors of this groundbreaking work comment upon their method of collection: "We have looked for depth of experience, for imaginative use of language, and for treatment of the important themes of Chicano life, past and present" (Shular et al. 1972: xxiv). The editors do not address in any way what the nature of that "Chicano life" is, do not problematize the notions of identity and experience, do not discuss the "textuality" of the literature.

One means of articulating a Chicano literary criticism comes to involve the analysis of the cultural and discursive practices embodied by that literature. Rather than presume the simultaneity of Chicano identity and its representation, this other analysis focuses on the significance of the mode of representation. This latest movement in Chicano critical practice might focus, for instance, on the use of mythic figures in the early Chicano poetry as a means of political unity and a measure of the archetypical. Clearly, this cultural creation served a particular need, and it is on this need that critical attention might fix its gaze. Gloria Anzaldúa, for example, as a Chicana lesbian poet, in her turn appropriates mythic images in order to articulate a sense of identity long absent from discussions of the "Chicano." In *"La herencia de Coatlicue,"* she states: "*Coatlicue* is one of the powerful images, or 'archetypes,' that inhabits, or passes through, my psyche. For me, *la Coatlicue* is the consuming internal whirlwind, the symbol of the underground aspects of the psyche" (1987: 46). In "Chicana Feminism," Norma Alarcón argues that this use of myth does not represent a desire for a lost utopia or an essence of being. Instead, the evocation of myth forms a strategy marked by a number of political projects. Anzaldúa appropriates the techniques developed by the founding Chicano fathers who enlisted mythical figures to consolidate cultural identity and pride. She assumes the patriarchal privilege of naming and identifying, but in order to name her own experience and to foreground female figures. Not only does this strategy mark positively, it marks negatively as well. Alarcón notes that "by invoking the 'dark Beast' within and without, which many have forced us to deny, the cultural and psychic dismemberment that is linked to imperialist racist and sexist practices are brought into focus" (Alarcón 1990: 251).

This is to suggest that Chicano literary criticism seems to be moving in a direction that more intimately links its practices with the historical, political, and cultural particularity of Chicano experiences. Recent critical practice responds to a need not just to study the hermeneutic meaning of the text, but also to discuss how that text is inscribed by historically determined practices. To discount the historical dimension of Chicano literature is not merely to remove it from its context. To deny the history imbedded in Chicano literature is to displace its aesthetic significance. In one form or another, the literature is traced by an intricate play of historically marked discursive practices. It moves through an odd nexus where popular culture – folk poetry, indigenous lore, balladry, religious ritual – meets an elite cadre of European–American cultural products – the "high" art that is the currency of institutional education – and the alienated forms of late-capitalist culture. This meeting rings with the clash and consonance of an anxious confluence at once part battle, part panic, part rebellion, part reconciliation.

Historically, Chicano literature forms that discontinuous region where the territories of the various colonizations of North America meet. This clashing of worlds raises a whole range of social and cultural issues that form what has been called "the Chicano." Chicano creative and critical writers have sought to negotiate the contours of this conflicted cultural terrain. Their work demonstrates that the struggle to function as a creative, engaged, intelligent individual within violent systems is a serious and ceaseless journey. Whatever gains Chicanos, Latinos, and other internal postcolonials have managed over the years, an adequate articulation of a personal and cultural subjectivity of the subaltern has still to be voiced within a more encompassing reconceptualization of American identity.[42] The struggle to critique and replace metaphors of "us" and "other," "majority" and "minority," "center" and "margin," "First World" and "Third World" is yet underway. At stake in this quincentenarian epoch is an understanding of the "American" as part of a larger culture of the Americas comprised not of a First World and a Third World, but rather of four or five highly complex, conflicted, and one hopes complementary worlds.

3

From the Homeland to the Borderlands, the Reformation of Aztlán

This is the place where everyone takes command:
No man's land.

– Latin Alliance

IN DELANO, CALIFORNIA, in 1965, a procession of campesinos walked away from the heat and dust of non-unionized grape fields into the stark sun of historical scrutiny. The group, organized and led by César Chávez, demanded the right to fair wages, legal protection, and decent working conditions – "basic, God-given rights as human beings." These demands were outlined in "El Plan de Delano" issued by the National Farm Workers Association (NFWA, later to become the United Farm Workers, UFW). On September 16, 1965, the NFWA voted to join Filipino grape pickers in their strike against wealthy landowners. As one of its first actions, the group undertook a 250-mile pilgrimage to Sacramento, during which "El Plan de Delano" was issued: "Our sweat and our blood have fallen on this land to make other men rich. This Pilgrimage is a witness to the suffering we have seen for generations" (1965: 198).

"Land," once again in the history of the poor and dispossessed, sparked demands for reform and change. "Land" again incited the sense of rightness and passion for justice necessary in engendering political action. The strike in Delano triggered the events known variously as El Movimiento or La Causa and incited calls for justice and empowerment that, variously muted or amplified, are still sounded today.[1] The claims for land, which informed one strain of Chicano nationalism through the 1960s and 1970s (and which resonated in the call for a Chicano cultural nationalism), mark a point of connection between Chicano discourses and those of other postcolonial groups. As with those other groups, the claim to land walked hand in hand with a hearkening to cultural and indigenous antecedents. The call for reform and recognition in Delano was based upon a prior claim linked to the history of Mexican laborers toiling in the fields of San Joaquín. This claim, in turn, became linked to one even more previous arising from the dispossession enacted by the Treaty of Guadalupe Hidalgo in 1848. And this event, finally, led back to an even more originary claim to land: "Aztlán."

"Aztlán" names, according to legend, the Mexican homeland – the land of seven caves (Chicomostoc), the place of the Twisted Hill (Colhuacán), the place of whiteness (Aztlán) – from which the Mexica migrated southward toward the central plateau in 820 A.D.[2] The ideas embodied in Aztlán draw together geography, culture, history, genetics, migration, tradition, heritage, unity, authenticity. It crystallizes in one term the history of dispossession endured by Mexicans, Mexican-Americans, and Chicanos alike. Or, as Rodolfo Acuña puts it in his characteristically blunt manner, Aztlán not only reaffirmed the Indian heritage of Chicanos but also "the fact that Chicanos were indigenous to the Southwest; therefore, if the Anglo-Americans did not like it there, they could go back to from where they came" (1972: 229). The invocation of pre-European links to indigenous ancestry valorized a claim to land that was home prior to invasion and dispossession. Although the skin tone and physiognomy of many Chicanos manifest this link, the significance of pre-European connections to the Americas is not circumscribed simply by genetic encoding. Nor is it bound by territorial claims; the myth of Aztlán as a compelling strategy of reclamation has long fallen out of favor. The significance of indigenous ancestry, ultimately, is constructed and reconstructed, the crystallization of historical and personal memories interjected into contemporary social and political conditions.

In 1981, Luis Leal, looking back a dozen years to the introduction of Aztlán into Chicano discourse, traces the traditions and effects of Aztlán. He notes, for example, that in one of the earliest European accounts of the Mexica, Fray Diego Durán reports that Aztlán represents a utopian vision of the Mexica homeland. There, the earth goddess Coatlicue lives, her fecundity manifested by the fact that men in her service never become old. Leal goes on to note that within pre-Cortesian symbolic economies, Aztlán functions on two levels: "As a symbol, it conveys the image of the cave (or sometimes a hill) representative of the origin of man; and as a myth, it symbolizes the existence of a paradisiacal region where injustice, evil, sickness, old age, poverty, and misery do not exist" (1981: 17). Within the more contemporary economy of Chicano symbolic exchange, Aztlán functions within both geopolitical and cultural orders: "It represents the geographic region known as the Southwestern part of the United States, composed of the territory that Mexico ceded in 1848 with the Treaty of Guadalupe Hidalgo; second, and more important, Aztlán symbolizes the spiritual union of the Chicanos, something that is carried within the heart, no matter where they may live or where they may find themselves" (1981: 18). Leal points out the crux of the problem with Aztlán in the early articulation of Chicano cultural and political identification. Its representations reveal its role as a split between a strategic critique of sociopolitical reality and an iconographic instrument of cultural unity.

A Land Divided

The notion of Aztlán was introduced to Chicana discourse with "El Plan Espiritual de Aztlán," drafted in March 1969 for the Chicano Youth Conference held in Denver, Colorado. It represents one of several plans – including "El Plan de Delano" (1965), "El Plan de La Raza Unida" (1967), "El Plan de Santa Barbara" (1969) – adopted by farm workers, community organizers, and university students in a flurry of activity defining and refining El Movimiento. "El Plan de Delano," as we have seen, accompanied the farm workers march and strike that eventually propelled the United Farm Workers into national prominence and politics.[3] "El Plan de La Raza Unida," demanding equal representation and affirming a role for Chicanas within "the framework of constitutional democracy and freedom" (1967: 331) marked a new level of Chicana self-determination by establishing La Raza Unida, an independent and, to a degree, efficacious political party. The party was for a time to play a significant political role in Crystal City and other towns in Texas, winning community control of schools and city councils and enabling the development of Chicana businesses in what had essentially been an apartheid system.[4] "El Plan de Santa Barbara," adopted, after six months of planning, at a statewide student conference held at the University of California, Santa Barbara, California, outlined programs for the development of self-determination within institutions of higher education. It led to the establishment of Chicano studies programs guided by the belief that "Chicano students, faculty, administrators, employees, and the community must be the central and decisive designers and administrators of those programs" (1969: 86). This emphasis upon community involvement and empowerment forms a central motif informing the Plans associated with El Movimiento.

Consequently, the failure of these plans – all articulating essentially reformist demands – to make immediate and lasting influences on the life of the community led to disillusionment and disintegration among the various waves of El Movimiento. As Sonia López notes: "Though some changes did occur in the areas of awareness of racism among the general public and the revival of cultural pride for certain sectors of the Chicano community, these activities and programs did not eliminate the conditions maintaining the Chicano population in subservient and dependent status. . . . Mexican communities still have a high rate of drug abuse, poverty, unemployment, low quality health care, low educational achievement, and no political power" (1977: 21). Despite their lack of long-term efficacy, these Plans nevertheless mark milestones in Chicana cultural identity. They represent moments at which Chicana constituencies assumed for themselves an agency within economic, political, and educational systems in ways previously denied to them. They articulate claims to self-affirmation carved out of and against exploitative sociopolitical systems.

The question in regard to "El Plan Espiritual de Aztlán" is how precisely – if at all – it marked a real move toward actual self-affirmation and determination. In part, the idea of Aztlán forms a matrix where two seemingly contradictory strands of Chicana thought meet. On the one hand, the term "Chicano/a" signifies an identification with struggles for change within or the transformation of socioeconomic and political systems that have historically exploited Mexicans and people of Mexican ancestry. The focus along this trajectory is on the transformation of material conditions, on gains in a real economic and political sense.[5] On the other hand, the term "Chicano/a" identifies a subjectivity marked by a heritage and culture distinct from and devalued by Euramerican society.[6] The interplay between these two meanings of the term Chicano/a is complex and not entirely resolved. Although the claims for Chicana cultural agency have been to a greater or lesser degree effective, their translation into social empowerment has, as Sonia López notes, been largely unsuccessful. This tension between the social and cultural polarities within Chicana activism is made evident in the various articulations of the term Aztlán.

Aztlán as the signifier marking the completion or return of the Chicano to a homeland suggests both cultural and social signification. As the representation of place, Aztlán makes claims to a political and economic self-determination not dissimilar to claims asserted by indigenous populations throughout the world. As a symbol of unity, Aztlán asserts a type of cultural nationalism that is distinct from – though meant to work hand-in-hand with – social activism. The sense of a double signification resounds in "El Plan de Aztlán":

> Brotherhood unites us and love for our brothers makes us a people whose time has come and who struggle against the foreigner "Gabacho," who exploits our riches and destroys our culture. With our heart in our hands and our hands in the soil, We Declare the Independence of our Mestizo Nation. We are a Bronze People with a Bronze Culture. Before the world, before all of North America, before all our brothers in the Bronze Continent, We are a Nation, We are a Union of free pueblos, We are Aztlán. (1969: 403)

The Plan rails against the Euramerican, the "Gabacho," who "exploits our riches" and simultaneously "destroys our culture." These two spheres in which violence occurs are – within the logic of the Plan – equitable but not identical. One represents the riches of land and labor, commodities within sociopolitical and economic systems of exchange. The other manifests self-identity and cultural independence. The tension between cultural and political autonomy makes itself felt in the image of the Chicano communities that affirms culture ("With our heart in our hands") and nation ("and our hands in the soil") as coming together to "Declare the Independence of our Mestizo Nation." What this Nation consists of – beyond the essentializing and vague vision of a "Bronze People" with a "Bronze Culture" forming a "Union of free pueblos" – remains unspoken.[7]

There are those who want to claim Aztlán as the embodiment of a successful unity between the cultural and political. Michael Pina, for example, argues:

> On one level Chicano nationalism calls for the re-creation of an Aztec spiritual homeland, Aztlán; on another, it expresses the desire to politically reconquer the northern territories wrested from Mexico in an imperialist war inspired by American "Manifest Destiny." These two mythic narratives merged to form the living myth of Chicano nationalism. This myth spanned the diachronic chasm that separates the archaic contents of cultural memory from the contemporary struggle for cultural survival. (1989: 36)

In effect, Pina argues that the evocation of Aztlán bridges "the diachronic chasm" between pre-Cortesian identity and contemporary social activism as well as spanning the gap between cultural and political agency. Rather than evoke a bridge beyond history, I would argue that Aztlán reveals the discontinuity and rupture that characterize Chicanos in history. Although it evokes a Chicano homeland, Aztlán also foregrounds the difficult relationship Chicanos bear with history – a history, after all, comprised of dispossession and migration.

Aztlán as it comes to be articulated forms something of a wish fulfillment, a dream of what could be: "through Aztlán we come to better understand psychological time (identity), regional makeup (place), and evolution (historical time). Without any one of these ingredients, we would be contemporary displaced nomads, suffering the diaspora in our own land, and at the mercy of other social forces. Aztlán allows us to come full circle with our communal background as well as to maintain ourselves as fully integrated individuals" (Anaya and Lomelí 1989: iv). Although the introduction to the fine critical collection *Aztlán: Essays on the Chicano Homeland* argues for the primacy of Aztlán as the completion of Chicano identity, I suggest that the notion of Aztlán – highly influential in the articulation of Chicano identity – marks less the wholeness than the heterogeneity evident in the subject position Chicano. It is impossible, for example, to ignore the role that Chicanos and Mexican migrant workers play within a diasporic history. One can no longer assert the wholeness of a Chicano subject when the very discourses that go into identity formation are themselves contradictory. It is illusory to deny the nomadic quality of the Chicano community, a community in flux that yet survives and, through survival, affirms its own self.

This is not to dismiss either the significance of Aztlán or the relevance of "El Plan Espiritual." The Plan does – owing much to Frantz Fanon – articulate an ambitious (if ambiguous) nationalism suggesting that the spiritual longing and physical needs of the subaltern "native" are inexorably bound together. Although Fanon argues in *The Wretched of the Earth* that the immediate effects of a cultural nationalism are difficult to gauge – "I am ready to concede that on the plane of factual being the past existence of an Aztec civilization does not change anything very much in the diet of the Mexican peasant today" (1961: 209) – he goes on to argue that "this passionate search for a national culture which existed before the colonial era finds its legitimate reason in the anxiety shared by native intellectuals to shrink away from that Western culture in which they all risk being swamped" (1961: 209). By Fanon's argument, the search for an "other" space proves not to be simply an escape from the present. On the contrary, since colonial processes wish to impose rule upon the past as well as the present and future of a colonized people, the quest for a past proves to be a great act of resistance and self-affirmation: "the native intellectuals, since they could not stand wonderstruck before the history of today's barbarity, decided to go back further and to delve deeper down; and, let us make no mistake, it was with the greatest delight that they discovered that there was nothing to be ashamed of in the past, but rather dignity, glory, and solemnity" (1961: 210). The affirmation of a glorious past becomes the condemnation of a repressive present.

Evoking a similar sentiment, "El Plan Espiritual de Aztlán" declares:

> In the spirit of a new people that is conscious not only of its proud historical heritage, but also of the brutal "Gringo" invasion of our territories: We, the Chicano inhabitants and civilizers of the northern land of Aztlán, from whence came our forefathers, reclaiming the land of their birth and consecrating the determination of our people of the sun, declare that the call of our blood is our power, our responsibility, and our inevitable destiny. (1969: 402–3)

The Plan hearkens back to the "forefathers" as a basis for reclamation, a tenuous position at best given the diverse indigenous past of actual Chicanos. However, the Plan serves to highlight the role of history – "the brutal 'Gringo' invasion of our territories" – as a trope one finds over and over in Chicano cultural criticism. History, after all, has proved to the Chicano that U.S. society has no patience or respect (when it has time to take notice at all) for people of Mexican ancestry, U.S. citizens or not. Chicano artists and critics constantly write themselves into this history.

The invocation of ancestry by the Plan reclaims a position and a heritage that lays claim to integrity and agency. This claim suggests, through the "call of our blood," an essentialized and biologically determined nationalism that was finally to prove an untenable position. So problematic was this essentialization that, a decade after the Plan, one of its drafters – the poet Alurista – felt compelled to defend it in his explanation of cultural nationalism.[8] The Plan, he argues in 1981, "clearly stated that 'Aztlán belonged to those who worked it' (not only Xicano workers) and that no capricious frontiers would be recognized – an important point which, in the fervor of an exclusivist narrow nationalism, was quickly overlooked" (1981: 25). Alurista disavows what could be interpreted as the most racist elements of nationalism evident in the Plan's articulation of Aztlán. At the same time, he insists upon a type of transnational "nationalism," a cultural nationalism distinct from the "exclusivist narrow nationalism" of strict political delineation.

This distinction helps explain the tension between two (ultimately contradictory) veins of Chicana "nationalism" strongly influential in subsequent movements of cultural and political identification. Did Aztlán signal a rationally planned nationalist movement, or did it evoke a mythopoetic cultural entity meant to enable some future political action? Although the drafters of the Plan, after Fanon, seem to view a cultural nationalism as simultaneous with a political nationalism, Aztlán came to be the hotly disputed terrain on which either one or another type of nationalism was ostensibly founded. Elyette Labarthe, discussing the development of Aztlán, notes the importance of these disputes in the early development of Chicana self-identity: "On one side an oracular voice crackled over that of reason, on the other side a dispassionate voice piped up above that of the inspired poet, but could not quite blot it out" (1990: 79). As Labarthe points out, militant factions in El Movimiento viewed Alurista's nationalism as a hollow and romanticized vision that subverted real claims to Aztlán, real political–nationalist interests. The tensions between the locally political and the universally cultural form one of the faultlines that runs through the terrain of early Chicana cultural articulations.

This tension and rupture between cultural and political nationalisms had some of their most durable effects, Jorge Klor de Alva implies, in the breakdown of leadership among Chicana communities. He notes:

> On one side are leaders with a humanist bent, often schooled in literature or fine arts, who tend to focus on cultural concerns while emphasizing the cultural autonomy of the individual. Their naive cultural nationalism is ultimately too chauvinistic to promote the unification efforts needed to overcome the divisive forces of monopoly capitalism and the seductiveness of modern fragmenting individualism. On the other side are those primarily trained in the social sciences, whose research is delimited by a preoccupation with economic and political issues, and whose eyes are fixed on social structures and the work force. The radicals among them disparage the importance of culture and nationalism while focusing primarily on the significance of class. (1989: 137)

Although Klor de Alva goes on to elaborate that this schema is "deceiving in its simplicity," it nevertheless reflects a distancing between "two valuable and necessary camps" (1989: 138).

This schema is indeed deceptive, as Klor de Alva astutely notes. The tensions that inform the schism between "the political" and "the cultural" within Chicana discourses run deeply. They spread out over a larger historical and geographic terrain not divided neatly into camps like "political" versus "cultural" or "historical" as opposed to "mythical." The fissures involved in Chicana nationalist claims derive from a number of different historical sources: the nationalist movements – American Indian and Black – current in the political climate of the late 1960s; the Third World struggles for national sovereignty in the 1950s; the "nationless" status of Chicanos who, after fighting in World War II, returned to a country where they were still considered foreigners in the 1940s; the institutionalization, following the Mexican Revolution, of Mexican national culture in the 1920s and 1930s; the usurpation of Mexican territorial rights in 1848; the history of Mexican independence from Spain begun in 1810. All these form influential trajectories that cross at the matrix of Chicana nationalism.

The influence of the Mexican Revolution on Chicana thinking in particular cannot be minimized. As Leal and Barrón note, "Immigration from Mexico to the United States from 1848 to 1910 was negligible. After 1910, however, and especially during the critical years of the Mexican Revolution (1913–1915), which coincided with the outbreak of World War I and the consequent expansion of American industry and agriculture, large numbers of immigrants crossed the border" (1982: 20). The influences on the economic and social conditions of Chicano life in the United States certainly changed as a result of the Revolution. Not the least of these changes was the backlash against Mexicans that was to come in the 1920s.[9] Moreover, the events following the Revolution provided some of the models upon which Chicana self-identification would be founded.

The nativism so valued by Chicana cultural discourses, for example, clearly draws its influence from the construction of postrevolutionary Mexican nationalism. The affirmation of native roots in the cultural identification of the Mexican begins with José Vasconcelos's service as Minister of Education under President Alvaro Obregón (1920–4).[10] Other movements toward Chicana empowerment are prefigured in the Mexican postrevolutionary world as well. In the politicocultural realm, one finds a strong conflict between Mexican intelligensia who wish to ally themselves with an international Marxism and those seeking to discover the true character of Mexico. Samuel Ramos began *Profile of Man and Culture in Mexico* (1934) as a personality study of Mexico, and Jorge Cuesta's anthology of modern Mexican poetry (1928) undertook an investigation into the meaning of Mexican cultural tradition. Octavio Paz notes: "They both reflect our profound desire for self-knowledge. The former represents our search for the intimate particulars of our nature, a search that was the very essence of our Revolution, while the latter represents our anxiety to incorporate these particulars in a universal tradition" (1950: 162).[11] As we saw in Chapter 2, the desire to articulate "the intimate particulars" of the Chicana national character as well as the incorporation of "these particulars in a universal tradition" resounds in the projects several Chicana critics have undertaken in articulating Chicana cultural identity.

These strong intellectual and cultural associations with Mexico, according to Genaro Padilla, arise from a profound sense of disconnection experienced by Chicana writers and thinkers. They have, Padilla argues:

> suffered from an "orphan complex" that led, in past generations, to an idealization of the Spanish forebearers, and more recently to a nostalgia for the Mexican homeland, especially as it has been imagined in that mythical realm of Aztlán. This impulse has manifested itself intensely in the last two decades, a period during which the Chicano, feeling deeply alienated from the foster parent United States, wished to maintain a vital spiritual link with Mexico, the model of language, culture and social behavior. This explains, in part, why Chicano cultural nationalists not only appropriated the pre-Columbian mythology of Mexico, but also its Revolutionary heroes – Benito Juárez, Emiliano Zapata, Pancho Villa – and affected a kinship with Mexico's common people and their history. (1989: 126)

This kinship informs the construction of cultural nationalism and its alliance to progressive economic, social, and political agendas. What specific course those agendas should take – and the role that the culture should play in relation to those agendas – forms part of the discontinuity apparent in the realm of Aztlán.

Aztlán stands as that region where the diverse political, geographic, and cultural concerns gripping the Chicano imagination of the late 1960s meet. Alurista, as we have seen, views Aztlán as a sign whose referent is unproblematically apparent. From Alurista's view, the conflation of a nation and a culture seems to provide no tension. Thus he can assert that Chicano literature "is a national literature, and will have to reflect all the levels that our nation implies, all that IS our people" (Bruce-Novoa 1980: 284).[12] The fact of Aztlán as a Chicano nation stands as an ontological certainty. The literature that will emerge from it will reflect the same nationalist concerns as any other national literature. There is a curious eliding of nation, literature, people in Alurista's configuration of Aztlán. The term comes to represent not just the fact of sovereignty, but the fact of existence, the very being that is the Chicano – a reflection of the essentializing moves manifested by this strain of Chicano cultural articulation, an essentialization that Alurista seems to speak against elsewhere.

In "In Search of Aztlán," Luís Leal looks upon the idea of Aztlán, and the Plan Espiritual specifically, from a more historical perspective. He traces the effects and traditions of Aztlán, most particularly by documenting "the rebirth of the myth in Chicano thought" (1981: 20). "El Plan Espiritual de

Aztlán" forms an important document and turning point in the articulation of Chicano consciousness. In it, Leal argues that the Chicano "recognizes his Aztec origins" as well as "establishes that Aztlán is the Mexican territory ceded to the United States in 1848" (1981: 20). The Plan articulates the affirmation of origins, both indigenous (though reified in the idea of "Aztecs" as original tribe) and nationalist. He goes on to note that "following one of the basic ideas of the Mexican Revolution, it recognizes that the land belongs to those who work it," making explicit the connection between Aztlán and the cultural history that enabled its articulation. Leal's comments thus point toward the historical loci and salient components that make up the discursive practices associated with Aztlán. This historical perspective quickly dissolves, however, into a more essentialized and reified notion of Aztlán.

Leal concludes "In Search of Aztlán" with the admonition "whosoever wants to find Aztlán, let him look for it, not on the maps, but in the most intimate part of his being" (1981: 22). His discussion, which begins as a historical project, becomes a rhetorical one. Aztlán ceases to exist except as a vague search for spiritual centering. Six years before Leal, Sylvia Gonzales had made a similar discursive move, dissolving the historical ground of Aztlán in favor of an essential and ultimately romantic notion of universal "culture." In her essay "National Character vs. Universality in Chicano Poetry," Gonzales begins by articulating a sociohistorically bound notion of Aztlán: "In recognition of our oppression, the Chicano people . . . searched for identity and awareness as a group, as a nation within a nation. This became the cultural, psychological, philosophical and political nation of Aztlán" (1975: 15). Aztlán thus represents a contested, resistant site. Not specifically bound to a geographic reclamation, Aztlán in Gonzales's view is a discursive construction arising out of political necessity. However, her argument quickly moves from a project of political resistance to one of eschatological dimensions. Her vision of Aztlán leaves us with a messianic vision of cultural universality: "The world awaits the appearance of a disciple capable of propounding the message, interpreting the underlying language of their work, which has already been proscribed. That disciple will have to be a priest, a magician or a poet" (1975: 19). This articulation of Aztlán moves from issues of self-determination to a dream of cultural salvation.

In the end, the terrain termed Aztlán comes to represent less a specific geographic locale – though various discourses viewed it as such – than a means of counterdiscursive engagement. Its efficacy from a strictly political perspective remains questionable. When compared with the other Plans marking El Movimiento, "El Plan Espiritual de Aztlán" did not leave as distinct a political legacy. Labarthe argues that the power of "Aztlán" lies in its imaginative conceptualization of Chicano unity: "The socio-economic debate was to be awarded a spiritual dimension and a dynamism that were sadly lacking. The symbol of Aztlán had the power to legitimize the struggles to cement the claims. It was a compensatory symbolic mechanism, fusing poetico-symbolic unity to socio-cultural concerns. The Chicanos who were divided by history, found in it an ancestral territory and a common destiny" (1990: 80). Its compensatory function served to make it a lasting image. But as a compensatory strategy, its political effects proved less than prepossessing.

Finally, as the arguments by Gonzales and Leal indicate, the function of Aztlán was to pronounce a minority position that staked claims for legitimacy through a cultural and ancestral primacy. In immediate terms, however, as Juan Gómez-Quiñones argues, the Plan "was stripped of what radical element it possessed by stressing its alleged romantic idealism, reducing the concept of Aztlán to a psychological ploy, and limiting advocacy for self-determination to local community control – all of which became possible because of the plan's incomplete analysis which, in turn, allowed its language concerning issues to degenerate into reformism" (1990: 124). The political vagueness of the Plan allowed it to dissipate its energies along the small faultlines of numerous cultural discourses. And this dispersal, although causing tremors in the cultural terrain of Euramerican society, did little to shake the walls and bring down the structures of power as its rhetoric so firmly proclaimed.

Aztlán as a supposed "common denominator with the claims to the vatos locos, pochos, pachucos, cholos and other mestizos" (Labarthe 1990: 80) fails. Purportedly invoked as a politically unifying metaphor, Aztlán becomes something quite different. Although politically and ideologically vague, "El Plan Espiritual de Aztlán" did help establish the discursive habits by which Chicano culture asserted its autonomy. It thus helped form not a national but a critical region for El Movimiento.[13] At its most efficacious moments, it comes to represent a cultural site expressing pride in origins and heritages. The investigation of the past, the reclamation of history, the pride of place embodied in Aztlán, manifests itself in the idea of Chicanismo.

The poet José Montoya explains: "*Chicanismo* is a basic concept which embodies both the Indio and the Spanish aspects of our heritage. As Chicano people we now accept the Indio side of our heritage. We somehow never had too much of a problem with our Hispanitude one way or the other. But to be considered an Indio!" (1986: 25). The mestizaje of Montoya's exclamations forms a nexus of cultural and personal identity that first gained currency in the nationalist movements of postrevolutionary Mexico. Although the impetus for the celebration of nativism emerges from the politicocultural discourses of Mexico, hegemonic views on race and culture die long and agonized deaths. Despite the ideological valorization of mestizaje, the racism inherent in both U.S. and Mexican societies certainly circulated in the "Mexican-American" communities. In a North American context, this meant that the members of these communities were under pressure to assimilate particular standards – of beauty, of identity, of aspiration. In a Mexican context, the pressure was to urbanize and Europeanize. Which is to say that in order to belong to larger imagined communities of the nation – particularly in the United States – "Mexican-Americans" were expected to accept antiindigenous discourses as their own.

In this respect, Aztlán allowed for a subjectivity that reclaims the connection to indigenous peoples and cultures. Although it did not offer a platform that would allow for a reclamation of a nation, it did provide an alternate national consciousness.[14] It allowed for another way of aligning one's interests and concerns with community and with history. This may prove to be the most lasting legacy of Aztlán. In crystallizing a sense of rightful place and identity, it sought to enable a newfound agency. Though hazy as to the precise means by which this agency would emerge, Aztlán valorized a Chicanismo that rewove into the present previously devalued lines of descent.

A politics of locality centers around Aztlán – a locality that finds its expression in notions of Chicanismo. As Gómez-Quiñones notes:

> Although "Chicanismo" was often a loosely expressed concept, it did translate as a radically political and ethnic populism. . . . "Chicanismo" referred to a set of beliefs; in particular, a political practice. The emphasis of "Chicanismo" upon dignity, self-worth, pride, uniqueness, and a feeling of cultural rebirth made it attractive to many Mexicans in a way that cut across class, regional, and generational lines. (1990: 103–4)

The sense of pride and connection, rebirth and respect implied in the term Chicanismo is nowhere made more manifest than in Rodolfo Gonzales's opus classicus *Yo Soy Joaquín*. The poem manifests a Chicanismo comprised of cultural nationalism and connectivity to Mexican history and culture. It prefigures both the empowerment and contradictions inherent to Aztlán as a concept central to Chicano consciousness.

An Other Country: Rodolfo Gonzales

Published as a leaflet, a mimeo sheet recited as a form of agitprop at Movimiento rallies, *Yo Soy Joaquín* represents a "quest for our roots, the renewal of a fierce pride and tribal unity" as the introduction to the published version of the poem proclaims.[15] Although it does not invoke the name of Aztlán, the poem expresses a number of concerns that Chicana nationalism articulates through Aztlán. Rodolfo Gonzales, a community organizer, a founder of the Crusade for Justice, a candidate for mayor of Denver, Colorado, wrote the poem in 1967 as a catalyst for galvanizing political action. Attempting to fortify the image of the community, the poem seeks to represent an empowering vision of Chicana subjectivity. Although it proclaims itself "a mirror of our greatness and our weakness," it seeks finally to stand as "a call to action as a total people, emerging from a glorious history, traveling through social pain and conflicts, confessing our weaknesses while we shout about our strength" (1967: 1). The introduction thus suggests that the poem touches on points of rupture in the articulation of Chicana subjectivity and culture but that it finally affirms Chicana identity and activism through history.

The reclamation of history offers agency, a propulsion into an empowered and empowering future. Presenting a variety of historical vignettes and portraits of contemporary exploitation, the poem asserts the heritage that goes into making the speaking subject of the poem: "Joaquín." The entire poem, then, represents a reiteration and elaboration of the title *I am Joaquín*. The poem is an assertion of self. "Joaquín" and *Joaquín* collapse into a single entity characterized by a history of pain, struggle, ultimately triumph. The collapse of speaker and title signals a collapse as well of history into culture. The poem works to make these realms coterminous so that culture is history is heritage is "Joaquín" is *Joaquín*.

The poem therefore offers itself as the embodiment of history, a node at which all the lines of descent that make up the "Chicano" coalesce. In coming together, these lines are meant to propel the "Chicano" into action. In this sense, the poem forms a prefiguration of Aztlán, for, as Anaya and Lomelí argue:

> Aztlán became a collective symbol by which to recover the past that had been wrestled away from the inhabitants of Aztlán through the multiple conquests of the area. It should be kept in mind that by reappropriating Aztlán the Chicano did not choose to live in the past; rather, the community chose to find its tap root of identity in its history so that it could more confidently create the future. (1989: ii)

Joaquín manifests the same sense of purpose and spirit. Introducing the poem, Gonzales notes that it represents "the psychological wounds, cultural genocide, social castration, nobility, courage, determination, and the fortitude to move on to make new history for an ancient people dancing on a modern stage" (1972: 1). The poem represents history in order to propel Chicanos – by making them see themselves as agents in history – toward a more empowered and gratifying future.

The invocation of dance and performance in Gonzales's introduction reveals the ethnopoetic impetus standing behind the poem's production and dissemination. (In addition to being read at rallies, quoted by speakers, and performed by theater groups, the poem was represented in a film version that enjoyed wide circulation during the 1970s.)[16] As is characteristic of Chicano poetry in the late 1960s and early 1970s, the performative function of the poem inflects its language and style. Juan Bruce-Novoa notes that the "writing is simple, free of complicated poetic tropes; the language easily accessible, communicating a readily memorable impression. Hence, repetition is a key technique. As in oral tradition, reiteration insures listeners' retention. Repeated material forms permutating motifs that, nevertheless, remain essentially constant" (1982: 48).[17] These motifs include the evocation of Mexican historical icons, among them Zapata, Juárez, Villa, Cuauhtémoc. The call to history, the reconnection of present struggle to past turmoil, the affirmation of spirit and a sense of defiance all are meant to rouse the listener toward action.

Despite its call to power and its self-positioning as the summation of all that is "Chicano," *Joaquín* reveals the discontinuities and contradictions inevitable in a history of dispossession and disempowerment. This is not to cast aspersions upon a classic text in the poetry of El Movimiento. Rather, it is to reveal how complex the claims to national culture and self-determination can be, given the numerous discourses interpellating the subject position "Chicano." Which is to say that although Aztlán as a site of Chicano nationalism is ostensibly articulated as one country, its actual performance results in the construction of another. So the stated aims of the poem give way to something other.

Several critics discuss the poem principally as a search for Chicano identity informed in part by the trope of self-identification.[18] The poem does after all open with the phrase "I am Joaquín" and goes on to proclaim "I am Cuauhtémoc" (16), "I was part in blood and spirit / of that / courageous village priest / Hidalgo" (25), "I fought and died / for / Don Benito Juárez" (30), "I rode with Pancho Villa" (34), "I am Emiliano Zapata" (34).[19] Joaquín is also the rich landowner, the conquering Spaniard, the dictatorial tyrant Díaz. So identity is undoubtedly an issue here. The "search" for identity within the poem, however, is less a search than an affirmation. And what the poem affirms is the entire history of Mexico as a political and cultural heritage that Chicanos not only inherit but actually embody. The poem, as Bruce-Novoa painstakingly charts, moves through the course of Mexican and American history to indicate that "the paradigmatic process of definition is *mestizaje*, or miscegenation, achieved through the spilling of blood. One must be willing to spill blood – a ritual hierophany according to the poem – for the good of the people" (1982: 49). The blood, which ran from the "back of Indian slavery" (54) to

> the ice-caked
> hills of the Alaskan isles,
> on the corpse-strewn beach of Normandy,
> the foreign land of Korea
> and now
> Vietnam (62)

mingles the physical being of the Chicano with the national political agendas of both Mexico and the United States. The poem stakes a claim for self-identity based on selfless sacrifice; and the right to be "Chicano" is validated by this history of sacrifice, which mixes the blood of the Chicano with the histories from which "he" arises.[20]

The poem turns at about half point. Although it still flashes back into history, the chronological tracing of history from pre-Cortesian to revolutionary Mexico ends. The second half of *Joaquín* concentrates instead on the significance of struggle and sacrifice as a means of achieving political ends. The speaker claims:

> I stand here looking back,
> and now I see
>   the present,
> and still
>   I am the campesino,
>   I am the fat political coyote –
>   I,
> of the same name,
>   Joaquín,
> in a country that has wiped out
> all my history,
>   stifled all my pride,
> in a country that has placed a

different weight of indignity upon
my
age-
old
burdened back.
Inferiority
is the new load. . . . (51, ellipses in original)

The reclamation of history the poem undertakes is in reaction to the country that has wiped out "all my history" and "stifled all my pride." The response is one of discursive resistance, a lesson that re-collects and remembers lost heroes and events. The inclusion of villains and exploiters as antiheros serves to construct a lesson by negative example. The villains in the poem are all selfish and self-serving, acting to exploit the community of Chicanos and Mexicanos that forms "Joaquín." The history told in the poem allows the community of auditors, along with "Joaquín," the opportunity to "stand here looking back" in order to make sense of the history of sacrifice the poem articulates. This in order to construct out of that history a story of pride and resistance, one that will fortify the auditor against the "new load" of inferiority imposed by this country that has "wiped out / all my history." Finally, the poem conflates the Chicano community ("I am Joaquín"; "I am the masses of my people") with its history ("I am Cuauhtémoc"; "I am Emiliano Zapata").

The poem affirms an identity in which "Joaquín" stands at the culmination of entropic historical processes: "lost in a world of confusion, / caught up in the whirl of a / gringo society" (6). The dilemma for the speaker thus comes in having to choose between two worlds. He can either ally himself with the world of his fathers who "have lost the economic battle / and won / the struggle of cultural survival" or "exist in the grasp / of American social neurosis, / sterilization of the soul / and a full stomach" (7), a world that seeks to wipe out cultural identity and history. The victory of the spirit "despite physical hunger" becomes the goal. The "struggle of cultural survival" exemplified by the reconstructed history in *Joaquín* represents the life of the spirit yet manifest in the face of economic and political disempowerment. As Felipe de Ortego y Gasca puts it, the poem represents "a choice between cultural apostasy or cultural loyalty." He goes on to argue that, not surprisingly, Joaquín opts for La Raza, becoming "the enduring spirit of the Chicano soul buffeted by alien winds in the land of his fathers, where he is considered a stranger by hostile Anglos" (1979: 115). History as a manifestation of "culture" represents a trajectory of resistance revealing the "soul" of

Chicanos. History becomes the expression of an internal spirit surviving the external realities of exploitation and discrimination.

Thus Juan Bruce-Novoa suggests that the temporal sites of present and past inform the organizing principle behind the poem (1982: 48–50). It moves from images and events in history to portraits of present culture – mariachi music, mural art, Mexican food. The poem sketches the positive and negative influence of the past on the present in relation to territorial dispossession, economic exploitation, and racial inequality. Most importantly, *Joaquín* seems to posit Chicano history as one that moves inexorably toward repossession and empowerment, one in which resistance most firmly makes its presence felt in the rich cultural heritage bestowed by the Mexican past to the Chicano present. José Limón argues that, on the contrary, the poem articulates a rejection of the past and the present. He states that the poem "generates a self-inflated, hyperbolic, male-centered nationalist rhetoric that stands at a great rebellious distance from . . . an engaged social critique" (1992: 128). His characterization is quite correct. The poem affirms self rather than critiques society. It seeks, however, not so much to deny the past as to allow, through an uncritical and perhaps reified cultural celebration, for a confluence of the past and the present – to trigger a temporal union. It reveals the heritage of Chicanos as one of exploitation and struggle marked by a heroism of perseverance and fortitude.

Although the temporal element does help organize the shifts in the poem, there exists as well a spatial metaphor informing the poem. Scrutinizing this spatial dimension helps locate sites of conflict within the poem. For it is, as Bruce-Novoa points out, the loss of land that most severely afflicts the Chicana community. The poem serves to validate the claim to the land on which we live. Although the notion of Aztlán had not yet entered the discourse of Chicana activism in 1967, the central tensions that led to Aztlán are clearly present in the poem: self-determination, cultural empowerment, political action, geographic reclamation.[21] The poem suggests that a connection to the land – as its previous owners, as its present cultivators – not only distinguishes Chicanas from the rest of the U.S. population, but empowers Chicanas and imbues them with a spirituality and understanding lost to a technologically enslaved North American culture. The spatial dimension of the poem thus underscores the cultural power at hand for Chicanas. The idea of Aztlán that will soon emerge after the composition of the poem represents a terrain marked by a confusion between geographic claims within a system of property exchange and cultural claims within a system of symbolic exchange.

The poem relentlessly asserts that Chicanas have a right to the land on which they work. An image of the Spanish conquest, for example, is not treated as an invasion or usurpation of territory. On the contrary, "Joaquín" claims that

> I owned the land as far
> as the eye
> could see under the crown of Spain,
> and I toiled on my earth,
> . . . [even though] THE GROUND WAS MINE
> I was both tyrant and slave. (19)

The poem invokes the image of Emiliano Zapata and his proclamation "'This land, / this earth / is / OURS" (34). Finally, it bemoans the fact that because of the broken Treaty of Guadalupe Hidalgo "My land is lost / and stolen" (66). The land that was rightfully claimed in Mexico – and from which sprang the rich culture and heritage of dignity that forms the background of the Chicana people – is in the United States usurped. Thus the United States represents a land in which the heritage and culture that have made the Chicana strong is erased, the land which the Chicana works is stolen, and the sterility of technology consumes the Chicana in a fruitless process of work and token reward. The tension between the geographical markers "Mexico" and the "United States" traces a history of endless exploitation commencing with the invasion of the Spanish and ending with the migration of the Mexican worker. Within the poem, the United States is never home, only a menace from which "Joaquín" recoils in a reaffirmation of the real home: Mexico.

The tension between the "real" home and the land of menace becomes this poem's vision of Aztlán, one that arises from the contradictions inherent in the identity "Chicano/a." The "Chicana/o" is from but not in Mexico, in but not of the United States. The geographic dislocation of Chicanas marks their history of dispossession and migration. Chicana culture, meanwhile, is meant to represent the last realm of spirituality, the embodiment of the absent homeland that allows for a space of resistance against Anglo incursion. The "internal" component of the Chicana – "the safety within the / circle of life – / MY OWN PEOPLE" (12) – stands in contradistinction to the "external" component of the Chicana – "American social neurosis, / sterilization of the soul" (9). Although gringo society exploited the Mexican and Chicana and "took what they could use," they ignored the art, literature, music and "so they left the real things of value" (70). Chicana culture stands as a pure and resistant force, an internalized locus of value otherwise missing in an existence bound by exploitation and violence.

In its prefiguration of Aztlán, the poem marks a tension in which the cultural and the geographic become, finally, distinct realms. The geographic represents a site of dispossession that, although making claims for it, Chicanas have lost. Only culture remains as a site of complete inheritance, of possession and richness, an area that proves itself to be the ultimate source of resistance.

The sense of discontinuity manifested in the spatial schema of the poem – between north and south, internal and external, home and exile – problematizes the function of the Chicano. The opening of *Joaquín* foregrounds the importance of choice in determining the proper course "Joaquín" should take: "And now! / I must choose" marks an insistence upon agency that suggests the speaker can become a player working in opposition to the sterility and vacuity of North American society. The fact of identity is already present, agency implied. This move undoubtedly reflects the uses of the poem as an instrument in political mobilization. However, the speaker also states

> I have come a long way to nowhere
> unwillingly dragged by that
> monstrous, technical,
> industrial giant called
> Progress
> and Anglo success . . . (10, ellipses in original)

Agency is denied "Joaquín," and it is this role as victim that lends some pathos to the struggle of self-determination the poem advocates. It also speaks against the declaration of agency that has come before. The poem marks the site of tension between a sense of self imbued as an agent for change and a self that is the victim of historically determined economic exploitation. It thus reveals a contradiction it does not explicitly address: Are Chicanos victims of their fate or agents of their destiny?

Ultimately, the poem attempts to resolve this contradiction by combining a sense of inevitability and affirmation signaled by the final lines: "I SHALL ENDURE! / I WILL ENDURE!" (100). As is characteristic of Movimiento poetry, these statements blend the affirmative with the imperative, expressing a statement of fact that will be a player in the creation of that fact. The poem hints that this endurance will result from the revolution that is just beginning and in which it wishes to involve its audience. Yet their activity in it – what their roles of agency will be – remains a vague issue. The final section of the poem claims that "now the trumpet sounds, / the music of the people stirs the / revolution" (93). The revolution begins moving "like a sleeping giant" that slowly "rears its head" at the sound of the trumpet sounded not by Gabriel (although the allusion is unmistakable), but by a mariachi band, an emblem of Mexican and Chicano culture. The revolution commences, the poem implies, at the behest of culture: "Mariachi strains / fiery tequila explosions / the smell of chile verde" (93). In the fields and cities "we start to MOVE" (96). The people are stirred, but a clear sense of their function and their agency is curiously absent from the poem. Almost as if by accident, and certainly as if by a heavenly mandate, the revolution "awakens" at the sound of marching feet and mariachi music. The "masses of my people" who "refuse to be absorbed" (100) are cast by the poem in an oddly passive role. They stand as the inheritors of a history that finally seems to propel (rather than enable) them to move boldly into an independent and active future.

In this respect, the poem articulates the dream/nightmare of Chicana subjectivity and political action, one that will carry over into the following decades of Chicana self-determination. While Chicanas have penetrated U.S. national space – or been usurped into it – that national space has likewise traversed the "Chicana/o" who has been controlled by that "industrial giant called / Progress" (10). *Yo Soy Joaquín* constructs this position of victim and posits against it the agency of cultural self-determination leading to revolution. The poem marks a central tension in a postrevolutionary – or at least post-sixties – Chicana identity. This tension runs along two possible trajectories. Within an economic system that is interminably self-differentiating and self-reproducing, Chicana resistance to exploitation may very well function as an important element in allowing for the development of a more complex and totalizing capitalism. Or Chicanas may represent new players in history who, by resisting, force that economic system against the direction of its own internal logic. These positions result in either new reforms in the interest of sustaining capitalism, or significant internal modifications that alter the structure and direction of postindustrial society.[22]

In its contradictory evocation of agency and change, *Joaquín* brings home the dichotomy of Chicana political resistance that continues to haunt Chicana thought. Has El Movimiento brought about real change? Has it enabled Chicanas a degree of self-determination previously not possible? And if it has, has that empowerment led to a clearer inscription or greater erasure of Chicana culture and differentiation? Mario Barrera argues that "Chicano political struggles were aimed at breaking the patterns of discrimination in order to provide access to the dominant institutions and to allow individual upward mobility to take place" (1988: 68). Consequently, "as the institutionalized barriers slowly erode, so do the cultural patterns that they have played a major role in maintaining. The contradiction here is that the partial achievement of the egalitarian goal has further undermined the prospect for attaining the communitarian goal" (1988: 68–9). The very success of political activism has led to a dissolution of the culture those politics are meant to protect.

The political work for which *Joaquín* was composed leads, ironically, to the very dissolution of the cultural values and ties *Joaquín* celebrates as the locus of Chicano resistance and self-identity. The poem prefigures a problem its author and its auditors could not foresee. *Joaquín* does not signal the coming of the winds of revolution, as it claims to do. It does not prefigure a liberation or the articulation of a cultural nationalism. It signals instead the discontinuities that will mark the procession of Chicano culture as it confronts a series of complex questions over the course of the next quarter-century. How does one avoid the construction of a culture against the margin that leads to an erasure of marginality but is not coterminous with an erasure of cultural distinction? How can one address the relationship between cultural self-identification and the history of territorial dispossession from which it arises? Are the cultural and the geographic locales invoked by *Joaquín* and imbued with contradictory qualities fated forever to remain discontinuous realms? How, finally, does Chicano cultural production in the years following the Movimiento imbue their construction of Aztlán as the site of cultural self-identity with a political charge that can bring home the promises of liberation and independence made in the "Plan Espiritual de Aztlán"?

Retribalization: Jimmy Santiago Baca

One of the most talented voices in the contemporary scene of Chicano poetry, Jimmy Santiago Baca writes poetry that can be seen to address – albeit in a mediated and complex form – some of these pressing questions. His poetry offers a vision of Chicano identity that has a great deal to do with the terrible interplay between historical and contemporary political oppression. Baca brings to us images of violence and violation on a personal level that Gonzales's poem only suggests. While voicing an outrage characteristic of much Movimiento poetry, Baca's poetry moves beyond simply casting blame on "America" or "the system."[23] The forms of oppression scrutinized by his poetry result from specific historical regimes in which indigenous values and peoples are erased through violence and malevolent neglect. Aztlán, within the logic of Baca's poetry, becomes a terrain inscribed by history, a terrain that marks but is also marked by the speaker and the subject of his poems. Gonzales's poem suggests a grandeur to history as a trajectory propelling the Chicano masses into a revolutionary future. The vision of community and cohesion offered by *Joaquín* gives way in the poetry of Baca to an intimacy with the particular and a personalization of history. Baca does not write of a "Joaquín" who embodies the history and represents the populus of the Chicano community. In quick strokes, his poetry fills out the multiplicitous dramas, conflicts, and tensions evident in the lives of its subjects. The history that emerges is one in which the answers to cultural decimation do not descend from the heavens with the blast of a trumpet. Salvation, where it exists, occurs on a personal level whereby individual rather than mass empowerment becomes the small response to the detribalization Baca's poetry addresses.[24]

The collection *Black Mesa Poems* offers a series of poems written between 1986 and 1989 that reflect on the relation between humans, history, and land – the three concerns marking Aztlán in its various avatars. The poems construct a sense of history not, as in Gonzales's poem, as an inertia-driven inevitability. History in Baca's poetry is dynamic and developing. It represents several currents within which Chicanos move and function. Rather than a singular trajectory leading directly from pre-Cortesian civilization through Mexican nationalism to contemporary struggle, history in *Black Mesa Poems* is a varied terrain marked by heterogeneity, a mosaic of violence and beauty that crystallizes in the land of the Black Mesa, a contemporary realm of Aztlán.

An excellent example of the discontinuity and diversity of history characteristic of Baca's poetry can be found in "Invasions," a poem that traces the various incursions into the territory that has become New Mexico. The poem's narrative is spoken by an individual alive to the influences of history. As he fishes the Jemez, he meditates on the fact that this is where "Coronado rode / through this light, dark / green brush." The terrain is marked by history, infused with the reality of the human activity that has led to the violence and disruption of cultural confrontation. The speaker imagines how "Back then the air / was bright and crisp / with Esteban's death / at the hands of Zuñi warriors." Esteban, an African slave who had survived with Alvar Núñez Cabeza de Vaca the first European exploration of the present American Southwest, served as a point man for Fray Marcos de Niza's expedition in 1539. Esteban moved ahead of the main party and sent reports and directions back to Fray Marcos. The first outsider to have contact with the Zuni, Esteban met with death at the hands of the suspicious warriors.[25] The speaker, fishing these same waters, realizes "I am the end result / of Conquistadores, / Black Moors, / American Indians, / and Europeans." The various bloods representing the different heritages and races that comprise the Chicano come together within the figure of the speaker,

> rainbowing
> and scintillating
> in me
> like the trout's flurrying
> flank scales
> shimmering a fight
> as I reel in.

In addition to being highly evocative, the vitality of the images describing the trout's fight reflects the tumultuous history that has brought the speaker to this point. The speaker "reels in" his history like the fish on his line, fighting and twisting yet comprising the heritages and battles that have marked the land as they have marked the speaker. These heritages, of which the speaker is the end result, evoke a history of violence and conflict evoked explicitly by the poem.

Moving from the sixteenth to the seventeenth century, the poem describes how the speaker walks south "like Jemez and Pecos pueblos / during 1690 uprisings, / when Spanish came north / to avenge their dead." The uprisings and their subsequent suppression led to the flight of the Indians and their "settling in present day / open plains." Violence and violation again mark the relationship between people and the land upon which they reside. The people who inhabit Baca's Aztlán traverse it both to escape its violence and to find a relationship with it. The speaker reconstructs the history of the land as he walks across it, meditating upon the present condition of Aztlán:

> Peace here now. Bones
> dissolved, weapons rusted.
> I stop, check my sneaker prints
> in moist sandy bank.
> Good deep marks.

The history of violence and confrontation that the speaker entertains and sees present in the landscape about him comes together in the last section of the poem, suggesting a sense of resolution. The violence gone, the agonies ended, all that remains are "Bones / dissolved, weapons rusted." The speaker after a manner inherits this calmed world. Unlike Gonzales's poem, in which the people are passive inheritors of a history of resistance and self-empowerment, this poem's speaker is an active player within his world.

Marked by history – "the end result / of Conquistadores, / Black Moors, / American Indians, / and Europeans" – the speaker inscribes the land with his tracks. His sneakers making "Good deep marks" in the sand signal his own participation in the processes of history.

The speaker, then, constructs his own history:

> I clamber up an incline,
> crouch in bushes
> as my ancestors did,
> peer at vacation houses
> built on rock shelves,
> sun decks and travel trailers –
> the new invasion.

He does not stand as an object propelled by history into liberation. Rather, history instructs the speaker how to confront new movements, new stories of migration and conquest being played out across the land of Black Mesa. The construction of history connects the speaker to that history, allowing him to identify with his ancestors as he crouches in the bushes peering at vacation homes. Here the migration into the sunbelt forms a seemingly benign and yet unmistakable invasion that marks the land. This latest invasion – humorously evoked by the image of "sun decks and travel trailers" – forms another wave in the historical currents running through the Jemez. The antagonism one finds in *Joaquín* between "genuine" Mexican culture and "sterile" American technology seems about to resurface in Baca's poem. Yet the lessons the poem teaches about the history of invasion underscores the notion of mestizaje as the end result of historical movement, as the process that has constituted the speaker's own sense of self. Vasconcelos's Raza Cósmica that informs other Chicano writing emerges in Baca's poem not as some ideal mixture of a super race, but rather the inevitable result of a history characterized by waves of invasion, violence, domination, and survival. The previous invasions led to the "rainbowing" and "scintillating" of the speaker's blood. The blood that marks his self results from historical movements. And the present invasion as well, if the history evoked by the poem teaches anything, leads to a new unfolding of union and fusion.

The poem marks a different sense of the relationship between Chicano and Other. The Other becomes in time the Self. The movements evoked by "Invasions" are of interpenetration and interweaving, processes that highlight transformation and deterritorialization – the dissolution of repressive order. The sense of history the poem evokes does not launch the Chicano into the culmination of some teleology; instead, it forces a confrontation with the processes of history. The Chicano stands as the endpoint of a mestizaje that is not a blithely utopian cosmic race. It is instead the genetic inscription of a history of invasion and conquest, of conflict and bloodshed, of repression and resistance. Thus the fusion to which the poem's resolution points does not imply a gentle union. The antagonism and violence that characterize the relationship between Anglos and Chicanos in the Southwest is nothing if not a tedious expression of racism and xenophobia. History here is not glamorized nor romanticized. As traced by Baca's poem, it reveals a series of asymmetrical power relations in which Indians, Mexicans, and Chicanos have consistently found themselves on the wrong end of a bayonet, an unjust legal suit, an anemic paycheck, a cocked rifle.

This history – and the story of resistance to it – informs another of Baca's poems in *Black Mesa*, *"Mi Tío Baca el Poeta de Socorro."* The poem is a tribute to the speaker's uncle Antonio, whose grave marker – significantly shorn of birth and death dates – forms the image that opens the poem. It is also a meditation on how the history that imbues the landscape of Aztlán must be confronted by those who are the inheritors of its darker effects. The speaker's uncle was the "Poet de Socorro, / whose poems roused *la gente* / to demand their land rights back." Directly addressing Antonio, the speaker describes how his uncle is awakened by the thunder of hooves as "lantern flame / flickered shadowy omens on walls" with the sound of "guns glimmering blue / angrily beating at your door" and the presence of "Black boots [that] scurried round four adobe walls." Antonio's agitation for the empowerment of the pueblo leads to the vigilante action by "men wearing remnants of Rinche uniforms." These "Rinches," characterized as disembodied lights and sounds, are the terroristic Texas Rangers.[26] The boots and lights and guns representing the Rangers imbue the opening portion of the poem with a sense of impending violence. The Rinches as a disembodied presence suggests that their power lies beyond individuals, manifests inhuman forces. The technique underscores the impersonality of repressive power. Although these are "arrogant young boys" who "held torches and shouted, / 'Shoot the Mexican! Shoot him!'" the forces the poem describes are both overwhelming and faceless and more frightening for it. The first section of the poem ends with the speaker telling how Tío Antonio turned to face his persecutors to meet "the scream of rifles with your silence."

As with "Invasions," the poem moves into a quieter mood in the final section. The speaker – still addressing his uncle – comments that "Your house still stands" but that it is returning to the earth as "weeds grow on the dirt roof / that leans like an old man's hand / on a cane *viga* . . ." (ellipses in original). Images of decay are all that remain of Antonio's home. The physical marks he has made on the land – his physical presence in Aztlán – fade and are erased through the passage of time. The ellipses that close this description lead, however, from an image of decay to one of connection. The speaker walks to church with "a prayer on my lips [that] bridges / years of disaster between us." This invocation of prayer marks a significant move in differentiating Baca's vision of "Aztlán" from those of his predecessors. The prayer foregrounds the use of words and imagination as modes of connection, just as the words of one poet connect him to the deeds of another. This is not an invocation of the past through the direct access of historical appropriation. This is not the grand vision offered by Gonzales's epic *Joaquín*. Rather, the connection here emerges from the prayer for an ancestor, words stirred by a memory that bridges years of disaster. Baca's poem highlights a history marked by discontinuities, unequal power, violent eruption. It constructs a sense of the past as an uneven and perilous terrain that the incantation of prayer and the power of words can simultaneously evoke and bridge, trace and erase.

This movement allows the speaker to wonder "Maybe things will get better. / Maybe our struggle to speak and be / as we are, will come about." The dream of reformation and freedom – of that which was denied Tío Antonio – haunts the speaker as a possibility. These dreams are not inevitabilities. These are not immediately attainable ends. These are the visions of a world that is not a part of the historical world evoked by the poem. These are visions of a world, in other words, not of Aztlán. "For now," the poem goes on, "I drink in your spirit, Antonio, / to nourish me as I descend / into dangerous abysses of the future." The speaker stands at the end point of history not as a trajectory being propelled into a future of liberation. Rather, the future becomes a hellish and dangerous abyss into which the speaker must inevitably descend. He descends into those fires, however, fortified by the ability to drink in the spirit of his uncle. The solace and succor offered by the power and bravery of his uncle gives sustenance.

The poem concludes with the speaker telling Tío Antonio that he had come to the cemetery "to walk over my history." This image crystallizes what the poem has already suggested: The land and history merge into one within the poetic imagination. Thus speaker, history, and land fuse in a moment of imaginative connection that, the speaker makes clear, forms a vision – but only a vision – in the "dangerous abysses of the future." Moreover, the vision is not one of utopian liberation and freedom. Instead, the speaker imagines his uncle – "face sour with torturous hooks / pulling your brow down in wrinkles" – walking by him toward the church. The speaker sees Antonio leaning "forward in haste / as if angels really did await us" at the end of their walk, at the end of time, at the end of history. This image of salvation and apocalypse is formed conditionally, a tone that permeates the final lines of the poem.

The speaker wants to believe "whatever problems we have, time will take / its course, they'll be endured and consumed" as he follows his uncle up the hill and into the old church that "slumps on a hill, somber and elegant." The repeated connection between decay and dignity, between dissolution and rebirth, forms a central tension in the poem. This underscores the sense of history the poem conveys, a history of destruction and dispossession leading to dignity and resolve. Clearly these are hard lessons, evidenced in the picture of Tío Antonio trodding up the hill to kneel

> before La Virgen De Guadalupe,
> bloody lips moving slightly
> . . . great gray head poised in listening,
> old jacket perforated with bloody bullet holes.

The prayer offered by the speaker earlier in the poem returns on the bloody lips of Tío Antonio praying to the great icon of Chicano and Mexican identity, the Virgin of Guadalupe. Antonio kneels in prayer with his head "poised in listening" – for what? The response of the Virgin? The voice of the angels? The answers to history? The suffering and the bleeding remain, a fact of history though the uncle prays, waiting for response. This response is one the speaker – and the reader – never hears.

The poet leaves Antonio at the altar of the old church, whispering, waiting, listening: "I close the door, and search the prairie, / considering the words *faith, prayer* and *forgiveness,* / wishing, like you, I could believe them." Significantly, the speaker scans the landscape for the answer his uncle searches for in prayer. The history of persecution and violence that marks the speaker's recollection of Tío Antonio causes him the difficulty with these three words of strength and salvation: faith that the future will not be like the past, the words of prayer that could make that faith manifest, and the forgiveness necessary to absolve the society and the people who have most benefited from Antonio's spilled blood – the owners of the sun decks and travel trailers that appear on the horizon in "Invasions." The final line of *"Mi Tío Baca el Poeta de Socorro"* remains ambiguous – does the speaker wish he could believe, as his uncle believes, in these words? Or does the last line indicate doubt and knowledge that, wish as they might, neither the speaker nor his uncle can believe them? The ambiguity remains opaque.

Yet the transformation of Aztlán in Baca's poem reveals itself clearly. The gravestone that opens the poem – a gravestone on which "Dust storms faded the birth and death numbers" – represents the markings which those who traverse the land leave upon it. The marker connects present to past; it is not bound by the dates of birth and death that would delimit its temporality. The poem underscores the recurrence of history, the return of stories that speak of pride and resistance against the violence and violation of imperial power. Baca's poetry takes up and transforms a number of issues established by earlier poets of Aztlán: history, land, cultural reclamation, hope, advancement, the future. Renouncing apocalyptic or utopian visions of Aztlán, the land for Baca is the Black Mesa of New Mexico. It stands as a terrain that has been marked and crossed by the forces of history, by the players of that history, by the dreams and pains of those players. There is a great deal of interpenetration and fluidity in Baca's vision of history and its relation to people and communities. History is constructed and reconstructed by humans through the poetry. In this imaginative reconstruction, the connection to the past and the claims to a place are reaffirmed. These claims are based less on the rights of previous ownership and ancestry, though elements of this view are evident in Baca's poetry too. Rather, the claims rest on the simple fact that the land has marked and been marked by previous nomads and settlers. This interaction, played out through time and reconstructed through history, connects person to place, present to past. Aztlán in Baca's poetry represents this rough terrain from which the past has been forged and into which, with resolve and with doubt, the Chicano is fated to proceed.

Alien Nation: Lorna Dee Cervantes and Ana Castillo

Aztlán reveals itself to be again and again a discontinuous region. The collision of historical forces with human needs, the collapse of history into teleology, the affirmation of rightful claims, the incessant recognition of bedeviled migrations – Aztlán within Chicana cultural discourses assumes different guises and significances. Certainly between Gonzales's early portrait of the intersection of history and land in 1967 and Baca's meditations some twenty years later, the terrain of Aztlán can be seen to buckle and break in a number of different and divergent ways. Within this span of time, the nationalism – literal or symbolic – implicit in Gonzales's configuration of Aztlán gives way to a more subtle and complex vision of the interaction between land and history in Baca's poetry. The Black Mesa as Aztlán becomes a site where the poetic imagination recasts and reclaims a history that simultaneously disempowers and offers a vision of hope. This poetic vision conceives of the land as a text telling a story not so much about a return to home as about nomadic passage. The land plays an integral part in the articulation of Chicana identity and forms the terrain through which march the figures and migrations populating Chicana poetry. These passages form not a return to origin but a ceaseless engagement between Self and Other. The history of Spanish incursion, of Indian resistance, of Anglo invasion influence the present construction of Chicana space and identity. The engagement between Self and Other – marked by the space between "Mexican" and "American" – manifests itself in myriad ways: historical conflict, economic exploitation, cultural mestizaje.

Chicana poetry during the 1980s and early 1990s emphasizes more clearly than ever that Chicana subjectivity is always becoming. The articulation of Chicana identity reveals a sense of spirituality and historical connectedness not necessarily incumbent upon the finding of the "source" of identity. The land does not represent a site of emergence. It stands as the physical marker that connects people to history, a history involving dispossession and repression, bullets and bloodshed. The land evinces a connection between the various populations that inhabit and traverse it and the devalued histories that speak of both oppression and resistance. Not a place of origins, "Aztlán" in Baca's Black Mesa and other imaginative configurations becomes a land marked by the unequal and asymmetrical power relations inherent in invasion and dispersal.

Durable as it has proven itself to be, the terrain encompassed by the Chicano imagination not only strains and breaks – it stretches. The geographic imagination of Chicano literature allows for a revisioning of "Aztlán" that bridges the historical with the utopian, the desperate with the hopeful. Lorna Dee Cervantes reveals this dual vision in "Poem for the Young White Man Who Asked Me How I, an Intelligent, Well-Read Person Could Believe in the War Between Races." Her poem, published in 1981, serves to mark the discontinuity of "Aztlán" in its portrayal of divergent lands. The poem opens with a utopian vision of a homeland in which "there are no distinctions" and the "barbed wire politics of oppression / have been torn down long ago." Her imagery evokes and denies the effects of a historical and political repression epitomized by the barbed wire border between the United States and Mexico. The poem thus calls forth once again a history of dispossession and rupture that Aztlán in its original deployment sought to redress. "In my land," the poem asserts, there are no boundaries, "no hunger, no / complicated famine or greed." Borders protecting the First from the Third World, violence used to maintain those divisions, greed that drives and feeds the history of that separation – all are simultaneously called up and denied by Cervantes's poem. The tension between evocation and denial resounds throughout the poem, which dances in a land between what is and is not.

The speaker claims "I am not a revolutionary," but goes on to state "I believe in revolution." The speaker refuses the potentially empowered position of "revolutionary," stating that she doesn't "even like political poems." The dream of revolution that drove factions of El Movimiento disappears here. And yet, at the same time that she denies her status as a revolutionary, the speaker asserts her belief in revolution and that it is at hand. Indeed, the realization that there is yet a revolution at hand propels the poem forward.

The speaker thus assumes a contradictory position in relation to the revolution her words evoke. This tension echoes the contradictory stance toward the land the speaker also expresses. The speaker can deny a belief "in a war between races" only "when I'm safe, / living in my own continent of harmony / and home, but I am not / there." The poem constructs a vision of salvation in which races do not war, but it can exist only when the speaker stands on a "continent of harmony" where she is not: a land imaginable but unreachable. In the land where the speaker stands, the historical conditions of exploitation persist. The imagery of borders and lands and wars evokes the history of dispossession and homelessness that marks a disjuncture between the desire for peace expressed by the poetic imagination and the flat reality ruled by regimes of violence and violation which prevent peace.

The continent of harmony that opens the poem gives way to a nightmare terrain where "the crosses are burning," where "sharp-shooting goose-steppers round every corner," with "snipers in the schools." The speaker addresses the "young white man" of the title, telling him parenthetically "I know you don't believe this / . . . / But they / are not shooting at you." The bullets are aimed at the speaker who is "marked by the color of my skin," bullets that "bury deeper than logic" aimed at her children. The speaker's proof that the "bullets are discrete and designed to kill slowly" are the wounds inflicted upon her:

> my stumbling mind, my
> "excuse me" tongue, and this
> nagging preoccupation
> with the feeling of not being good enough.

Suggesting a history that was written by the blaze of bullets and the flames of fire, the poem notes that the physical oppression and murder endured by Chicanos in the past have been transformed into a more insidious and equally destructive form of personal violence. The violence that is the instrument of discrimination and inequality becomes internalized. The pain and doubt that mar the speaker's sense of self manifests the scars inflicted by the enemy outside her door, "a real enemy / who hates me." This enemy, armed with racist beliefs and ready to lash out in combat, causes real harm and inflicts real pain. This pain, of course, can be felt only by those who find themselves at the wrong end of that gun, who feel in the flesh the bullets forged in history and fired by ideology.

Cervantes's poem maps a terrain that is both an internal landscape scarred by racism and an external battleground that sounds with "blasting and muffled outrage." These two lands, representing the dichotomies of internal/external, desire/reality, utopia/dystopia, harmony/battle, converge in the final lines of the poem:

> Every day I am deluged with reminders
> that this is not
> my land
> and this is my land.
>
> I do not believe in the war between races
>
> but in this country
> there is war.

Aztlán becomes in Cervantes's poem a region between violence and peace, a site of tension between possession and dispossession. The poem constructs Aztlán as a realm of discontinuities, the ruptured terrain of the Chicano homeland: a land that "is and is not" claimed by the speaker; a land in which external violence traverses and scars the integrity of self; a place where the dream of escape is perpetually confounded by the blasts and outrage of historical violation. These discontinuities come together in the dichotomous phrases that this "is and is not" the speaker's land, that there "is and is not" war in this country, this region, this homeland of "Aztlán" which is and is not home.

Aztlán ceases to be the reclaimed territory of a homeland envisioned by Alurista and other early proponents of cultural nationalism. Culture in Cervantes's poem is not going to trigger the revolution needed to reclaim and salvage the Chicano territory. Her poem cannot even begin to claim that its presence works – except imaginatively – to traverse the gap between this country and the continent of harmony the speaker so desires. Here Aztlán is the impossible interstitial realm that stands amid the disparity between the historical reality of racial war and the utopian dream of a world beyond war. Aztlán is an imaginative reclamation of land, but not in the name of some Chicano or Mexican nationalism. It captures the sites of tension at which the Chicano subject in the guise of the speaker is most vulnerable. The capture is a small victory, a resistant move in a war meant to silence even outrage. The revolution the poem textualizes, however, is one turned against the people. "Aztlán" is not the land of liberation in "Poem for the Young White Man . . ."; it is instead the gap between liberation and enslavement.

Evoking as well the tensions and gaps stuck in Cervantes's poem, Ana Castillo's "In My Country" opens with the simple line: "This is not my country." The poem, published in 1988, goes on to articulate how the speaker's country is markedly different than "this" country. There, in the other country, "men / do not play at leaders" and "women do not play at men." In that other country, roles specified by gender no longer haunt individual behavior. The cruelty of the world disappears in the other country of the speaker's imagination. Consequently, "there is no god / crucified to explain the persistence of cruelty." The country – simultaneously imagined and ostensibly lived by the speaker, as becomes clear in later lines – is characterized by practices of liberation and freedom. The world of the speaker's imagination represents a realm in which self-fulfillment, culture, and ethnic identity all flower in its rich terrain.

The speaker articulates a series of negative images that do not exist in her country. There, she is not afraid of sitting alone in a park or going to the store at night. She is not afraid of layoffs and men do not need to sleep with guns. There in that other country children are not abused. The violence and indignity that comes with poverty are gone. Significantly, the speaker shifts from the present tense to the past as she describes how it once was in her country:

> In my country
> i did not wait in line for milk
> coupons for my baby, get the wrong
> prescription at the clinic, was not
> forced to give my ethnic origin,
> nor died an unnatural death.

The speaker shifts tense to indicate that her world not only exists in her imagination, but that her country at one time actually existed. Where and when was this world?

The answer emerges after a shift back for three stanzas to the present tense in which the speaker proclaims how in her country she is "not exotic," does not "go artificially blonde" and the "sun that gravitates to my dark / pigmentation is not my enemy." This evocation of racial categorization –

and its subsequent self-loathing manifested through the fear of dark skin and hair – leads to an idealized meditation on the world that was. There, "Mesoamerica / was a magnificent Quetzal, / Africa and its inhabitants / were left alone." The shift to the past tense again suggests an evocation of origin, a reconnection to a world before European invasion and colonization. The poem thus suggests that the speaker – somehow, sometime – existed in a world that did not live through a history of colonization, that did not experience the effects of racism, that did not suffer the conflation of a social with a racial order. The evocation of the Quetzal suggests that the poem may reflect a blind nativism, that strain within Chicano thought that posits the pre-Cortesian world as a wholly positive and wholly attainable element of integral self-identification.

However, Castillo's poem complicates this vision by once again shifting away from the native past into a present tense. In the world imagined by the speaker,

> Arab women
> don't cover their faces or
> allow their sexual parts to be
> torn out. In my world,
> no one is prey.

Although the world the poet envisions/remembers seems to connect the speaker to a prelapsarian precolonial society, this is not a simple retreat into cultural purity or authentic origins. The poem refuses the easy retreat into a simplistic cultural nationalism that blindly asserts the correctness of ethnic tradition and cultural heritage no matter the cost to human – and here specifically women's – freedom and dignity. The vision the speaker offers conveys a complex and not unproblematic world in which no one is prey. This means not simply a blind recuperation, but a staunch refusal of those traditions that delimit rather than empower women.

Instead of relying upon an unproblematic invocation of the past as its ideal, the poem instead turns to an extended refutation of myths and mystifications of all kinds:

> Death is not a relief.
> i don't bet on reincarnation
> or heaven, or lose the present
> in apathy or oblivion.

The speaker articulates a skepticism toward beliefs in rebirth or paradise as a part of a vision that seeks to empower rather than enervate. This other world, utopian in its sense of integrity and yet firmly grounded in its sense of the present, allows for dreams of such a perfect existence that the speaker does not attend "conferences with academicians / who anthropologize my existence," who "find the differences created / out of Babel interesting." The mystifications of false promises – whether cultural with the reification of tradition or religious with the promise of heaven or intellectual with the useless infatuation of minutae – cease to exert influence on the speaker's other world.

Finally, shifting in the last stanza one last time to the past tense, the poem resolves into a discussion of that other world as a cultural haven. There "the poet sang loud / and clear and everyone heard / without recoiling." Evoking again a world that once was, the poem speaks of poetry in transformative terms as a song "sweet / as harvest, sharp as tin, strong / as the northern wind, and all had / a coat warm enough to bear it." The poem resolves into a final image in which the poet's world becomes a past world where both poetry spoke the cold blast of truth and its auditors possessed the fortitude to bear it.

As the shift in tenses suggests, the speaker stands at the interstices between an imagined world, a world that ostensibly once existed, and the world as it is actually lived. The poem bespeaks a weariness with the brutality of this present world by negating its violence through an incantation of all an other world is not. Yet that other world itself is a conflicted space. On the one hand, the poem suggests that it is a world that actually once existed, thus indicating that the speaker has a capacity to reconnect and revivify that lost world through her voice. In a sense, this represents an infatuation with tradition and the "native" of which contemporary Chicana poetry seems suspicious. On the other hand, the poem simultaneously makes quite clear that this other world, where "no one is prey," exists nowhere but in the imagination of the speaker. The world the poem constructs is made alien, made a dream that both suggests the necessity of alternate spaces for Chicana self-affirmation and points to the impossibility of that dream. The poem, simply put, moves between worlds of affirmation and desperation.

As with Cervantes's poem, Aztlán in Castillo's poem becomes that space between nations, one that straddles two terrains – one of hope, one of despair. In both poems, the poetic imagination encompasses and is encompassed by these worlds. The speaker of "In My Country" – by constructing an anticountry of imagined beauty and harmony – recasts a vision of the historical world from which the poet speaks. Aztlán as the borderland between these countries marks again the site of a profound discontinuity where racial, sexual, gender, economic regions delimiting human freedom converge.

Borderlands: Gloria Anzaldúa

In the examples of Chicana poetry produced by Castillo and Cervantes, the poetic imagination functions as a bridge between the various realms in which the speakers of the poems live and desire to live. This imaginative leap is no escape from terror. Quite to the contrary, the poetry casts anew the shadows of repression and violence that cross the scarred landscape of Aztlán. Aztlán as a signifier still reaches out to the geography of the American Southwest, attempts to reflect its distinct physical qualities. Yet the notion of physical reclamation within the majority of contemporary Chicana poetry no longer represents a driving force within the discourses of Aztlán. Partly, a refutation of the nationalist dreams of El Movimiento was the result of the Movement's conflicted message in which revolutionary rhetoric articulated what quite quickly became reformist demands. These reformist positions ultimately offered neither genuine self-determination nor universal liberation. Partly, the refutation of nationalist demands is due to the fact that Latinos, as the fastest growing minority in the United States, have in a sense already reclaimed the Southwest. Partly, there remains the unshakeable belief that the Southwest was never lost. Raymund Paredes notes about Chicana fiction that it moves easily across the border between the United States and Mexico, "for Chicano writers regard the boundary as an impertinence. To them, the southwestern United States and northern Mexico compose a single geographical and cultural entity. 'Greater Mexico,' Américo Paredes calls this land, and its northern regions thrive precisely to the degree Chicanos preserve Mexican traditions" (1977: 33). Paredes goes on to argue that the Chicano writer has "one foot planted solidly in Mexican culture and another planted – somewhat more tentatively – in American culture." The argument charts an Aztlán that does not permit for space in between, that precludes a Chicano consciousness that understands itself as belonging to and being neither of the United States nor of Mexico. Though his work is heavily influenced by Américo Paredes's on Chicano folklore as a hybrid and resistant cultural object, Raymund Paredes's position affirms a connection to and perpetuation of origin that casts Aztlán as a space of cultural purity and essence.

Chicano poets in the 1980s affirm the influence of Mexican culture and history upon their articulations of Aztlán. Simultaneously, in focusing on the interactions and reactions between dominant society and the variegated spaces of Chicanos, they foreground the processes of rupture that mark a discontinuous landscape. Jimmy Santiago Baca writes poems that textualize a history of dispossession and violence, that highlight the processes of power and struggle that have carved the land. Most explicitly in *"Mi Tío Baca,"* the poetry reveals a connection between discourse and repression. Baca's poems as discursive acts and evocations of silenced discourses thus situate themselves within and against the processes of history they evoke. This relationship to history marks, in a more mediated form, the poetry by Lorna Dee Cervantes and Ana Castillo as well. Both these poets position Aztlán in the impossible interstices between imagination and history. In their negative recollection of repressive social forms, their works indicate how historically grounded the Chicano poetic imagination is. This history constructs a fluid mending and blending, repression and destruction of cultures. This tempestuous sense of motion marks that region termed the "borderlands." Not a homeland, not a perpetuation of origin, the borderlands allude to an illimitable terrain marked by dreams and rupture, marked by history and the various hopes that history can exemplify. The borderlands represents the multiplicity and dynamism of Chicano experiences and cultures. It is a terrain in which Mexicans, Chicanos, and mestizos live among the various worlds comprising their cultural and political landscapes.

Sergio Elizondo, among others, seeks to give voice to the idea of the borderlands. He discusses a relationship to land that Chicana literature has often expressed (one thinks immediately of Tomás Rivera's *y no se lo tragó la tierra*) but which – as Cervantes and Castillo indicate – has come to engage Chicana imagination like never before:

> We understand now the Border between the United States of America and the Estados Unidos Mexicanos; now we would do well to consider that Borderlands might be a more appropriate term to designate the entire area over which the Chicano people are spread in this country. In so doing, we would come also to understand that the mere physical extension between the U.S.–Mexico border and, let us say, Chicago, is a fact of human dispersion, and not a diaspora of the Chicano people. It is not static for us, but rather it has always been a dynamic and natural motion motivated by laws and processes common to all cultures. Our migrations north of the old historical border have extended the geography and social fabric of Aztlán northward in all directions; we have been able to expand our communal life and fantasies. (1986: 13)

Elizondo speaks to a number of the issues that emerge during the 1980s as central to the Chicana literary imagination. The problematization of heritage and tradition, the dynamism of Chicana cultural and social experiences, the connection to land and to other cultures, the expansion of "homeland" and "fantasies" all inform the various movements of contemporary Chicana culture. It is interesting that Elizondo suggests the movement of Chicanas through the United States is "motivated by laws and processes common to all cultures." The desire to make Chicana identity "universal" still finds a voice. Nevertheless, Elizondo's statement indicates that the notion of Aztlán has given way to a broader and more diverse vision of Chicana cultural terrain. This cultural terrain expands the realm of desire for Chicanas, moving it as it does across the entire face of the United States and beyond, but it also closes the book on a chapter of cultural identity. No longer grounded exclusively in the Southwest or border region, the borderlands expand the territorial claims of Chicanas. Elizondo portrays this expansion as simply the extension of "the geography and social fabric of Aztlán." His conceptualization does not address at all what that sign "Aztlán" signifies.

As I have sought to suggest, Chicano nationalism failed in its ability to perceive the multiplicity and discontinuity evident in the histories and geographies it sought to encompass within Aztlán. Aztlán as a place, or even as a unifying symbol or image, erases the vast differences that form the richness and variety of the term "Chicano." The histories of the Chicano populations in this country are marked by a series of tensions and ruptures – cultural, linguistic, political, economic, racial – that come from cutting across various social and national terrains, calling everything and nothing home. The interstitial becomes the liminal where the living between becomes a way of moving through such definitions as Other, native, foreign, gringo, pocho. The performance artist Guillermo Gómez-Peña addresses the multiplicity that makes up identity in the borderlands:

> My "identity" now possesses multiple repertories: I am Mexican but I am also Chicano and Latin American. At the border they call me *chilango* or *mexiquillo;* in Mexico City it's *pocho* or *norteño;* and in Europe it's *sudacap.* The Anglos call me "Hispanic" or "Latino," and the Germans have, on more than one occasion, confused me with Turks or Italians. My wife Emilia is Anglo-Italian, but speaks Spanish with an Argentine accent, and together we walk amid the rubble of the Tower of Babel of our American postmodernity. (1988: 127–8)

The identities Gómez-Peña exposes lead to a decentering of subjectivity accompanied by loss – of country, of native language, of certainty. But this leads as well to gain: a multifocal and tolerant culture, cultural alliances, "a true political conscience (declassicization and consequent politicization) as well as new options in social, sexual, spiritual, and aesthetic behavior" (1988: 129–30). The desire to rediscover a homeland within the current climate of Chicano culture fades; the reclamation at hand is much more complex and extensive. It calls for a reclamation of all that is cast between, devalued by other nationalist identities. Chicano culture traces "lines of flight," movements toward deterritorialization.[27] Chicana writers and critics most powerfully enabled this type of cultural configuration as they sought to articulate the defficiencies of a Chicano nationalism that presumed male subjectivity as central. Their experiences suggested a more textured and multifaceted sense of self than that proffered by the first representations of Aztlán.

As one Chicana academic has articulated her own position within Aztlán, "I was aware from the very beginning that the establishing of a Chicano intellectual tradition was very male dominated. . . . It was often the case that women were only being included in this tradition if their point of view fit under the cultural nationalist banner" (quoted in Chabram 1990: 229). The tension between a "global" Chicano nationalist agenda, concerned with the position of the Chicano community within society at large, and the "local" concerns expressed by Chicanas center on the realization that "women have first to achieve recognition *within* their own community" (Rocard 1988: 130). As a result "the themes of subordination and exclusion are exploited at length by the Chicana writer" (Rocard 1988: 130). The multiple marginalizations the Chicana has endured in terms of gender and sexuality, race and ethnicity, linguistic and cultural identification, enable a vision of self that must constructively engage with the discontinuities already present but left unspoken in the realm of Aztlán.

No Chicana author addresses the borderland more frequently than Gloria Anzaldúa. Caught between the worlds of lesbian and straight, Mexican and American, First World and Third World, Anzaldúa constructs poetry that seeks to exemplify and reflect the condition of the interstitial and liminal – of being simultaneously between and on the threshold. In the poem "To live in the Borderlands means you," the speaker visits the various characteristics of the borderland. The title reads as the first line of the poem, a device immediately signaling the transgressions between borders that informs the thematics of the poem. The title also allows for a shifting in syntactical meaning. Taken alone the title signals a conflation between the "you" the title addresses and the Borderlands of which it speaks. Melding into the poem, the title also signals the mestizaje inherent to the borderlands:

> To live in the Borderlands means you
> are neither hispana india negra española
> ni gabacha, eres mestiza, mulata, half-breed
> caught in the crossfire between camps
> while carrying all five races on your back
> not knowing which side to turn to, run from. . . .

The borderlands in the poem become a zone of transition and not-belonging. You are not Hispanic, Indian, black, Spanish, or white, but mestiza. Identity emerges from the racial, cultural, sexual mixture. It is a land of betrayal where "*mexicanas* call you *rajetas*" and "denying the Anglo inside you / is as bad as having denied the Indian or Black." A mestizaje of linguistic and sexual identity emerges in the borderland as well: "*Cuando vives en la frontera* / people walk through you, the wind steals your voice, / you're a *burra* [donkey], *buey* [mule], scapegoat / . . . / both woman and man, neither – / a new gender." The poem's interlingual expression and evocation of interstitial spaces represents the power of transgression. The borderlands do not represent merely a cultural or national transgression. As the imagery evoked by the poem suggests, sexual and gender identities give way before the transformative forces of a true mestizaje. To live on the borderlands means transgressing the rigid definitions of sexual, racial, and gender definitions.

The battleground finally of the borderlands is similar to that proposed by Lorna Dee Cervantes's poem. Here, however, the dream of a utopia is not proffered as some critical other space. The enemies here are not without. In the borderlands

> you are the battleground
> where enemies are kin to each other;
> you are at home, a stranger,
> the border disputes have been settled
> the volley of shots have shattered the truce.

As with Cervantes's poem, the series of contradictions serve to indicate the discontinuity inherent to the borderland. From this perspective, Elizondo is right in conflating Aztlán with the borderland; they meld one into the other as regions of rupture where self and other perpetually dance around and through one another.

Although one enemy remains the homogenizing elements of society that seek to erase any trace of "race" – the mill that wants to "pound you pinch you roll you out / smelling like white bread but dead" – these enemies do not stand wholly without. These are the lessons internalized through the history of racism and violence that marks the borderland. The borderland stands as that region that is home and not home, the places where all the contradictions of living among and between worlds manifests itself. Anzaldúa's poem offers a series of vignettes lending a sense of the difficulties and problems inherent to this realm of discontinuity. Not offering a vision of another land as the utopian hope for peace or justice, all the poem can offer is advice on how to negotiate through the ruptured terrain of the borderland: "To survive the Borderlands / you must live *sin fronteras* / be a crossroads." To live without borders means that the subjectivity to which Anzaldúa's poetry points constantly stands at the intersection of various discursive and historical trajectories. The crossroads that subjectivity becomes allow as well for the self to venture down various roads, follow trails that will lead across numerous – often discontinuous, often contradictory, often antithetical – regions: European, Indian, Mexican, American, male, female, homosexual, heterosexual. The quest suggested by Anzaldúa's sense of the borderlands is not toward a fixed or rigid identity. The Chicano becomes a fluid condition, a migratory self who reclaims not merely the geographic realm of Aztlán. Instead, Chicanos come to be seen as transfiguring themselves – moving between the worlds of indigenous and European, of American and Mexican, of self and other.

The transformation of "Aztlán" from homeland to borderland signifies an opening within Chicano cultural discourse. It marks a significant transformation away from the dream of origin toward an engagement with the construction of cultural identity. As the U.S.–Mexican border represents a construction tied to histories of power and dispossession, the construction of personal and cultural identity entailed in any multicultural project comes to the fore in Chicano cultural production. The move represents at this point a liberating one that allows for the assumption of various subject positions. The refusal to be delimited, while simultaneously claiming numerous heritages and influences, allows for a rearticulation of the relationship between self and society, self and history, self and land. The geographic Aztlán as a site of origins and nation has been rejected. But Aztlán as a realm of historical convergence and discontinuous positionalities becomes another configuration embraced and employed in the borderlands that is Chicano culture.

4

Locality, Locotes, and the Politics of Displacement

The tradition of the oppressed teaches us that the "state of emergency" in which we live is not the exception but the rule.

– Walter Benjamin

Born out of the dissolution of homeland represented by the borderlands, the various regions that have made up Chicana experiences in the United States must of necessity be recast if we are to treat their specificity and diversity with any accuracy and sensitivity. As is evident in the notion of "Aztlán," the idea of land and its relationship to the notion of community has exerted a strong force on the Chicana imagination. It is clearly indisputable that before 1848 the U.S. southwest belonged to Mexico. This claim to the land, resonating as it does with the claims of Aztlán as a pre-European homeland, still informs Chicana thought. The ways of reclamation, the varied significances of "land," change when the land ceases to be Aztlán and becomes the borderlands instead. In an age where notions like "home" and "center" come under question, Chicanas traverse a varied social and cultural terrain that places them simultaneously in numerous locales and regions. The lived practices of a people mark a literal rather than theoretical form of crossing.

This movement is both liberating and enchaining. Although it offers the possibility of living synchronically under the sway of a variety of discourses and cultural configurations, our celebration of deterritorialization cannot blind us to the fact that literal and figurative migrations also remain linked to economic and political necessity. As Alfredo Mirandé argues, "the American take-over of the Southwest is best seen, not as a clash between cultures or a military victory, but as a clash between competing and conflicting economic systems" (1985: 46). This clash does not end with the Treaty of Guadalupe Hidalgo nor with the final usurpation of Chicano land by U.S. courts. The economic wars whose front is the U.S.–Mexican border represents an ongoing battle in which Mexicanos and Chicanos become both foot soldier and booty. This position, as Mirandé notes, places the migrant in an unusual position regarding power relations: "The proximity of Mexico and the economic dependency of this nation on the United States meant that the Mexican would constitute a permanent and virtually inexhaustible supply of cheap labor, but it also meant that they would actively resist assimilation and incorporation into the melting pot" (1985: 47). Belonging to the work force but not to society as a whole, marginal in the quotidian political sense, a source of readily exploitable labor and lower-level management, Chicanos have (though making minor gains) remained at the periphery of power in the American scenes of national politics and corporate networks. That is, the relation to land Chicano culture seeks to make manifest is inflected by the uses to which land has been put.

Chicano cultural production both reflects upon and represents this condition of Chicano "power." Early, more nationalistic Chicano poetry like that by Rodolfo Gonzales implied that a revolutionary project was underway that would transform the dual exploitation of land and labor into something powerful and emancipating. The poetry stood as a clarion call, a prophecy, a catalyst of change. Other poetry, like that by Raúl Salinas, celebrates the events and organizations that peopled the political terrain of the Movimiento.[1] Whereas these poems inform, celebrate, and exhort national and global political change, by contrast, texts produced during later movements of Chicano poetry suggest that incessant exploitation of land and labor require strategies for empowerment and agency that function on a local or molecular level. Poetry, by and large, can no longer in good faith incite global revolution. It can and does, however, present sites where resistance to exploitation continues to take place. It also affirms, through representation, the small and significant processes of empowerment undertaken by various constituencies within the Chicano population. Delimited by repressive, exploitative, discriminatory social forces, segments of this population employ strategies for empowerment and resistance at personal and interpersonal levels. The local rather than the global becomes the site for Chicano political activity and change, the location where new claims to land take place.

Buscando Justice

Micropolitical responses arise in part because the political legacy of El Movimiento – and Chicano political activism more generally – has been mixed. A long-term and large shift in the organized U.S. political arena has yet to react to the needs and demands of Chicano communities. Juan Gómez-Quiñones in his study *Chicano Politics* explores the efficacy of the Chicano political process. His work draws the conclusion, "Periodically, group unity and resistance have been expressed sufficiently to defend and advance group interests. More often, however, class divisions and negative negotiation have intertwined to mitigate political gains" (1990: 5). Divisions marked primarily by class within the Chicano communities contribute to the continual political dispossession of Chicanos within U.S. society. However, Quiñones argues that this is not the only or even primary factor in restraining Chicano progress in traditional political realms: "A latent or overt anti-Mexican ideology is always being propagated by certain circles. Concomitantly, there are the recurring practices of deportation, anti-Mexican legislation, continued exploitation on the job, the deployment of the ever-present police power against Mexicans, and the continual scapegoating and pursuit of undocumented workers – all attacks on the Mexican community" (1990: 207–8). Chicano politics have failed primarily because of the hostility and repressiveness manifested in dominant U.S. society. Thus the persecution of various segments of the Chicano community at various sites – the workplace, the legislature, the barrio, the border – as well as internal dissension crystallizing along class lines, constrain potential advances that even the poetic voice cannot overcome. Despite the revolutionary and separatist rhetoric associated with El Movimiento, and the advances at the local political level in various sites throughout the Southwest, real world effects at a national or international political level have yet to be felt. Against this backdrop, changes are sought by Chicano and other Latino groups whose efforts, felt locally, may eventually affect a larger national picture. At the moment, this influence remains distant, though advances – the election of Chicano representatives to Congress, the redistricting following the 1990 census, the incessant demographic changes – suggest a more powerful future. Soon, the question will not be when Latinos will assume greater power within the United States, but how.[2]

The poetic field has for Chicanos historically formed a cultural site where the issues surrounding power and oppression are held up for scrutiny. The various forms of folksong, theater, and poetry flowering along the border often represent a critique and counterposition to the violence and injustice perpetrated by Euramerican invaders. This counterdiscursivity provides a realm of imaginative resistance, expressing a discontent with asymmetrical social configurations and locating the matrices of disempowerment. These expressions of a Chicano political unconscious certainly found fruition in the days of El Movimiento.[3] At its most basic, Movimiento poetry – evidenced by the work of Rodolfo Gonzales, Ricardo Sánchez, Alurista, and others – served an agitprop function.[4] This poetry may be understood at various interpretive levels. It sought to unify and inspire a diverse constituency. It also functioned within a politics of representation. The struggle for power on the level of representation is implicated in the cultural nationalist projects that arose in tandem with agitation for social reform. The fact that members of disempowered communities spoke their concerns and represented their visions of the world within the aesthetic realm remains in itself a powerfully resistant act. The affirmation of a vision and a voice stakes a claim within systems of symbolic exchange that cannot be turned back.[5]

The vision of politics and the voices used to express relationships of power have, however, changed over the years. Gone is the sense of didacticism or exhortation that marked the most forceful examples of Movimiento poetry. In its place, a quieter and more personal vision of the political emerges. In part, as I have noted, this response is due to the uneven legacy of El Movimiento. What direct political gains were made as a result of the Movement were often scattered or temporary. Although the processes of empowerment that were put into place as a result of the Movement cannot be denied, the overall political scene for Chicanos has only slowly been changing. This change corresponds to the altered economic and political realities of Mexicanos and Chicanos within the borderlands. The sense of Movement and project – of revolution – that informed so much of Movimiento poetry is clearly absent from the current Chicano sociopolitical horizon. In its place, a network of micropolitical engagements emerge.

Local micropolitical groups have developed as a way of meeting the immediate needs of particular constituencies or communities. These range from neighborhood-based groups sometimes associated with particular parishes, to worker groups advocating for improvement of work conditions, to parent groups lobbying for educational change. These groups are marked by an emphasis upon the local, the self-empowering, the self-supporting.[6] Some cross a populist tradition of North American political practices with a pedagogy for the oppressed resonant of Liberation Theology. Whatever their influences, the strategies of these groups form effective if ultimately reformist political projects.[7] This reformist tendency – one which Gómez-Peña traces through various organizations and positions evident from the end of World War II to the rise of the Chicano Movement – finds voice in such disparate places as Boston, where Latino parents have pressed school officials for more attention to Latino students not in bilingual classes (Diesenhouse 1988: 72), and East Los Angeles, where women of the parish Dolores Mission form base communities to rid their neighborhoods of drugs and gang violence, to feed the hungry, and to house political refugees (Hendrix 1991: E6).

The micropolitical characterizes life not just amid the barrios of Latino neighborhoods. The type of dynamic and localized politics found in neighborhood groups also manifests itself in certain political configurations along the border. Discussing the need for transnational labor organizations, Elizabeth Martínez and Ed McCaughan note the interpenetration of contemporary socioeconomic conditions along the border. The political challenge emerging from the left in Mexico since 1988, new U.S. immigration legislation, the influx of Central American political refugees, the coming together of Chicanas and Mexicanas to organize against such issues as the disposal of toxic waste all engage each other and engender internationalist agendas among women's workers' groups (1990: 57–8). The need for international engagement is a response to the Fordist maquiladora system that arose out of the Border Industrialization Program. The Border Industrialization Program, created in 1965 with the termination of the Bracero Program, is the result of governmental planning meant to stimulate job growth along the border and to discourage undocumented immigration.[8] As of 1990, 1,800 factories, representing such companies as RCA, Xerox, Chrysler, ITT, IBM, and Eastman Kodak, employed half a million Mexican workers, at a savings of between $16,000 and $25,000 per worker annually (Tolan 1990: 18). Along with the money saved by these international organizations, the maquiladora system has brought with it a high price that local workers and residents have had to pay.[9] The imposition of transnational capitalism does nothing to improve the social infrastructure of its workers.[10] Workers – setting up homes in areas with little or no public services – must lay claim to land, water rights, and sewage privileges. These basic necessities, which ensure a minimally acceptable standard of living, the assertion of the right to a healthy and dignified quality of life, are claimed in localized moments of political activity. Whatever minimal gains are made result from locally organized insurgences and negotiations.

Within the workplace, as Devon Peña indicates, maquiladoras often combine Fordist organization with patriarchal hierarchies to delimit the resistance among a primarily female Mexican workforce. Her research indicates that a "dozen or more independent worker coalitions are emerging as formidable autonomous networks of struggle in Juárez" (1986: 85). Moreover, Peña goes on to note, these efforts do not end at the factory gates: "Prior research demonstrates that former maquila workers, trained as 'external promoters' (community and cooperative organizers) . . . circulate struggles and organizational initiatives through . . . intensive primary education centers in marginalized areas, . . . various self-managed cooperatives in the Juárez area, and strike support groups" (1986: 85). Maquila workers develop their own organizational priorities and struggles. The effect of these workplace efforts radiates outward into the community. At very basic levels, these workers and their coalitional groups are transforming the material conditions of their lives. By attempting to take control of local conditions, they resist forms of social and cultural manipulation. Astute local political organization challenges the effects of global Fordism and other transnational labor processes.[11]

The labor organization of postmodernity – the diversification and appropriation of alterity and cultural specificity in order to enhance productivity – finds its counterpart in the local and community-specific responses of postmodern politics. These struggles and successes must be brought into an academic discursive arena both to mark significant moments in the political self-affirmation of the dispossessed and to remind ourselves of the precious privilege we enjoy.

More germane to the argument here is to note that these political battles do not mark a takeover of the means of production, nor do they place Chicanos, people of color, or other members of the "Third World" in executive or administrative positions. Nor do they ensure that all constituencies benefit from even marginal gains. For there is no group among Chicanos who more clearly manifests the call for justice in the workplace than the farm workers. Yet, despite the position of privilege the campesino has traditionally held within the Chicano imagination, the reality is that little has improved to alleviate the hardship of fieldwork. Despite the best efforts of the United Farm Workers and other advocacy groups, "migrant laborers continue to be exposed to dangerous pesticides as they work in the fields and denied access to toilets and drinking water. . . . At the day's end, many still go home to shacks, with minimal enforcement of housing codes" (DeParle 1991: E3). These conditions exist from California to Pennsylvania, Florida to Maine. The struggles are long and continuing.

Nevertheless, the advocacy and agitation occurring at local levels help form the bases for "strong 'operational unity' coalitions, which can be vehicles for the national community on specific issues."[12] A micropolitical project may indeed form a new and potentially effective basis upon which to build a totalizing political program. These nodes of micropolitical activism carve out niches within exploitative systems that provide for more livable conditions and greater personal empowerment. These organizations do not simply represent, as Fredric Jameson tends to believe, "the willed euphoria of some metaphysical permanent revolution" (1991: 330). Rather, they form a powerful local response to insufferable conditions of impoverishment and exploitation. Although the likelihood is remote that these efforts will immediately result in capturing exploitative modes of production, they represent radical and effective challenges to the effects of contemporary capitalist organization.

They also offer a crucial and encompassing critique of capitalist exploitation. This critique allows for a fruitful cross-pollination between cultural expression and social action. The new configuration of social activism distinguishes the contemporary Chicano political terrain from that evident decades back and finds voice in a variety of poetic modes. The marriage of politics and poetics in Chicano history has, as we have seen, proven a productive if tempestuous union. One central discursive feature focuses on the power of representation, which allows for the type of cultural and political assertion exemplified in the production of recent Chicano poetry. Like its predecessors, this recent poetry indicates that the scrutiny of power and politics remains a rich vein in the Chicano poetic imagination. The poetry reexamines the historical conditions that have positioned Chicanos within systems of exploitation. It also inserts discursive practices unheard by dominant cultural formations. Through the various movements of contemporary Chicano poetry, discrete figures have formed loci at which poetic and political discourses cross. Three figures in particular help crystallize the political concerns of Chicano poetry: the migrant worker, the pinto or prisoner, and the pachuco – the vato loco found in urban centers and big city barrios during the 1930s, 1940s and 1950s. As Barbara Harlow observes:

> "Immigration, deportation, prison, and exile," each differently, but nonetheless complicitously, indicate what might be called "extradiscursive formations," institutions and mechanisms initiated by state bureaucracies to control the borders of dissent within their territorial domain. As such, they also serve to manipulate a "discourse of boundaries" from within the sites of hegemonic power. (1991: 150)

Within poetic texts, these figures help crystallize a critique of those "discourses of boundaries." These figures help map at least three localities in which a resistant Chicano politics becomes engaged with the cultural field.

The Migrant: Abelardo, Sánchez, Villanueva, Corpi, Baca, Soto

Cutting right down the middle of a road marked by political, cultural, economic, and social ruptures, the migrant within Chicana poetic discourses crystallizes numerous political positions. As labor force, immigrant, undocumented worker, and "illegal" alien, the mojado highlights the discontinuity inherent to the term "Chicano" as it emerges from a cultural legacy of migration. The history of the majority of Chicanas involves some permutation of movement into the United States. It is small wonder the image of the migrant holds such a dominant position in the retablo of the Chicana imagination. The Mexican Revolution began a process of immigration – ebbing and flowing over the course of the twentieth century – that initiated the modern era of Mexican–American relations. Following the establishment of an independent and self-determining state that nationalized its major industries, Mexico became a trading nation with the United States. One commodity it could not afford to export was its labor force. Consequently, the movement between the United States and Mexico has been fluid, testy, marked most of all by an anxiety that was translated into the Bracero Program – a compromise between factions in the United States that wanted an open border in order to ensure a steady and cheap labor resource and the Mexican government's attempt to regulate the treatment of its citizens abroad. The twentieth century has been an era of intense migration and immigration in which millions of Mexicans have moved in and out of the United States. For the majority of Chicanas the image of the immigrant strikes an intensely personal and familial note.

There is no doubt that following "1848" the plight of Mexican landowners in the new "American" territory involved terror and horror as their land was taken from them through force, intimidation, fraud, and the manipulation of the legal system. In this period, racial violence – associated with attempts to acquire land holdings and often carried out under the guise of law and order by Texas Rangers – escalated. As a consequence, individuals, families, and communities once economically and politically powerful found themselves dispossessed and forced to find employment. Once proprietors, Mexican-Americans between 1848 and 1910 found themselves a largely landless class who, despite a doomed series of resistances within and without legal systems, were transformed into a mobile colonized labor force.[13]

The reality for the majority of Chicanos is that this past represents a culturally reconstructed history, one in which their families played little part. For most Chicanos, especially those in California and the Midwest, the history that brought them and their communities to the United States has more to do with migration and immigration than with invasion and manifest destiny. Thus the migrant figures as a metaphor for the position of Chicanos whose movement across the United States – whether literal or figurative – connects with economic and social displacement. The weaving together of various geographic, economic, and national sites helps explain the pervasive power of the migrant image. Although the claims of Aztlán as original homeland and the invocation of "1848" as territorial dispossession were discursive attempts to lessen the sense of foreignness implicit in the Chicano history of migration and immigration to the United States, the reality remains that most Chicanos stand as the end result of twentieth-century Mexican migration. Tracing ancestral and cultural ties to a country outside the territorial borders of the United States, Chicanos find themselves washed ashore the United States, propelled by waves of migration successively crashing into the North American economy and consciousness.

To maintain the metaphor of migration as a phenomenon of nature: The United States has sought to control the floodgates of the border so that enough Mexicans are allowed into the United States to form labor pools without flooding the markets and deluging the workplace with overly cheap labor. The figure of the migrant, in addition to evoking personal or family histories of entrance into the United States, crystallizes the sense of displacement and decentering that comprises something of Chicano experience no matter what employment, no matter what social class, no matter where situated. This displacement is crossed with a sense of disempowerment. The migrant is the pawn in geopolitical games of economic planning and control. Alfredo Mirandé notes:

> Throughout history Mexican immigrant workers to the United States have been at the mercy of fluctuations within the American economy. Their movement has depended on the operation of a number of "push" and "pull" factors. As American capitalism has expanded, the demand for Mexican labor has intensified, but during times of economic contraction the demand decreases. (1985: 52)

Migration is dependent not just on the vicissitudes of the Mexican economy in order to produce an excess of labor; the United States economy as well must create the demand. The Mexican migrant must work within and against these two impersonal forces (at the very least). The image of movement, dispossession, and powerlessness helps locate in the figure of the migrant an abiding image in the political consciousness of modern Chicano poetic imagination.

This figure emerges in several early examples of Chicano poetry. Abelardo Delgado's "El Imigrante" (1969), for example, evokes the image of the migrant as a locus of morality and spirituality. The poem equates the migratory patterns of the farmworker with those of the sparrow, meditating on the position of "golondrinas cortando betabel, / Americanos de papel." These sparrows cutting beets are, according to the poem, Americans "on paper" – in name only. The poem celebrates the goodness and endurance of the fieldworkers who migrate with their whole families from camps in California to Illinois to Michigan and back.

As the text attempts to construct a gentle paean to the incessant wanderings of this laboring group, the portrait of the migrants proves dissonant. They are curiously passive subjects for so active a life as the poem describes. Why they move the speaker says he does not know. It may be "El cariño a la tierra" (their affection for the land) or "El corazón libre / que dicta la jornada" (the free heart dictating the journey) that impels the migrant.[14] The poem concludes with a simple observation of the migrants: "good people, honest people, people who are the victims of their need to migrate, / lettuce or justice is what they are going to plant."[15] Evoking the UFW lettuce strike, the poem celebrates the fortitude and sense of justice exemplified by the migrant workers. However, it also suggests a passivity and victimization that robs from the workers their agency. They are portrayed as being subject to the forces of nature and the economy, bound fully by necessity and trapped within a system of endless movement and ceaseless arrival. Although the invocation of the lettuce strike suggests that the workers may indeed "plant" the seeds of justice, representations of their actions – and a clear sense of agency motivating their migrations – are entirely absent from the poem.

Slightly more aggressive and yet equally celebratory, Ricardo Sánchez's "migrant lament. . . ," composed in 1970 and published in 1973, agonizes over the deprivation and endless work suffered by migrant workers. Typical of Sánchez's work, the poem locates in "gringoismo" and "priests genuflecting / to pobreza" the source of the agony the poor migrants suffer. The poem goes on to proclaim "a new age / has dawned" and, as the work of the migrant moves "from grape boycott / to lettuce strike, / you laugh with new machismo." In conclusion, the poem calls for the migrant to "weep not over past desmadres," urges them to "pick up coraje y cojones" (courage and balls) and go forth to create a global social change. This testosterone-imbued view of the migrant's new struggle exemplifies a machista attitude toward the migrant. He becomes a "new man" venturing forth to construct a new world order despite past disasters and setbacks. The poem exhorts the worker to greater action. Although the migrant represents a much more active figure here than in Abelardo's gentle celebration, the exclamatory style and exhortations, and the vague vision of a world transformed, places the migrant in a realm of utopian other, the vanguard of a revolutionary future. Their connection to the present, the flesh and bone locality of their condition, remains absent.

Tino Villanueva's "Que hay otra voz" (1972) examines the "other voice" that wants to speak out of the Mexican migrant experience. As with Abelardo's poem, Villanueva's locates the source of the migrant's inalterable schedule in the necessity of economics: "hay que comer, hacer pagos, sacar la ropa / del *Lay-Away; '55 Chevy engine tune-up;* / los niños en *seventh-grade* piden lápices / con futuro." Against the need to eat, to make payments, to get the clothes out of lay-away, to tune up the car, to buy the children pencils, the poem posits another voice that wants to speak: "Hay otra voz que quiere hablar." The poem addresses the migrant, describing his physical appearance, his sweat-filled days, his new blue jeans, relating how he appears to sprout every year "como fuerza elemental, / temporal. . . ." This description of the migrant as elemental and seasonal echoes Abelardo's naturalistic vision of the migrant. The poem concludes with an image of the migrant in the fields and vineyards where brave shouts arise: "las huelgas siembran un día nuevo. / El *boycott* es religión, / y la múltiple existencia se confirma en celdas." Incapable of resisting the metaphor already explored by Sánchez, the poem suggests that the field strikes plant a new day. The boycott becomes religion, and multiplicitous existence is confirmed in cells, echoing the sense of religious order with a monastic cell and evoking the civil disobedience and persecution of a jail cell. The poem portrays an essential vision of the migrant as a part of nature, a player within larger forces, a figure who will somehow, almost organically, bring forth justice into the world.

The lack of agency evident in these three poems is matched by a lack of specificity. All three portray a migrant farmworker who is at the mercy of grand forces, who remains a voiceless manifestation of nature's way. The migrant workers are imagined much as Rodolfo Gonzales's *Yo Soy Joaquín* imagines Chicano political resistance: as somewhat inert and inevitable players in the irreversible revolutionary processes of justice. In these migrant poems, the imaginary conflates revolutionary change with seasonal change. In either case, the poems skirt the issue of empowerment.

Similarly, the poems avoid the issue of gender. Or rather, they represent an image of the migrant who is quite specifically gendered. At the time of their composition, these migrant poems sought to describe a labor force of which 40 percent was female (Rosaura Sánchez 1977: 10). The erasure of

Chicanas and Mexicanas from poetic portraits of labor reinscribes the ideology of domesticity that delimits Chicana subjectivity. The androcentrism exemplified by these poems, the curious passivity of the migrants themselves, the sense that agency forms a condition beyond the capabilities of the farmworkers each poem celebrates, constructs a limited image of the migrants. They become objects within larger process of growth and change. Although the migrant assumes a forceful and central presence in these early examples of Chicano poetic imagination, the picture that emerges is finally distorted, romanticized, and distant.

The march on Delano, the lettuce boycott, the grape strike, all the various forms of activism by the UFW and César Chávez placed the image of the farmworker in the cultural repertoire of Chicano poets. At the same time, it is clear that the migrant's vocal political activism found a silent double in the aesthetic arena. The political resistance and claims for justice associated with the migrant worker certainly crystallized a figure who embodied the claims for equality, dignity, and empowerment sought by the various movements of El Movimiento. At the same time, the poetic reproduction of these workers reduced the function of the workers to passive objects of natural forces.

As I have suggested, the power of this overtly politicized figure to capture the imagination of Chicano culture derives from a history of immigration. Rodolfo Acuña estimates that as much as one-eighth of the Mexican population emigrated to the United States between 1910 and 1930. This movement certainly meant gains both materially and representationally for the Chicano communities of long standing in the United States (Acuña 1972: 123). However, it also brought with it some harder times for Chicanos. Because of the perceived "flood" of uncontrolled immigration and the darkening of the American socius, one result of this movement was a backlash and tightening of immigration controls – accompanied by a rise in racist attacks upon Mexicans – during the 1930s and 1940s, a pattern one finds repeated in the 1990s. Historically, the migrant stands at the contradictory nexus of economic and social forces. Desirable as a laborer, the Mexican migrant was equally repugnant as a member North American society. Although more Mexicans migrated to the United States to meet the demands for increased labor as a result of World War II, the Zoot Suit or Pachuco "Riots" of 1943 indicate a continued resentment and violent rejection of people of Mexican descent. The "Riots" consisted of gangs of U.S. servicemen rampaging through numerous Chicano communities in and around Los Angeles, beating Chicano youth and spreading terror. Often as a result of these attacks, in a predictable perversion of justice, many Chicanos were arrested, but none of the servicemen was ever charged (McWilliams 1948: 244–54). The Sleepy Lagoon Case (which Luis Valdez dramatized in his play *Zoot Suit*) similarly represents an example of the miscarriage of justice for Chicanos. The trial, which found members of the 38th Street Club guilty of the murder of José Díaz on 1 August 1942, proved itself to be a racist sham. The defendants became icons of fearfulness and barbarity, ultimately incapable of self-control because of their violent "Aztec" ancestry.[16]

Where there was social revulsion against the Chicano and Mexicano, there was also a strong commercial attraction to the Latino. In 1942 the Bracero Program began; by its termination in 1964, it had imported four million Mexican workers as "temporary" laborers into the United States. When the U.S. economy suffered several reversals in the 1970s, public opinion again turned sharply against immigration. Although it has been shown often enough that immigrants, both legal and illegal, have slight impact on the earnings or employment prospects of American residents, with the economic downturn came a new wave of antiimmigration legislation.[17]

Antiimmigration laws prove ineffective in part because migration has become so integral to both Mexican and American life. Douglas S. Massey argues that after 40 years of steady development, "migration is now so institutionalized, so widespread, so much a part of family strategies, individual expectations, and community structures, in short, so embedded in social and economic institutions, that the idea of controlling it is probably unrealistic" (1987: 1399). The failure to control immigration is inevitably linked to the metaphors used in conceptualizing the border as a floodgate. Simply, the metaphor does not hold water. Migrants are not part of a natural force ebbing and flowing like a tide of humanity toward the shores of the United States. They are a part of a highly diverse and dynamic social group whose migration decisions are based on a complexity of issues. Consequently, visualizing the border as a "floodgate" to "stem the tide" of migration proves ludicrous. Massey notes that the surprise registered at the persistence of immigration "stems from a basic misunderstanding of the nature of international migration. It is not something that can be turned on and off" (1986: 670). In part, this control is impossible because the traditional notion of Mexican migrants as "sojourners" rather than "settlers" is premised upon a falsehood: "The utilitarian conception of migrants as economic beings divorced from a social setting ignores the social context of migration." Thus the social ties that come with obtaining jobs, housing, and support "inevitably expand and ramify, binding [migrants] more closely to people and institutions in the United States and progressively drawing them into settled life abroad" (Massey 1986: 671). The migrant as a social being rather than *homo economicus* indicates that the image of the migrant is not one wholly circumscribed by powerlessness and despair.

The historical conditions of migrant life indicate a sense of agency and complex decision making absent in the early portraits of migrant life. Nevertheless, during the days of El Movimiento, the migrant inspired the search for social justice and equality. Much of the moral core that grounded the actions of the Movimiento could be located in the simple and profound claims for humanity demanded by the farmworkers. The distance between the world of the workers and that of the poets is made evident in the position the migrants assume within the poetry. Although several writers worked closely with the workers – Luis Valdez most notable among those – the reality of the experiences each lived was profoundly different. The differences also mark a historical tension that runs throughout the relationship between Chicanos and migrant Mexicanos. As John Chávez notes, undocumented workers have traditionally competed for the same low-paying jobs and low-cost housing that sustain Chicanos. In the 1930s and 1950s, Mexican-American organizations supported restrictions on Mexican migration because of the undue competition. After the rebirth of Chicano consciousness and the interest in social, political and economic justice that the Movimiento had instilled, the presence of undocumented workers in the country by the 1970s and 1980s led to some tenuous form of solidarity between migrant Mexicans and settled Chicanos. Although the relationship is still highly fluid, in the face of overt racism both Chicano and Mexicano shared the brunt of North American panic, overt racism, and widespread xenophobia arising from continued migration and the increasing presence of Latinos in "Aztlán."[18]

This sense of connection and solidarity is made nowhere more evident than in the poetic imagination of Chicano writers during the 1980s. Lucha Corpi, herself a Mexican immigrant, celebrates the resistant strains of Mexican migration in "Underground Mariachi" (1980). The brief dramatic poem opens with images of abandoned instruments hanging from the wall and lying mutely on the dresser. Music no longer sounds:

There are no musicians
there are no singers
la migra picked them up
and sent them to their land
(because they say that California
is no longer ours).

The speaker reports that she told this story to an old man in the park who assures her they will be back "'hands open and ready arms stretched across the Rio Grand.'" The poem asserts a continued cultural connection to the motherland, reaffirms the permanent regeneration of cultural forms within the California that "they say . . . is no longer ours." The poem connects this fact of cultural regeneration with a dream of other, more empowering forms of transformation: "'we may have our first / underground mariachi band / Ah, the sweet music / of the revolution!'" Corpi's poem expresses the same discursive conflation of the cultural and political played out by various poets of "Aztlán." Although this collapse of culture and politics is charming coming from the mouth of an old man seated in the park, Corpi's poem nevertheless reveals the immanent ruptures running through the idea of a Chicano homeland.

Although Corpi's version of the migrant experience is romanticized, it does convey somewhat more clearly the processes of choice and tenacity involved in the migrant condition. The choice of movement itself – informed but not fully determined by the various "push" and "pull" factors in Mexico and the United States – indicates a limited but nevertheless efficacious agency to the life of Mexican migrants. Within Corpi's poem, the choice of movement, the certainty of the old man that the musicians will return, suggests an agency and insistent resistance to cultural separation. Thus, with "hands open and ready arms" the mariachis represent active agents within a complex process of social and economic relations. Although Corpi's poem recasts the significance of this complexity in cultural terms, a strategy we have seen earlier poets undertake in relation to the cultural nationalism associated with Aztlán, the poem does offer a vision of the migrant not passively subject to larger natural and economic forces. The sense of agency evident in the numerous ploys used to enter the United States – even as simple a strategy as bursting in clusters through the border checkpoint and rushing down the center of the San Diego Freeway – indicates that the power of this constituency to make decisions and take risks exceeds their earlier poetic portrayals.

This revision of the migrant as a locus of empowerment and resistance in the face of oppression and impersonal forces makes for a compelling and complex image of Chicano subjectivity. This image appears in the 1981 poem by Gary Soto, "Mexicans Begin Jogging." The poem expresses a strong sense of optimism over the dissolution of borders and the recasting of a border region. It offers a humorous narrative in which the speaker describes his misadventures working at a rubber factory raided by the border patrol. When his boss tells him to run, the poet responds by telling him he is American: "'No time for lies,' he said, and pressed / a dollar in my palm."

The speaker goes along with the escape: "Since I was on his time, I ran / And became the wag to a short tail of Mexicans." The poet as wag proves correct, not just in his punning description of the line of running Mexicans before him, but also in his response to his run "from the industrial road to the soft / Houses where people paled at the turn of an autumn sky." For, while these faces pale in the day's dying light – perhaps paling in the face of demographic changes throughout the southwest, certainly paling as the speaker runs from the inner industrial area of the city to outer more suburban climes – the poet shouts with joy. "What could I do" he asks "but yell *vivas* / To baseball, milkshakes, and those sociologists / Who would clock me / As I jog into the next century / On the power of a great, silly grin." The affirmation by this deterritorialized American fond of baseball and milkshakes provides a humorous counterpoint to the celebratory and ethnically marked *vivas* he yells into the pale autumn sky.[19]

This poem, characteristic of some of Soto's more humorous sketches, reveals the problem of dispossession felt and resistance voiced by many Chicanos in the twentieth century. The strategies for empowerment and self-worth come from an affirmation of the numerous cultural particularities of being born Mexican – born other – in the United States. Not only aliens in another country, Chicanos are made alien in their own. This theme, recurrent throughout the history of the Chicano in the United States, helps to engender the sense of placelessness so influential in the development of Chicano self-identity. The historical memory of dispossession and displacement marked by "1848" burns so brightly in the minds of many Chicanos and Mexicanos because of the constant reminder of difference and alienation. In the Chicano imagination "1848" and its aftermath come to represent a Benjaminian monad in which the crystallization of dispossession and displacement finds a historical home. The date serves as a marker that invokes a historical reality and resonates with a contemporary politics. The connection of self to a history involving dispossession becomes manifestly clear with the type of reclamation Soto's poem so successfully portrays.

More pertinent to the present discussion, the poem complicates the image of the migrant by blurring the line between migrant and nonmigrant. It continues the practice of identifying the Chicano with the Mexican migrant as sharing distinct parts in a contiguous historical experience of displacement and settlement. In Soto's poem, however, the migrant does not represent a distant and inactive object within larger social processes. He becomes a conscious and humorously self-deprecating subject in the person of the speaker as "wag" to a tail of Mexicans. All are involved in a movement forward into a future in which the historical memory of Chicano dispossession and displacement finds its vengeance through the reclamation of baseball, milkshakes, and the power of a great silly grin.

Although Soto's poem does not precisely treat the image of the migrant worker, it does suggest a connection between self and future that implies an agency we do not find in earlier evocations of the migrant. The connection of self to a past – likewise implying a sense of agency – is made evident in the poetry of Jimmy Santiago Baca. Even for Baca, who so strongly identifies with the indigenous populations and cultures of New Mexico, the migrant resides in his repetoire of poetic icons. In "A Better Life" (1989) he portrays the thoughts of a migrant worker holding onto the hope of change that drives so many north to the United States. The poem centers the reader in the mind of the migrant, opening with the dominant image of the poem: "My life is a lover's breathing / on embers of dreams / for a better life" (115). The speaker assumes a curious position in relation to his life. As if nurturing fragile embers, the speaker's life stokes his dreams in the face of institutionalized oppression. The sense of tenderness and fragility that opens the poem contrasts with the images of persecution the speaker endures at the hands of immigration officers who detain him for months in "American jails [that] armored my flesh / with steel skin." Despite the processes of dehumanization endured by the speaker – a dehumanization suggested by the image of metamorphosis whereby the speaker's biological body and institutional identity blend into one – the speaker rejects "their iron/concrete skins." The poem expresses an agency that can deny the manifestations of repression and containment "for my own / embers of a dream / for a better life." This last phrase becomes like a chant through the course of the poem, drawing the speaker on, assuring him when all else seems to fail.

The processes of incarceration and detention become the identity imposed upon but finally rejected by the speaker. The poem passes from the enamored relationship between the speaker and his life to his armored condition as an inmate in American jails. The migrant in Baca's poetic vision remains a site of resistance and dignity. The interaction between oppressive – and politically motivated – institutions and the figure of the migrant as a figure of resistance and liberation is here an intimate one. Unlike much early Chicano poetry, Baca's poem does not rail against systemic violence. The violence evoked by the poem occurs on an immediate and personal level. As the jails become the steel skin of the speaker, the interpenetration between politics and the subject here is complete. Although an oppositional stance still makes itself manifest, the collapse of the political into the personal is made vividly plain in Baca's poem.

One reason the speaker maintains a resistant stance is simply because

"Dreams do not corrode or rust / like the gun in an officer's hand / or the knife of a violent man." The dream that propels the speaker does not extinguish like the pleasure of tourists "who buy and sell children for sexual play." Pointing toward the practices of dehumanization and violation at work in the border region, the poem seeks to highlight a realm of desire that outlasts the explosions of violence and sexual pleasure. This realm, marked by a desire for a better life, outlasts the destruction by knives and guns and prostitution. "Instead," the poem continues, "when I am desperate / and see no future for me," the refrain returns: "then my life / is a lover's breathing / on embers of a dream / for a better life."

In the face of despair, the tenacious hope for a better future permits the speaker to drive forward. Baca's poem transcends the image of the migrant as an almost mystical locus of power and transformation. Subjectivity reveals itself to be intricately connected to the complex historical, social, and economic influences that circumscribe the life of the speaker. The forces that "push" and "pull" the migrant become, within these poetic evocations, quite conscious decisions rather than the inevitable results of impersonal forces. It is the pull and push of the future and past, these poems indicate, that move the migrant onward across the treacherous terrain of the borderlands. The intimacy conveyed by these poems, the sense of agency they convey, the subjectivity influenced but not determined by various political and economic trajectories – these distinguish the poetic treatment of the migrant from the exhortative poetry of its predecessors.

The Pinto: Sánchez, Lucero, Baca, Salinas

The migrant within Chicano poetic imagination asserts dignity and empowerment despite the displacement, dispossession, and exploitation involved in a migratory life. The migrant stands as a locus of political discourses: the point at which international treaties, transnational labor movements, economic forces, military action, racist fears converge. Among the many dangers the "illegal" migrant encounters in coming to the United States, the final one is the violence and repression that lurks behind the veneer of North American "civilization." In November 1988, for example, two teenagers playing war games on the border shot and killed, while "hunting hispanics," two young Latinos standing by the side of the road. Both victims were in the United States legally (Davidson 1990: 558).

Civilians are not the only perpetrators of violence. Three immigrants were shot to death and three wounded by the Border Patrol, two killed and one wounded by the San Diego police. Eerily evocative of the Palestinian

Intifada, both 15-year-old Eduardo García Zamores – shot through the lung, liver, and spleen (Mydans 1991: 9) – and Francisco Ruíz – trying to prevent a Border Patrolman from stepping on the stomach of his seven-months-pregnant wife (Davidson 1990: 560) – were shot for allegedly attempting to throw rocks at the Patrol.

The violence that haunts the border finds its institutional twin in the prison systems that house migrants and Chicanos. A tradition of "pinto" poetry, composed by Chicano poets/prisoners, runs through the movements of Chicano poetry. Abelardo Delgado, Ricardo Sánchez, and Raúl Salinas were among the early poets whose writings began during and continued to be influenced by the imprisonment they endured. The prison within Chicano poetic expression comes to represent the embodiment of industrialization, control, and technological vacuity. It stands as the quintessential product of contemporary American society, with its dehumanizing processes, its violence, its rigidity, its sterile and murderous environment. As such, pinto poetry scrutinizes the underside of American power. Whereas the migrant represents a figure striving to arrive to America – an image associated with endurance, ingenuity, earnestness – the pinto becomes a figure trapped by America. The prisoner is the individual who has been caught twice: once in a network of criminal activity that comes from the outlaw position which dominant society configures as his or her identity, and once in a system that perpetuates processes of punishment and dehumanization.

Ricardo Sánchez, serving time twice during the 1960s, remains the grandest of the pinto poets.[20] Imprisonment as a condition of life in the United States is a theme his poetry returns to over and over again. As is evident in a poem like "Reo Eterno" (1971), the processes of injustice and punishment meted out by the judicial system represent but a small part of a systemic violence and violation. Thus the subject of his pinto poetry is not simply a personal expression of his own suffering as a prisoner – though the poetry performs that function as well – but a commentary upon the condition of contemporary American society. Humanity as a whole suffers the oppression of economic and political exploitation undertaken by the United States. From the point of view of Sánchez's poetry, everybody stands as a type of prisoner, an eternal convict, as the title of his poem suggests.

"Reo Eterno" opens with the repetitious "reo reo reo reo," intoning the monotony of prison life. This life, the poem argues, represents a larger reality:

> the loneliness life is
> caught in the mesmerizing words

you are now sentenced
to die day by day
in the sordid world
of cement and bars.

The "sordid world" of the poem represents the physical conditions of prison and simultaneously suggests the inescapability of human existence sentenced, as it were, "to die day by day." The world of Sánchez's poetry becomes one circumscribed by a gray and dehumanizing institutionalization. The poem, however, does not simply offer an existential vision. It voices a sharply political critique. The poem invokes Rodolofo Gonzales, citing *Yo Soy Joaquín:* "and corky rapped of / being 'lost in the swirl / of a gringo world.'" The institutional world of Sánchez's poem resonates with the technologized one of Gonzales's. In both cases, these worlds represent all that the United States has to offer as a nation of mechanization, capitalism, institutionalization. Sánchez's poem makes explicit its thematic intent: "all humanity / but an eternal convict / suffering the binding of its soul." This suffering results from the "hard nosed justices" meting out "measured eternities / from capitol hill to wall street jungle." The poem thus casts blame for the processes of dehumanization on the legislative and economic powers of the nation.

Although the connections the poem makes are significant, one cannot turn a blind eye to its limitations as well. The poem evokes the condition of the prisoner only to cast judgment upon all humanity. The grandiose statement finally proves too melodramatic to be effective. The object of its criticism, and the voice it uses to convey its criticism, makes the poem distant and abstract, a pronouncement rather than a meditation. The failure of the poem to move beyond simplistic generalizations manifests itself most clearly in the bloodless ending: "humanity doesn't have a chance . . . / and no one seems to give a damn . . ." (ellipses in original). The poem closes on this rather empty note that leaves behind little emotional impact.

Somewhat more powerfully rendered is "Out/parole," published in 1973 but written ten years earlier. The poem is a meditation on Sanchez's getting out after his first stint in prison. The speaker thinks of his getting out as a chance to taste freedom. He finds instead "a freedom / that even now hides / . . . / in this hideous factory" where "women hurry, / tired and old / at 24." Prison, he notes, he could understand – "after all convicts commit crimes." What does not make sense are the lives of these workers, worn down by poverty and drudgery who commit no crime yet haunt this "nightmare" where the poor are "sentenced by fate / to toil out empty lives / in cavernous factories." The hell of ceaseless toil the poor endure forms a parallel oppression to that suffered by the pinto. The institutionalization and numbing drudgery kills the spirit as effectively in a factory as in a prison. Each is the manifestation of a spiritless social configuration.

The significance of Sánchez's pinto poetry is also the source of its weakness. In drawing parallels between distinct forms of social institutions, the poems move toward easy overstatement. The attempt to link the personal experience of the prisoner with larger processes of social control – and consequent dehumanization – suggests a type of universalizing that proves ultimately resistant. As the poems suggest connections across experiences, they offer a vision of Chicano life in the United States that allow for a sense of alliance and allegiance. All Chicanos become victims of institutional drudgery and bureaucratic control. Implicit in Sánchez's pinto poetry is a call to break through that control toward freedom. At the same time, Sánchez's poetry, beyond the tediousness of its often bombastic style, is weakened by its overgeneralized view of Chicano life. The specificity and vibrancy of the different experiences his poetry seeks to evoke is lost in a tendency toward sweeping pronouncements about the overall conditions of humanity, illustrated by the dehumanizing experiences of the pinto.

As does Sánchez, Judy Lucero underscores the dehumanizing qualities of prison in her own pinto poetry. A heroin addict, ex-convict, and battered woman, Lucero died at the age of twenty-eight. Out of this life of violence and violation, she constructed enough space for herself to write a series of poems all signed with her prison identification number: #21918. This mark of dehumanization resonates in the themes and structure of her work. The title of one poem, "Jail-Life Walk" (1973), indicates that Lucero shares Sánchez's vision that institutional incarceration forms a homology for social order. The poem's military cadence echoes a march through the corridors of prison: "Walk in the day . . . Walk in the night / Count off the time . . . One to Ten / Then you'll be free. . . . Free again" (ellipses in original). The regularity of the rhythm and the repetition of the phrasing binds the poetic content, creating a numbing pattern that almost erases the contours of the poem. The speaker intones the result of this incessant walking: "Walk without pain . . . Walk without care . . . / Walk till you see. . . . See the sign / Look at the sign. . . . Walk in Line!" (ellipses in original). The repeated rhyme and meter suggest an incessant monotony, represent the drudgery that Sánchez finds in both prison and the factory. Lucero's poem likewise indicates that the numbing effect of the jail walk also informs the life walk. Numbness and monotony form the conditions people endure both within and without prison walls. Significantly, the poem is written in an imperative voice, evoking the powerlessness of those constituencies that make up the prison and social populations the poem addresses. The "sign" that the addressee sees marks a structural break in the poem. The poem shifts to a series of irregular and abrupt statements: "Then walk in hate / Walk without the world / Walk in fear . . . / See the anger / In their eye / just walking by . . ." (ellipses in original). Left only to walk in fear, noting the anger of others, the addressee is finally advised that "The only thing free / is your mind." This seeming affirmation turns back upon itself. The mind that ostensibly forms a realm of escape and liberation proves in the final lines only "Free to count / As U walk in Line." The distance from quotidian reality, the escape from the degradation and numbing repetition of "the world" works to free the mind only to maintain a mental count of the monotony characterizing institutional life. The poem evokes a limited sense of freedom indeed.

Both Lucero and Sánchez dwell upon the numbing effects of institutionalized life. They attempt to construct some meaning out of the dreariness of that life by connecting it to processes occuring throughout society. In this respect, their work functions counterdiscursively. The poetry empowers the poetic voice to transform and connect through the process of aesthetic creation.

These poets both represent part of a tradition in which poetic and political consciousness grow out of the institutional confinement endured by many Chicanos. They speak with two different voices – different, but both limited in their range and tone – that serve to underscore the connections between the practices of prison life and social order in the larger world. In each realm, the regimentation and monotony wear down the human spirit, crush the desire for liberation, lead to a deadened sensibility that permits subjects to endure but accomplish little more. The violation of unified subjectivity and agency represented by prison life returns in modulated tones in later Chicano poetry. In this later poetry, the pinto ceases to be a strongly evocative figure. Nevertheless, the legacy of pinto poetry resounds in various manifestations of Chicano poetic expression.

Perhaps more than any other contemporary poet, Jimmy Santiago Baca most clearly writes out of the pinto poetic tradition. The story of his early life tells an all too common tale of poverty and despair: abandoned to an orphanage at the age of five, a runaway at eleven, a mother murdered by her second husband, a father who died of alcoholism, a prison sentence of five years when he was twenty that became six and a half for "incorrigible behavior," a refusal to perform forced labor, a series of stints in solitary confinement that added up to four years, a series of shock treatments that left him unable to pronounce his own name. In the face of this brutality, Baca also responds with acts of affirmation and empowerment. In prison he taught himself to read, took to "birthing a way out through the poetry" that he came to write. He used the word as a weapon against oppression:

> In prison I saw all these Chicanos going out to the fields and being treated like animals. I was tired of being treated like an animal. I wanted to learn how to read and to write and to understand. . . . I wanted to know how to function in this world. Why was I so ignorant and deprived? The only way of transcending was through language and understanding. (Krier 1989: V6)

This search for transcendence led Baca to the power of the word, the force behind poetic discourse and reclamations of history.

Although several of his poems written in the 1980s – collected primarily in *Martín and Meditations on the South Valley* (1987) and *Black Mesa Poems* (1989) – refer to prison, most of the poetry dealing explicitly with pinto experiences comes from the early part of Baca's career. Most of these poems were written in prison and touch on the process of dehumanization and the struggle for dignity Baca undertook within the walls of maximum security. The chapbook *What's Happening* (1982) collects a number of these early poems, including "I Applied For the Board," which powerfully conveys the complexity of institutional dehumanization. The poem opens with a brief meditation on liberation: ". . . a flight of fancy and breath of fresh air / is worth all the declines in the world" (ellipses in original). The poem signals a small hope, a minor power in the face of demoralization and setbacks. This general reflection gives way to the specific dramatic situation that the body of the poem treats. The poem reconstructs the moment when the speaker – touchingly and humorously constructing an image of himself that is slightly befuddled and ragtag – appears as a prisoner before the Board of Appeals:

> It was funny though when I strode into the Board
> And presented myself before the Council
> With my shaggy-haired satchel, awiry
> With ends of shoestrings and guitar strings
> Holding it together, brimming with poems.
> I was ready for my first grand, eloquent,
> Booming reading of a few of my poems –
> When the soft, surprised eyes
> Of the chairman looked at me and said no.

The poet hauls in his "shaggy-haired satchel" held together with the practical shoestring and the slightly more musical guitar string. The disarray becomes even more complete with the adjective "awiry" – suggesting both "awry" and "wirey" and resonating with the guitar string that wraps the satchel.[21] Evoking an image of a modern if scruffy bard, the poem juxtaposes the pretension of the "first grand, eloquent, / Booming reading" the poet imagines he will give against the "soft, surprised eyes" of the chairman who replies with a simple but devastating "no."

The poem contrasts the vitality and wildness of the poetic spirit – made present in the person of the speaker – and the bureaucratic coldness and blandness manifested in the chairman's soft eyes and anticlimactic no. This contrast, humorously evoked, shifts into another more frightening and violent scenario: "And his colleagues sitting on each side of him, / Peered at me through bluemetal eyes like rifle scopes." The soft eyes of the chairman harden and sharpen into the "bluemetal eyes" of his colleagues. This leads to an extended metaphor that, in a move similar to that undertaken by Sánchez and Lucero, serves to convey both the dehumanization of institutional life as well as the violence of incarceration. The poet, no longer the ragtag minstrel, becomes instead a hunted animal:

> And I like a deer in the forest heard the fresh,
> Crisp twig break under my cautious feet,
> As they surrounded me with quiet questions,
> Closing in with grim sour looks, until I heard
> The final shot burst from their mouths
> That I had not made it, and felt the warm blood
> Gush forth in my breast, partly from the wound,
> And partly from the joy that it was over.

Through consonance, the poem conveys the tension and volatility of the hunt. The crisp twigs that break under the deer's cautious feet, the quiet questions that close in around the poet, resound with a crackling that announces the coming of the hunters. This image resolves into the "final shot [that] burst from their mouths." After the dynamic poetic and imagistic tension, the final shot, "I had not made it," forms an anticlimax combining the pedestrian pronouncements of bureaucratic institutions with the devastating violence those pronouncements engender. The shot leads to the gush of blood in the speaker's breast, partly from the denial of parole, partly from the joy that the hunt was over.

Although the poem opens with the statement that a flight of fancy "is worth all the declines in the world," it presents the events before the Board as perhaps a setback not worth the fancy: "It was funny though when I strode into the Board / And presented myself before the Council." This decline may be distinguished from others in the complexity of the final resolution. For it is not just the denial that fills the speaker's breast with blood, but the joy as well that the tribunal has ended. This devastating joy at the conclusion of battle causes as much damage as the Board's decision. The reversal the poem traces may serve to disprove the opening observation of the poem that "A flight of fancy and breath of fresh air / is worth all the declines in the world." This signals a contradiction that juxtaposes the bravado of the opening line with the devastating effects the events in the poem have. This contradictory move suggests something of the complexity and nuance evident in Baca's poetry. It marks a significant shift in the form and function of Chicano pinto poetry.

"I Applied for the Board" represents institutional power fully capturing and transforming the lives of its victims. The poem portrays diverse discourses intimately involved in power traversing and binding the speaker. In its eloquence, it certainly suggests the injustices and destructive effects that diverse political practices can have. It also indicates that these effects are felt not in an abstract realm, but in the very visceral experiences of those who are most severely positioned by those discourses.

More immediately, Baca's poem suggests the intricacy of feeling that prison life might bring with it. Beyond the obvious evocations of violence and bureaucratic sterility, the poem does not focus so much on prison as an allegory for contemporary social order but looks instead at the profound and complex effects that bureaucracy has on an individual. It is important to keep in mind that this focus on individual experience does not represent a simple advocation of individual feeling and personal experience. Instead, the move toward examining individual responses to systemic violence in Baca's poetry indicates a counterdiscursive quality that resides in an insistence upon subjectivity and agency. Baca's poem empowers by giving voice to a complicated and contradictory consciousness in the humble struggle with injustice. The stridency, verbocity, and shrillness of a Lucero or a Sánchez give way to a self-deprecating humor and an antiheroic stance in Baca's poetry that nevertheless does not diminish a sense of the suffering endured by humans subject to the sordid world of cement and bars.

In a similar spirit, Luis Omar Salinas explores the repercussions of another type of institutionalization. "On a Visit to a Halfway House after a Long Absence" (1987) treats the speaker's experiences upon returning to the site of his "treatment" for a mental breakdown. Gary Soto notes in his bio-critical review of Salinas's poetry that its themes are governed by a willingness to reveal the personal "with such conviction and honesty that it is almost impossible not to be moved by what he has to say" (1982: 65). Salinas, like Baca, thus writes poetry that evokes individual experience – implying a sense of subjectivity – bound by bureaucratic and institutional practices. "On a Visit" portrays the despair and terrible sadness born of the memories of mental illness. The poem treats the process of return and refusal the speaker undergoes on his return to the halfway house:

> I am here bright eyed
> and night is here also
> with its cold and awful memories.
> No news is brought here
> that will save anybody.
> The damned and the defeated
> share coffee here
> like lost apostles, but
> no saint or prayer can
> change the hunger or the cold.

The powerlessness expressed by the poem manifests itself in the visceral. The hunger and cold that are impervious to change, to divine intervention, delimit the lives of the "lost apostles" wandering the halls of the house. The halfway house becomes a fixed point where no news penetrates, where no intrusion into the timelessness of suffering can seemingly occur. Nevertheless, this place has some appeal to the speaker: "Winter and the devil / have conspired, / for to step into madness / has its wry smell / and romance." The "smell and romance" of madness draws the speaker, but ultimately proves not strong enough to hold the speaker. The speaker removes himself:

> I leave this place and its
> aroma of suicides, for the lost
> have gathered here
> like wounded sparrows;
> and the inhuman
> and the human
> suffocate in this air,
> in this terrible refuge.

The "terrible refuge" of the mental institution forms a physical site where the personal destruction of mental illness freezes time into an endless point of suffering. The sense of suffocation and paralysis conveyed by the poem shades its portrait of the halfway house and echoes the outlines of dehumanization and powerlessness portrayed in other forms of Chicano pinto poetry.

Clearly, Salinas is not writing directly out of a pinto tradition. Nor is this poem an explicitly political one. Yet the scenario the poem presents here arises out of institutional practices similar to those that inform the work of the pinto poets.[22]

The poetry by Baca and the later Salinas serve to convey the complexity of power in practice. The systemic violence of imprisonment that Sánchez's poetry critiques from without becomes, in these later poets, a fully interiorized condition which positions the speaker in an ambivalent place. Although the injustice and violation championed by pinto poetry are clearly abominable, Baca's poem highlights the contradictory subject position of the prisoner. The speaker proves to be bound as much by the bars of jail as by an ideology of oppression and victimization. The image of the disheveled and vital poet stands, then, as a small image of resistance against – but also as a complicitous player within – ideology. The poetry complicates the overtly oppositional position evoked by Sánchez and Lucero. On a formal level, this complication manifests itself in the humorous tone that shades into quiet despair in Baca's poem, as opposed to the exuberant outrage of Sánchez's pinto poetry or the smoldering anger of Lucero's.

Even more clearly, Salinas's poetry moves toward an interiority in which institutional conditions become a realm seemingly separated from social networks. The effects of political decisions that inevitably affect the conditions of institutionalized life in the prison and in the halfway house are played out in more recent "pinto" poetry through the interiorized space of individual experience. Like a ghostly remnant, the political configurations of power haunt these interiorized spaces. The poetry still evokes a vision of political inequity and social injustice. The effects of institutionalization – the dehumanization, the sense of hopelessness, the stultifyingly endless passage of time – evoked by the early and later poetry remain the same. Only the perspective and implications of these effects change in the later poetry. Chicano poetry comes to construct an image of the political as a realm whose discourses traverse life experiences. The poetry by now no longer critiques the vast systemic oppression that institutional confinement represents. Instead, it looks at the local effects of oppression, the immediate results of dehumanizing practices, the small resistances and acts of survival that manifest a bravery and power that – for all their bravura and pain – the work of early pinto poets like Sánchez and Lucero do not convey.

The Pachuco: Montoya and Vigil

Whereas the migrant becomes a central victim of injustice, the pinto a primary image of political persecution, the pachuco – with his stylized clothes, gangster image, creole language – more than any other figure within the pantheon of Chicana symbology represents the quintessence of nonconformity and resistance. In his by now infamous essay on the pachuco, Octavio Paz argues that, standing outside both U.S. and Mexican society, the pachuco "actually flaunts his differences. The purpose of his grotesque dandyism and anarchic behavior is not so much to point out the injustice and incapacity of a society that has failed to assimilate him as it is to demonstrate his personal will to remain different" (1950: 14–15). Certainly in these times of poststructural hangover, the "will to remain different" conveys a very positive charge of defiance and deterritorialization. George Yúdice, for example, notes that poststructural thought "has taken the old 'myths of marginality' and turned them on their heads, endowing them with a 'positive,' 'subversive,' sense. The 'laziness,' 'shiftlessness,' and 'cynicism' attributed to the 'marginal' by liberal sociologists and anthropologists of the fifties and sixties are transformed here into 'radical' and 'subversive' tactics of resistance and advantage" (1989: 216). In this respect the pachuco represents a political avant-garde whose presence in the barrios of the 1930s, 1940s, and 1950s transcends simplistic social critique and reformist paradigms. The celebration of difference and otherness suggests that the pachuco serves a subversive function within the social and cultural networks of Chicana life. Undoubtedly, it is this subversive spirit that Octavio Romano-V. offers in his vision of the pachuco: "*The* Pachuco *movement was one of the few truly separatist movements in American History.* . . . The Pachuco indulged in a self-separation from history, created his own reality as he went along even to the extent of creating his own language" (1973b: 83).

The use of "movement" may, as Juan Bruce-Novoa suggests, indeed be misleading since pachucos were not engaged in an organized program of social change.[23] However, one must admit a more focused critique than the pouty "dandyism" Paz ascribes to the pachuco. Not a protest over not belonging, the pachuco's actions were aimed toward a cultural self-expression and identification. To suggest their cultural separatism was not a form of resistance and refusal erases the pachuco's significance. The positions taken by Paz and Romero, however, are not the only ones to take. Carey McWilliams argues that the sartorial clothing such as the zoot suits worn by pachucos is "often used as a badge of defiance by the rejected against the outside world and, at the same time, as a symbol of belonging to the inner group. It is at once a sign of rebellion and a mark of belonging. It carries prestige" (1948: 243). The construction of a self-identity in the face of dominant social rejection or erasure serves a powerful function.

Striking figures in Chicana communities between the 1930s and early

1950s, the pachucos lived as loci of rebellion sporting zoot suits made of voluminous amounts of material even in the days of World War II rationing. Their very dress and speech bespoke cultural resistance. In part, this rebellion derived from the history of the pachuco. The term "pachuco" is a colloquial way of saying El Paso, and the jargon or caló of the El Paso underworld formed the source for much of the pachuco's vocabulary (Baker 1950: 21).[24] Caló and its speakers followed the tracks of the Southern Pacific railroad throughout the southwest, moving most notably to Los Angeles, where a large group of young Chicanos from El Paso settled in 1942 (Baker 1950: 22).[25] Their petty criminal activities continued, and though the cultural manifestation of their dress and speech spread, the pachuco remained marginal to the law as well as the community. To argue that their drapes – long coats, pancake hats, baggy pants with narrow cuffs – fomented political movement and revolution is a little extravagant. That the pachucos manifested an image of nonconformity seems more valid. That this identity bespeaks a profound discontent is undeniable.

For many men and boys who left the barrio and the world of the pachuco behind, drawn into the conflagration of World War II, the return to the barrio was often disheartening. The social inequities, the discrimination, the suspicion they had left behind they found anew. Felipe de Ortego y Gasca notes that discrimination followed Chicanos despite their extensive participation in the war:

> The tragedy for Chicanos was that even though they responded patriotically to the colors during the war, they were still considered "foreigners" by Anglo Americans most of whom had themselves "recently" arrived from elsewhere, particularly Europe. Ironically, the first draftee of World War II was Pete Aguilar Despart, a Mexican American from Los Angeles. Chicanos were to emerge as the American ethnic group having won more medals of honor than any other group of Americans except Anglos. (1981: 12)

Despite the enthusiastic response to the war effort by Chicanos, the case of Felix Longoria – denied burial service in 1949 by a funeral home in Three Rivers, Texas, because of his Mexican ancestry – was not unusual.[26]

In the face of such discrimination and rejection, many Chicanos returned to the clubs and gangs that had provided them with a sense of place and identity before the war years. This led to a postwar pachuquismo that, according to George Baker, differed from the wartime brand in two important ways. Young Chicanos began to glamorize the pachucos as Robin Hood figures rather than as criminals, and caló become an important part of a colloquial rather than an underworld slang. It came "to symbolize the ways and attitudes of the pachucos and of Mexican-American youth in general" (1950: 23). The pachuco became a cultural icon and caló a means by which a group identity was forged and maintained. At this level of cultural distinction, the pachuco became a figure who helped define an aggressive and assertive Chicano self-identity.

Yet one wants to problematize the social and cultural role of the pachuco. Although consistently an icon signifying rebellion, he simultaneously represents a conflicted figure. Beyond the obvious glamorization of petty criminality and the underworld, the pachuco assumes a position of hopeless rebellion. The poem that best captures the conflicted role of the pachuco within Chicana poetic movements remains José Montoya's much discussed "El Louie" (1970).[27] The poem forms an elegy written using caló to express sorrow over the passing of "un vato de atolle" from the small town of Fowler, California. In marking his death, the poem celebrates the remarkable life of Louie Rodríguez, who was "class to the end." Louie cuts a stylish figure of pachuco cool. Wearing fashionable clothes and surrounded by girls – "buenas garras and always / rucas" – Louie has a penchant for nicknames: blackie, little Louie, Diamonds. Louie ends up in Korea, an experience characterized by "heroism and the stockade," and afterward hocks his bronze star "for pisto en el Jardín Canales." Indeed, it is the "booze and vida dura" that the speaker indicates does Louie in. He becomes "slim and drawn, / there toward the end" and dies alone in a rented room.

Traditionally, Chicana critical attention has focused on the pachuco as a locus of rebellion and cultural resistance, precisely as McWilliams does. Whereas Juan Bruce-Novoa sees in "El Louie" a paradigmatic expression of cultural salvation and affirmation (1982: 14–25), Cordelia Candelaria, acknowledging the potentially resistant qualities of pachuquismo, suggests that the poem "casts a floodlight of truth on the essential escapism of *pachuquismo,* an aspect that is frequently overlooked in discussions of the poem" (1986: 116). Louie constructs a self-identity forged out of the mass cultural images that surround him:

> En Sanjo you'd see him
> sporting a dark topcoat
> playing in his fantasy
> the role of Bogard, Cagney
> or Raft.

These movie heroes form the models by which Louie articulates his own sense of self-bravado. As Teresa McKenna notes, the poem draws on the corrido tradition that celebrates the life of an exemplary individual.[28] In "El Louie," the life of that individual is a highly complex and ultimately ironic one. Louie "moves deliberately outside the events of his own life to define himself," McKenna argues. The result is "that he turns to those consumerized images of bravery fabricated by the society which impinge so destructively on his selfhood. By choosing these images, Louie entrenches himself further in the domination which is making him extinct." Thus, in contrast to traditional corrido heroes who are shown within the events which define and link them to a communal center, "Louie's link to this center is mediated and ultimately ironic" (1991: 195).[29]

The figure the pachuco has cut within Chicana poetic and critical discourses thus reveals the intricate processes by which Chicana culture forms itself. Multifaceted and fascinating, the poetic evocation of the pachuco still binds the historical figure of the pachuco to forces beyond his own agency to affect. The limited subject-position ascribed to the pachuco most clearly crystallizes with the sense of loss and irony that emerges in Louie's death scene, a death that proves "an insult / porque no murió en acción." Neither the other vatos nor the enemy in Korea kill Louie "in action." Instead, he dies "alone in a rented / room – perhaps like a / Bogard movie." The speaker pictures Louie within the context of his role-playing, assigning him glamour through the framework of poetic expression when the scene itself conveys no such glamour. The speaker admits as much in the final declaration: "The end was a cruel hoax." However, the speaker does go on to affirm el Louie: "his life had been / remarkable! / Vato de atolle, el Louie Rodríguez." This last phrase – signifying the high esteem in which the speaker holds the dearly departed – forms Louie's epitaph.

Ignacio Trujillo suggests that when "one places Louie's struggle in historical perspective, one sees that this individual type of revolt was doomed to self-defeat, although it was one of the seeds of the present Chicano Movement" (1979: 159). This comment emerges from a sociohistorical perspective common to a particular current of Chicano literary criticism. The view assumes that language and literature possess a transparent quality, as if "Louie's struggle" could be placed in a historical perspective. Language here represents a window through which reality can be perceived rather than a means by which mediated aesthetic products are produced. Despite the limitations of Trujillo's assumption, his observation is true that the pachuco represents a germinal character in the development of Chicano self-affirmation. His observation, however, is not true exactly as Trujillo seems to intend it. Certainly "El Louie" stands as an instance of Chicano self-representation. It does so while simultaneously recognizing – as Cordelia

Candelaria and Teresa McKenna indicate – the limitations of the cultural repertoire upon which Chicanos have historically been allowed to draw in constructing a self-identity. Montoya's poem evokes and complicates the vision of a resistant Chicano culture. Although this culture, embodied by the language and dress of the pachuco, stands apart from mainstream society – revels in its difference, as Paz points out – it simultaneously draws upon the mass cultural products that belong to the very society against which the pachuco stands. The complicitous critique, the curious position of a self that stands apart yet also unwittingly belongs, becomes emblematic of the complexities inherent in articulating Chicano subjectivity. This becomes a place of mestizaje, a place of impurity: the borderlands.

Evangelina Vigil takes up the image of Montoya's pachuco in her poem "to the personalities in the works by José Montoya and the chucos of the future." The poem, published in 1985, further explores the complex figure of the pachuco by examining the historical conditions which inform his position. What proves problematic in Montoya's evocation of the pachuco becomes in Vigil's a means by which to interrogate the historical reasons pachucos and other Chicanos are allowed an impoverished cultural repertoire from which to construct a sense of self. Vigil's poem scrutinizes the processes of historical identity construction and cultural self-determination. The poem, composed of three stanzas, opens with an imperative:

> recall that memory
> that keeps calling you back in time
> but will not show itself:
> invisible fiber connected to the past
> needled through your ombligo
> it pulls you onward
> but at the same time
> aback

The recalling of memory triggers another calling back, which forms the invisible fiber of connection. The result is a visceral tie, a memory needled through the bellybutton – an image suggesting birth and prenatal connection. This tie moves in two ways at once, pulling simultaneously onward through the affirmation of cultural identity and backward into history. The double movement indicates the position of Chicano culture that ceaselessly seeks to connect the historical past with a potentially empowered future.

The memory of the pachuco forms a locus of cultural identity. This connection is made explicit as the word "aback" closing the first stanza opens the second, echoing and leading back "like a bato loco from the barrio" who strides confidently "clicking rhythmically forward / but head swung back some."[30] The confident move forward and the cocking back of the head – "as if poised to say '¿qué pajó, ese?' / 'what's happenin' home!'" – signals the condition of Chicano culture. At every moment, in its most bold assertions, it returns to the past, questions its origins, expresses an anxiety about what has vanished, what remains.

The connection of memory is strongly affirmed in the final stanza as the speaker confirms the lessons that need to be learned by an illuminated and empowered Chicano community. Where the poem opens with an imperative statement, it closes with an explanation why this imperative – to recall the memory that keeps calling "you" back in time – proves so important:

yes, head swung back some
because string of consciousness
pulls him back in time
although the dude
is really walking forward

The "consciousness" – of the past, of rebellion, of confidence, of self-assurance – compels the "bato loco" back into time. This glance backward signals an awareness of the disempowerment and exploitation that has caused the pachuco to emerge as a figure of rebellion and resistance. The pachuco simultaneously evokes a historical consciousness and abjures a political one. The position of outsider and rebel precludes a communitarian political consciousness, let alone political activism.

However, the pachuco's condition is not a fully apolitical one. Although his consciousness draws him back into an awareness of historical disempowerment, it accompanies his movement into the future. Ultimately Vigil's poem validates and affirms the figure of the pachuco as an image of self-assurance and cool control. The poem employs the chuco as an icon that affirms a consciousness of resistance and self-empowerment. Whereas the historical figure of the pachuco was certainly a highly complex and multidimensional character – part gangster, part hero, part conman, part rebel – the discursive reconstruction of the pachuco serves to affirm a sense of Chicano identity that foregrounds an agency and a historical consciousness. Precisely because of this affirmation, the pachuco becomes a figure whose grounding in a complicated and complicitous history makes him an appropriate if conflicted cultural icon.

Dispossessions: Romero and Mora

The marked change in tone and perspective in Chicano poetry that addresses issues of power and politics underscores the transformation from the voice of outrage present in the early part of the Movimiento toward a wider range of discursive registers available in the later political climate. In the heyday of Chicano activism, the political within the poetic was often worn like a badge. The street theater of demonstrations, the public display of discontent, the righteous hostility manifested in the activism of the day – all powerful expressions of a type of radical politics – set the tone for much of the politically engaged poetic expression. Although the issues involved in those political configurations – balanced justice, fair housing, economic opportunity, racial equality – have yet to be resolved, the tenor by which those demands are made has changed. The quiet reflection, the humor, the self-deprecation that contemporary poets include in their palette allow for a wider range of expression.

Chicanos – subjects well aware that they stand at the intersection of a variety of economic, social, and political discourses – have time and again pointed out the violence committed on the person when he or she is subject to the injustices of those discourses. When dominant society configures the Chicano as an outsider instead of a constituent, a foreigner instead of an American, a labor force instead of a complex human being, an awareness of the limitations and delimitations of social discourses grows. Chicano literature and literary criticism have been functioning out of this perspective in a variety of ways for many years. Luís Leal points out that in order to understand Chicano literature, "we must consult the large bibliography that already exists regarding the social, racial, linguistic, and educational problems which the Chicano has confronted since 1848. The social and literary symbols, as we shall see, are the same. Their origin is found in the sociopolitical struggle, from where they have passed on to literature" (1981: 16). This connection between the sociopolitical and the literary forms an essential, though mediated, link in understanding Chicano culture. Although we have seen the debate between those arguing for the universal against the historical as the literary critical horizon of Chicano culture, the specificity of Chicano literature arises from the conditions of its production. Ramón Saldívar points out that history in relation to Chicano literature "cannot be conceived as the mere 'background' or 'context'. . . ; history turns out to be the decisive determinant of the form and content of the literature" (1990: 5).

The greater intimacy in the portrait by contemporary Chicano poetry of the political and its associated institutions and movements – prison, mental institutions, legal and illegal immigration – suggests an insight into the complexity of political conduct. The expanded tonal range available to Chicano poets underscores a diverse range of experiences between the personal and the political. More significantly, it indicates the numerous ways that individuals standing as a complex of subject positions can respond to the effects of political maneuvering. Humor, anger, resignation, and horror comprise some of the poetic moods that sound with the diversified responses to injustice and oppression.

Which is not to say that this indicates a loss of heart, an acceptance of a dehumanized condition, the quelling of rage. The figures of the dispossessed – the prisoner, the migrant, the vato loco – run with equal anger throughout early and late Chicano poetic expression. The sources of dispossession evident in Chicano history resonate through the many forms of identity Chicanos assume. Economic dispossession informs the configuration of the migrant. Political dispossession informs the image of the pinto. A cultural and social dispossession informs the figure of the vato loco, the wild man, the loose canon running roughshod across an urban terrain marked by prejudice, injustice, and violence.

Craziness, the image of the pachuco suggests, results from tyranny. This tyranny manifests itself in the erasure of difference within the social and historical configuration of the United States. Reaction against this exclusion marks a sense of outrage and seething anger that represents a strong current in the movements of Chicano poetry. Leo Romero, for example, wrote "I Too, America" in 1971 as a demand for cultural and social recognition. Though Romero's later works – *During the Growing Season* (1978) and *Agua Negra* (1981) – are primarily lyrical evocations of the land in his native New Mexico, his early poetry resonates with the political tenor of its times.[31] "I Too, America" addresses the dominant image of the United States as "blue eyes and blond hair / America from England / Protestant America." The poem goes on to evoke grade school images of America: George Washington "on every dollar" and Lincoln "on every penny," images of bombs exploding in air, Daniel Boone, Davey Crockett. These last figures lead to the Alamo and the history of American imperialism in Latin America beginning with the notion of Manifest Destiny. The poem runs through the last century and a half of warfare and murder, of San Juan Hill and Castro, the Bay of Pigs, Vice-President Nixon's stoning in South America.

Nixon's image allows for a shift into domestic figures of resistance to American capitalist domination: César Chávez and Reies Tijerina. The poem concludes with the speaker's proclamation

> I too
> live on this continent
> and in this country
> I too am an American
> and my eyes are brown and my hair
> obsidian black.

Where the poem opens with the incantation of "American" heroes like Washington and Lincoln, it closes with "Simón Bolívar los Incas / los Aztecas / Juárez y Villa y Zapata."

"I Too, America" counters the erasure of cultural and social identity for Chicanos in North America with an affirmation of an identity integrally tied to antiimperial sentiment. The Chicano becomes a member of a social order that runs north–south rather than east–west. Intervening against Manifest Destiny and the Monroe Doctrine, the twin policies of nineteenth-century imperial claim, Chicano identity moves against dispossession by advancing a sense of self linked to alternate social, political, and cultural systems. In allying the Chicano with the Latin American and the indigenous populations, Romero configures a constellation comprised of self, social network, historical trajectory, and resistant movements. Romero's poem moves easily between these spaces but does not consider the problematic relationship the Chicano has with Latin America. Although Romero's work seeks to connect inner and outer colonial struggles by connecting the Chicano Movement with Latin American resistance to imperialist U.S. policies, the poem simultaneously erases the often difficult movement between north and south that forms the axis of resistance within the poem.

For all the ease with which the poem constructs connections between "First World" minority struggle and "Third World" antiimperialist struggles, this formulation remains a rich vein in Chicano poetic production. As should be expected, the overt political stance of this connection diversifies and goes, so to speak, underground over time. Nevertheless, the dream of liberation tied to other cultural and social spaces permeates Chicano poetry. "Now and Then, America" (1986) by Pat Mora echoes the sentiment – even the title – of Romero's "I Too, America." The poem moves through three stanzas, linking a meditation on literal death with a spiritual death that results from adherence to North American social order. As the title of her second collection of poetry – *Borders* – attests, Mora expresses a keen awareness of difference in her poetry. A native resident of El Paso, she has noted that life in the border area "forces one to see the problems of people facing serious economic hardships . . . these people become a part of your life" (Alarcón 1986: 121). Using a trope common to Chicano poetry, the economic hardships of Mexico are offset by the cultural richness it has to offer.

In "Now and Then, America," the impoverishment of "America" is made evident in the image of death that opens the poem. "Who wants to rot" the speaker queries, "beneath dry, winter grass / in a numbered grave / in a numbered row / in a section labeled Eternal Peace [?]" The first stanza concludes: "Grant me a little life now and then, America." The life the speaker pines for resides in the difference between her and the stolid order of North American society. Rather than "rot" "in a "pin-striped suit / neck chained in a soft, silk bow / in step, in style, insane," the speaker desires to be in "board rooms wearing hot / colors, my hair long and free, / maybe speaking Spanish." This freedom is marked by an economic and cultural difference that "America" refuses the speaker. These differences are meant to supply the speaker with life, with an experiential world alien to the mechanized and sterile portrait of America (conveyed through images highly evocative of the sterility that the poetry by Sánchez, Gonzales, and Lucero associates with North America) that forms another common trope running through Chicano poetry.[32]

Mora's poem concludes by conflating the social and cultural differences she desires to express with the richness of indigenous flora and fauna. Cultural affirmation shifts into the natural realm. When she dies, the speaker requests that the addressee of the poem, America,

> plant *zempasèchitl,*
> flowers of the dead, and at my head
> plant organ cactus. . . .
> Let desert creatures hide
> in the orange blooms.
> Let birds nest in the cactus stems.

The delineation and precision of North American burial practices described in the first stanza forms an obvious cultural contrast to the burial of which the speaker dreams. The richness and life that sprout around the imaginary grave of the speaker grants the "little life" the poem requests. The poem's plaintive tone shifts in the last few lines to one slightly more affirmative as the speaker concludes with a final request: "Let me go knowing life / flower and song / will continue right above my bones." Flower and song are the *flor y canto* which in Nahua culture metaphorically referred to poetry, metonymically to culture.[33] The union of nature and culture – an ideal union for the Mexica in which the spiritual and physical find fusion – resounds in Mora's poem. The dream of the speaker that life and poetry continue around her suggests the richness of autochthonous life and culture. The poem reinscribes the contrasts between an enriched and connected vision of life provided by the Mexican and the sterility and decay suggested by the American. This dichotomy – evident in as early a poem as Rodolfo Gonzales's 1967 *Yo Soy Joaquín* – indicates the pervasiveness within Chicano poetic discourse of the political critique established by early Movimiento poetry.

The small cultural acts of resistance that Mora's poem evokes – wearing hot colors, growing long hair, maybe even speaking Spanish – form personal acts of rebellion against the ordered social organization found in North America.

As with several recent poets, this vision of personal liberation forms the inheritance of the political didacticism of early Chicano poetry. Bursting like a sun from the crucible of political activism, Chicano poetry has in its various movements through the last quarter century not lost the burning sense of injustice and inequality that gave rise to its creation. The manifestations of its politics has changed with the face of political engagement. More diversified, more local, more site specific, the political configurations current in Chicano communities find their parallel in poetic expression whose scrutiny of power and its various institutions focuses on the personal. Political and other discourses of power have always traversed and delimited Chicano subjectivity. The multiplicity and specificity of those discursive effects forms the topic of current "political" Chicano poetry. What becomes apparent in the examination of political currents in Chicano poetry is the continued commitment to social change and resistance. Moreover, given that Chicano poetry manifests the intimate connection between history and literature, the distinctions between political poetry and poetry treating the political becomes blurred. As Teresa McKenna suggests, "All that we can do at this point is to recognize and to reaffirm the force and importance of 'event' in forging the uniqueness of Chicano literature as it has been underscored through history" (1991: 201). In order to hear the full political resonance present in the poetry produced in the 1980s, the reader needs to keep in mind the powerful "event" poetry has historically represented in Chicano culture. The political within the poetry has not evaporated. It has migrated into other forms for other effects. Where it no longer rings with the clamber of revolution, it yet sounds with the call of those who speak with the voice of certainty: Where injustice exists, winds of change must blow.

II

The Postmodern

5

Migratory Readings: Chicana/o Literary Criticism and the Postmodern

And these are the days
when our work has come asunder
And these are the days
when we look for something other.
– U2

WE HAVE SEEN the multiple worlds of the Chicana/o, the rocky terrain of Aztlán *cum* borderlands, construed in a number of different ways. In Chapter 2 those worlds, considered from a critical perspective, break down roughly into the Anglo-American, the Spanish, the pre-Cortesian indigenous, the Mexican-American, and extant North American indigenous cultures. In Chapter 3, that terrain is viewed from a postnationalist perspective, shifting from a search for homeland to a migration across borderlands. The landscape here is mapped along the lines of separatism, foundationalism, essentialism, resistance, and migration. Chapter 4 configures those worlds in terms of the regions in which Chicana cultural figures engage and resist antagonistic sociopolitical systems. These worlds break down into micropolitical realms where particular figures – the migrant, the pinto, the pachuco – search for justice and empowerment. The politics of locality evoked by poetic texts do not abjure a vision of global change; they do focus on the immediacy of political configurations.

From a discursively theoretical perspective, the worlds explored in the previous chapters of this book can be viewed as three distinct but interrelated realms: the postcolonial, the postnational, the postrevolutionary. I would like to offer a couple more terms – the postmodern and the multicultural – as signs for two of the critical landscapes across which Chicano poetry moves.

The Red and the Black

Postmodernism and multiculturalism, seldom discussed as if they belong together, might remind us of bickering partners. Each of these contested terms serves as a center of attraction, collects friends, makes enemies, coordinates allies, sets up networks of information. These networks seldom cross. The camps that identify themselves with these positions offer each other only the most cursory nod of recognition. This, despite the fact that postmodernism and the multicultural share many affinities: a valuation of marginality, a suspicion of master discourses, a resistance to empty conventions.

Perhaps part of the problem is that these polysyllabic terms – postmodernism and multiculturalism – seem to engender more questions and tensions than answers and resolutions.

Is postmodernism primarily an aesthetic or historical condition? Does it describe the site of elite cultural interests or define a more general system of production and consumption? Does postmodernism really exist at all as a significant epistemological break from modernism? A breakdown might schematically run something like: Ihab Hassan and Brian McHale (aesthetic postmodernism), Jean-François Lyotard (constructively decentering postmodernism), Jean Baudrillard (nihilistically decentering postmodernism), Hal Foster (critical postmodernism), Andreas Huyssen (culturalist postmodernism), Fredric Jameson (repressive postmodernism), Jürgen Habermas (modernist postmodernism). This list, however, does little to resolve the question: What do we enact when we utter the word "postmodern"?

All this indicates that what postmodernism "is" and how one positions oneself against, in, or through it proves volatile. Postmodernism is like a clear night sky, full of twinkling critical positions that seem to form patterns slowly but endlessly spinning and shifting. Each point of light representing a nexus of the postmodern seems to join one constellation. Yet, when viewed from a slightly different angle, another pattern and potential seems to emerge. Against this black night, the stars of the postmodern burn but do not freeze into a fully coherent pattern.

By contrast (but no less problematically), notions of the multicultural seem so clear that no conflagration rages about its definition. Although a stormy debate still continues about what to do with the multicultural, the term itself within both academic and popular discourses generally invokes notions of "diversity." Multiculturalism seems to rise like a bright red sun, unproblematic, uncomplicated, obvious in its burning simplicity. Multiculturalism implies a recognition that North American societies have become more culturally, racially, and ethnically diverse. Cultural configurations therefore need to address this reality. Perhaps, if one were seeking an even more adventurous version of multiculturalism, one might acknowledge not just a present demographic diversity but a historical reexamination in which past contributions to American culture by nonwhite, non-European peoples are acknowledged. What controversy exists over the term arises out of the way we are to treat multiculturalism: Does its acknowledgment by cultural institutions corrupt or enhance or challenge institutional knowledge?

At the root of these controversies, obviously, lay the issues of cultural power and the politics of signification. And these issues circle back to postmodernism.

Although they should be viewed as sympathetic conditions, postmodernism and multiculturalism are neither coterminous, nor should they be understood as synonymous with poststructuralism. The point finally is that a discussion of multiculturalism and postmodernism can help construct an inclusive discourse about cultural empowerment.

Rather than view the crossing of the multicultural with the postmodern as a "grafting" of one interest unto another (or subordinating one under another), the concerns associated with the multicultural and the postmodern interpenetrate and traverse. They come finally to shape one another. Multiculturalism must refuse the position of civilizational Other in relation to the dominant cultural field. It cannot be used, as Susan Suleiman suggests, simply as a "political guarantee postmodernism needs in order to feel respectable as an avant-garde practice" (1991: 116).[1] The margin cannot be required to act as the conscience of contemporary cultural discourse.

Consequently, the postmodern valuation of difference – informed by poststructuralist thought – must come under scrutiny by "minority" discourses. This is true if the "margin" is to claim any constructive and empowering space within academic and cultural institutions. It is also true if postmodernism is to do something more than resurrect a hollow monument to abstract difference and a reified margin. In their introduction to the volume of *Cultural Studies* devoted to Chicano cultural production, Rosalinda Fregoso and Angie Chabram argue that the invocation of difference within poststructuralist discourses should be viewed closely:

> poststructuralism's concept of "difference" as a category imposed on and used to describe the cultural identities of people of color . . . subsumes ethnic identity into a universal category of difference without attention to our specific historical internal differences. Furthermore, this notion of difference is predicated on a singularity which takes as its center the Western speaking subject and which posits that all people of color are different to this subject yet transparent among themselves. (1990: 207)

Difference, as Fregoso and Chabram (and Spivak and hooks and West and others) argue, becomes within some poststructuralist discourses a reified category. This does nothing more than to reinscribe the centrality of those who define difference. More damaging, as George Yúdice argues in "Marginality and the Ethics of Survival," the deployment of marginality by poststructuralism becomes "the condition of possibility of all social, scientific, and cultural entities . . . that constitutes the basis for a new, neo-Nietzschean 'freedom' from moral injunctions" (1989: 214). Under the poststructural, everything is marginal, so the margin can no longer serve a critical function. Everybody dances across a Brownian cultural universe, fragmentary and decentered.

Some critics refuse this diffusion of the margin. Speaking from a self-defined radical marginality, bell hooks seeks to distinguish qualities of marginalization: "Postmodernist discourses are often exclusionary even as they call attention to, appropriate even, the experience of 'difference' and 'otherness' to provide oppositional political meaning, legitimacy, and immediacy when they are accused of lacking concrete relevance" (1990: 23). The postmodern looks to the historically marginal in order to supply a politically relevant dimension. The position hooks takes as regards the postmodern conflates the postmodern with the poststructural, a move of which one must remain suspicious. Bracketing for the moment a discussion that distinguishes postmodernism from poststructuralism, hooks's observation about the abstraction of difference by contemporary cultural discourse is well taken. This stand cannot, however, serve as an excuse to cast off the postmodern as a problem that does not involve the historically marginal. Indeed, hooks refuses disengagement. She seeks instead to recuperate the critical potentiality of postmodernism for constituencies positioned by dominant discourse as "different" and "other." These constituencies, hooks argues, engaging with the postmodern condition of decentered subjectivity, can clear space for oppositional practices. The discontinuous terrain of the postmodern allows for Others to stake a claim in a new cultural order.

From a strategic standpoint, the postmodern infatuation with alterity breaks ground on which the multicultural can build a critical discourse of marginality. For example, Guillermo Gómez-Peña – Mexican-born performance artist and MacArthur Fellowship winner – treats in his work the transnational and transitional identities to be found in the borderlands. As a Mexican who identifies with Chicano issues, Gómez-Peña resists any easy categorization of identity:

> I believe in multiple identities. Depending on the context I am Chicano, Mexican, Latin American, or American in the wider sense of the term. The Mexican Other and the Chicano Other are constantly fighting to appropriate me or reject me. But I think my work might be useful to both sides because I'm an interpreter. An intercultural interpreter. (Carr 1991: 43)

This vision of the multicultural self as translator suggests that the subject of the borderlands crosses numerous cultural and historical configurations. Rather than underscore place, this view foregrounds the movement inherent in a constructively decentered subjectivity: a marginality that is both critical and powerful, but one that is multiplicitous and in flux.

The vision of multiple identities articulated by Gómez-Peña clearly resonates with the issues of schizophrenia that characterize postmodern discourse. Viewing postmodernism critically, Fredric Jameson sees schizoid disconnection as the near-triumph of late capitalist hegemony. Jameson argues that in modernism, reification "liberated" the Sign from its referent. In this way modernist culture could play with systems of meaning separate from connections to an "outside world." In postmodernism, reification liberates the Signifier from the Signified. The systems of meaning themselves break down. Postmodernism thus begins "to project the mirage of some ultimate language of pure signifiers which is also frequently associated with schizophrenic discourse" (Jameson 1984a: 200). Language becomes language disorder. Syntactical time breaks down, leaving behind a succession of empty signifiers, absolute moments of a perpetual present. The links of the signifying chain snap, leaving behind nothing but the rubble of distinct and unrelated signifiers:

> The connection between this kind of linguistic malfunction and the psyche of the schizophrenic may then be grasped by way of a two-fold proposition: first, that personal identity is itself the effect of a certain temporal unification of past and future with the present before me; and second, that such active temporal unification is itself a function of language, or better still of the sentence, as it moves along its hermeneutic circle

> through time. If we are unable to unify the past, present and future of the sentence, then we are similarly unable to unify the past, present and future of our own biographical experience or psychic life. (1991: 26–7)

The rupture within the linguistic realm finds its homology in all epistemological realms. The rubble of language functions in the same way that the rubble of history or the rubble of identity function, sites of dissolution in which all things, now detached and free-floating, collapse into – within Jameson's conceptualization – the marketplace.

Jameson, simply put, overstates the case. The equation of schizophrenia with postmodernity neutralizes any historical memory. This process of historical amnesia may be at work within the general discourses of mass cultural hypnotism. (Media representations of the noxious 1992 presidential "elections" serve as good an example as any. Where in the mass media were stored memories of the war with Iraq, the savings and loan bailouts, the upward redistribution of wealth?) As the 1992 insurrection in Los Angeles showed, historical memory cannot be erased with the punch of a button. This is particularly true among those communities and constituencies who have borne the brunt of history.

Gilles Deleuze and Félix Guattari give schizophrenia a more positive spin than Jameson. Schizophrenia characterizes a revolutionary tendency of desire that produces liberating movements against the structures of systemic order. Modern societies are caught "between the Urstaat that they would like to resuscitate as an overcoding and reterritorializing unity" and the schizophrenic "unfettered flows that carry them toward an absolute threshold" (1972: 260). Our societies organize themselves around systems that can either move toward a regime of stratified order or dissolve into fluid movement toward a joyful chaos. Societies thus "recode with all their might, with world-wide dictatorship, local dictators, and an all-powerful police, while decoding – or allowing the decoding of – the fluent quantities of their capital and their populations. They are torn in two directions: archaism and futurism, neoarchaism and ex-futurism, paranoia and schizophrenia" (1972: 260). Deleuze and Guattari speak persuasively of the potentially empowering movements a dissolution of systems – deterritorialization – can entail. However, the fact that these deterritorializations also resonate with dispossession and displacement delimits the "lines of flight" along which desire moves. The anti-oedipal model – strung between paranoia and schizophrenia – does little to ground the historical effects of capitalism. The driving forces of capitalism and its reterritorializing processes always haunt migrations, invasions, enslavements, and other multicultural deterritorializations. It is very easy to value schizophrenia when it doesn't drive you crazy.

Neither the conceptualization by Jameson nor the one by Deleuze and Guattari adequately addresses the multiple subjectivities – constrained by historical conditions but constructively empowering nonetheless – suggested by Gómez-Peña. His description of a multiple subject-position is neither simply a dissolution of self nor anarchic transgression; it is a position of translation, of interpellation, of liberation, of confinement. As a historically inscribed position, it manifests the numerous discontinuities and disruptions inherent to its various localities.

Overlapping the grids of postmodernism and multiculturalism changes their configurations. It brings each discourse into sharper focus so that the diversity and multiplicity of each terrain becomes clearer. For example, Hal Foster, Jürgen Habermas, and Andreas Huyssen have noted – each in his own way and for different ends – that there are at least two discernible strains of postmodernism: the culturally resistant and the neoconservative.[2] The neoconservative postmodern rejects modernism, reduces it to a style, and elides the pre- and postmodern in "a resurrection of lost traditions set against modernism, a master plan imposed on a heterogeneous present" (Foster 1983: xii). The nostalgia for tradition – rather than the critical examination of what tradition means – marks a neoconservative agenda that seeks to impose social control based upon words like "morality" and "justice" and "quality." Empty convention returns in force (antichoice arguments, the idea of reverse discrimination, bashing "political correctness").

To counteract this neoconservative construction of the post/antimodern, the critic must articulate what comprises a resistant rather than reactionary postmodernism. Hal Foster provides an incisive sketch of this critical cultural practice:

> A postmodernism of resistance, then, arises as a counter-practice not only to the official culture of modernism but also to the "false normativity" of a reactionary postmodernism. In opposition (but not *only* in opposition), a resistant postmodernism is concerned with a critical deconstruction of tradition, not an instrumental pastiche of pop- or pseudo-historical forms, with a critique of origins, not a return to them. In short, it seeks to question rather than exploit cultural codes, to explore rather than conceal social and political affiliations. (1983: xii)

In a move sympathetic with multicultural concerns, resistant postmodernism seeks to problematize the bases – "morality" and "justice" and "form" and "quality" – upon which exclusivity rests. What "justice" means within a suburban courtroom suffused by the promises of a dominant social discourse might very well mean something quite different on a street corner in

South-Central Los Angeles smoldering with social discontent. Multicultural concerns and a resistant postmodernism seek to scrutinize the political and cultural affiliations that terms like "justice" and "quality" enable.

The attention to detail and locality implicit to Foster's concept of resistant postmodernism resonates with the demand for specificity and historical acuity voiced by multicultural critics. Wahneema Lubiano, for one, argues that the general celebration of the multicultural by postmodern critics serves to collapse a highly textured space. She argues against a blind affirmation of African-American cultural products that ostensibly give voice to demands for justice and morality: "morality for whom, when, and under what circumstances? It seems to me more useful to think of African-American postmodernism as a way to negotiate particular material circumstances in order to attempt some constructions of justice" (1991: 157). The discourse of African-American (and may I add multicultural) postmodernism serves to work toward the construction of justice, not the proclamation of some originary source of justice. Similarly, in his skeptical and engaging essay on the postmodern and the postcolonial, Kwame Anthony Appiah employs a trope of deferral that might indeed prove the dominant rhetorical strategy of postmodern academic discourse: "I do not (this will come as no surprise) have a definition of the postmodern to put in the place of Jameson's or Lyotard's [or Habermas's or Baudrillard's, or . . .]" (1991: 341). In the end, however, Appiah does argue that the break between the modern and the postmodern is indeed real and that a consensus has been reached about postmodernism in the various cultural domains in which it has been invoked: "In each of these domains there is an antecedent practice that laid claim to a certain exclusivity of insight, and in each of them 'postmodernism' is a name for the rejection of that claim to exclusivity, a rejection that is almost always more playful, though not necessarily less serious, than the practice it aims to replace" (1991: 342). Rejecting exclusivity, postmodern discourse opens the field of cultural play after the jealous guarding of the modernist treasure house.

Yet, while roughly outlining the shape of a resistant postmodernism, pointing toward issues of multiplicity and locality as possible sites of postmodern and multicultural confluence, I've avoided a singularly thorny issue: What do I mean by "multicultural"? Where the term "postmodern" has stimulated an academic critical industry, "multicultural" has not. What it has done, of course, is create a pedagogical industry in which it seems every anthology or panel discussion strives to be multicultural. The voice of the Other in the academy is a big ticket item.

The ideological category "diversity" collapses into notions of the multicultural and brings home – in these post-sixties, post-civil rights, postmodern times – in a new guise the dream of *e pluribus unum*. Reed Way Dasenbrock, for example, defines multicultural literature as "both works that are explicitly about multicultural societies and those that are implicitly multicultural in the sense of inscribing readers from other cultures inside their own textual dynamics" (1987: 10). The multicultural serves an educational purpose. It makes manifest the dream of a benign liberal plurality and draws diverse constituencies together through greater understanding.

This blithe use of the term "multicultural" ultimately leads to an evacuation of any critical potential. In Dasenbrock's argument, the multicultural is coterminous with diversity. This sense of empty pluralism is nowhere more apparent than in the conclusion to Dasenbrock's essay. Although he is quite correct to argue that a multilingual multicultural text cannot simply be attacked for resisting "universality" or celebrated for its hermetic "localism" that closes out uninitiated readers, his article notes that a "full or even adequate understanding of another culture is never to be gained by translating it entirely into one's own terms. It is different and that difference must be respected" (1987: 18). This "respect for difference" manifests itself in the demand made by particular multicultural texts that readers broaden their horizons of understanding. The counterdiscursivity of multicultural texts – their refusal to engage in a dominant system of symbolic exchange – is reduced in Dasenbrock's argument to a heuristic element "teaching" readers about multicultural difference and making them "literate" in the multilingual "world" of the characters. All differences can be understood; all differences can be overcome.

The introduction to one of the many multicultural anthologies published in the last few years similarly typifies the pluralistic bent behind much academic use of the term "multicultural." This particular collection, *Braided Lives*, emerges from a collaboration between the Minnesota Council of Teachers of English and the Minnesota Humanities Commission:

> Both organizations share a mission of promoting the study of literature as part of the humanities and of contributing to quality education for all Minnesotans. Both also agree that the multiplicity of American views, beliefs, and histories is a story that always must be heard. . . . We dreamed of a strikingly beautiful collection of stories and poems that would reveal the abundance and diversity of American writing. (1991: 9)

Here again, hollow diversity. Everyone is different and let us celebrate that difference.

Within the body of the collection, however, something else occurs. The stories collected in *Braided Lives* are divided into four sections: Native American, Hispanic American, African American, and Asian American. The representative stories reprinted in the collection undercut the empty pluralism promised by the introduction. Each of these multicultural groups is marked racially, economically, and ethnically as a contemporary "other" in the United States. Each presents devalued cultures that historically have been silenced or marginalized in the rush to develop and expand Euramerican capitalist interests.

The incorporation of historically silenced voices into this collection (which, it must be said, is an excellent anthology, obviously thoughtfully collected, full of fine literary texts) indicates that the power behind the term "multicultural" does not lie in its reliance upon simplistic notions of plurality and diversity. This forms a neoconservative position in which the multicultural can be appropriated as the logical extension of the Melting Pot. All Americans are different equally. Hence the clichéd move taken by a number of conservatives like Dinesh D'Souza and Lynne Chenney, who bemoan the ostensible "fact" that the rush to political correctness limits personal freedoms and makes p.c. a new McCarthyism. Real "diversity," they argue, means that everybody – from WASPs on down – should function on a level playing field. This vision of a colorless, classless, sexless world represents the type of ahistoricity and easy revisionary politics for which postmodernism – a reactionary postmodernism – is rightly attacked.

"Multicultural" as used to designate devalued cultures inserts a historical consciousness into discussions about cultural representation. It serves to reconnect the present to the past, but in a critical way that highlights absence and dispossession. These absences and dispossessions are replicated in the institution of culture according to master narratives invoking "great traditions" and "universality." In this respect, the multicultural thus engages with postmodernism in ways that challenge institutionalized notions of culture, knowledge and tradition. In this regard, Houston Baker has made the exceedingly important observation: "Fixity is a function of power. Those who maintain place, who decide what takes place and dictate what has taken place, are power brokers of the traditional. The 'placeless,' by contrast, are translators of the non-traditional. . . . Their lineage is fluid, nomadic, transitional" (1984: 202). Simultaneously, we want to keep in mind that the "placeless" multicultural are "non-traditional" only from a central hegemonic perspective. Multiculturalism negotiates with other traditions, employs and deploys discredited knowledge as part of a strategy for survival and resistance. Multiculturalism does not simply involve the recuperation of "lost" traditions in order to prove the richness and diversity of "America," as so many suggest. Rather, multiculturalism interrogates which traditions are valorized and by whom, which are devalued and by whom, which serve to empower marginalized peoples, which serve to disempower even further, which traditions provide strength, how traditions provide agency, when traditions provide knowledge. Thus, engaging with issues of cultural power and the politics of signification, scrutinizing the ideas of history and tradition, the constellations of multiculturalism and postmodernism inevitably intersect and overlap.

Most academics react to these critical clusters – the red sun of multiculturalism, the black night of postmodernism – as if they were unconnected systems. Individuals interested in one issue tend to negate the relevance of the other to their own projects.[3] I would argue that to theorize successfully about and intervene in contemporary American culture, one must come to understand these systems – the red and the black – as integral parts of a highly complex and textured terrain often all too blithely called "contemporary American culture." Nevertheless, it is imperative – especially from a minority position within American society – that critics undertake the project of imagining and theorizing about this seemingly unimaginable terrain. Edward Said argues in "Opponents, Audiences, Constituencies and Community," that "one thing to be tried – out of sheer critical obstinacy – is precisely *that* kind of generalization, *that* kind of political portrayal, *that* kind of overview condemned by the present dominant culture to appear inappropriate and doomed from the start" (1982: 2). Multicultural critics must undertake the process of overviewing the various realms of North American culture in order to place (and displace) their own cultural and critical projects. This is one of very few outlets by which the "voices" of devalued knowledge may be heard in a larger cultural realm. As Wahneema Lubiano – speaking within an African-American critical framework – astutely notes, cultural practices by "minority" groups "matter in the academy and in the 'real' world of prisons and bombs. . . . If the other 'others' cannot speak, and I (who at least under some circumstances used to be an 'other') allow myself to be admonished into silence, then who is left speaking? And who or what will interrupt business-as-usual?" (1991: 150). Voices speaking from histories of discord and disruption must intervene into the discursive realms of cultural critique even though these voices cannot fully represent – and may only approximate – the diversity of multicultural groups.

Although Chicano literary criticism has not fully conceptualized itself as necessarily engaging in the definition of "American culture" – in fact often positioning itself in opposition to it – those who identify themselves as Chicano cultural critics and academics must insist upon reclaiming this home that is not home. As I have argued, Chicano literary criticism forms a multicultural practice that privileges a politics of locality, that insists upon a critical cultural practice, that problematizes notions of tradition and history. As such, it is not only at home within the American scene of contemporary culture, it functions within and through postmodernism as a key player always already addressing and defining the *critical* issues that emerge from debates over the postmodern.[4]

Traveling Jones

Historically, the two-way dispersal of information and knowledge in a post–World War II context marks the double emergence of multiculturalism and postmodernism. This double emergence became most apparent in the realm of the university. It was in the the university of the 1960s that knowledge produced both by the colonized (nationalist agendas, civil rights reform, Third World Marxist praxis) and the colonizers (universal humanism, individualism, military-industrial technology) converged. Moreover, it was in the university that trenchant social and political demands – the Civil Rights movement, postcolonial national liberations, internal nationalisms claimed by various racial and ethnic groups – found their most powerful voices and greatest legitimation in the United States.[5] The university structures responded to student and faculty demands that discredited forms of "other" knowledge must be incorporated into educational institutions. Hence the establishment of "special" programs: women's studies, African American programs, Chicano studies, Native American studies, Asian American studies.

The same historical conditions that impelled universities toward inclusion defined the larger cultural terrain – of which the university is but one manifestation – called the postmodern. Andreas Huyssen suggests that the postmodern forms a critically pluralistic cultural site:

> It was especially the art, writing, film making and criticism of women and minority artists with their recuperation of buried and mutilated traditions, their emphasis on exploring forms of gender- and race-based subjectivity in aesthetic productions and experiences, and their refusal to be limited to standard canonizations, which added a whole new dimension to the critique of high modernism and to the emergence of alternative forms of culture. (1984: 27)

This fragmentation of the cultural scene beginning in the 1960s allowed Picasso's African masks to no longer stand as silent witnesses to the master's craft. They could now speak. One might argue that Huyssen too readily elides demographic diversity with genuine institutionalized cultural transformation. However, his argument is compelling. In the construction of postmodernism, the colonized, by refusing silence, gave voice to the knowledge and experience not only long absent from the halls of museums and universities but which, quite literally, built those halls. From this perspective, it is impossible to talk about either postmodernism or multiculturalism as if their rejections of institutional culture were entirely isolated events.

The problems posed by this position – a few of which form the topic of this discussion – may yet be necessary if we are to begin to conceptualize Chicanas and other multicultural groups as more than marginal or ancillary to dominant North American culture. Chicana literary criticism has, as we have seen, from the first insisted that it be understood as something other than Other. However, part of the problem in discussing Chicana culture against and through postmodernism implies some violence committed against the concerns of the former as one explicitly or implicitly promotes the "hegemonic" theoretical and cultural positions of the latter. The generalizing implicit in this approach seemingly violates the demand for specificity and historicity that marks multiculturalism.

Dealing with a literature forged in the heat of economic and political struggle and engaged with processes of empowerment and agency, as is Chicano poetry, makes for a testy relationship between academic discourse and literary production. To be flip, ivy-covered walls are far removed from rows of poisoned lettuce or from graffiti-scrawled walls of the abandoned inner city. However, it must be remembered that the Chicano student movement spawned such activist groups as MEChA (Movimiento Estudiantil Chicano de Aztlán) and MAYO (Mexican American Youth Organization) as well documents like the Spiritual Plan of Aztlán and the Plan of Santa Barbara. The connections between the academy and the community is a strong and long one. One of the founding fathers of the contemporary Chicano novel, in fact, was the Chancellor of the University of California at Riverside and an educational activist working for the betterment of the community from which he came – Tomás Rivera.[6]

This is not to suggest that the cultural production and political activism of Chicano communities absolutely identifies and aligns itself with Chicano academic activity. Ricardo Sánchez writes scathingly about academics like Juan Bruce-Novoa and Juan Rodríguez who "continue pushing the works of academically trained poets" and persist "in promoting the Gary Sotos of Anglicized Hispanic America" (1990: 11). Of the works of academics, Sánchez suggests,

it seemingly
cannot matter much,
when one is hired
to replace
a pretty face from new haven, ct.,
what one writes
as long as it is pleasing
or soothing
and somehow makes a point
about the intricacies
of constructions and fabrications created neath a burnishing sun.
(1990: 16)

The "pretty face from new haven" is, of course, Bruce-Novoa – a mean-spirited personal attack that presents the ugliest face of prejudice evident among Chicano communities. Sánchez's verse, however, serves to indicate that the suspicion of academics – and even more so, of academic discourse and practice – holds a firm place in the Chicano imagination.

Theorizing about multiculturalism leads inevitably to problems of domination and hermeticism. Multiculturalism tends to be forged outside the ivy walls of academe. Theory tends within those walls to turn in on itself. Edward Said is correct in noting: "Left to its own specialists and acolytes, so to speak, theory tends to have walls erected around itself . . ." (1983: 247). There is no getting around the fact that most critical theory is an elitist and exclusive project meant to address, as Said notes, the three thousand academic workers harvesting in ever smaller fields of intellectual engagement.[7] This does not preclude the potential uses of theory, however:

> To measure the distance between theory then and now, there and here, to record the encounter of theory with resistances to it, to move skeptically in the broader political world where such things as the humanities or the great classics ought to be seen as small provinces of the human venture, to map the territory covered by all the techniques of dissemination, communication, and interpretation, to preserve some modest (perhaps shrinking) belief in noncoercive human community: if these are not imperatives, they do at least seem to be attractive alternatives. And what is critical consciousness at bottom if not an unstoppable predilection for alternatives? (1983: 247)

Toward this end, theories of postmodernity and the multicultural provide powerful tools by which to explore the expanding limits of each other. Each project ultimately seeks to walk skeptically in the broader political world of contemporary American culture. The goal, then, in crossing postmodernism and multiculturalism, is to employ theory as a generalizing practice,

> "to make us see" connections, homologies, similarities, and isomorphisms among disconnected and disparate realities. . . . In this sense then, the capacity of theory to generalize and travel among constituencies can have a positive and progressive impact on the constituencies themselves, each of which is enabled to look beyond its immediate area or zone. (Radhakrishnan 1987: 17)

Theory constructs bridges (problematic, "abstract," elite, "intellectual") cultural critics cross as they articulate a vocabulary by which to understand the expanded field of "the Americas."

In this regard, I propose a migratory sensibility. What proves to be a metaphorical notion in the poststructural (a deleuzeguattarian "deterritorialization") can be used to trace the relationships between postmodernism (a cultural condition connected to, though not identifiable with, poststructuralism) and the multicultural (a cultural identity premised upon a history of voluntary or enforced migrations). Rather than allow the term "migration" to remain metaphorical, therefore, one must insist upon the fact of deterritorialization as a historically grounded, painful, and often coerced dislocation. This dislocation can enact another form of deterritorialization – the dissolution of ordering systems valued by Deleuze and Guattari. These dislocations result from political and economic disruptions solicited and supported by the very centers of empire – Europe and the United States – in which the turmoil over multiculturalism erupts. The term "migration" therefore marks the nexus where economic, social, linguistic, political, theoretical, and discursive fractures converge.

A migratory reading in order to move across this treacherous terrain of literal rupture suggests a strategy of continual negotiation. The landscape permits only tentative articulations. No firm foothold ensues. Lisa Lowe, in articulating the discursive field of Asian American identity, notes that Peter Wang's film *A Great Wall* performs a filmic "migration" by "shuttling between the various cultural spaces; we are left, by the end of the movie, with a sense of culture as dynamic and open, the result of a continual process of visiting and revisiting a plurality of cultural sites" (1991: 39). The term "migration" here, while evoking a history of actual displacement and economic exploitation, again becomes a metaphor characterizing the movement between fixed cultural sites. The different cultural spaces among which Wang's film moves seem, by Lowe's description, to exist as static sites. The description does not highlight the interpenetrability of these different cultural sites, an interpenetrability that forms the openness and dynamism of culture. (Only the film – and Lowe's discussion of the film – as cultural objects convey a sense of that dynamism.) Despite these minor limitations, Lowe's use of "migration" does help articulate a cultural identity – in this case Chinese-American – that moves in ways elsewhere called postmodern:

> We might consider as a possible model for the ongoing construction of ethnic identity the migratory process suggested by Wang's filming technique and emplotment: we might conceive of the making and practice of Asian American culture as nomadic, unsettled, taking place in the travel between cultural sites and in the multivocality of heterogeneous and conflicting positions. (1991: 39)

This heterogeneity arises not merely from undifferentiated "difference." The multivocality that marks a migratory process arises from conflicting systems of signification. These significations emerge from the crossing of contestatory discourses, contradictory positions. What can a Chicano do when the forms of knowledge passed along at home – folklore, legend, ballad, spirituality – are discredited from a socially dominant perspective? Yet that dominant social perspective forms one that informs identity construction as well. One reaction is to deny the discredited knowledge, as Richard Rodriguez does in his much-publicized *Hunger of Memory.* Another reaction is to embrace all that is nondominant, a move that sometimes results in an unexamined nativism. The multicultural, as I propose it, resides in the tension between these two poles. The result is a multiplicity of identities, a perpetual movement among numerous subject positions. None forms a fully privileged realm.

Mappings

The landscape of postmodern debate is itself, of course, one of discontinuities and ruptures. One realm of the postmodern emerges from the well-known debate between Jürgen Habermas and Jean-François Lyotard. Habermas posits the postmodern moment as a crisis in the longer history of modernity. He warns against shattering epistemology into fragments of knowledge – science, morality, and art – which become "autonomous spheres separated from the life-world and administered by experts" (1983: 14).[8]

Although Lyotard questions this critique, suggesting that Habermas posits a sense of unity that is more teleological than real, his argument too raises a specter of the postmodern that becomes more of the same: "*Post modern* would have to be understood according to the paradox of the future (*post*) anterior (*modo*)" (1984: 81). His argument suggests that modern aesthetics as a nostalgic aesthetic of the sublime "allows the unpresentable to be put forward only as the missing contents; but the form, because of its recognizable consistency, continues to offer to the reader or viewer matter for solace and pleasure" (1984: 81). The postmodern takes this project a step further by searching for new forms of presentation – not to enjoy them, but in order to impart a stronger sense of the sublime. It puts forward the unpresentable in presentation itself and thus engages in a game of one-upmanship.

It is but a small step to a critic like Marjorie Perloff, who argues for a "poetry of indeterminacy" embodied by the work of Beckett and Ashbery but traceable to Pound and Stein and Rimbaud. The "indeterminacy" of this poetry lies in its undermining the relationship between signifier and signified: "the symbolic evocations generated by words on the page are no longer grounded in a coherent discourse, so that it becomes impossible to decide which of these associations are relevant and which are not. This is the 'undecidability' of the text" (1981: 18). One wants to point out that this analysis functions only when the textual product stands in a completely ahistorical context. The analysis makes the (modernist) assumption that the text represents a privileged and isolated event out of time, as it were. For although there is no ultimate textual authority to clarify Perloff's sense of "indeterminacy," there are historical, political, and economic authorities that authorize discourses. And, indeed, a common perception of postmodernism is that it rejects the discursive authority of institutionalized modernism and its "indeterminant" discourses. So Perloff's critical stance assumes an aesthetic innocence, a cultural practice divorced from history. Postmodernism becomes enfolded within modernism as the "Other Tradition" – aesthetically distinct from but simultaneous with the symbolist or "High Modern." From this view, postmodernism as a cultural condition has no meaning but as an inevitable aesthetic development. This leaves unexamined the historical conditions of postmodernity: its cultural conditions, the developments that have led to it, the exercise of its influence at the nexus of contemporary cultural and political fields, its potential as a resistant cultural practice. Although the position articulated by Perloff falls short of the mark, the stance it represents certainly finds good company in a number of critical studies about literary postmodernist aesthetics.[9]

Interestingly, although from a critical perspective like Perloff's postmodernism becomes (in the most pejorative sense) an academic question, it is precisely within the North American academic space that the cultural import of postmodernism becomes evident. The university as a "multiversity" becomes the supreme example and disseminator of postmodernism. It embodies the fragmentation and hyperdistribution of information and knowledge that characterizes the operations of multinational capitalism. It also serves as the site into which issues of identity and representation centering on racial, sexual, and gender differentiation were most prominently intromitted during the 1960s. The university as both a product and a producer of culture responds to the modes of production developed and disseminated in the years following World War II.[10]

This conjuncture of multiculturalism and the postmodern university led in the 1980s to a neoconservative backlash that yearns for a return to the good old days of premodernism, an expression of reactionary postmodernism. For critics like Roger Kimball, the multicultural represents an abandonment of traditional humanistic culture as the price paid in homage to that academic mantra of the 1960s: relevance. For others, such as the overly publicized National Association of Scholars, multicultural issues are just another degeneration of academic rigor in which solid scholarship gives way to political necessity.

From a position more benignly liberal/democratic, the multicultural is one more (maybe final) step along the long road to academic and social reform and rehabilitation. The rush to embrace the multicultural from this perspective becomes a sign of beneficence and goodwill, the embodiment of (at least within the institutional academic sphere) a true "family of man."[11] An almost blind or reverential acceptance can replace a response of active neglect. And, in fact, the response to multiculturalism is often a mixture of both at once: a distracted (perhaps even insincere) embrace.

These positions toward the multicultural, divergent as they may appear, move toward a common end. One side advocates a tacit ghettoization, marginalization, erasure sometimes masked behind a defense of the "canon" or of "quality" or of "literary" (as opposed to "sociological" or "political") study.[12] Another side proposes the inclusion, celebration, and ultimately commodification of diversity in the name of academic growth. Each side serves the same purpose: to erase, distort, or rewrite the historical, cultural, and social specificity of multicultural groups.

From both friend and foe, the multicultural within postmodern academic terrains often finds itself relegated to that essentialized sphere of the "Other," an image of pure alterity. If the postmodern questions "the very bases of any certainty (history, subjectivity, reference) and of any standards of judgment," as Linda Hutcheon argues, then the "ex-centric, the local, the regional, the non-totalizing, are reasserted as the centre becomes a fiction" (1989: 142). The "margin" does not displace the "center," but neither does it free itself from its gravitational pull. Hutcheon argues that "postmodern difference is always plural and provisional" and that the multiple, the heterogeneous, the different, form a "pluralizing rhetoric of postmodernism" that rejects essentialism and universalism (1989: 150). Yet even her belief in a "critical difference" flattens and equalizes cultural, racial, sexual, and gender differences. Thus, notions of cultural pluralism represent an essentialization ("all others are equally Other") often imposed upon the multicultural from a poststructuralist position. Gayatri Spivak, for one, has done much to theorize a resistance to this type of reified valorization of difference. She suggests that the attempt of Subaltern Studies to retrieve the subaltern consciousness is "the attempt to undo a massive historiographic metalepsis and 'situate' the effect of the subject as subaltern. I would read it, then, as a *strategic* use of positivist essentialism in a scrupulously visible political interest" (1988: 205). The essentializations necessary to theory form part of a political strategy that constantly foregrounds its delimitations. In part, this strategy serves to emphasize rather than erase the historically inscribed particularities of distinct multicultural groups, and in this resists the processes of erasure enacted by so many who wish to "celebrate difference."

In fact, the only factor one can count on to be common to all U.S. multicultural groups is their being positioned by dominant cultural discourses as "other"; the center defines where the margins lie. Michael Omi underscores this point in his discussion of racial distinction: "distinct and different groups have encountered unique forms of racial oppression. . . . What is common to the experiences of these groups is that their particular 'fate' was linked to historically specific ideas about the significance and meaning of race" (1989: 114). The particular forms of violence committed by discourses of exclusion and their agents – the Chinese Exclusion Laws, the Texas Rangers, the KKK – are unique to and go a long way toward defining the particular spaces occupied by each multicultural group. As we have seen, the multicultural is often misrepresented as a cultural pluralism whereby all cultures, despite their distinctly marked histories of unequal relations to power, are equally valuable, equally valid, equally privileged. This representation enacts the type of historical and discursive erasure that has marked issues of race throughout American history.

Some defining points of the multicultural, then, cluster around issues of subjectivity, of agency, of distinct cultural identity, of racism, of silenced histories, of exploitation and repression of many forms. These issues help comprise the multiple discourses available to individuals seeking to articulate a multicultural identity. "Multicultural" here signifies not just the multicultural makeup of a diverse North American society. It serves to signal the multiple cultures available to historically marginalized racial and ethnic "others." Because of their unequal histories, multicultural "others" negotiate through social–cultural–economic–political spaces that are both "marginal" and "central."

The concept of the borderlands, the perilous no-man's-land between First World and Third World, the area of flux in which Chicanas and Chicanos negotiate between numerous subject-positions, represents the metaphor and emblem and reality of multiculturalism. Chicano subjectivity, as is any multicultural subjectivity, is interpellated by a "series of different, competing and overlapping ideologies, including class and non-class ideologies." As Rosaura Sánchez goes on to argue, the subject positions and identities Chicana historical discourses seek to articulate "emerge from a complex material reality which includes class, ethnicity, national origin, religion, gender, age, family, locality and education" (one might also add language, sexuality and racial identity) (1983: 5). Thus the Chicana/o stands at the nexus of numerous subjectivities "between borders." What distinguishes this radically decentered subjectivity from other postmodern decentering is its strong and continual link to a history of dispossession and disempowerment. Hence the position of Chicanos and Mexicanos as a transnational labor force within the economies of mercantile, monopoly, and finally corporate capitalism links the current condition of identity construction to a powerful and painful history.[13] This position is historically specific, yet it links the Chicano to other multicultural identities.

Multicultural identity ends up a dynamic condition that radically questions the issue of "origins." On the one hand, the influences of limited and limiting dominant social discourses like "race" and "ethnicity" complicate the process of multicultural subject construction. Inflected by their repressive and exploitative function, these discourses obviously cannot form the bases of a multicultural identity that encourages agency and empowerment. What is it to value cultural, racial, ethnic traditions over which dominant discourses – belittling, demeaning, and dehumanizing – seek to speak? Concurrently, the construction of a multicultural subjectivity must necessarily be negotiated through those discourses. It is possible to resist the truth-value of these discourses, but it is impossible to deny their historical influence.[14]

The problem for the multicultural becomes a clear one: how to begin to inscribe a multicultural terrain without fixing it, without replicating the same discursive violence that tends to construct all "minority" discourses identically, or without casting it in the powerless and reactive subject-position of victim? One tactic, suggested by Homi Bhabha's postcolonial theorizing, is to consider the multicultural a Derridian *supplement* to dominant discourses: "The power of supplementarity is not the negation of the preconstituted social contradictions of the past or present; its force lies . . . in the renegotiation of those times, terms, and traditions through which we turn our uncertain, passing contemporaneity into the signs of history" (1990: 306). Hence we return again to the multicultural as a migratory condition. The multicultural moves between, among, and toward two or more cultural practices simultaneously without negating the positions and contradictions of power embedded in those practices. The term thus serves to mark those spaces, discourses, individuals where one culture reveals itself to be discontinuous with another. This migratory discontinuity, I would further argue, forms an experience invariably marked by historically circumscribed categories like "race" and "ethnicity." Hence the multicultural can become visible as such only in the afterglow of the 1960s and America's racial and ethnic "enlightenment."[15]

As Bhabha's example suggests – and our previous discussion of the relationship between Chicana communities and the academy illustrates – the cultural space occupied within academic institutions by postcolonial and multicultural critics is discontinuous and in tension with their other cultural spaces – the home, the street, the church, the bar – due to the way dominant discourses define those spaces. More than one literary critic has heard from friends or family that, although they are proud of the critic's academic work, they cannot understand a single word of it. The multicultural critic thus stands in a privileged though difficult position, for the fractures that mark the intersection between the personal and the professional reveal disjunctive points where a type of genealogical project can unfold. This type of project, as proposed by Michel Foucault, entertains the "claims to attention of local, discontinuous, disqualified, illegitimate knowledges against the claims of a unitary body of theory which would filter, hierarchize and order them in the name of some true knowledge and some arbitrary idea of what constitutes a science and its objects" (1980: 83).

An example of this attention to disqualified knowledge is the work undertaken in the field of ethnopoetics. Critics like Tey Rebolledo, Marta Sánchez, Cordelia Candelaria have undertaken the analysis of resistant, nonhierarchical poetry that relies on religious rite or tribal unity as an integral part of its community function. Cordelia Candelaria, for example, notes that one defining element of Chicano poetics is its ritualistic quality, which places it at the intersection of primitive, communal, and shamanistic impulses: "This ethnopoetic dimension conforms with the post-modern rejection of the Eliotic emphasis on the poem-qua-text" (1986: 76). As articulated by processualist anthropologists like Victor Turner, the study of culture is shifting its stress from concepts like structure and system to process and reflexivity, from a "being" to a "becoming" vocabulary. He argues, therefore, that culture needs to be understood as situated at the juncture of various systems and is thus

> to be seen as processual, because it emerges in interaction and imposes meaning on the biotic and ecological systems (also dynamic) with which it interacts. I should not say "it," for this is to reify what is, regarded processually, an endless series of negotiations among actors about the assignment of meaning to the acts in which they jointly participate. Meaning is assigned verbally through speech and nonverbally through ritual and ceremonial action and is often stored in symbols which become indexical counters in subsequent situational contexts. (1977: 63)

Chicano poetry at one level seeks at times to lay bare the various systems with which it interacts: ritualistic, poetic, alienated literary, communal, oral, performative. The poetry re-collects (though not unproblematically, as I discuss later) pre-Cortesian forms of artistic expression as a rejection of "true knowledge" about the function of poetry. Neither fully of the people nor a hermetic negative critique (to invoke Adornian categories of modernist valuation), Chicano poetry exemplifies a critical poetics that cannot be understood in terms of modernist hermeneutics. As an interventionary poetics Chicano poetry does not rely simply upon a revision of tradition in the name of a purer original moment. It employs the forms of premodern culture to critique the contemporary condition. As such, the Chicano as multicultural critic gives voice – within the essentially white, elite, Eurocentric space of the North American academy – to those points at which cultural rupture occurs, at which illegitimate and disqualified knowledges reemerge.[16]

As I previously suggested, multiculturalism has been an academic player primarily in the already very tired game of curricular reform. I insert this topic not simply as an example of equine flagellation. Rather, debates over the curriculum are always about power. They revolve around the control of cultural reproduction: Who is to be the gatekeeper of knowledge, who the one to determine what concerns characterize that national body? One element of resistance among the various decentered subjectivities of our postmodern and multicultural worlds centers on the reexamination of the idea of tradition. Unlike the impression left by the media and the misinformation surrounding curricular reform, it is not proponents of multiculturalism who clamor for the destruction of the canon. The perceived threat to academic rigor, the much publicized loss of "tradition" and "reason" wrongly and even purposely associated with multiculturalism, proves little more than a smoke screen. This screen covers an anxiety over a perceived loss of cultural control.

Multiculturalism cannot seek to negate tradition or the canon since it cannot deny – on the contrary, it tries to foreground – preconstituted social contradictions. Rather than decry canonical literary forms – a move, one might note, associated with the now canonized historical avant-garde – multicultural artists often embrace and transform and intervene in the canon. In addition, as evidenced by the constant return to forms of folk knowledge, oral literature, legend, myth as literary precursor and inspiration, multicultural artists bring to the cultural field other traditions and canons heretofore absent from institutional study.

All this is not to say multiculturalism does not question (the metaphor is often "explode") the canon. It does so, however, only as it lives at the rupture – of histories, of cultures, of social and aesthetic practices – with which it cannot do away. Rather than bury, exile, or fire the canon, the multicultural critic seeks out the discontinuities made evident through its deployment within institutionalized academic spaces. Rather than deny the centrality of Shakespeare, Chaucer, Milton (or Eliot, Pound, Stein) – those great figures in the pantheon of "English" literature that burn brightest in the constellation of Anglo-American literary tradition – the multicultural critic scrutinizes their prominence. Why are they central? How does this preclude multicultural literature from gaining a foothold in the canon? What type of dialogue is being created between canonical and multicultural literatures?

Curricular controversy is just one site where issues of the postmodern and the multicultural clearly converge. Postmodern suspicion of master narratives and empty tradition provides the multicultural with ammunition as it seeks out the discontinuities – historical, aesthetic, linguistic, institutional – inherent in the controversy.

From the other side, the multicultural provides an insight into the critical potential of postmodernism. Postmodernism, several critics note, is plagued by its seeming inability to offer a position beyond the diffused and defused webs of social organization. In the slippery ground of the postmodern, no archimedean point exists from which to construct an effective critical discourse. Although multiculturalism does not offer a purely Other space, its compromised and interpenetrated position does allow for a historically inscribed space that is not like this one. The multicultural explores ways that enable forms of agency and identity within a decentered world. It points toward a resistant postmodernism already at hand.

The dissolution of self from Self marked within the postmodern as the "death of the subject" stands within the multicultural as a (always-already present) form of alienation. The decentralized subject finds its perfect and painful analogue in the decentered migrant displaced by economic and/or political violence. Alienation is not a condition unique to multicultural subjects, as the critic and poet Rafael Jesús González observes: "The question of identity, the desire for integration of the self, the preoccupation with recovering a sense of ontological potency is a theme that runs through all 20th century [modernist] Western poetry" (1977: 130). The Chicana as multicultural member of contemporary society stands at the alienating but familiar rupture between industrialization and human value. However, the Chicana stands in this alienated landscape with a difference: "What is interesting about Chicano poetry is not its preoccupation with alienation as such, but that it is so conscious of it, that it so clearly links alienation with cultural dislocation" (1977: 130). The migratory experience – the negotiated journey of agency, the quest for justice, the reconfiguration of community and family – reveals strategies for empowerment with which the rest of the postmodern socius might do well to catch up. The troubled histories of economic displacement and political persecution that haunt the migrations of Mexicans and others to this country provide a glimpse into strategies of survival in which decentered subjectivity is not replaced with a simplistic paradigm of origin or tradition. Rather, a highly dynamic and fluid form of social organization, cultural affirmation, and personal identification emerges.[17]

Those critics interested in multicultural issues who dismiss postmodernism as a "white problem" err in one of two ways. By refusing to theorize multicultural issues within the postmodern space of the university, they deny their own assigned position in the institution, their "unavoidable starting point," as Gayatri Spivak articulates in "Theory in the Margin." Thus they wield power blindly. Or, conversely, they posit their position as beyond the institution, banishing themselves to a margin that "as such is wholly other," and so deny academic power altogether.

Either position prevents them from capitalizing on Lyotard's observation: "To the obsolescence of the metanarrative apparatus of legitimation corresponds the crisis of metaphysical philosophy and of the university institution which in the past relied on it" (1984: xxiv). The conditions of postmodernity and the exigencies of the multicultural can function symbiotically if the concerns of those historically configured as other, alien, or marginal are inserted into this ruptured cultural space. The power of this relationship is readily evident in the unease demonstrated by the Hilton Kramers, the Allan Blooms, the Roger Kimballs of academia. It is no wonder they feel under siege. Needless to say, these defenders of culture seem to invest their energies so fully in keeping the hordes at bay that they (willfully?) forget some important truths. Their treasured "culture" has only ascended its privileged throne thanks to a very dirty history of armed confrontation, warfare, economic imperialism, and colonial exploitation. Their defense rests on the separation of the best that is thought and known from the rest of the dirty world. This rationale masks what Walter Benjamin's theses on history reveal so brilliantly: "There is no document of civilization which is not at the same time a document of barbarism" (1940: 256). The canon debate comes down to this: Who serves a political master more, those who assert Benjamin's observation or those who deny it?

The multicultural within the institutional space of the academy seeks to reveal the barbarity implicit in the cultural documents encased and replicated by the university. More importantly, scholars working within multicultural fields help to reveal not just the discontinuities present in the institutional creation and preservation of culture. They present configurations of power and knowledge based in marginal communities and histories. They explore realms of justice and morality constructed locally, specifically, often in opposition to master narratives. They work within the larger cultural movement that rejects master narratives of Western Culture in order to give voice to (among others) the illegitimate knowledges of the multicultural. Here the trajectories of postmodernism and multiculturalism most clearly converge.

Movement

Yet no sooner do they meet than they again seem to diverge. For the postmodern dissolution of the subject – a fact viewed as either inevitable (à la Jameson) or desirable (à la Baudrillard) – runs counter to the needs expressed by the multicultural. In the margin, subjectivity is a condition still staunchly to be sought.[18] Postmodernism, if it is understood as a poststructural position, fails to allow for the construction of self-identity. In his discussion of the postmodern condition, for example, Lyotard claims: "The narrative function is losing its functors, its great hero, its great dangers, its great voyages, its great goal" (1984: xxiv). He slides from the dismissal of *grands récits* (a useful move for advocating the multicultural) to a questioning of agency *in toto* (a move not so useful). His conflation of postmodernism and poststructuralism marks the weakness of his definition. As Radhakrishan underscores:

> Post-structuralist thought perpetuates itself on the guarantee that no "break" (Althusser) is possible with the past even though its initial intentional trajectory was precisely to make visible this very "break," valorize it *qua* "break," and then proceed towards a different and differential creation. Post-structuralist intententionality thus dessicates itself, allegorizes this dessication, and offers this allegorically perennial revolution as the most appropriate defense against the reproduction of such categories and structures as, Self, Subject, Identity, etc. (1989: 190)

Radhakrishnan's critique of poststructuralism underscores Andreas Huyssen's observation that "French theory provides us primarily with an archeology of modernity, a theory of modernism at the stage of its exhaustion" (1984: 40). The endless subversion of metanarratives within certain forms of poststructuralism has – as critics from Seyla Ben-Habib to Christopher Norris note – led to an endless playfulness, a polysemic perversity in which agency and empowerment can be judged only by their performative power. Lyotard's devaluation of all narrative functions *en masse* – his refusal of a break that would allow for a privileged social–political–cultural creation – represents an allegorization of his refusal of grand narratives. Multicultural texts are the products of a discontinuous history marked by an asymmetrical relationship to power. Exploited and dispossessed, the multicultural within history reveals the breaks – the contradictions, the limitations, the barbarity – of master narratives. And this is done in order to "proceed towards a different and differential creation."

Lyotard's work exemplifies the most pernicious poststructuralist traits: ahistoricity and decontextualization. The grand narratives he is so quick to dismiss yet stimulate the cultural, social, and political systems that define and regulate our lives at almost every level. But these master narratives do not represent *all* narratives. Micronarratives, migratory readings, articulations of the local perpetually divide and reproduce themselves. These narratives must, if postmodernism is to save itself, be given privilege. Although "justice" and "liberation" may be terms linked to metanarratives, the construction of these terms within particular localities and among people who have not received justice or achieved liberation is a process that will continue.

The narratives that seek to enact justice proceed, fully aware of but not hamstrung by the knowledge that the Enlightenment project may at times manifest itself in cancerous eruptions of blind inhumanity, violent upheaval, and spiritual desecration. Nations and cultures still struggle for freedom from colonial and neocolonial denigration and exploitation; the disempowered still try to articulate an affirmative identity of self and of agency; the dispossessed still hope for a more equitable distribution of food and funds.

Postmodernism – in order to be resistant, critical, and finally compatible with multicultural issues – cannot dismiss notions of narration, subjectivity, agency. These topics must be subject to scrutiny, contextualization, and reconceptualization within a postmodern multicultural space. The problem for the postmodern critic, as Huyssen argues, is "to redefine the possibilities of critique in postmodern terms rather than relegating them to oblivion" (1984: 9). However, what we understand the Self to be cannot be dismissed as a nostalgic ideological construction employed to perpetuate capitalism.

One critical trajectory Huyssen traces, intersecting both postmodern and multicultural terrains, follows the construction of subjectivity, especially in terms of cultural formation. The self-assertion of minority cultures and their emergence into public consciousness, for example, have helped collapse the strict modernist separation of high and low culture: "such rigorous segregation simply does not make much sense within a given minority culture which has always existed outside in the shadow of the dominant culture" (1984: 23). In the 1960s, "minorities" and "marginals" finally entered into the consciousness of the university and other cultural institutions. The repercussions of this entrance are yet with us.

We see, for instance, the emergence of nationalisms among both the inner and outer colonized – minority groups in the United States and nationalist movement groups throughout the world – in the postmodern 1960s. We see the formation of academic fields created within and against academic and other institutions in the 1970s. We see an increase in the numbers of professionals and intellectuals of color in the 1980s. None of these phenomena is without its contradictions, dislocations, and ruptures: genealogies that are as conflicted and potentially violent as any other. We can agree with Huyssen, however, that "to reject the validity of the question Who is writing? or Who is speaking? is simply no longer a radical position in 1984 [let alone now]. It merely duplicates on the level of aesthetics and theory what capitalism as a system of exchange relations produces tendentially in everyday life: the denial of subjectivity in the very process of its construction" (1984: 44).

To reposition subjectivity within theoretical discourses – especially those focusing on the postmodern – remains an obviously complex matter. At one extreme, we find a Jamesonian postmodernity populated by subjects in a corporate, collectivized, postindividualistic age. This conceptualization leaves small room for those constituencies that, like multicultural groups, have historically led collectivized (and marginalized) lives. At another extreme stands the poststructural position that subjectivity represents a constructed, ideologically infused text. This offers little to the historically marginal, who posit a sense of agency as an empowering rather than a repressive act. When performed by those (inner and outer) colonized or postcolonized groups who have been denied representation and subjectivity, the reclamation of a self proves a resistant act. The emancipatory potential of that perpetual demystification machine, poststructuralism, as well as liberal humanism's empowering notion of individuality and agency, changes when applied to those who have suffered the greatest violence spawned by the expansionist policies of European Enlightenment.[19]

Fredric Jameson's discussion of precisely this issue betrays a useful and problematic dimension to theoretical positionings of postmodern and multicultural subjectivity. The focus on Jameson here results from the convergence of a number of issues. Obviously, he is one of the first cultural critics to connect postmodernism to postmodernity; that is, to view postmodernism as a manifestation on the cultural level of deeper social issues.[20] His work has helped formulate the defining issues in debates over postmodernism. Finally, the theoretical positions he articulates – those in *The Political Unconscious* even more than his work on postmodernism – have influenced the work of many contemporary Chicano cultural theorists, anthropologists, and critics.[21] In this vein, and as a way of broadening the theoretical borrowings from Jameson within a Chicano context, I turn to Jameson's theories regarding locality and marginalization.

Jameson notes that inner and outer colonized "subjects" – women, "minorities," postcolonialists, nationalists – frequently repudiate the very concept of postmodernism itself as the universalizing "cover" for what are really narrow class-cultural concerns serving a white and male-dominated elite. Postmodernism preserves positions of privilege and power by replicating strategies of dissociation and disempowerment among those groups traditionally made marginal within capitalist production: workers, people of color, women (1991: 318). Indeed, a number of multicultural voices register ambivalence, suspicion, and outright dismissal of postmodernism. Cornel West, for example, rejects postmodernism insofar as it does not seriously acknowledge the distinctive cultural and political practices of oppressed peoples: "I do not displace myself from the postmodern debate, I simply try to keep my distance from its parochialism and view it as a symptom of our present cultural crisis" (1989: 92). West questions whether debates about postmodernism can cast light on the complex relations between race, class, and gender, whether it can enable potentially resistant and empowering practices of the multicultural. Drawing a distinction between the multicultural as some "Third World" struggle and postmodernism as another form of "First World" angst, I would argue, precludes an engagement between inexorably bound fields within contemporaneous academic and cultural spaces.

From another perspective, suspicion toward postmodernism is evident in those skeptical of the rush toward theories and theorizing ultimately associated with an elite (and somewhat rarefied) institutional sphere. At its most vulgar, a current crosses the multicultural terrain that posits a dichotomy between "practice" and "theory" and valorizes the former over the latter. As if, of course, practice were some form of pure action behind, around, and through which no textuality runs. From a more sophisticated critical position, Barbara Christian rejects the demand by the dominant academic ideology to produce a complete and universal theory of the multicultural condition: "Some of us are continually harassed to invent whole-sale theories regardless of the complexity of the literature we study. I, for one, am tired of being asked to produce a black feminist literary theory as if I were a mechanical man" (1990: 43). The race for theory, Christian suggests, involves a dehistoricizing that serves to erase the complex heterogeneity and particularity of multicultural texts. The rush toward theoretical positionings can be viewed as replicating the processes of domination within an intellectual and cultural sphere.

These claims against theory by the multicultural are true. Those in the margin or in the minority are correct in their suspicions of a central postmodern theory. It is an elite project discussed in elite circles. Nevertheless, scholars of color interested in working against the grain cannot avoid postmodernism and its theories. This cannot mean, however, that postmodernism subsumes the interests of the historically marginal. In articulating the relevance of postmodernism to marginal spaces, Jameson points out, "it is no less true that the 'micropolitics' that corresponds to the emergence of this whole range of small-group, nonclass political practices [based on gender, sexuality, environmental concerns, race, ethnicity] is a profoundly postmodern phenomenon, or else the word has no meaning whatsoever" (1991: 318–19). Well, yes and no. The political practices of these groups as they have emerged in a postmodern world are profoundly postmodern: A world of micropolitics derives but is distinguishable from exclusionary modernist discourses defining national and cultural identity. To suggest, however, that these groups had no sense of identity (much less "political practice") previous to the postmodern is inaccurate. That they did not exist fully within the logic of capitalism may be true. That their political practices are a phenomena of postmodernism is patently absurd.

Clearly, as is evident in his "Third-World Literature in the Era of Multinational Capitalism," Jameson privileges a totalizing and resistant cultural vision in response to the unifying force of contemporary history: the economic control by American bankers of the world system. This vision, as Aijaz Ahmad points out in his response to Jameson's piece, posits a binary opposition between "First" and "Third" World cultural production that transforms each into the civilizational Other of the other. Jameson motions toward the specificity of the various constituencies that form an inner- and inter-national "Third World," but time and again elides these differences in his examinations of a repressive postmodernity. Thus, his point that a whole range of small-group, nonclass political practices over the last twenty years stands as a profoundly postmodern phenomenon subsumes the variety and specificity of those practices.

Nevertheless, despite the violence of his theoretical practices, Jameson does raise an issue about the position of these new social movements central to the "Third World" practices of postcolonialism and multiculturalism. Of the new social movements he asks: "Are they generated by the system itself in its interminable inner self-differentiation and self-reproduction? Or are they very precisely new 'agents of history' who spring into being in resistance to the system as forms of opposition to it, forcing it against the direction of its own internal logic into new reforms and internal modifications?" (1991: 326). That is, is the multicultural another movement in the endless process of capitalist appropriation? Or, is it a force fully resistant to powers of political dominance?

This supposed opposition, Jameson notes, is false. Both positions are right. The choice between these two poles is a sterile one that precludes "the simultaneous possibility of active political commitment along with disabused systemic realism and contemplation" (1991: 330). Jameson's "new social movements" therefore can fruitfully function only at the nexus between agency and causality. They must be aware of historical necessity, but able to act as agents capable of creating the conditions that both establish and capitalize on historical necessity. This forms the useful dimension of Jameson's theorizing about subjectivity. It helps those interested in a resistant multiculturalism participate critically in the economies of cultural capital.

One area in which issues of agency and empowerment play themselves out resides in the field of politics. Given the decentralization and fragmentation of the postmodern condition, how can political agency prove effective? On what principles does a political movement base itself? Having given up on master narratives like revolution, liberation, and Marxism, how can political action occur?

Fredric Jameson argues that the type of local politics available within the postmodern precludes any real political engagement. From Jameson's Marxist position, politics can work only when coordinating local and global struggles for a transfiguration of the here-and-now. The purely local cannot successfully challenge that which forms the global dimension – economics. By focusing on the micropolitics of the local – the politics of postmodernity – we are left with a politics marked by a willed euphoria of some metaphysical permanent revolution. This euphoria, from Jameson's view, is a compensation formation for our times when genuine or "totalizing" politics are no longer possible.

Jameson does offer some slight consolation. It will be "politically productive" and "a modest form of genuine politics" to attend to such things as the waning of a visible global dimension, the ideological resistance to the concept of totality, the shearing away of such apparent abstractions as the economic system and social totality (1991: 330).

This sort of "secondary" or "minority" politics may indeed prove to be the political legacy of postmodernism, but not exactly as Jameson envisions it. The challenge posed by the postmodern is to employ the legitimate concerns of the local in reshaping the global without reproducing forms of discursive violence. How to move from local concern to global change without, for instance, reinscribing the marginal? Boaventura de Sousa Santos observes that postmodern knowledge "favors the near to the detriment of the real. To be pragmatic is to approach reality from [William] James's 'last things,' that is, from consequences, and the shorter the distance between acts and consequences, the greater the accuracy of the judgment on validity" (1991: 100). In other words, the total can be at hand. The ethics of a self practiced in solidarity with others lends a legitimacy to immediate political struggle and action. In this sense (among others) postmodern knowledge can be understood as "local." Modernist foundationalist epistemologies, to borrow Rorty's term, cease to function.[22]

Postmodern knowledge – local, proximate – although not totalizing is, Santos argues, total: "The localism involved is the localism of context, not the localism of static spaces and immemorial traditions. It is an internationalist localism, without a solid genius loci" (1991: 100). Postmodern knowledge works at the interstices of paradigms, negotiates through (historical, cultural, economic) contexts. The specificity of the local does not preclude connections to larger systems of social organization. The local and its politics need not remain superficially "local." Not a politics of populism, the politics of the local represents a politics of rhizomic resistance.

Thus Wahneema Lubiano scrutinizes David Harvey's invocation of the 1960s "revolutionary" slogan, "Think globally. Act locally." This scrutiny emerges from the concern over what precisely a politics of rhizomic resistance may signify. A multicultural postmodern political practice of the local, Lubiano finally admonishes, "in cultural resistance terms, might require some lack of sureness, confidence, some awareness of what Spivak [in *The Post-Colonial Critic*] calls 'vulnerability' (18), or, to paraphrase Foster [in *The Anti-Aesthetic*] a willingness to recognize that a representation may 'mean' differently in place, in moment, and in particular minds" (1991: 159). A multicultural postmodernism foregrounds the localism of context, the specificity of devalued knowledges and histories repressed by the hegemonic "political unconscious," and the potential for the local to achieve some significant and lasting social change.

From Jameson's view, however, there is no escaping the need for a global (class-bound) vision of politics. To describe the longing for class politics of some older type as simply some "nostalgia," he notes, "is about as adequate as to characterize the body's hunger, before dinner, as a 'nostalgia for food' " (1991: 331). We might admire the metaphor but remain suspicious of its point.

Jameson incessantly privileges class over race as a site upon which to contest discourses of oppression. In "Periodizing the 60s," Jameson argues that the merger of the AFL and CIO in 1955 formed:

> a fundamental "condition of possibility" for the unleashing of the new social and political dynamics of the 60s by forcing the demands made by blacks, women and other minorities out of the classical institutions of an older working-class politics. Thus "liberated" from social class and released to find new modes of social and political expression, their concerns could only focus on the local rather than global. (1984a: 181)

Kicked out of the global political arena, the marginal are left to squabble among local issues that preclude any genuine systemic transformation.

Boaventura de Sousa Santos counters that "the relative weakening of class practices and of class politics has been compensated for by the emergence of new agonistic spaces that propose new social postmaterialist and political agendas (peace, ecology, sexual and racial equality) to be acted out by new insurgent groups and social movements" (1991: 97). He goes on to note that the discovery that capitalism produces classes, and "that classes are the organizing matrix of social transformation" was a nineteenth-century discovery: "The twentieth century enters the historical scene only when it discovers that capitalism also produces racial and sexual differences and that these can also be nodal points for social struggles" (1991: 97). The multicultural provides critical insight into the processes by which racial and ethnic others can form and have formed "nodal points for social struggle." This represents a vision of politics beyond class, one which moves away from a showdown between a powerful master discourse (Marxism) with a contradictory or negating discourse (radical locality). Politics of locality do not seek to overthrow a Marxist revolutionary project with another master narrative. Rather, the narrative of locality functions to supplement other narratives, other political configurations.

Migration

Multiculturalism can form a discourse that, as it critiques violence, precludes the violence of replication. To be an effective discourse, it cannot propose the substitution of one master discourse for another. Homi Bhabha, therefore, argues for a supplementary minority position. Bhabha seeks to articulate agency and empowerment for the marginal but not couched in terms of overthrowing (and so replicating) or capturing (and therefore employing) the powers of the state: "Insinuating itself into the terms of reference of the dominant discourse, the supplementary antagonizes the implicit power to generalize, to produce the sociological solidity" (1990: 306). The multicultural critic must be aware of avoiding the processes that replicate, reflect, and reproduce the tyranny of globalizing discourses even as they are combated.

Hence the significance of negotiation as a technique associated with the migratory. In a migratory reading, one employs and thematizes the essentialism of intellectual activity while traveling from constituency to constituency implicated in the multicultural and postmodern. Simultaneously, this reading highlights the discontinuities and fractures inherent in the literal journey of migration. The movement across linguistic, cultural, and political boundaries undertaken by groups forced to endure the violence of decentering power represents the factual condition of deterritorialization. This placelessness stems from the histories and processes of exploitation and repression alive within and without centers of empire. The point becomes not to deny the potentiality of postmodern thought for multicultural issues, nor to erase one's position as a compromised critic of dominant culture, nor to negate multiculturalism's ability to speak to and with and through postmodernism. Rather – caught between the rock of practice and the hard place of theory – one might want to attempt a series of negotiations that wed a contractual sense of power and a navigational sense of journey. A migratory reading wends between the Scylla of the local and the Charybdis of the total, between the devil that historical and cultural specificity can be and the deep murky seas of essentialization and homogeneity. In short, it steals.

From those who can least afford to be exploited (and whose lives are nevertheless delimited by exploitation), a migratory reading steals strategies from the lived practices of the dispossessed. This intellectual exploitation tries to profit from the improvisation and negotiation born of necessity in the hard and hostile world of transnational survival. Ironically – or perhaps not so ironically – this profit is made in order to enable more critical interpretations of current social and political fields. The profit born out of this exploitation is meant for those from whom it steals. This rough passage, Linda Hutcheon suggests, is "inside yet outside, inscribing yet contesting, complicitous yet critical" (1989: 158).[23]

A complicitous critique at various levels, the migratory represents a model by which difficult cultural and political terrain can be successfully traversed. More to the point, the migratory also evokes within its discursive strategies the same process of negotiation undertaken by migrant groups caught between poverty and repression in their homelands and cultural dislocation and oppressive marginalization in the centers of power to which they flee.

A practice already implicit to the multicultural condition becomes the necessary element for deploying multicultural issues within a postmodern cultural space: continuous critical negotiation, an endless engagement with contradictory positions. These engagements seek neither to refute nor to overthrow particular historically inscribed concepts. Instead, they attempt "to engage with the 'anterior' space of the sign that structures the symbolic language of alternative, antagonistic cultural practices" (Bhabha 1990: 313). This engagement takes the form of a type of genealogy, the tracing of the discontinuous region of multicultural subjectivity, the retelling of stories otherwise forgotten. To form a resistant practice across the fields of the multicultural and the postmodern involves a process that discovers or recovers the discredited histories of groups circumscribed by regimes of repressive discursive practices.

This proposal does not posit a clear field of cultural play. It is more like a heavily guarded borderland, a potential threat at every step. There stands at one point the poststructuralist valuing of difference as a dissociated and ahistorical quality bearing no relevance to the actual histories of those constructed as racially or sexually different. At another point, there stands the suspicion of postmodernity as a new, subsuming, and repressive master narrative sacrificing historical and cultural specificity for a project of elite self-interest. Again, at another position, one finds those who would privilege class at every turn over race as a compelling catalyst for social and political change. Compound these issues with the postcolonial valuation of such modern notions as "nation" and "agency"; add a fear of the homogenization of difference; join this to the problematic dismissal of narrative as a compelling and powerful force. We are left with a terrain scarred by discursive and political rupture.

Yet this should not deter us from explaining and exploiting the potentialities inherent in a crossing of sympathetic – although not synonymous – intellectual projects. Theories of the postmodern form an academic discourse by which to interject multicultural issues into the boardrooms and backrooms (to say nothing of classrooms) of institutionalized educational systems. George Yúdice, in his essay "Marginality and the Ethics of Survival," persuasively concludes that intellectuals "need not speak for others, but we are responsible for a 'self-forming activity' that can in no way be ethical if we do not act against the 'disappearance' of oppressed subjects" (1989: 230). Though academics cannot always speak to economically, racially, and politically oppressed peoples at home and abroad, we can speak about and against their dangerous and denigrated positions. An engagement of the multicultural with the postmodern acts, finally, as a self-conscious and self-critical move against disappearance.

6

Mythic "Memory" and Cultural Construction

As long as the world will endure, the fame and glory of Mexico-Tenochtitlán will never perish.

– Domingo Chimalpahín Cuauhtlehuanitzin

LIKE A PERSISTENT DREAM that returns vaguely during daytime, the notion of an ancestral memory has haunted contemporary Chicano cultural production. The claim for rights and land, intensified during the political activism of the 1960s, brought with it a re-collection and re-valuation of indigenous cultures both contemporary and pre-Cortesian. The procession of campesinos in Delano who walked from the grape fields into the stark sunlight of history marched – just as their ancestors had since *el Grito de Dolores* in 1810 – behind both a firm sense of justice and the outstretched banner of Our Lady of Guadalupe. This connection to a Mexican political past resonates with a spirituality invoked by the beneficent presence of the Virgin. The Virgin of Guadalupe also evokes a more distant spirituality since the image of the Virgin represents a postconquest confluence of pre-Cortesian and European religious imagery.[1] Ancestral "memory" thus merges with mythic "memory," and a central trope in the articulation of Chicano culture emerges.

Whereas folk-legend and indigenous cultural practices form a living cultural memory for many Chicano writers – one thinks immediately of Rudolfo Anaya and Jimmy Santiago Baca, to name but two – the "recollection" of Mexica and (less commonly) Mayan myths and images by Chicano poets employs pre-Cortesian cultures and values as a foil, as a rejection of the most pernicious influences of the Enlightenment and capitalism, as a source of alternate and empowering forms of social organization, as a dream for contemporary Chicano life. This mythic "memory" with its resultant storehouse of imagery and symbolism has helped shape the discourse of contemporary Chicano poetry.

Finding the Center

Cordelia Candelaria in her excellent study, *Chicano Poetry: A Critical Introduction*, divides symbolism in Chicano poetry into four areas: the pre-American, mestizaje, El Movimiento, and non-raza Other (1986: 74). Chicano poetry, especially that produced in the 1980s and 1990s, resists easy categorization. Nevertheless, Candelaria's grouping of these symbolic images can be especially useful for analyzing the poetry of the 1960s and 1970s. For the purposes of this discussion, I am most interested in the focus on the first of these areas, pre-American imagery, which functions, according to Candelaria, on two levels. It conveys specific information about pre-Cortesian cultures before European influences became pervasive, and it conveys "a sense of the uninterrupted continuum of human experience from the earliest legends about Aztlán to the Chicano adaptations of the meaning of Aztlán for contemporary purposes – a millennium's span in time, a continent's span in space" (1986: 74–5). From this perspective, the deployment of pre-Cortesian symbology invokes a mythic "memory" that implies an unproblematic and uninterrupted recuperation and "remembering" of devalued knowledge made manifest through myths and legends. Chicano literature thus seems to "reveal" connections between the troubled and unfullfilling present of Chicano disempowerment and a richer, fuller, more holistic but lost past. This connection and contrast help identify and articulate the "unique" and "authentic" qualities of Chicano identity.

As we have seen from earlier critics, anxiety about authenticity runs throughout a good deal of Chicano literary criticism. Candelaria, implicitly writing out of this anxiety, suggests it is possible to isolate three primary characteristics of Chicano poetics:

> *It is multilingual.* This characteristic promotes both social verisimilitude and literary foregrounding in the poetry. *It is symbolic in an identifiably Chicano way.* Its symbols stem, for the most part, from the culture's pre-American heritage, from contemporary *mestizaje*, from Movement history and values, and from the culture's experience of the dominant society

> defined largely in colonialist terms. *It is grounded in ritual.* Both in its overt replication of a communal rite through the poem/performance and in its recognition of an ethnopoetic tradition extending from the present to the primitive past, Chicano poetry is most fully comprehensible within a context of ritual. These characteristics of Chicano poetics derive directly out of the poetry, and although not every poet or poem exhibits every one of these features, in general we find aspects of them (singly and combined) throughout the work. (1986: 77)

These characteristics mark the chicanismo of a given poetic text. As a generalized statement, and based on Candelaria's encompassing familiarity with Chicano poetry, this description of a Chicano poetics moves toward a useful definition. (It does not, however, address the significance of a Chicano poetics as a resistant or critical practice. Nor does it address the problem of the Chicano poem that does not evince these particular poetics. Nor, finally, does it take into account the presence of Chicano poetry as a historical product. These are, for the purposes of this discussion, not of immediate importance.) Implicit in Candelaria's analysis of a Chicano poetics lurks the question of "authenticity," of the clearly definable "Chicano" character of a text. This may very well be the inevitable result of attempting to frame an introduction to Chicano poetry, especially one that provides as astute and insightful a framework as *Chicano Poetry: A Critical Introduction*.

Although I am in complete sympathy with Candelaria's project, and agree with much of her analysis, it could prove productive to problematize the idea of a pre-American heritage from which Chicano poetry draws its symbology. This heritage proves central to the idea of a mythic "memory" forming and informing "authentic" Chicano poetic practices. The pre-Cortesian elements that populate Chicano literary production – Aztlán, flor y canto, eagles, serpents, cactus fruits, quinto sol – are appropriations of an indigenous culture that in its pre-European context ceased to exist over four centuries ago. The fragments and shards of this original culture form archeological and historical evidence that scholars have taken great pains to reconstruct. This heritage, then, as with all heritages, is discursively constructed. The constructed quality of a Chicano heritage proves doubly apparent since its symbolic system does not form a part of the residual culture of the Mexica: There are no more warrior clans, there is no reverence for Huitzilopochtli the god of war, there is no Nahua flor y canto. For the most part, the symbology associated with the Aztec empire must be garnered from museums and books.[2]

The notion proposed by Candelaria that pre-Cortesian symbology lends "a sense of the uninterrupted continuum of human experience from the earliest legends about Aztlán to the Chicana adaptations of the meaning of Aztlán" (1986: 74–5) seems a little overstated. What emerges from the history of Mexico and the southwest United States are narratives full of discontinuities: imperial devastation, economic exploitation, racist vituperation, and an incessant devaluation of indigenous cultures by European-identified settlers. In order to construct a literary critique premised on resistance and historical representation, the Chicana critic might want to focus on the pressing issue of discontinuity. In the end, the disruption between past and present – marked by military attacks, invasions, conquests – forms one primary theme of Chicana poetry. The use of pre-Cortesian symbology, therefore, does not represent "an uninterrupted continuum of human experience." On the contrary, it represents a resistant response to rupture and violence, to cultural imperialism and discursive erasure. One of its strategies of resistance, the formation of a counterdiscourse, resides in the idea of mythic "memory." The disrupted, the discontinuous, the devalued – these qualities become foregrounded as Chicana poetry invokes indigenous cultural practices that have been made marginal. This invocation helps to focus the privileged critical lens of a Chicana counterdiscourse.[3]

In addition to the recuperation of pre-Cortesian symbology, the ethnopoetic tradition with which Chicana poetry engages forms a locus in which the trajectories of history, politics, and aesthetics converge. Within the context of contemporary Euramerican literature, interest in ethnopoetics dates to the 1950s and 1960s with the work of Gary Snyder and Jerome Rothenberg. Their influence, as well as poetic performances such as the corrido and other forms of public poetic expression, form a confluence that shapes the ethnopoetics of contemporary Chicana poetry. Chicana poetic expression problematizes this connection to "tradition" as it works with and through ethnopoetic forms. A good deal of Chicana poetry has been performed as event. Rodolfo Gonzales's *I am Joaquín* was written for and recited at numerous rallies before it ever found its way into book form. Hector Calderón points out that:

> Chicano artists and writers chose public forms of expression. Much of this literature was enjoyed in an oral, communal setting. These community readings endure today. As in one of the founding poems of Chicano literature, "El Louie" by José Montoya, a new pride in the language was reflected by writers who have continually returned to the lived speech act to capture in print the oral quality of Chicano Spanish and English vernaculars. (1990: 218)

And Tomás Ybarra-Frausto notes that Chicana poetry is often meant to be spoken rather than read (1979: 118). The use of ethnopoetics and public, performative modes does not exclude other forms of poetic expression from the repertoire available to Chicana poets. Even a cursory look at Chicana poetry indicates that a dialogue rather than an antagonism exists between the ethnopoetic and other traditions within the field of Chicana poetic practices: Bernice Zamora's "And All Flows Past" was influenced by Theodore Roethke (himself interested in Native American cultures), Gary Soto studied with Philip Levine and borrowed liberally from his use of narrative poetic form, Jimmy Santiago Baca owes a debt to both John Donne and Ezra Pound, among others.

If we are willing to take into account a dialogic relationship between Chicano poetry and "tradition" (indigenous, pre-Cortesian, European, Euramerican), the object of Chicano poetry becomes much more dynamic than the recuperation of lost or noncanonical poetic practices. What emerges is a system of interpretation and reinterpretation in the articulation of cultural empowerment and identity. Chicano poetry forms a counterdiscourse by which claims for agency and empowerment, scrutiny of subject positions and interpellation, examination of devalued knowledges and histories, all come into play within the aesthetic field. The idea of a Chicano mythic "memory" manifested in ethnopoetic expression represents less an unproblematic recuperation of indigenous culture than a complex cultural construction of self identity. From this view, the myths and legends that tend to infuse Chicano literary products cease to be collectable fragments of a non-European Other and become instead part of a larger cultural palette from which Chicano artists draw as they scrutinize the complex and contentious identities comprising the subject-position "Chicano/a."

Closing the Circle: Alurista

The attempt to demarcate the "space" of Chicano culture, the move to note its distinct and unique qualities, the desire to define its formal and thematic concerns drive one trajectory of Chicano literary critical thought in the 1960s and 1970s. Often working from an ethnopoetic or archetypical point of view, this trajectory sought to create a Chicano cultural identity based on a reconnection with a world of spirituality, linked to a pre-Cortesian world infused with indigenous myths and legends. The move is an empowering one, one which allows for the imaginative reconceptualization of human activity. As Arnold Krupat observes, "the reverential stance toward 'ordinary' life, the sense of human responsibility to nature, the commitment to a relationship of 'participant maintenance' (in Robert Redfield's phrase) toward the universe: these are all attitudes familiar to the Native tradition" (1989: 125). The nativist dynamic of Chicano poetry certainly seeks to connect with this tradition, and it does so often through the invocation of a mythic "memory" as a remembrance/expression of pre-Cortesian power and might.

What is sometimes overlooked in the articulation of Chicano mythic "memory" is its status as cultural product. The desire to articulate what "is" Chicano, the need to define and delimit its cultural space, leads oftentimes to an essentialist notion of the culture. Several Chicano critics, as we have seen, fall into an essentializing trap when seeking to articulate the peculiar values of Chicano literature. As we have also seen, this move proves ultimately to be a political response to the academic and cultural marginalization of Chicano literature.

In a similar vein, the production of early Chicano poetry worked toward the articulation of a cultural identity distinct and disengaged from dominant Euramerican traditions. Primary among the poets of this phase stands Alurista. His poetry – whose influence resonates throughout the field of early Chicano literary production – seeks to empower through the invocation of spiritual strength and cultural origins that are non-European, antirational, and historically devalued.[4] Alurista's poetry is often meant to represent the angry outcry of the pueblo. Constructed through indigenismos interwoven with chicanismos – pre-Cortesian stories, myths, and phrases intermixed with the caló and phraseology of the barrio – the poetry articulates an unproblematized voice of "the Chicano" blithely arising from an essentialized identity. This production of a community and community voice – interesting as a strategy of resistance and a tool for political activism – ultimately delimits the "space" of Chicano experiences.

In his poem "libertad sin lágrimas" from *Floricanto en Aztlán* (1971), Alurista demonstrates the processes of poetic recuperation favored by early Chicano poets:

libertad sin lágrimas
        sin dolor
and with pride
la Raza
        nosotros
we won't let it
        freedom shall not escape us
libertad en mano
        frente erecta
we shall

now
are
libres
albedrío of our self assertion
and our will
to be men
caballeros
clanes tigres
proud guerrero plumaje
free like the eagle
y la serpiente

The poem calls for a "freedom without tears," without pain, "and with pride / la Raza / nosotros / we won't let it / freedom shall not escape us." The nosotros who form the locus of agency in the poem are represented as though speaking through the poetic voice. This communal voice proclaims in the declamatory style of Chicano protest poetry.[5] The call for liberation – specifically from what or toward what is left unclear – concludes with an affirmation of "our will / to be men / caballeros / clanes tigres / proud guerrero plumaje / free like the eagle / y la serpiente." The poem, characteristic of much of Alurista's work during this period, makes a claim for the idealized dual identity of Chicano mestizaje. Tomás Ybarra-Frausto notes in "Alurista's Poetics" that his poems "create a structure of recollection where cultural heroes, mythology, and values from the Chicano's indigenous heritage are evoked as sources of pride and identity. The poems chart a spiritual journey aimed at achieving an organic, almost pantheistic, relationship between man and nature" (1979: 131). The caballero evoked in "libertad sin lagrimas" refers to the Spanish horseman of the conquest. It is also a term that signifies gentleman. Part of the Chicano mestizaje that Alurista's poem invokes suggests connection to the formality and courtly manners of Old World conduct. In addition to this European aristocracy, the clanes tigres invokes one of the aristocratic Mexica warrior clans, the jaguar warriors, wearing their "proud warrior plumage." The poem thus alludes to two worlds of order – the courtly society of Spain, the warrior society of the Mexica – as immediately available loci of cultural pride.

The cultural roots defining Chicanismo are eminently accessible. These merge with the power of "our will / to be men" to construct an unmediated bridge between cultural origin and its unproblematic access through personal agency. As the poem states that "we won't let it / freedom shall not escape us," the poetic voice oscillates between registers at once declamatory and imperative. The speaking voice asserts an agency that erases its contradictory position in relation to the community for which and to which it ostensibly speaks. Does it articulate a community position, or does it stand beyond, exhorting it? How the power to "will" and to "be" manifests itself, just as whether the speaker assumes the role of voice or conscience of the community, remains in the poem an unspoken issue.[6]

Implicit in the declamatory style of the poem is that the poetry itself will enact agency, will provide the impetus, will will itself into becoming reality. As Alurista articulates it, "part of what literature can do, or at least what I'm trying to do, is make it a healing art, not only a reflective art. It is also a surgical tool. . . . By now I'm convinced that, given the power to describe reality, we can construct a more human reality beginning with a more human description" (Bruce-Novoa 1980: 279–80). Certainly this is a function of the ethnopoetic in which the literary becomes shamanistic. However, this poem does not function within social or economic or political spaces where shamanism is a valued form of knowledge. It thus finds itself in a position where its expression is discontinuous with its modes of reception. The poem works within a cultural system of exchange in which literature is predominantly not shamanistic. In this respect, the poem helps reveal the silences and absences within the social, economic, and political systems of exchange, implicitly broaching a counterdiscursive move. Still and all, the poem seeks to speak outside dominant socioeconomic systems of exchange. Its shamanistic invocations, its declamations of will, its affirmation of agency are in essence expressions that function at the level of wish-fulfillment. Implicit to the poem is the assumption that by simply stating agency and liberation, these conditions will be so. The invocation of a mythic "memory" centering on the cultural clash and pride to be found in mestizaje thus serves a performative function that closes the circle between word and world.

As a part of a contemporary symbolic system, however, "libertad sin lágrimas" reveals its own discontinuous position not only in relation to the exploitative systems outside of which it ostensibly stands, but also in relation to the original culture instigating agency. The phrase "proud warrior plumage" leads a bit too obviously into the final allusive lines of the poem: "free like the eagle / y la serpiente." The eagle associated with flight and the snake as representative of the earth-bound represent the central tension in Nahua thought between the spiritual and the physical. These images are united in the image of Quetzalcoatl, whose name means "Precious-Feather Snake." This god was, for the Mexica, the personification of wisdom. According to Nahua myth, Quetzalcoatl engaged in a quest for a beyond where, unlike on earth, there would be no sin and people would not age. Through penance and meditation he discovered that the dual divinity, Ometéotl – emblematic of masculine and feminine principles, of earth and sky, of day and night – maintains and gives order to the universe and makes itself apparent in the red light of day and black darkness of night. Hence within Nahua symbology, the colors red and black come to represent writing and wisdom. Quetzalcoatl, who according to legend was light-skinned and fair haired, was tricked by the god of war Huitzilopochtli into committing incest with his sister. Shamed, he felt compelled to wander toward the east, eventually crossing the ocean, promising to return to his people one day. It is this god with whom some Mexica confused Hernán Cortés at the beginning of his advance into Mexico.[7]

Beyond the immediate instrumentality of instilling cultural pride in the Chicano reader, the purpose of Alurista's symbology – the evocation of the eagle and serpent – in this poem remains vague. The poem represents a type of fetishization of pre-Cortesian themes and icons that Jorge Klor de Alva critiques in his essay "California Chicano Literature and Pre-Columbian Motifs." Chicanos, he notes, "have consistently emphasized the form over the content of native ideology and symbolism by oversimplifying both to the point of caricaturing the intricate and enigmatic codes that veil the meanings of the original texts" (1986: 24). Alurista's poem represents a historical and cultural decontextualization of pre-Cortesian symbology that disrupts the hermeneutics of his text. The invocation of pre-Cortesian symbols and images in "libertad sin lágrimas" neither undermines the relationship between signifier and signified as a way of achieving a modernist "undecidability," nor functions within a coherent system of symbolic exchange. What does the evocation of the eagle and the snake suggest? An allusion to a new-found wisdom to be had as the result of political struggle; a meditation upon the incommensurable tensions evident in human existence as part physical, part spiritual; a reference to the idea that an emergent Chicano populous will represent the second coming of a new spirituality; a simple nationalist allusion to the figures portrayed on the Mexican flag? Or does the allusion serve as a convenient and recognizable – though decontextualized – image that, like a bell, rings when struck but proves hollow?

Alurista's poem constructs an essentialized identity that stands outside and beyond history. This untenable position ultimately sends the poem crashing back into history. Although the poem proclaims agency and celebrates alterity, it reveals itself as an instrument articulating a sense of identity it does not suspect. The poem invokes, but does not possess, shamanistic qualities. It does, however, present the impossibility of its claims, and at this level functions counterdiscursively. In its silence on the issue, the poetic voice speaks of the disempowered historical position of Chicanas. In its inability to achieve the transformative incantation its words imply, the poem deconstructs both the silence imposed by dominant cultural discourses and the ethnopoetic heritage from which its symbology ostensibly emerges.

Obviously, the culture of Chicanas does not derive directly nor literally from this Nahua past. There were hundreds of tribes throughout North and Central America at the time of the conquest, and the cultural identity of Chicanas is as complex and diverse as the identity of any other people tracing their ancestry to the original inhabitants of the Americas. Alurista's poetry attempts to activate and articulate a Chicana identity through an appeal to the glories of a common indigenous civilization. He looks to the Aztec empire as a cultural icon that can form a locus of pride. Nahua symbology helps form a cultural nexus about which members of disparate Chicana communities can find common cause. As Alurista has noted: "There has been an antagonistic relationship between [Chicana communities], specifically [in] California and Texas, that I think in order to wage and to forge a national consciousness, we must overcome. Our unity is not bound to, let us say, homogeneity. I mean we aren't all the same, and because we recognize that, we looked for something older than us and that had more future than us, that was based on the present" (Monleón 1981: 442). His articulation of that something older, although motivated by historical political demands, nevertheless serves to strike a cultural chord that has resonated throughout the entire range of Chicana cultural production.

Alurista's later poetry still invokes Nahua cultural forms, but loses the strident and declamatory tone evident in "libertad sin lágrimas," as well as any manifestation of counterdiscursivity. "Wild butterflies" from *Timespace Huracán* (1976), for example, glides along a number of poetic trajectories – from the lyrical to the allegorical, the allusive to the polemical. In the end, however, the poem resolves into a simple programmatic political project. The poem opens with the projection of an action that will occur in the near future: "wild butterflies to fly / sobre campos / alegres / sun butterflies / all about the wind / every moment / bringin' / poquito más / sol / every person / behind / out front / toda mariposa challenges." The poem opens with the evocation of wild butterflies, which are to fly over fields, happy, bringing sun. (The forced colloquialism of "bringin'" is better left without comment.) People "behind" and "out front" – suggesting political engagement, perhaps social hierarchical positions – are challenged by the butterfly. Why Alurista focuses on the butterfly who brings sunlight as the unifying image in this poem becomes apparent in its second half.

The poem moves through a series of four repeated lines: "viento colibri /

viento colibri / viento colibri / viento colibri / viento marxiano." The repetition of the lines mimics a sense of ritual inherent to the ethnopoetic. The "hummingbird wind," meanwhile, represents a symbolic evocation of Huitzilopochtli, the Mexica god of war. The poem conflates the power of this god with a Marxist wind, blowing undoubtedly toward revolution. In case one should miss the point, the poem goes on in Spanish to describe how Huitzilopochtli brandishes a machete to cleave walls in savage evenings and to lacerate arrogance.[8] The poem thus moves from a seemingly lyrical moment toward a pastiche of dynamic conflict and violence, invoking the pre-Cortesian god of war, conflating him with Marxism, moving through violent revolution and overthrow. The poem then closes with a seemingly incongruous image. After this hurricane of Marxian/Huitzilopochtlian revolution, the reader is told that the "healing butterflies flutter." The incongruity is, however, simply another manifestation of the poetic voice invoking Nahua symbology. The butterfly and the hummingbird are in Nahua thought manifestations of the spirits of dead warriors returning to earth in order to enjoy the beauty and sweetness of flowers.

Although the poem requires some literacy in Nahua symbology to make sense, it does not employ Nahua symbology or pre-Cortesian ways of being as loci of cultural pride. "Wild butterflies" does not trace a Chicano heritage based on alterity, on devalued forms of knowledge. On the contrary, the poem calls for Marxist revolution, connecting with the battles for liberation fought throughout Latin America and other parts of the "Third World." The struggle of Chicanos, the poem suggests, will be a part of these wars of liberation, not the primary means of liberation. The symbolic function of its images – the butterfly, the hummingbird – is interwoven more integrally to the structure of the poem than in "libertad sin lágrimas." In the earlier poem, the images incorporated in a strategy of cultural self-definition prove ultimately to be gratuitous evocations of mythic "memory" meant to connect the present moment to a historical past in a counterdiscursive strategy of cultural empowerment. "Wild butterflies" encodes its revolutionary message through the use of Nahua symbology rather than, as does "libertad sin lágrimas," evoke the symbology as a way of effecting revolutionary change. The significance of the pre- Cortesian cultural codes is completely erased, leaving in its place an instrumentality that does nothing to help articulate the counterdiscursivity of Chicano literary production.

Even within the work of a single author, the function of mythic "memory" becomes muddled and unfocused. Early on, its embodiment in the form of Nahua imagery harkens to a proud and golden age as the touchstone for a contemporary identity. The imagery articulates a resistant position with respect to Euramerican cultural traditions. However, the use of mythic "memory" is problematic on two levels. As exemplified by "libertad sin lágrimas," the use of mythic "memory" makes apparent the rupture between the system of symbolic exchange – an implicit quasi-shamanistic invocation of agency and will – and the social and political economies that will ostensibly be affected by its incantatory powers. In problematizing the complicated function of an ethnopoetics, the poem successfully represents the discontinuous position of Chicano culture. In its move toward a dehistoricized vision of cultural and political agency, the poem crashes against historically produced asymmetrical power relations in the conflict it embodies – a conflict between desire and reality. The poem wants to function within a shamanistic culture. It instead circulates in a world in which its own mode of expression is made marginal. The invocation of a pre-Cortesian heritage is problematic on a second related level as the poem employs Nahua symbology as a dehistoricized fetish, a veneer of "origin" and "authenticity" gilding a polemic exhorting "us" to struggle for the abstract notion of "liberty."

In Alurista's later poetry, we see Nahua imagery used expressly to codify Chicano political struggle but no longer to function as an integral part of it. This poetry represents the problematic dehistoricizing aspect of mythic "memory." It fails, however, to articulate the productive quandary it represents: the discontinuous position of a Chicano poetic voice employing devalued forms in order to assert its own identity. The imagery in "wild butterflies" works on the level of a coherent poetics, more clearly integrating the "butterflies" and "hummingbirds" within the significatory processes of the poem as a call to armed revolution. However, the poem does not position itself within a counterdiscursive strategy of resistance. In its call for political revolution, it abjures cultural revolution.

Influential in the movements of Chicana poetry, Alurista's construction of a poetics reliant upon mythic "memory" ultimately falters. In its attempt to unite disparate communities, this type of poetics ultimately results in "the glorification of a remote past [that tends] to obscure the historical contradictions of Indio–Chicano relationships within the United States" and to "make barrio vatos think of themselves as descendants of Aztec nobility without focusing on the basic realities of pre-Hispanic life" (Ybarra-Frausto 1979: 130).[9] Mythic "memory" as it was constructed by Alurista's poetry finally abjured the political reality of Chicano communities in struggle. Although it proclaimed an allegiance to global revolution, Alurista's poetry represented to "Chicano militants, marxists, leftists or anarchists . . . an invitation to evade the world in a hazy wonderland where the daily reality of the oppressed worker/labourer was made to vanish" (Labarthe 1990: 81).

Not only on an instrumental political level does the escape into pre-

Cortesian cultural affirmation delimit strategies of resistance. Within processes of identity-formation, the valorization of mythic "memory" with its imaginative leaps into the past constructs a cultural identity blind and mute to the important distinctions between and among the different cultural communities supposedly served by the invocation of that "memory." Immigrant or long-term resident, New Mexican or Californian, feminine or masculine, gay or straight, young or old, poor or affluent, rural or urban, the needs and peculiar perspectives afforded through difference within a community become – in the facile identification of the pre-Cortesian with the contemporary Chicana – elided. Only an essentialist vision of identity remains. Finally one is left with a notion of "memory" that unproblematically links past and present without foregrounding the contradictions and discontinuities inherent to the history that connects that past to this present. The "re-membering" of fragmented pre-Cortesian and indigenous cultural icons – myths, legends, tales, figures – becomes coterminous with the "recuperation" of those icons.

Claiming the Present: Ana Castillo

This discussion has focused so incessantly on Alurista because his literary production has been terribly influential in the construction of a Chicana poetics. Moreover, his work marks a turning point in the history of contemporary Chicana literature as its interests broaden from a strict political instrumentality and strident didacticism of Movimiento poetry. Since the passing of the Movimiento and its influence on poetic production, Chicana poetry has made two moves in terms of its ethnopoetic practices. One, exemplified by poetic texts from Gloria Anzaldúa to Bernice Zamora, reworks the idea of ethnopoetics in order to make of it anew a resistant practice. The other, although not negating the importance of ethnopoetic form, downplays the quest for an original or authentic voice and opens a wider poetic field by which to articulate the subject positions "Chicana/Chicano." Consequently, one can discern in Chicana poetic production a greater concern with notions of appropriation rather than of recuperation.[10] The construction of a mythic "memory" through the appropriation of such cultural artifacts as Nahua symbology is no longer treated as a connection between the multiplicitous term "Chicana" and some clearly definable cultural identity. Rather, "the Chicana" is constantly under construction and revision. Not a return to "Aztlán," to a homeland, "to be" Chicana becomes more and more a journey toward a "becoming" across North American contemporary cultural landscapes. The shift in the idea of mythic "memory" serves to mark this significant transformation in the changing terrain of Chicana cultural production.

As is evident in the poetry of Alurista, the mythic "memory" imagined by a Chicano poetics turns on the construction of heritage, a move that forms a part of a larger counterdiscourse of cultural self-identification. It need not require that those of us who – for better or for worse – are critically suspicious of carte blanche mysticism embrace the mythoreligious underpinnings this mythic "memory" evokes. This embrace, after all, would rely upon a rather straightforward mimetic model whereby the invocation of the Quetzalcoatl myth somehow makes present the "universal truths," "deep structures," or "archetypical models" that myth represents. Speaking against the traditional view that Chicano novels can be read as "reflections" of a minority experience, Ramón Saldívar argues that the textuality of Chicano literature must be taken into account. "Reflectionism" fails, he argues, on four counts. It "reduces the acts of reading and writing into non-dialectical, isolated experiences. It decomposes the laws of composition. It presupposes that readers will find in the work of art only what authors have put there. And it limits our understanding of a work (and therefore of the historical world it represents) to the investigation of only one of its aspects" (1981: 36).[11] In addition to these very severe limitations, the crystalline connection between signifier and signified marks an even more violent system of repression. "Reflectionism" represents a tyrannical regimen of meaning that, in mediated but pertinent ways, functions out of the same rationale that has historically delimited the meaning of words like "race" and "heritage" and "tradition" and "history."

Rather than reinscribe this ideology, one might want to look at the relationship between the signifier and signified of Chicano mythic "memory," look at how the conventions of meaning are constructed and employed in specific cultural acts of empowerment, how symbolic exchange functions within and against social and political economies. I would argue that the crossing of communal, archetypical, spiritual, ancient forms of communication with isolated, creative, alienated, modern forms of expression presents a point at which genres, cultures, histories, and epistemes cross. The literature becomes a sundial of history.[12] A criticism that seeks to articulate the historically resistant tendencies of Chicano literature might best abjure the quest for the "universal" within Chicano literary practices and focus more sharply on the ruptures implicit in the construction of mythic "memory." Which is to say, it is no longer necessary to shed light on the "universality" behind the myth of the plumed serpent; but it is productive to examine how that serpent is constructed.

The poetry of Ana Castillo – spanning from the late 1970s to the present – provides us with an opportunity to contrast how notions of mythic "memory" have changed as they are constructed and reinscribed within a changing Chicano cultural space.[13] Her 1976 poem "Our Tongue Was Nahuatl" represents an exemplary attitude toward ideas of Chicano identity clearly incorporating the type of mythic "memory" worked by Alurista. In both its almost mechanical invocation of Nahua culture and its simplistic view of oppression, the poem becomes a near parody of ethnic outrage.[14]

"Our Tongue Was Nahuatl" takes the form of a dramatized first-person account told by a Chicana as she encounters a Chicano: "You. / We have never met / yet / we know each other / well." An immediate recognition occurs, and a bond is forged in that fleeting moment. The speaker's connection with the young man is based on physiognomy as she recognizes his "high / set / cheekbones" and his "slightly rounded / nose." A communal bond is activated by the physical presence, a connection founded upon biology. The Chicano's

near-slanted eyes
follow me –
sending flashback memories
to your so-called
primitive mind.
And I know
you remember.

This spark of supposed recognition marks a mythic, nearly genetic "memory" of a pre-Cortesian past. The racial and the cultural thus conflate, forming a quintessential image of an essentialized identity.

The spark of "memory" serves to connect Chicano to Chicana, present to past, the discontent of contemporary life with a near-Edenic time

of turquoise blue-greenness,
sky-topped mountains,
god-suns
wind-swept rains;
oceanic deities
naked children running
in the humid air.

The evocation of "turquoise" as an indigenous stone symbolic of (among other things) life and water in Nahua symbology mimics the moves made by earlier Chicano poetics. This move is undercut somewhat by odd terms like "god-suns" and "oceanic deities." The poem creates a generic vision of pantheistic pre-Cortesian life evocative more of Greek than Nahua myth.

The poem presents a utopian image of fecundity and harmony, posits a "remembered" time of plentitude and sacred worship of "our / rich golden / Earth" when "our tongue was Nahuatl" and "we were content – / With the generosity / of our gods / and our skins." This remembrance is marked by a domestic tranquility and gendered division of labor that relies more on post–World War II ideology than it does on Nahua social organization:

> I ground corn
> upon a slab of stone,
> while you bargained
> at the market
> dried skins.

The woman, the good mother watching "our small sons / chase behind your bare legs / when you came home those days," prepares the evening meal and basks in the glow of domestic and social tranquility.

The utopia of pre-Cortesian life abruptly ends as the Spaniards cross "the bitter waters" and enact a process of racial, political, and economic denigration. The "white foreign strangers / riding high / on four-legged / creatures" force the natives to bow before them in submission and defeat, to bow in "our ignorance to the / unknown / . . . / until our skin became / the color of caramel / and nothing anymore / was our own." This miscegenation and erasing of "color" marks on a genetic level the fall into a postlapsarian world. The erasure of color also signifies a lack made present on a material level in which all possessions, all indigenous religious worship, all forms of integrity are lost: "Raped of ourselves – / Our civilization – / Even our gods turned away / from us in shame." The speaker incorporates the trope of rape in order to highlight the sense of cultural alienation inscribed by a metaphorical as well as literal rape. The trope, suggesting violence and violation, activates the sense of domination inherent in the Spaniards forcing the natives to bow before them and triggering as well the forced process of mestizaje.[15] This domination and violation, the speaker indicates, is yet evident in the present helpless economic position in which Chicanos find themselves:

> Yet we bowed,
> as we do now –
> On buses

going to factories
where 'No-Help Wanted' signs
laugh at our faces,
stare at our hungry eyes.

Yet we bow . . .
WE BOW! (ellipses in original).

An economic submission returns in the present as a repetition of the original moment of conquest. Against this continual conquest, the mythic "memory" of a utopian other, a prelapsarian age, stands as an icon of empowerment ostensibly resisting the present condition of humiliation and violation. The poetic voice concludes: "But I remember you / still – / It was a time / much different / than now. . . ."

Castillo's poem exemplifies the contradictory comfort inherent in this construction of mythic "memory." That time that was "much different than now" represents a time irrevocably in the past. Ruptured by conquest, it is made more distant as the first moment of conquest returns in the disempowering present. Mexica forced to submit physically are now Chicanos forced into economic submission. The speaker's moment of recognition opening the poem represents an imagined nostalgia for a time and culture with which the speaker of the poem is obviously not terribly familiar. That time, for the speaker, represents a praxis impossible to recuperate. Even the imaginative powers of literature can only leave us with the impotent realization that "it was a time / much different / than now. . . ." The ellipses underscore the dissociation between the mythic "memory" of pre-Cortesian life and contemporary reality.

Although speaking of connection and cohesion, the poem throughout serves only to fix alienation. The edenic qualities the poem associates with the pre-Cortesian world remain inexorably disconnected in a time and space separated by a double conquest. The potentially liberating qualities of mythic "memory" (liberating within the logic of the poem's discourse) – the integrated relationship with nature and the gods, the clearly defined gender roles, the fecundity and productivity of the Mexican past – is undercut by the hopelessness of ever connecting that mythic "memory" in any transformative way to the present. Just as the idealized vision of the past is dissociated from the historical reality of the present, the poem sunders its mythic "memory" from a historic one. It evokes a hazy but ideal portrait of a native past that the title – "Our Tongue Was Nahuatl" – ties to a historically specific and socially complex group, the imperialistic Mexica. The invocation of harmonious economic and familial relations does little to make present the historical specificity of the very people it ostensibly evokes.[16]

This vision is further complicated by the evocation of sexuality and economics in the poem. The speaker's mythic "memory" is activated, it would appear, through an action implicated in sexual desire. While subjected to the power of the male gaze ("Your near-slanted eyes / follow me"), the Chicana speaker evokes an image of harmony between male and female within the fecund confines of pre-Cortesian family and home.[17] Sexuality – safely domesticated within a strictly heterosexual reproductive role – is contained and controlled. Similarly, economic exchange is controlled through a system of use-value implied in the bartering of "dried skins / and other things / that were our own." Ownership and domesticity go hand in hand, a vision not too dissimilar from the dominant ideology of the American Dream.[18] The male gazer, whom the speaker has never met but nevertheless "recognizes," follows her with his near-slanted eyes in an act of possession and, ultimately, domination.

Implying a spark of recognition from the speaker's perspective, the gaze – most reasonably sparked by desire – serves a highly objectifying and containing function. We might think of Luce Irigaray's discussion of the repressive power of the masculine gaze: "The predominance of the visual, and of the discrimination and individualization of form, is particularly foreign to female eroticism. Woman takes pleasure more from touching than from looking, and her entry into a dominant scopic economy signifies, again, her consignment to passivity: she is to be the beautiful object of contemplation" (1985: 25–6).[19] The speaker so reifies the dramatic situation that prompts her reveries that the reality of gender relations in the present fade from sight. The speaker enters into a scopic economy in which she becomes the possessed, the consumed, the passive object.

Castillo's poem projects onto the male gaze a function not of containment but of liberation: the mythic "memory" of a harmonious and empowered time. This projection is at odds both with the presumable reality of the gaze within the poem and with the historical realities from which the poem arises. Masculine power manifests itself through the gaze. Rape forms another more violent more violating means of masculine power. Thus the trope of rape employed by the poem to describe the alienation of one's (lost) self from one's (lost) civilization remains blind to the asymmetrical power dynamic inherent in the "near-slanted eyes" following the woman speaker. This is not to say that the poem evokes and misreads a rape in the making. But it does suggest that the poem – essentializing the condition and identity of "the Chicano" – blindly asserts a sameness about the discontinuous subject position "Chicano/a."

Twelve years later, Castillo returns to an evocation of pre-Cortesian iconography in the title of her collection *My Father Was a Toltec* (1988). The opening poem, "The Toltec," suggests that the problematic valuation of mythic "memory" exemplified by "Our Tongue Was Nahuatl" has given way to other, less romanticized concerns:

> My father was a Toltec.
> Everyone knows he was *bad.*
> Kicked the Irish-boys-from-Bridgeport's
> ass. Once went down to South Chicago
> to stick someone
> got chased to the hood
> running through the gangway
> swish of blade in his back
> the emblemmed jacket split in half.
>
> Next morning, Mami
> threw it away.

The term "Toltec" here is highly ironic. Rather than an evocation of a pre-Cortesian historical reality, "Toltec" here does not refer to the cultural antecedents of the Mexica. Instead, a mythic "memory" gives way to familial memory. The dream of cultural connection implied by the Nahuatl language is replaced by the reality of complex but very present cultural manifestations like neighborhood gangs and their identifying clothing. The utopian vision of a lost world before conquest results here in a world of ethnic and racial strife. And the sense of epic defeat implied by the invasion of the Aztec empire becomes the mock-epic adventure of the speaker's gang member/warrior father. The term "Toltec" here serves as an ultimately diminished evocation of the lost world of Meso-American indigenous populations. The discourse of a racial–ethnic identity traced back to the bronze roots of pre-Cortesian cultures undergoes a revision and rewriting in this poem that reverses the heroic impulse implied through an indigenous genealogy of la raza. Neither murdered nor subjugated, the hero of this narrative suffers the indignity of having his Mami throw his ruined gang jacket away. Given the move away from mythic to personal memory, the voice of the speaker has changed as well. It no longer betrays the sense of outrage and melancholy we hear in "Our Language Was Nahuatl." Here the speaker employs the jargon of the street, cool and clipped phrases creating a swift and concise narrative.

This questioning of cultural strategies represented in Castillo's later poem is not a complete rejection of the idea of connection and mythic "memory." Rather, it serves to mark a general problematizing of the construction of cultural identity among more recent Chicana poetry. Instead of positing an ethnic self that derives directly from a by now mythologized past, Chicana poetry articulates the mediated processes of desire and representation. As exemplified by "The Toltec," the use of pre-Cortesian cultural artifacts scrutinizes the class and ethnic tension evident in the contemporary urban scene. "Toltec" as a marker fully reified from any historical grounding signifies an ethnic identity. The poem foregrounds the fact of reification, focusing on the social configurations of gang membership and family dynamics. The mythic "memory" developed in early Chicana poetry as an unproblematic locus of cultural pride and political action is transformed into a cultural icon, ironized in the antiheroic world of street fights and a mother's disapproval. Unlike her earlier work, Castillo's poem does not rely upon a romanticized "memory" to serve as a foil against which the problems of the socioeconomic present become more visible. Instead, an indigenous cultural past is used as an icon, quoted in order to construct a humorous and subtle commentary on the problems, conflicts, and inadequacies of the Chicana present. Rather than locate the defining content of a Chicana mythic "memory," "The Toltec" explores what the cultural construction of a mythic "memory" does.

A more complex and enigmatic poem in Castillo's collection *My Father Was a Toltec,* "Ixtacihuatl Died in Vain" serves further to expand the significance of cultural memory and its function as an articulation of Chicana identity. In Mexican legend, Ixtacihuatl is a princess who falls in love with Popocatépetl, a warrior from a rival tribe. Upon hearing of his death in battle, reported erroneously to her, Ixtacihuatl kills herself out of sorrow. Popocatépetl returns victorious from his military exploits only to find his beloved dead. He takes her up in his arms and carries her to the mountains where he stretches her out and hunches beside her, guarding her pregnant body by the fires he burns eternally for her. Thus are explained the twin volcanoes, Ixtacihuatl and Popocatépetl, that loom above the Valley of Mexico.

In an explanatory footnote, Castillo's poem evokes the legend to serve as a foil for the poem's main topic: the subject position of women in the speaker's family. In the first of its three sections, the poem articulates the difficult position of Chicanas who are "hard on the mothers who've died on us / and the daughters born to us":

> Hard are the women of my family,
> hard on the mothers who've died on us
> and the daughters born to us,
> hard on all except sacred husbands
> and the blessings of sons.
> We are Ixtacihautls,
> sleeping, snowcapped volcanoes
> buried alive in myths
> princesses with the name of a warrior
> on our lips.

The women of her family – described by that most unfeminine adjective "hard" – interiorize and manifest a schizophrenic subjectivity. They are hard to and on each other, mother and daughter, hard on all except "sacred husbands" and "the blessings of sons." The antagonism and tension beneath a patriarchal order causes the women to turn hard against each other. Thus the first section concludes: "We are Ixtacihautls, / sleeping, snowcapped volcanoes / buried alive in myths / princesses with the name of a warrior / on our lips." Myths and legends, frozen in the stillness of some reified and unchanging realm of "tradition," bury the speaker and the women of her family and (by extension) Chicanas generally beneath the weight of a subject-position meant to be self-sacrificing and reverent. The legend of Ixtacihuatl serves to instruct the Chicana on the great Mexican truth about woman: She must be willing to sacrifice herself for her "warrior," to die with his name on her lips as a proper tribute to his stature and to her devotion. She should be prepared to either live through her man or die.

The second section speaks from a greater position of power, one that asserts a lesbian agency in the face of patriarchy.[20] The speaker becomes a suitor struggling for the hand and heart of her loved one:

> You, my impossible bride,
> at the wedding where our mothers were not invited,
> our fathers, the fourteen
> stations of the cross –
>
> You, who are not my bride,
> have loved too vast, too wide.
> Yet I dare to steal you
> from your mother's house.

It is you
I share my son with
to whom I offer up
his palpitating heart
so that you may breathe,
and replenish yourself,
you alone, whom I forgive.

Opening with a reference to "the wedding where our mothers / were not invited, / our fathers, the fourteen / stations of the cross –" this section conflates the exclusion of female antecedents with a patriarchal evocation of pain, suffering, sacrifice: Christ's passion. The marriage between women is impossible, because the institution of marriage is reserved for the preservation of patriarchal control. Thus the fathers of the would-be spouses become the suffering of the fourteen stations leading to Calvary. Beyond the allusion to Christ's crucifixion and consequent marriage to his bride the Church, these lines suggest that conventional marriage is a terrible culmination of sacrifice: a death that gives rebirth. The progeny of this renascence is, however, left unclear.

This "impossible bride" who is "not my bride" has "loved too vast, too wide." The prospective fiancée refuses to limit her devotion to a single object, a single love, and instead defies conventions. The speaker meets this defiance with her own rebellion, abducting the bride from her mother's house. The taking of the bride asserts a female aggressiveness in the face of an incessant male aggression and possessiveness. For the marriage that is not a marriage leads to the female speaker sharing her son with her would-be bride. In an act of sacrifice that implies renewal, she offers her son's "palpitating heart / so that you may breathe, / and replenish yourself." In a conflation of Christian and Nahua ritual, the "son" is offered in order to enact a rebirth. The section thus closes with a moment of impossible communion between two women, women forbidden the sanctity of church and home. Their love and sacrifice resolves in an image of forgiveness. The absolution exonerates the impossible bride, leaving the speaker free to ruminate upon that which is possible. And that which is possible is, ultimately, a world of limitations and diminishment.

The tension evoked by this twin production of sacrifices seeks some synthesis in the third and final section of the poem:

Life is long enough
to carry all things
to their necessary end. So

if i am with you
only this while,
or until our hair goes white,
our mothers have died,
children grown,
their children been born,
or when you spy someone
who is me
but with fresh eyes that see
you as Coatlicue once did –
and my heart
shrivels with vanity;
or a man takes me out to dance
and i leave you at the table
ice melting in your glass;
or all the jasmine in the world
has lost its scent,
let us place this born of us
at Ixtacihuatl's grave:
a footnote in the book of myths
sum of our existence –
"Even the greatest truths
contain the tremor of a lie."

The speaker, in a tumble of images strung together by conjunctions and prepositions, notes that "Life is long enough / to carry all things / to their necessary end." The process of rebirth implied in the first sections begins in the rush of the third section to make itself manifest. If, the speaker notes, "i am with you / only this while, / or until our hair goes white," the lovers will leave something behind as a tribute to the history of sacrifice inscribed in the pre-Cortesian/Christian myths evoked by the rest of the poem. It is worth noting that the personal pronoun "I" in the second section of the poem gives way to the "i" of this last section, a diminution that speaks to a sense of identity overwhelmed and dwarfed by the myths against and through which it is forged. For the "i" suggests that someday the addressee may spy "someone / who is me / but with fresh eyes that see / you as Coatlicue once did." Coatlicue, the Mexica god who gave birth to the powerful and destructive god of war Huitzilopochtli, is an androgynous figure represented with shrunken breasts wearing a skirt of snakes and a necklace of human hearts. Decapitated, from her neck twin snakes sprout signifying the blood and sacrifice necessary to the perpetuation of life and abundance. Coatlicue thus sees all as a process of death and rebirth, as a tension between the reciprocal actions of destruction and fruition.

Just as the speaker in the second section ambiguously portrays the woman as an "impossible bride / . . . / You, who are not my bride," here the speaker maintains a sense of ambiguity and denial. She identifies and does not identify herself with Coatlicue. She imagines that she will "with fresh eyes" see her lover "as Coatlicue once did," and yet she immediately imagines a time when her "heart / shrivels with vanity." This last image suggests both the sin of pride and the hopelessness of futility. Her identification with the god that is also not an identification causes the speaker to recoil from such weighty subjects, to realize the uselessness of such a project. This position recalls the title of the poem, as the sense of futility infuses the signifying process of the poem. The speaker goes on to evoke the more mundane image of herself going off with a man who "takes me out to dance / and i leave you at the table / ice melting in your glass." Does this suggest that the tensions in the relationship signal necessary forms of destruction to engender a more powerful union? Or could the sense of necessary sacrifice suggested by the images of Coatlicue and Christ stand in juxtaposition to the petty jealousies evoked by the deserted dance partner, watery drink in hand? Does the poem suggest a heroic or ironic posture? From either perspective, the pre-Cortesian symbology becomes a cultural icon employed to scrutinize the difficult and contradictory position of the contemporary Chicana.

This last section of "Ixtacihuatl Died in Vain" is constructed around a conditional framework: "So / if i am with you / only this while, / or until our hair goes white, / . . . / or when you spy someone / who is me / . . . / or a man takes me out to dance / . . . / or all the jasmine in the world / has lost its scent." If any or all of these things – mundane and cosmic, immediate and eternal – occurs, the speaker has one last request. She urges that they place at Ixtacihuatl's grave "this born of us." The process of creation activated in the first section reaches its conclusion. What is born is a simple "footnote in the book of myths / sum of our existence – / 'Even the greatest truths / contain the tremor of a lie.'" The evocation of myth serves less to suggest a connection and active memory of an alternative and better world existing sometime in the past than to help construct an ambiguous and complex portrait of the present. This present is infused with the demands of mythic "memories" that help make up the complex subject-positions of Chicanas. The image created by the poem is one of victimization and victimizing, one which reveals the tension between models of identity – the "greatest truth" – and the failure of those models – "the tremor of a lie." Against this tension, the speaker negotiates the treacherous terrain that serves to comprise the space of Chicana subjectivity.

"Ixtacihuatl Died in Vain" forms a striking departure from the use of mythic memory in Castillo's "Our Tongue was Nahuatl." The evocation of myth in the more recent work serves neither to glorify myth nor to signal a lack the myth seeks to fill. Instead, it becomes an icon employed in the revision and scrutiny of Chicana cultural and personal identity. The desire is not to return to some holistic and wholesome past evoked by mythic "memory." There is no yearning that seeks to transcend the present. The present serves as a dynamic moment inscribed by a frozen mythic past which, because frozen, delimits the positions Chicanas can rightfully assume. The poem invokes mythic memory not to admire it or ironize it, but to scrutinize its power and to speak a counter-truth: That which is "born of us" and forms the "sum of our existence" is but a "footnote in the book of myths." The diminution (marked again by the use of the personal pronoun "i") can be read as a small, wry commentary upon the vanity of grandiose "mythic" visions propounded by earlier Chicano poetry.

Other Myths: Corpi, Cisneros, Cervantes

Demystifying, diminishing, the voice in several examples of contemporary Chicano poetry reworks a variety of mythic "memories." In these visions and revisions, the evocations of myth assume functions ranging from the critical – as with Castillo's use of "memory" – to the more simply lyrical or evocative. Lucha Corpi, for example, relies upon a pre-Cortesian mythological pantheon in order to portray a sense of rebirth and fruition. Her poem "Lluvia/Rain," published in 1980, is marked by a consciousness of Nahua symbology, but does not incorporate this symbology as part of an aggressive affirmation of Chicano national culture. This lack of cultural militancy may be due in part to Corpi's having migrated to the United States from Mexico in 1964 when she was nineteen. While living through the tumultuous 1960s in the San Francisco Bay area, Corpi's background and early education undoubtedly mark her relationship to cultural creation and the types of discourses she employs in her poetic production.[21]

Much of the poetry collected in her bilingual edition *Palabras de Mediodía/Noon Words* – a collection that represents ten years of writing – evinces a lyrical, nearly romantic quality.[22] Although the poems voice a concern with cultural iconography and subjectivity, the evocation of mythic "memory" occurs on a very intimate scale. Absent from her work is the polemical tone of other Chicano poetry that invokes pre-Cortesian symbology. Corpi herself says of this collection that it contains "much light, much color, and many contrasts. It is a poetry of feelings, it is sensual" (1989: 73). This sensuality is most clearly evident in the poem "Rain":

Slender reeds
Cadenced waterfalls
Intimate forms

Rupture and formation
in the cornfields

Offspring of Tlaloc
song of *teponaztle*
rising out of time.

On rainy afternoons
squash cooked with sugar
and hot *atole.*

Childish sins
Infinitives
wrapped
in antique green.[23]

The poem forms an intimate meditation on the pleasures of rain, on the comforts of sweets, on the fecundity of life-giving water conflated with "childish sins" like infinitive verbs ("Verbos infinitivos") wrapped in ancient green. This vision of birth and creation and comfort evokes Tlaloc only as part of a cultural repertoire. Tlaloc, the Nahua god of rain, appears here as the absent father of the rain that falls like the song played on the *teponaztle*, a flute used in indigenous ritual celebration. The poem relies upon a cultural specificity, drawing its imagery from indigenous Mexican arts, thus suggesting a sense of cultural continuity. This continuity, however, is manifested less in the mythic "memory" of Tlaloc than in the evocation of hot atole and candied squash ("dulce de calabaza"), foods native to Meso-America that derive from pre-Cortesian times.

The remnants of pre-Cortesian culture embodied by food and musical instruments lend an intimacy and connection to the past that is not an invocation of symbology or pantheons. This is an intimate portrait of rainy afternoons and the warmth of home. The memories here are associated less with myth than with childhood, and Tlaloc appears not as a locus of cultural pride but as a part of a cultural repertoire. The poem emphasizes how ancient these cultural artifacts are as "infinitive verbs" that the "antique green" wraps up in rainy afternoons. The poem thus offers intimate images of fecundity, continuity, and connection quite distinct from the cultural nationalism of earlier mythic "memory." All these images become associated with a language of infinite potential, the infinitive verbs waiting for conjugation. The ancestral becomes personal and potentially empowering.

Sandra Cisneros also contributes to the history of mythic "memory" in the movements of Chicano literature. Her collection *My Wicked Wicked Ways* (1987) speaks, with less romantic lyricism, to the same issues of intimacy and tradition as Corpi's poems. However, the tradition she evokes is one quite distinct from – some might say antithetical to – the tradition of pre-Cortesian culture so carefully cultivated by other Chicano letters. Cisneros's collection expresses itself through humor, irony, and understatement as it delves into the possibility and impossibility of relations between men and women. In particular, it explores the conflicted interaction between men who presume power and women who are expected not to claim it. In a tone at once dry and cutting, her poems generally evoke dramatic situations whose conflict is resolved in the quiet anger or humor of poetic expression.

A good example of this type of resolution can be found in "New Year's Eve." Addressed to a silent companion, the poem opens flatly: "I saw your wife tonight." The speaker goes on to make observations about this wife framed wholly in negative constructions:

> No Athena. No Medea.
> No Adelita nor Malintzín.
>
> From what I could observe
> she is a woman risen from a rib
> like any other –
> two eyes, two breasts, one uterus.

Mythic and legendary figures are simultaneously evoked and erased through the course of the poem as the speaker compares them to the unsuspecting wife. These figures become foils against which the poetic voice contrasts the plainness of the auditor's wife. She is, after all, "a woman risen from a rib / like any other – / two eyes, two breasts, one uterus." The simplicity of the language forges an understated commentary from the position of the "other" woman, she without the socially sanctified security of marriage and husband.

The rest of the poem is constructed through similarly negative statements. The speaker observes about the wife that "She did not arrive / wearing raiments of gold" and that "No Botticelli pearl is she." The speaker compares the wife negatively to Venus, to Cleopatra, to Carmen, to the Adelita figure of the Mexican Revolution, to the Sirens. This series of mythical and legendary figures forms points of unfavorable comparison, employed dismissively in the poem, which concludes:

> Her hands were clean.
> Her forehead modest, serene.
>
> How did I fail to understand?
> A female, like any common female.
>
> For a common male.

As the speaker turns her critical gaze from the unsuspecting wife to the philandering husband, the poem evinces a dramatic turn (matching the turn of the speaker's gaze), which resolves in a coldly ironic tone. What appears at first a biting criticism of a plain wife becomes instead an understated dismissal of the philandering husband. The title as well – "New Year's Eve," which at first appears to describe the setting in which the speaker sights the unsuspecting wife – undergoes a process of transformation as it becomes an allusive pun in which the speaker, realizing the condition of her relationship, becomes a new Eve "risen from a rib" into a new year. The attack against the wife transforms itself into a dismissal of the husband in a turn and resolution that, although clever, suggests that the poem works only through one reading. The cooly ironic trigger is pulled in the final line; the bullet that dispatches the husband cannot be reloaded.

The rhetorical structure of the poem, however, is not the main issue here. The iconography that the poem invokes – Athena, Medea, Adelita, Malintzín – forms a cross-cultural and multiethnic pantheon. Cisneros's poem uses the same type of strategy as many other Chicano poets, deploying a series of cultural icons as a frame or foil by which to construct signification in the poem. The noteworthy difference here is that the icons derive from a cross between European cultural traditions – Ancient Greek, Italian Renaissance – and Mexican – translator/traitor Malintzín, the legendary *soldadera* of the Mexican Revolution, Adelita. These figures are textualized by this poem and become obvious foils that allow the speaker to pull the rug out from under her unfaithful male auditor. This same strategy of iconic evocation, this same move at the construction of a mythic "memory," in other texts supposedly ground Chicano cultural identity in an indigenous heritage. What Cisneros's poem helps foreground is the constructed quality of that heritage.

This strategy is again evident in Cisneros's second collection of poetry,

Loose Woman (1994). Here once more the deployment of iconography reveals the constructed quality inherent to mythic memory. Especially in a poem like "You Bring out the Mexican in Me," Cisneros's poetry revels in icons: mythic, kitsch, popular, sensational. The poem serves as a list that indicates how much the addressee brings out the "Mexican" in the speaker, calling forth "the Dolores del Río in me" and the "eagle and serpent in me." The movement from mass cultural to mythic allusion reveals the strategy for what it is: the construction of cultural identity through a language based on iconography. The listing of events and disasters – from the 1985 Mexico City earthquake to the "tidal wave of recession" – leads the speaker to declare "I am the filth goddess of Tlazoltéotl."[24] Finally, the speaker invokes all the saints and goddesses "blessed and terrible, / *Virgen de Guadalupe, diosa Coatlicue*" in a passionate declaration of a woman's love for the object of her address. The iconography throughout the poem is marked by gender and ethnicity, and sets into motion a series of signifiers meant to position the speaker and her passion. That passion is revealed through the codified language of icons, pointing quite clearly to the interplay between cultural identity and cultural construction.

The play between myths and legends and subject positions is evident, to a different purpose, in Lorna Dee Cervantes's "Astro-no-mía." The title is a play on the Spanish word for astronomy, transformed by Cervantes into a phrase meaning "not my star." The suggestion of dispossession is manifested in the poem as the speaking voice addresses that "the closest we ever got / to science was the stars." The speaker articulates her position outside forms of knowledge like science, and outside mythical stories that are not hers, like those associated with the stars. She thinks of the stars that were diamonds

> for some Greeks
> long ago when law was a story
> of chased women set in the sky:
> Diana, Juno, Pleiades, las siete
> hermanas, daughters, captives
> of Zeus, and the children, the children
> changed into trees, bears, scared into stars.

The pastiche of Roman and Greek mythical figures serves to underscore the notion of dispossession woven throughout the text: These myths the speaker invokes are not hers.

This fact is made clear in the next movement of the poem. The speaker notes that "We wished ourselves into the sky" and "stopped dreaming, / stopped stories, our hearts and elevated / up into that ash-trip to heaven-seven / smoked rings of escape from the chase." The inversion of colloquial expression and punning on the idea of "smoke" places the poem firmly in the quotidian and earth-bound world of the street, a fact underscored by the resolution of this second section. For all the wishing to become "stars," and holding of breath, the result is clear: "Y nada. Punto. We were never stars." Parental figures – mothers who would call, the fathers "of fate, heavy like mercury" who "would trash / our stomachs into our wombs" – disrupt the hope, bring the speaker on a "roller coaster back down to the earth." This descent back into reality moves the poem into the third and final section where the speaker, cold, alone on the night before school and another failed exam, is left sitting in her room with Orion "helplessly shooting his shaft / into my lit house from the bow. / Y Yo? Hay bow. Y ya voy." The poem closes on word play, punning aurally on the word "bow" as verb and noun so that "I bow" and "there is a bow," a play that resolves into a final affirmative sense of movement with "ya voy": There I go. The impossible move into the stars and the night sky finally becomes an affirmation of some movement in the end.

Again, Cervantes invokes mythical figures, as does Cisneros, not to posit a sense of "memory," but to indicate the constructed quality of these myths as they are textualized in the poem and in the life of the speaker. These particular poems – "New Year's Eve" and "Astro-no-mía" – highlight the various traditions and heritages with and against which Chicana cultural identity constructs itself. Along with Corpi's "Rain," which employs myth in a most offhand way as an allusion subordinated to the intimacy and comfort of childhood memories, these poems demonstrate that the techniques in constructing a mythic "memory" can be employed in a variety of ways toward a variety of purposes. The function of mythic "memory" as a constructed rather than "natural" connection to a Chicana heritage allows for the types of moves these three poets make.

Other Memories: Baca and Anzaldúa

This is not to suggest that the desire for a spiritual connection represented by myth and its evocation is no longer an influential force within Chicana culture. A spiritual longing, even mysticism and recollection of lost gods, persists throughout Chicana literature and culture. However, the sense of stridency, insistence, and advocacy of an alternate space found in earlier poetry gives way to a more modulated and complicated evocation. The later poetry crosses alternate cultural expressions like curanderismo and indigenous forms of worship with politically charged and historically inscribed discourses. The evocation of mythic "memory" suggests a distinct and unique but nevertheless constructed cultural identity. The employment of myth becomes a strategy by which to present a critique of all-too-present forms of repressively interpellated subject-positions.

Seeking through highly concrete imagery and alliterative techniques a spirituality in the poetic realm difficult to locate in the quotidian, Jimmy Santiago Baca's poetry moves as if toward a union between the spiritual and physical – a union that poetry like Alurista's seeks to invoke through a mythic "memory" of indigenous culture. "Dream Instructions" from *Black Mesa Poems* (1989) makes four movements in the course of the poem that parallel four visions the speaker encounters in his dreams. The poem opens with a reference to an earlier poem in the *Black Mesa* collection, "From Violence to Peace." The earlier poem recounts the slaughter of a steer that leads the speaker toward a violence that results in him getting shot. The poem ends with the voice of the curandero telling the speaker that the "'bull's blood, / is either going to drown you or liberate you, / but it will not be wasted.'" The echo of these lines returns to open "Dream Instructions" as the speaker falls asleep thinking about blood wasted.

In his dreams, the speaker envisions himself entering prison "face cringing, hands tightening, / terrified, / saying *no, no, no . . .*" (ellipses in original). The state penal system is a site in which spirituality and hope are beaten and burned away. The experience of Baca in prison, the discrimination, the systemic violation of human rights, represent a social realm against which a spiritual quest becomes all that much more urgent. The vision of prison the poem offers, suffused with images of illness and enclosure, gives way to one in which the speaker sees himself and calls out. He realizes that "Men I once was want me to return to their skins, / want me to fill their bodies." The poem, after evoking these twin dreams of personal confinement and containment, moves into a vision of a winged serpent whose "wings warped and scarred / wrap round its skeleton." This serpent – Quetzalcoatl again? – beats blistering hot wind across the desert floor and settles in "the hollow / of a half-buried / petrified skull." The hellish qualities of the vision are taken up by the voice of the serpent who speaks to the poet: " 'Did you tell them / Hell is not a dream / and that you've been there, / did you tell them?'" In response to this dream, the speaker posits parenthetically: "(Is it the peaceful man / speaking to the destructive one in me?)" The poetic voice offers an analysis, removing the dream from the realm of memory, instead treating it as an icon or portent, a means by which to enact analysis.

The icon of the feathered serpent gives way to the final dream in which the speaker dives through his flesh:

past the bone's porous depths,
                                        a pearl diver
with knife flashing in my teeth,
and come to my heart.
Red throbbing fish
I cut open.

Diving into himself, the speaker "finds" a glowing sun – evocative again of the Mexica belief that human hearts fed the sun – and a tapering white horn of ivory; men made of cobwebs, flesh rotted away beyond which stretches an "eternity of airy darkness." And, at the far end, "all by itself," shines a "small sparkling bead of light, / where another way of life thrives." This light at the end of darkness shines with the promise of a life unlike this one. Although it certainly shines as the utopian promise of alternate praxis somewhere beyond this violent world, a vision of a potential spiritual fulfillment, this light at the end of the tunnel could also suggest the light shining through the door of solitary confinement. The image of prison at the beginning of the poem, the hell the speaker has known and about which the serpent reminds him, stands as the ultimate realm of spiritual emptiness. This version of hell stands in contradistinction to the death-haunted vision of potential rebirth that closes the poem. The resolution represents the horror and hope lying at "the heart" of the speaker's psyche.

"Dream Instructions" articulates the speaker's quest for a spirituality that manifests itself through the poetry itself. Although the vision of Quetzalcoatl is self-interpreted as the peaceful speaking to the violent self, we have seen that the plumed serpent stands as an icon for wisdom and culture. The vision thus weaves together the speaker's own dream analysis, a commitment to the production of cultural objects, and an affirmation of a spirituality that promises another way of life separate from the violence invoked by the opening lines of the poem. The ambiguity of "From Violence to Peace" (the poem ends with "The flood of that bull's blood, / is either going to drown you or liberate you, / but it will not be wasted") finds its resolution in the close of "Dream Instructions." Here the blood leads to a vision of promise and hope, one constructed through quasi-mythic iconography. But one which nevertheless calls for a genuine spiritual regeneration in the face of potential and actual destruction.

There is a danger in articulating such a vision. The poetry opens itself up to the allegation that it represents nothing more pertinent than a gossamer dream of liberation dissociated from the reality of human engagement. Gloria Anzaldúa, for example, constructs an ethnopoetic strategy that may at first seem as much an expression of wish-fulfillment as Alurista's "libertad sin lágrimas." In the essay "*Tlilli, Tlapalli:* The Path of the Red and Black Ink," Anzaldúa articulates the purposes of her artistic practice:

> In the ethno-poetics and performance of the shaman, my people, the Indians, did not split the artistic from the functional, the sacred from the secular, art from everyday life. The religious, the social and aesthetic purposes of art were all intertwined. Before the Conquest, poets gathered to play music, dance, sing and read poetry in open-air places. . . . The ability of story (prose and poetry) to transform the storyteller and the listener into something or someone else is shamanistic. The writer, as shape-changer, is a *Nahual*, a shaman. (1987: 66)

Of course, these are not pre-Conquest times. And an image of art as functioning integrally within social and religious as well as aesthetic and cultural systems represents an image that stands in contradistinction to what actually is the condition of art in contemporary society. As with Baca's work, Anzaldúa's writing evinces an awareness and discontent with these realities. As a result, mythic "memory" in her work plays a counterdiscursive practice within contemporary symbolic economies. Anzaldúa insists that we "stop importing Greek myths and the Western Cartesian split point of view and root ourselves in the mythological soil of this continent" (1987: 68). Her writing speaks against specific (Eurocentric) systems of appropriation and exchange.

For Anzaldúa, mythic figures allow for a vision of connection associated with but not inexorably tied to some distant, more authentic past. These figures provide an image, a cultural icon that can be employed in numerous divergent and even self-contradictory ways. As Anzaldúa explains in *"La conciencia de la mestiza,"* the "new" mestizaje of Chicano culture implies a radical pluralism where "nothing is thrust out, the good the bad and the ugly, nothing rejected, nothing abandoned. Not only does [the new mestiza] sustain contradictions, she turns the ambivalence into something else" (1987: 79). The "good the bad and the ugly" – a phrase evocative not only of Clint Eastwood but also of Oliver North – includes the clichéd, the tired, the worn, which flicker again with a form of life in a process of reconsideration and reconfiguration. Whereas early Chicano poetry would evoke myth as a primary strategy in locating cultural identity, Anzaldúa's work employs mythic elements as a part of a cultural pastiche that moves toward but never ultimately fixes Chicano identity. Her work exemplifies a complex position in which the "local, discontinuous, disqualified, illegitimate knowledges" of a society or culture are entertained.[25] The presence of this disqualified knowledge within Anzaldúa's poetry suggests a tenuous condition marked not so much by a faith in pre-Cortesian religious icons as by a need for spirituality.

Anzaldúa's poem *"Antigua, mi diosa"* provides an example of this use of icons. The poem, written in Spanish and italicized, forms a plea to the poet's ancient and dark goddess. The speaker, *"Dezcalza, gateando a ciegas* [Barefoot, blindly crawling]" like a newborn baby follows the faint footprints and ancient lineage of the goddess as she recalls previous visitations: *"En medio de un chillido de trenes / veniste a las ruinas de Brooklyn / con tu sonido de cascabeles* [Amid the screeching of trains / you came to the ruins of Brooklyn / with your tinkling of bells]."[26] The goddess came then, and she filled *"con tu luz . . . el hueco de mi cuerpo* [with your light . . . the emptiness of my body]." The poem discusses these visitations as having planted seeds of light whose harvest is *"esta inquietud / que se madura en agonía* [this restlessness / that matures into agony]" – an agony arising from the speaker's futile search for the now vanished goddess.

The evocation of the goddess conflates a spiritual longing with strong sexual imagery pointing toward a very worldly lesbian love as a means of spiritual salvation. Not only does the poem employ mythic "memory" as a signal of spiritual longing, it deploys that "memory" as an affirmation of a lesbian identity, which – like the image of the powerful and ancient goddess who was once hidden – now emerges into Chicano poetic practice as a response and rejection of the dead hand of received patriarchal tradition.

The speaker begs for another sign, another ray of light, another chance to *"brotar otra vez / en tu negrísima piel* [spring once again / in your blackest skin]." The poem signals a dissatisfaction that the goddess has abandoned the speaker and evokes a spiritual yearning that informs the poetic meditation on the lost goddess whose burning light has fled. The poem crosses this spiritual disaffection with images of the dark and unnamed goddess suggestive – of course – of Coatlicue.

As in Castillo's work, Anzaldúa's evocation of the goddess serves to mark a tension between creation and destruction. At one level, this tension can be read as that which characterizes the longing the speaker feels for her lost but driving goddess. Coatlicue both creates and destroys the spiritual life of the speaker. At another level, the tension reflects the process by which the poem itself is created. Although the poem marks the simultaneous presence and absence of Coatlicue, the actuality of the goddess herself is not at issue. Rather than suggest that spiritual need is *caused* by the loss of pre-Cortesian myth and actual Nahua gods, the poem indicates that the absent goddess *signals* a spiritual need.

The discursive practices characteristic of Chicana poetry – the evocation of mythic religion, the "memory" of lost cultures, the yearning for a glorious past – are employed by Anzaldúa's poem to convey a sense of a present spiritual rather than a nostalgic social or cultural longing. Indeed, the goddess to which the speaker pleas has already made herself present in the speaker's life. Instead of invoking a long lost culture or religious system – as does the early poetry by Castillo and Alurista – Anzaldúa's poem employs the image of the dark goddess juxtaposed with the screaming trains and urban decay of Brooklyn. By contrasting the spiritual power embodied by the ancient Coatlicue with the disintegration and emptiness of the modern city, the poem makes manifest the pressing need for a spirituality lost within the logic of dominant social practices. Moreover, it evokes the types of devalued knowledge that have been repressed by a history of disempowerment, repression, and cultural genocide. *"Antigua, mi diosa"* thus functions counterdiscursively, creating the space for spiritual transformation and the expression of spiritual need within and against the cultural practices of dominant North American society through the invocation of knowledge and poetic practices relegated to the "margins" of contemporary culture.

The cultural icons Anzaldúa employs to form this spiritual counterdiscourse are those that have accumulated through the various movements of Chicano poetry. Her poem dwells on some of the images and icons that evoke a "memory" of pre-Cortesian religion, but does so to mark the thematic concerns of the poem. As Norma Alarcón has noted: "For many writers the point is not so much to recover a lost 'utopia' nor the 'true' essence of our being. . . . The most relevant point in the present is to understand how a pivotal indigenous portion of the mestiza past may represent a collective female experience as well as 'the mark of the Beast' within us – the maligned and abused indigenous woman" (1990: 251). The evocation of myth in Anzaldúa's text does not exclusively signal a longing for a return to purity or essence. It represents a strategy that allows for the expression of a genuine longing integrally linked to the imperialist, racist, and sexist practices that have served to silence the disqualified knowledges her poetry evokes. Her work does not recuperate the iconography of a lost past in order to recover that past. It rather appropriates that iconography to signal the distress of a culture attempting to articulate the significance of its multiplicitous and devalued historical presence.

From the first, Chicano art and literature have relied on an aesthetic of appropriation and pastiche. In the 1980s, this aesthetic begins to focus more on the process of continuing cultural mestizaje and the abjuring of a lost native past. The invocation of a mythic "memory" that has so strongly marked Chicano cultural production finds its greatest fruition. The poetry no longer fixates on the articulation of an "authentic" Chicano identity or culture. Instead, it demonstrates a cultural identity constantly being transformed and shaped, perpetually finding itself in new positions, new locations. The terrain has shifted so that its ruptures and discontinuities become apparent. In this landscape, the migratory nature of Chicano culture, the multiplicity and diversity of Chicano experiences find voice. Here the uses of mythic "memory" no longer form strategies by which the connection to an original moment of identity is forged. Rather, the evocation of myth becomes a strategy that helps map additional realms through which Chicano culture and Chicano identity can move.

7

Mouthing Off:
Polyglossia and Radical Mestizaje

They can't handle this smooth roughness
Taking two words meaning totally opposite
The lyrical engineer will take 'em and make 'em fit
Create another definition out of the two.
– Latin Alliance

A PRIMARY CHARACTERISTIC of Chicano culture remains its ability to move across numerous textual terrains: the ritual, the mythic, the mass cultural, the popular, the folkloric, the hyperreal, the Mexican, the American. A strategy of pastiche and appropriation enables this movement, a strategy that manifests a cross between postmodern and postcolonial concerns and discursive formations. The articulation of Chicano cultural identity conveys an outrage and sadness, a humor and wryness that weave themselves out of the multiplicitous discursive practices surrounding and traversing the borderlands of Chicano experience. Some of the topics: the concern with reconstructing history, the desire to reconnect with an original moment, the construction of expressions that establish historical connections and simultaneously enable a sense of agency for movement forward, a piecing together of resistant and acquiescent social practices. All these constitute some of the features that mark the articulation of contemporary Chicano culture.

Chicano poetic expression interwoven – as both its metacommentary and meta-articulation – with and out of this experience manifests the highly textured character of the cultural landscape. We have already seen some of the poetic and critical configurations possible. Several poets evoke pre-

Cortesian cultural remnants in order to proffer a singular and empowering contemporary identity. Critics (Leal, Padilla, Pina, Alurista) have taken up this strategy, employing the name "Aztlán" to name the site of Chicano cultural production and political action. In a similar vein, many critics cite the connection between the narrative and folkloric tradition of the corrido and contemporary expressions of Chicano poetry. Some critics (Limón, the Paredeses, the Saldívars) argue that these connections convey a sense of tradition and generation; others (McKenna, Grajeda) propose that they signal decline and degeneration. Still other critics tease out the mythical and archetypical dimension deployed by Chicano poets, arguing that this reveals the underlying universality of the literature (Bruce-Novoa, Gonzales, González, Lomelí) or that it grounds the texts within particular historical, political, and cultural constellations (Alarcón, Klor de Alva, Chabram, Sommers).

Pastiche: Francisco Alarcón

Quite simply, Chicano culture moves dynamically through and between numerous spaces. The betweenness of Chicano culture, its interstitial quality, allows it to draw from a large variety of discursive practices that come to form its repertoire. From the histories and traditions it constructs to the motifs and speech acts it evokes, the poetic expression of Chicano culture employs a type of recuperative strategy akin to the pastiche associated with the condition of postmodernity. Within the postmodern debates, the contemporary deployment of different historical styles has been critiqued as a type of historical eclecticism that expresses a simplistic neoconservative nostalgia. Although it does employ a type of historical pastiche (exemplified by Rodolfo Gonzales's *Yo Soy Joaquín*, for example), the counterdiscursive quality of Chicano culture precludes the easy conclusion that cultural eclecticism necessarily signals a reactionary ideology. Indeed, as Andreas Huyssen argues, the postmodern invocation of historical styles can "express some genuine and legitimate dissatisfaction with modernity and the unquestioned belief in the perpetual modernization of art" (1984: 12). The demand to "make it new" cannot be an imperative when what is "old" – traditional forms of discredited knowledge passed on through families and communities – has from a "majoritarian" position been denied. The historical connectivity made evident in Chicano cultural production refuses to become either a meaningless play of empty historical signifiers or a neoconservative reinscription of a regime of tradition. It marks a profound reexamination and critique of history. It questions the narratives that comprise that history, proposing alternate and critical narratives that seek to counterpoise disempowering subject-positions and limiting discourses. Chicano cultural production provides, in other words, a counterdiscourse that draws on history and simultaneously interrogates it. Or, as Ramón Saldívar has articulated this process, Chicano literary production is marked by a double-move, the "paradoxical impulse toward revolutionary deconstruction and toward the production of meaning" (1979: 88).

This double-movement, at once interstitial (between hermeneutics and deconstruction) and resistant (advocative and interrogative) manifests itself in numerous ways. The celebration of the racial and cultural mestizaje that, during the 1920s and beyond, found valorization in the construction of Mexican national identity resonates, during the 1960s and beyond, throughout the development of Chicano cultural identity. The sense of joining and conjoining implied by mestizaje expands exponentially within a Chicano cultural space comprised of seemingly infinite conjunctions between the North American, the Native American, the pre-Cortesian, the Afro-Caribbean, the Spanish colonial, the popular cultural, the folkloric, and the rest of the by now familiar litany. Chicano culture becomes a radical mestizaje.

This is nowhere clearer than in the poetics of a figure like Alurista. Mestizaje forms, as we have seen, a dominant key in his poetic production. In addition to the concept of "Amerindia" and its celebration of nativism, Alurista's poetry (Tomás Ybarra-Frausto notes) forges "new images and a new vocabulary from the confluence of cultures that nurtures the Chicano experience, he sings of 'the radiance of our quilted heritage.' In his poems, pre-Cortesian images relate to barrio symbols. Culture heroes like Quetzalcoatl, Tizoc, and Zapata coexist with Pachucos, Vatos Locos, and contemporary pop culture stars like Jimi Hendrix" (1979: 118). The poetry both thematizes and becomes the embodiment of mestizaje, the manifestation of the multiplicitous discourses from which Chicanos create a sense of identity. Mestizaje becomes a racial/radical marker of self-determination.

Mestizaje as a cultural strategy has proven durable within Chicana poetic expression because of its interminably dynamic quality. The mixing and melding of cultures that defines the contemporary condition of world culture (we are all the bastard children of history, Salman Rushdie tells us) lends a global perspective to Chicana cultural production. Although its concerns are certainly local, regional, the conditions of its creation and the move toward empowerment which it implies resonates with other "local" projects of cultural identification globally.

The notion of La Raza Cósmica borrowed by Chicanas from Vasconcelos served a somewhat limited – and reified – notion of connectivity and multiculturalism. In Francisco Alarcón's "Mestizo" (1992), the idea of the mestizo as the universal man returns in a much-altered form. The poem opens with a disavowal of identity: "my name / is not / Francisco." This leads to a recitation of various inner identities – the "Arab / within me," behind the Roman nose "a Phoenician / smiling," and the eyes that "still see / *Sevilla*." This inner-identification suggests the various histories of invasion and contact that have served to form the populations and cultures of the Spanish peninsula. The multiracial mixture that becomes the Spanish results from the series of invasions and the history of violence that connects this first part of the poem to the second. The poem shifts from a description of the inner qualities of the speaker toward his physical manifestation; "my mouth / is Olmec / my dark / hands are / Toltec / my cheekbones / fierce / Chichimec." (As should be apparent, the poetics of the poem are fairly uninteresting; this is not the concern here.) The biological connection to indigenous pre-Cortesian tribes signals the result of mestizaje. The speaker's feet "recognize / no border / no rule / no code / no lord / for this / wanderer's / heart" – an image of absolute transgression and flight. Against all order, against limitations, against the rules of man, "this / wanderer's / heart" roams in an image of hypermestizaje.

The vision of absolute freedom implied by the poem should certainly be viewed with suspicion. The speaker's feet may recognize no border, but just let them actually try to cross one without proper documentation. The interest of the poem for our present discussion is its construction of mestizaje. The combination of races, ethnicities, and cultures results from an incessant and ruthless history of dispossession. This history leads to a profound deterritorialization, which enables possibilities for configurations of personal and cultural identification. The evocation of violent historical events points toward a mestizaje that acknowledges what it marks. "History cannot be reversed or erased out of nostalgia," Gayatri Spivak argues in "Who Claims Alterity?": "The remaking of history involves a negotiation with the structures that have produced the individual as agent of history" (1989: 282). Structures involved with invasion, diaspora, commercial exchange, xenophobia, and genocide create mestizaje. Alarcón's poem points toward the histories of conquest, violence, and dispossession that enable these structures; the text does not turn away from the past.

Mestizaje thus carries with it a cost. In Ana Castillo's "Our Tongue Was Nahuatl," for example, the valuation of the "native" so inflects the poem that mestizaje actually becomes a marker of economic and cultural servitude. The blanching of the race marks a debilitation and dispossession enacted in the past and repeated over and over within a contemporary social context. The poem signals the distress implicit in the mestizaje of cultural identity. (It also, to its discredit, suggests a nativist culturalism that succumbs to a certain helplessness. History has destroyed the origin of identity in that poem, and all the natives can do is bow and remember). The heritage of violation – as is also evident in Baca's "Invasions" – forms a complex history of simultaneous enrichment and impoverishment.

The tension between these two qualities revisits the historical conditions inherent in Chicano culture. Mestizaje cannot be separated from the histories of rape and violation from which it emerges. Simultaneously, it cannot be dismissed in search of an original indigenous identity that is not the condition of Chicano praxis. The cultural products that emerge from Chicano configurations of identity carry with them the conditions of mestizaje: conjunction, enrichment, violation, conquest, fusion, violence. Textualized, mestizaje enables a scrutiny of power and knowledge as these have been enacted or erased through history.

Within the literary field, the succession of conjunctions (not "either/or" but "and . . . and . . . and . . .") implicit in mestizaje finds its most material manifestation in its deployment of language. One practical problem in teaching Chicano poetry – or writing about it – has to do (*pace* reader) with the audience's proficiency in languages. At the very least, one would hope that an aversion to Spanish would not preclude communication. Although for many people responding to a "foreign" language on the printed page is disorienting, to find this "foreign" tongue *interalia* imprinted within native speech approaches a violation. Instead of understanding, the reader must confront a *horror vacui* – the most aggressively interlingual poem can become a meaningless void when approached monolingually. Even under the best of circumstances, a rapprochement between reader and text is difficult if the text forces a consultation with dictionaries or a glossary.

Fernando Peñalosa notes that the term polyglossia applies to Chicano speech because it employs more than two varieties in the languages Chicanos employ (1980: 42–3).[1] One manifestation of this polyglossia is the use of code-switching, the alteration of linguistic codes. Borrowing or substitution occurs, as Peñalosa explains, when an individual substitutes a word in one language for the corresponding word in the other. Incorporated borrowing or lexicalization occurs where the dialect has borrowed the particular word from another language.[2] This type of linguistic interpenetration on the sociodiscursive stage forms a type of bilingualism (more precisely polyglossia) in which speakers use code-switching to establish numerous social relations.

Simplifying to the extreme, the issue of bilingualism or code-switching within social discourse revolves around power relations – who is speaking to whom, and the proximity or distance one wishes to establish within the discursive relationship. L. A. Timm observes that "switching is frequently employed by bilinguals as a highly effective rhetorical or stylistic device" (1975: 475). Beyond these textual uses of code-switching – to set off quotations, to emphasize what was just said, to make a parenthetic aside, to mimic someone – code-switching signals a relationship between speaker and audience. Fernando Peñalosa notes that "Chicano code switching can also be a verbal strategy for conveying social information, such as a sociopolitical identity marker or intimate relationship, for signalling social distance from an Anglo role, and for implying that one's own interlocutor will not be offended by language mixture" (1980: 68). From a sociolinguistic perspective, this particular speech-act establishes or disrupts social roles, aids or precludes the construction of community.

What would be code-switching on a sociodiscursive stage becomes on an aesthetic level something more complex. Rather than "bilingual," Chicano poetry is better characterized as interlingual. As Juan Bruce-Novoa explains in *Chicano Poetry*, many poems draw together two (or more) languages within the text. These languages are thus positioned in "a state of tension which produces a third, an 'inter' possibility of language. 'Bilingualism' implies moving from one language code to another; 'interlingualism' implies the constant tension of the two at once" (1982: 226). The interlingual forms a highly fluid and complex textuality that lays bare the tensions at work in the articulation of Chicano poetic voices. These voices often derive authority and form from the traditional position of the balladeer, the village poet, the premodern messenger. Simultaneously, they produce texts that are reproduced and distributed through the familiar alienated forms of production and consumption characterizing modern and postmodern worlds. The mestizaje of linguistic form, interlingualism reveals some of the dichotomous conditions through and against which the Chicano poetic speaker voices the discontinuity of Chicano subjectivity and agency.

Reed Way Dasenbrock argues that an interlingual novel like *Bless Me, Ultima*, which deploys Spanish within a primarily English text, casts the reader on a voyage through the book that "mirrors" the protagonist's experience as a Spanish-speaker in an English-dominated world. Moreover, not only does the text provide the experience of "reality," it offers a valuable lesson about diversity and tolerance: "the reader is thrown into a world of Spanish without translation or cushioning, and even the monolingual reader moves toward a functional bilingualism, an ability to understand the world of the novel" (1987: 16). Dasenbrock's argument seeks to account for the particular multivocality of anglophonic multicultural texts. These texts construct a bilingualism (Dasenbrock's conceptualization) which foregrounds difference and makes the texts "difficult" for monolingual readers as an intentional strategy meant to broaden the reader's horizon.

This type of liberal reading seems inadequate for explaining the multivocality of Chicana texts. Dasenbrock's article treats – in addition to the Chicana text by Anaya – an Indian, a Chinese-American, and a Maori novel. One glaring problem with Dasenbrock's argument is its reification of alterity. It positions all these "multicultural" novels as the civilization Other of monolinguistic anglophone texts. This elision of difference (a difference the article ironically seeks to celebrate) does not adequately address the sociohistorical specificity of these texts, neither from the standpoint of production nor from that of consumption. I suspect that Dasenbrock's argument does not adequately address the significances of code-switching within Indian, Chinese-American, and Maori cultures. It certainly does not address these significances in relation to Chicana culture.

Bilingualism within Chicana social discourse is a much-studied and complex issue.[3] Dasenbrock does not deal with how these various novels intervene in a politics of representation implicit in the evocation of "minority" linguistic patterns. One reason these texts deploy bilingual strategies is because the communities from which they draw their discourses employ bilingual speech. At one level, these texts affirm and validate the practices they describe. The power of representation as an aggressively affirmative form of self-identification does not enter into Dasenbrock's argument. However, we know that these texts are mediated representations that more than replicate particular sociopolitical experiences. As such, the use of bilingualism – more precisely interlingualism – becomes even more complicated.[4] What role does code-switching play as a narrative or poetic strategy? What function does an interlingual text seek for itself within particular systems of symbolic exchange? Why employ code-switching to "thicken" or make difficult an aesthetic text when other linguistic strategies can be used for the same purpose?

The polyglossic within Chicano texts functions to establish a particular relationship with the reader. Through its processes of inclusion and exclusion, the interlingual Chicano text defines its readership. Although this may provide an exclusionist feeling, the more pressing issue has to do with representational power. The literary texts reconstruct a voice, portray a community, enact a union between linguistically apt readers. This does not mean that any reader proficient in Spanish immediately gains access to interlingual texts. The use of caló, the re-creation of regional dialects, the specificity of speech-acts that occur within the borderlands of Chicano social networks all are matrices that form the hermeneutic grids of a text, which inflect a range of Chicano poetic expression. Familiarity with and recognition of speech patterns forms one of the draws and requirements of comprehension within Chicano poetic discourse.

Let us not forget, however, that these re-creations exclude Chicana readers as well. While continued immigration brings fresh voices reinforcing the Spanish language, second and third generation Chicanas lose fluency and proficiency in their "mother tongue."[5] Interlingualism both affirms and denies a communitarian identity. Its function is to construct an imaginary community that transcends geography and time, that employs the specificity of linguistic acts to weave the image of community through the discursive warp of localized speech-acts. It celebrates the local while enabling a transcendent sense of community removed from that locale. The cultural nationalism of Aztlán returns with a vengeance, fully textualized within the interlinguistic codes employed by poetic texts. The texts reveal a tension between presentation and creation, between community voice and singular poetic creation, between invocation and evocation of speech. The poetic voice becomes both speaker for and speaker about the community, both within and without its social bonds.

Representing portraits of a community and simultaneously constructing that community, the Chicana poet deploys a multilingualism that operates within a realm of social drama. The text serves to form a liminal stage that highlights processes of becoming. The interlingualism forms an Other language that is always on the verge of being but which does not become. The tension between the public voice and the private poet creates a position of rupture that straddles but does not settle into premodern or postmodern modes of cultural production. The interstitial drama plays itself out in the use of transgeneric codes that resonate with the interlingualism of some Chicana poetry. The use of diverse poetic genres – the lyric, the epic, the dramatic, the ballad – are all available to a poetry that has no home but lives perpetually in the borderlands of a postmodern contemporaneity. The deployment of pastiche – not as a Jamesonian blank parody, but as a strategy of marginal survival – makes for an empowering move within the realm of the aesthetically available.[6]

The construction and deployment of linguistic codes within Chicana poetry forms a type of mestizaje in which a third language, a third possibility, a "line of flight" offers possibilities beyond simple dualisms. As Alarcón's poem indicates, Chicana culture constructs itself out of the consciousness that it arises from numerous origins. The interstitial quality of the linguistic mestizaje manifests itself in the continual crossing – of language, of voice, of genre – which moves toward the ritualistically liminal. The textualization of mestizaje becomes a condition of Chicana cultural expression that most clearly manifests the connections between history, text, self, community.

Minority Discourse: Deleuze and Guattari

The discussion through the previous chapters has motioned toward Gilles Deleuze and Félix Guattari's concept of minor literature. It may at this point be fruitful to re-collect some of the fragmentary comments made about minority discourse. Their analysis of Franz Kafka's description of "minor" literature highlights three main features: 1) a minor literature employs a language suitable for "strange and minor uses" because of its high coefficient of deterritorialization; 2) this literature has an immediate social and political function; and 3) it fosters collective rather than individual utterances (1975: 16–18).

The critical reception of Chicano literature has made it amply clear that culture has served a most important social and political function within the Chicano community and that, as a result, its utterances mark a collective position. For example, Carlota Cárdenas de Dwyer has noted that

> the narratives of [Tomás Rivera and Rolando Hinojosa] place increasing emphasis upon the regional and ethnic culture of the characters. . . . Paradoxically, the words of all these writers suggest that by shifting the focus from themselves to the region from which they came and to the people who inhabit the locale, the authors may find the locus of selfhood. (1981: 46)

The writer seeks out the voice of the collective, finds within the local and communal "the" locus of self-identification. Similarly, José David Saldívar in "Towards a Chicano Poetics" argues that the corrido tradition from which a good deal of Chicano poetry derives works toward the integration between self and collectivity:

> The nature of the corrido as form and content is social and revolutionary, drawing heavily on the deepest levels of what Fredric Jameson has called "the political unconscious," defining relationships between temporalities and ultimates. The corrido is sung by Chicanos who live throughout the Southwestern United States. The corrido's function is to reconcile individual experience into a collective identity. (1986: 12)

Although the collective and political nature of Chicano poetic expression has been noted by numerous writers and critics, what of the "high coefficient" of deterritorialization championed by Deleuze and Guattari? Linguistic deterritorialization is marked by an expression that "must break forms, encourage ruptures and new sproutings. When a form is broken, one must reconstruct the content that will necessarily be part of a rupture in the order of things" (1975: 28).[7] Chapter 2 has already served to highlight the process of simultaneous erasure and connection involved in the cultural self-definition of the Chicano. The deterritorializations of the self implicit in migration – the nomadic subject becoming always other – highlight the contradictory position of all subjects in flight. These subjects do not escape the structures or discourses that historically, culturally, socially, and economically bind them within particular territorializations. The systems of exchange and production continue. But migration allows another way of being, a line of flight along the faultlines of structures, modes that move along lines of neither/nor rather than either/or. This conceptualization – a theoretical and poststructural vision of historical and economic marginality – underscores the issues under scrutiny in relation to contemporary Chicano literary production. It ruptures the order of things.

This does not mean that Chicano literary criticism should embrace the theoretical project offered by Deleuze and Guattari. Nor does it mean that their perceptions somehow explain and validate Chicano culture. Quite the opposite. Chicano cultural production demands a reformulation of their theory. But to more clearly explain this observation, I need to make a detour through literature.

Kafka represents the closest Deleuze and Guattari come to articulating a sustained literary analysis. It also represents the most historically specific analysis they offer: "The breakdown and fall of the [Hapsburg] empire increases the crisis, accentuates everywhere movements of deterritorialization, and invites all sorts of complex reterritorializations – archaic, mythic, or symbolist" (1975: 24). Kafka, engaging in a process of deterritorialization, employs Prague German to write his literary texts.[8] In this "foreign" tongue, Kafka strikes in a minor key and makes the arid language "vibrate with a new intensity" (1975: 19). Clearly the linguistic strategies and imperatives behind an early twentieth-century Jewish writer in Czechoslovakia cannot be taken as a model for late twentieth-century Chicano poets in the borderlands of postmodern America. It is useful, however, to form a dialogue between these places and times. Moreover, it may be useful to consider the implications of the analysis offered by Deleuze and Guattari.

"How many people today live in a language that is not their own? Or no longer, or not yet, even know their own and know poorly the major language that they are forced to serve?" they ask. With this question as backdrop, I pose another: What is the Chicano language? Although numerous literary attempts have been made to define and reflect Chicano discourse – one thinks of Alurista, of course, of José Montoya, even of Jimmy Santiago Baca – where will these linguistic deterritorializations end? The condition of a minority language, that which is not yet and is not yet one's own, "is the problem of the immigrants, and especially of their children, the problem of minorities, the problem of a minor literature" (1975: 19). This interstitial condition, where one stands between a potentially liberating language not yet born and a territorializing language to which one owes servitude, may be thought to represent the condition of the Chicano. On the one hand, one might revert to an adoption of the master's language. On the other, one might revert to a language of origins, be it a reification of indigenous languages or (less commonly) a reversion to "pure" Spanish. More often the language is an Other language, a third language, one which the poetry seeks to record and create.

La Lengua Mestiza: Alurista and Tafolla

This mestizaje of language does not fully represent a pure alterity, however, as Deleuze and Guattari would seem to want to suggest. Whether it was true of the German Kafka employed or not, the English with which Chicana poets speak represents less a "paper" or "official" language (though it does that too) than a dominant one. The stratification implied in the differentiation between a Prague German and a paper German does not hold up – despite assertions otherwise – in the case of minority languages within the United States.[9] The condition of language must be scrutinized through a historical lens. For Mexicans, English is the language of a foreigner and an invader. For Chicanas, English often remains the "foreign" language of powerful and rich possibilities. We have seen Lorna Dee Cervantes in "Poem for the Young White Man . . ." describe her "stumbling mind" and her "'excuse me' tongue" which accompanies "the feeling of not being good enough." This aversion to the language, the dynamic of control, historical consciousness, and connection to dispossession reinforces a series of powerful discourses that surround the English tongue.

Cordelia Candelaria, for example, provides a simple but useful example in her analysis of Alurista's poem "address" (1971). The poem represents an exchange between an English-speaking bureaucrat and a Pedro Ortega who responds only in Spanish:

address
occupation
age
marital status
–perdone . . .
yo me llamo pedro
. . . .
zip code
i. d. number
classification
–perdone mi padre era
el señor ortega
(a veces don josé)
race

Candelaria argues that the exchange demonstrates "the sterile impersonality of Yankee culture in its dominance over ethnic minorities. Pedro Ortega, a metonym for all colonized raza, wishes to identify by reference to his name, his father, and his father's respectability. But his inquisitor perceives him solely in terms of external variables associated with an easily categorized, superficial *identification*" (1988: 93).[10] Interestingly, the title of the poem plays a pun. While it refers (as all the poems in *Floricanto* do) to the first line of the poem, it also suggests the speech-act of address. Ironically, no addressing occurs in the poem. Each voice speaks across rather than to the other, the unequal power dynamic concretized within the distinct linguistic utterances. Here language stratifies.

One register of code-switching within Chicana poetic discourse does serve – as Deleuze and Guattari suggest – as a line of flight, an escape toward a something else neither English nor Spanish. This stand problematizes somewhat the view about Chicana literature articulated by Francisco Lomelí: "We are dealing with a literature within a dominant culture, whose posture is to make a stand against what the latter dictates, and to reach for 'poetic autonomy' by resorting to two languages (and their variants) at will, and to their respective emotional substances" (1984: 106). The linguistic binary implicit in Lomelí's position – Spanish and English and their variants – denies the embrace of difference which interlingualism suggests. By accepting the otherness thrust upon us by dominant society, Chicanas do indeed "make a stand against what the latter dictates." This occurs in a way more thorough and subversive than simple opposition. As George Yúdice notes of *I, Rigoberta Menchú:* "Menchú describes the abject contempt and rejection that Indians experience and describes the practices by which they attempt to overcome these evils, not by separation, but by the acceptance of otherness. It is this otherness that opens them to the world; to survive, their very definition of identity must incorporate new elements" (1989: 226). Neither separate nor subsumed, the Chicana similarly survives by incorporating new elements into the definition of identity. The deployment of another language – an inter-language – manifests for the Chicana this other incorporating identity.

Carmen Tafolla's poem "La Isabela de Guadalupe y el Apache Mío Cid" (1985) conveys the sense of power and growth possible through this mestizaje of language and acknowledgment of an Other self. The persona of the poem – the speaker La Isabela de Guadalupe and the addressee El Apache Mío Cid – indicate immediately the conflation of subjectivities implicit in an identity of mestizaje. The name Isabela suggests the Queen of Castile who financed Christopher Columbus's journey to the New World. Guadalupe makes reference to the national Virgin of Mexico, herself a conflation of Catholic iconography and indigenous religious belief. The Apache, of course, refers to the indigenous tribe of nomadic warriors whose history straddles the borderlands between the United States and Mexico. Mío Cid evokes the legendary Spanish warrior whose exploits form the content of the Spanish national epic *El Cid*.

The mestizaje invoked by the appeal to cross-cultural iconography echoes in the temporal crossing undertaken by the poem. It opens with a question that will resound toward the end: "I, as an India, / And you, as a Spaniard, / How can we ever make love?" This problem informs the meaning of the poem. It also evokes the moment of contact and conquest between the Old and New Worlds. This passage back into time proves unstable. Later the speaker poses another pointed question: "Will we have to meet between the day and night, / enlazados, escondidos, entejidos en amor, / with two masks and jet-way tickets labeled 'Smith'?" The poem evokes but does not situate itself firmly within a single temporal moment. The contemporary condition of a love that has the lovers "bound, hidden, woven" blends with the historical, emerges from the historical, situates itself against the historical. Out of history, the speaker weaves together the dilemma of the poem.

These tropes of weaving and interstitiality make themselves explicit in the above passage. Isabel de Guadalupe wants to know if the lovers will have to meet between the nocturnal and diurnal, at the twilight that signals both the subterfuge and the liminality implicit in their journey. The passage through the jetway – into a flight toward something other – is marked by a procession of disguises: the masks, the tickets labelled "Smith." This move through is further complicated by the binding implied in the description of their relationship as "tied, hidden, woven in love." The alliteration of "enlanzados, escondidos, entejidos en amor" moves through the line just as the two lovers move disguised down the jetway toward some other future.

The primary tension of the poem manifests itself in the very different worlds with which the speaker and the lover identify:

I, by mecate tied
    to a red dirt floor
    y una casucha de adobe
    en las montañas de cool morning
    and the damp of the wet swept floor.
Y tú, with your fine-worked chains
    Tied from armor to iron post.
    White stallions and engraved gateways
    And a castle of hot night,
    Fine tablecloth, and chandelier etiquette.

These positions preclude union. The gap implied by the distinct indigenous elements – she tied to the dirt floor, a house of adobe in the mountains of cool morning; he tied to iron, to castles, to finery and manners – works to physically separate Isabela from Mío Cid. The distance is underscored by the speaker's use of "casucha" – a colloquial expression for house – which signals her ties to the local and regional.

The disjuncture between the two continues as the speaker repositions the "I" who likes to walk barefoot and the "you" who is embroidered in gold thread: "I, que me gusta andar descalza, / y tú, bordado en hilos de oro / How can we ever make love?" This leads to a meditation on the possibility of union, on the potential positioning of self necessary to a successful union. The speaker asks: "Will I have to crawl inside your armor?" Similarly, "Will you have to paint your feet with dirt?" The absurdity of assuming the binary position, of becoming the other, is underscored by the painting of the feet and the retreat to the oxymoronic womblike armor into which Isabela thinks of crawling. The absurdity is underscored by the interlingual pun between "armor" which prevents the "amor," the speaker's desire.[11] These possibilities vanquished, the speaker turns to the liminal image of the jet-way and traveling incognito.

The resolution in the poem emerges from questioning the notion that these two positions actually represent polarities – evoked by the mecate and chain, the red dirt floor and chandelier. The speaker commands the auditor to tell her: "¿am I really the criolla en manta? / ¿Are you really the apache in armor? / Who did this for us already?" The subject positions that delimit the agency of the poem's personae come under scrutiny. The speaker demands to know the authority behind the binaries she and her lover occupy. She has become the criolla en manta, the creole covered in coarse cloth. The term "criolla" also carries with it a sense of the domestic or native. It thus evokes either an individual of direct European descent or, colloquially, a native of the Americas. The slipperiness of the interlingual signs here serves to signal a move further into unfixed signification.

The speaker repeats the opening lines of the poem: "I, as an India, / And you, as a Spaniard, / How can we ever make love?" The problematic that opens the poem – how can diverse subjectivities implying binary positions come together in love and fulfillment – leads into a flurry of incomplete questions interrogating subject positions:

> I as an India and?
> – you as campesino and?
> – I as la reina and?
> – You as indito and?
> – Yo la azteca and?
> – Tú el tolteca and?
> – Yo la poblana y?
> – Tú Mío Cid y?
> – Yo la mora y?
> – Tú el judío y?
> – Nosotros la gente y
>   nosotros
>   la gente
>   y . . .
>   Amamos.

The resolution into the phrase "we love" results from the turns through the various subjectivities that could comprise their identities. From queen to peasant, indian tribe, epic hero, Moor, Jew – the poem passes through the same national, religious, cultural components of mestizaje evoked by Francisco Alarcón's poem "Mestizo." Here, after moving from interlingualism toward monolingual Spanish, Tafolla's poem resolves into the self-identification as "we the people and / we / the people / and. . . ." The invocation of the modern democratic ideal – a quotation from the Preamble to the U.S. Constitution – is colored and consequently transformed by the fact that it is articulated in Spanish. The move toward mono- rather than interlingual expression thus does not signal a retreat into an unexamined nativism. It rather reinforces the sense of appropriation and movement implicit in mestizaje. The phrase "la gente" also evokes a populist sentiment – la gente del pueblo – that conveys in Spanish a much stronger sense of community and unity than the phrase "we the people" would imply. The reclamation of "we the people" – for we the people who speak Spanish – conveys the empowerment of mestizaje, which allows a breakdown of rigid subject positions. Tafolla's poem ends hopefully with "Amamos" as a verb of connection and creation – desire (momentarily at least) fulfilled between speaker and addressee.

Mestizaje marks the poem: the "and . . . and . . . and . . ." construction that draws us tantalizingly toward love, the interlingualism that puns on words like "amor" and "armor," the conflation and clash of cultural iconography. The text signals the aleatory movements possible, the incessant acts of reclamation enabled, through the articulation of cultural mestizaje. The reclamation and flight, the resistance to binaries explicitly addressed in the poem, all suggest that mestizaje involves a process of becoming. Deleuze and Guattari say, "The act of becoming is a capturing, a possession, a plus-value, but never a reproduction or an imitation" (1975: 13). The endless plus value of "and . . . and . . . and . . ." bespeaks a refusal to make a choice between the either/or. In this sense, the deleuzeguattarian anti-oedipal stance does resonate within the dynamic Chicano production of culture.

However, it must be emphasized that this resonance does not mean that Chicano cultural production finds its affirmation only when French theoretical positions validate it. On the contrary, these theoretical positions fall short of enunciating fully the variety of movements available through cultural mestizaje. Discussing minor literature, Deleuze and Guattari argue for the complete deterritorialization implicit in the becoming-animal represented in the stories of Kafka:

> To become animal is to participate in movement, to stake out the path of escape in all its positivity, to cross a threshold, to reach a continuum of intensities that are valuable only in themselves, to find a world of pure intensities where all forms come undone, as do all the significations, signifier, and signifieds, to the benefit of an unformed matter of deterritorialized flux, of nonsignifying signs. (1975: 13)

This vision of pure alterity and unimpeded flight associated with minor literature fails.

Although the vision of a literature that moves incessantly toward the nonsymbolic and semiotic (to employ Kristevan terminology) or toward the anti-oedipal and nomadic (to employ deleuzeguattarian phrases) proves appealing on a theoretical level, it leaves behind the all-too-real conditions of confinement and delimitation suffered by the historically configured marginal. The "minor" as a key struck by Deleuze and Guattari cannot exist without the "minority" that lives and breathes the territorializations that its culture speaks against. The vision of pure alterity posited by poststructural thought fails precisely because it constructs an image of pure alterity. The margin has become apotheosized.

George Yúdice has very forcefully argued against the deification of marginality as a liberating force. He notes:

> "Marginality" is a concept that straddles modernity and postmodernity; it is operative in pluralist utopias and radical heterotopias, following a logic of exclusion in the former and a tactic of singularity in the latter. Now, because it is central to both modes of thought, its relevance to action – i.e., politics, which operates according to different, even contradictory logics – may become confused. On the one hand, liberal pluralism calls for the incorporation of the "marginal" into a framework that necessarily co-opts it. . . ; the postmodern tactician, on the other hand, often uses the "marginal" to make a case for his or her own subversive potential. . . . In both examples the concept is inflated to such proportions that it loses its critical edge, its contribution to concrete struggles against oppression and domination. (1989: 214–15)

The incorporation of marginality as either benign pluralism or reified alterity serves the same purpose: to erase, distort or rewrite the historical, cultural, and social specificity of that margin. That is, the "recuperation" of the marginal by both "liberal" and "radical" ideologies works against the interests of an ethics of survival. This ethics, Yúdice goes on to explain, involves a "'self-forming activity,' in which the 'self' is 'practice' in solidarity with others struggling for survival" (1989: 229). Self-identity takes on an aura of responsibility when it must enact a solidarity with others. This process opens and incorporates, enables a process of self-identity that involves an "and . . . and . . . and. . . ."

Thus the reification or pluralization of marginality precludes an ethical position. These strategies simply appropriate and remarginalize the oppressed subjects that form the sociohistorical margin. Deleuze and Guattari, for all the usefulness (and arcane expression) of their arguments, construct a "minority" position that reifies the margin. The presence of subjects within the margin demands a more critical use of marginality. Subjective and moral dimensions within the margin must find their expression through the process of identity-formation. Without a doubt, this has been the function of a great deal of Chicano poetry and its criticism. Yúdice argues that this "formation of consciousness-conscience" is denied the marginal within the logic of poststructural thought:

> Until recently, the "postmodern" has neglected "marginals" – defined in relation to oppression – either because their experience is not "modern" in the elitist sense of the European avant-garde or because . . . their identity is, it is argued, "fixed" in resistance to the power of domination. It would be equally problematic, however, to claim the "postmodernity" of the oppressed and subaltern, for that maneuver might serve to theorize the futility of a politics of empowerment. The attacks by certain poststructuralist intellectuals on a feminist empowerment respond to this double bind of the "marginal," who . . . is chastised for seeking the material conditions (equal rights, equal pay, institutional recognition, etc.) that the elites already enjoy. The very attack on the notion of identity is problematic in this respect, for identity is a major weapon in the struggles of the oppressed. (1989: 221)

The point Yúdice makes is extremely important to the relationship between historically marginal constituencies like Chicanos and the "postmodern." The reality is – as I have tried to indicate throughout this study – that much of poststructural thought has cast the marginal further into the margins through dehistoricized celebration and disempowering reification. This apotheosis of the marginal that propels it beyond the realm of the worldly cuts the ground out from any meaningful engagement with all the social, political, economic, and cultural issues that can enable the fulfilment of agency. It is small wonder, indeed, that Chicano and other multicultural critics distance themselves and their work from the rarefied airs of contemporary theoretical contemplation. Yúdice's argument makes a strong case.

It is equally important, however, to take exception with the implications of the above passage. For in essence, the point one can draw from refusing engagement between the "postmodern" and the "marginal" is another form of exclusion. Historical marginals have and should enter and supplement the discussions that map contemporary cultural production. This resistance to exclusion will ensure that the discussions proceed on other terms.

What problems I find with Yúdice's observation lie in a few terms: "until recently," "postmodern," and "identity." One hopes that the "recent" incursion by Gayatri Spivak, bell hooks, and Wahneema Lubiano, among others, into postmodern enemy territory serves to break down the walls (within academic–cultural institutions) between the politically engagé multicultural critic and contemporary cultural theory. The issue is not so much that the postmodern has neglected the marginal – which it has – but that the margins refuse to permit that negligence to continue. More to the point, Yúdice's conflation of the term "postmodern" with "poststructural" makes for an easy elision, but implies a monolithic and (always already) confirmed identification of postmodernism. The "marginal" who seeks space and identity within the multicultural dynamics of a contemporary North American culture – as I argue in Chapter 5 – needs to crash the pomo party. The insistence of inclusion and difference challenges notions of the postmodern and highlights the highly discontinuous and textured terrain of contemporary cultural production. In this same spirit, the construction of identity – personal, cultural, communal – against a postmodern terrain becomes the highly fluid and inclusive project that Yúdice implicitly values in his affirmation of Rigoberta Menchú's ethics of survival. As I have sought to demonstrate, Chicano culture and politics have moved to expand identity, reconfigure ways of "performing the self" in order to reclaim agency, and confirm solidarity with others struggling to survive. Part of this performance includes the construction of a Chicano poetic language that foregrounds its minority position. In this respect, although its practice is not precisely a homology, it does find resonances in French poststructural considerations of literature.

Vernacularization: Tafolla and Baca

The construction of an empowered identity means including and maneuvering the variety of terrains Chicana subjects must cross. This discontinuous terrain – formed by a history of exclusion and dispossession – is imagined and transformed by Chicana cultural products. Chicana poetry, for one, has sought to reimagine notions of self and place, of self and political agency, of self and tradition. Reconfiguring personal and community identities has required a reconfiguration of language. The deployment of the various vernaculars current in Chicana communities by Chicana poetic texts connects on an aesthetic level – through the incorporation of "standard" forms of English and Spanish, mexicanismos, slang and working class English, caló, regional Mexican Spanish, chicanismos, regional Chicano Spanish, indianismos – the processes of deterritorialization and reterritorialization evident on a socioeconomic and political level within Chicana communities. This use of terminology and analysis deriving from Deleuze and Guattari in the employ of Chicana literary criticism is not new. The French critic Marcienne Rocard, for one, has already made explicit the connection between Chicana literature and the deleuzeguattarian notion of "minor" literature.

Rocard asserts, "The mode of expression the minority writer resorts to in order to assert himself is 'deterritorialized' vis-à-vis the major language, it bears the mark of his irreducible distance from the 'territory' on which he has elected or been forced to live" (1986: 33). From Rocard's perspective, the deterritorialization marks the historical condition of dispossession and exclusion suffered by minority writers. This condition finds reflection in the language of Chicana poetry. Linguistic deterritorializations flow against the rigid stratification of systemic order – an act that speaks not just as an aesthetic act of rebellion but which moves against the processes of dispossession suffered by Chicanas. The marginalization and exclusion that Chicanas endure is countered by the literary production. Rocard thus argues that the Chicana "must become visible but his visibility can no longer be achieved through the traditional medium of the dominant language, since speaking the latter means assuming an alien culture and, to a certain extent, adhering to an ideology responsible for his own alienation" (1986: 35). Linguistic deterritorialization becomes an ideological resistance. The Chicana writer, according to Rocard, "resents the supremacy of the English language and chooses to keep his distance from it" (1986: 33). More than resent, the Chicana transforms the positions of power implicit in the choice of linguistic expression. Language becomes a marker of displacement and reclamation, a marker of self-identity and self-empowerment. It is also a way of manifesting history with every word. The presence of Spanish is a presence through history of discrimination and exploitation. Every Spanish word represents a refusal to capitulate to English ethnocentricity. Thus, "Writing in his vernacular is, for the minority writer, one way to do away with the supremacy of the English words" (1986: 36).

The return to a vernacular, to a mother tongue, does not represent the only form of refusal. The process of deterritorialization, the movement along the line of flight, means the search for another possibility. Thus Chicano poetry, beyond simply reclaiming Spanish, "consists in using the dominant language while perverting it by undermining, dismantling, exploding it" (1986: 36). The "perversion" of English is the condition of the marginal writing with the master's language. The perversion becomes a writing against the grain of oppression, against mastery – a counterdiscourse. Some skeptics might argue that this refusal of mastery masks the fact that Chicano writers are incapable of mastery. However, this position rests on a dream of universal identity. The mastery of the English language is minor compared to the multiplicity and richness of the multiple linguistic codes present in the margin. Thus the question of monolingual mastery, of control, of command becomes in the margin an empty question. The game, as Rocard points out, involves undermining, dismantling, exploding monolingual mastery by counterpoising it to the multiple linguistic codes that cross in the margin.

The use of caló – evidenced in a poem like Montoya's "El Louie" – represents one form of deterritorialization that does not so much seek to dissolve poetic form as to interfere in a politics of representation. In several poems – both those written early and those written late in the movements of Chicano poetry – caló becomes a form of affirmative self-representation. Poetry employing caló serves to valorize a particular sociohistorical condition, a constituency, a community generally marginalized by dominant cultural representations. "El Louie" conveys the particularity of the pachuco experience: the types of movies that offered role models, the names of specific towns and streets that formed the pachuco's terrain, the historical events like the Korean War that influenced the attitude of the pachuco. However, it does not link the use of caló – the formal qualities of the text – with the socioeconomic tensions evoked by the text. Caló and regional speech as a form of representation "continually returned to the lived speech act to capture in print the oral quality of Chicano Spanish and English vernaculars" (Calderón 1990: 218). Here Calderón argues that the Chicano poet still seeks public forms of expression. The use of caló represents a return to origins, a valorization (or critique) of a socioeconomic reality outside the text. As Calderón's remarks indicate, "El Louie" (unlike later uses of caló within poetic expression) does not foreground the disjuncture between the orality involved in public performance and the capturing in print of "the oral quality of Chicano Spanish and English vernaculars." A tension remains between written and oral expressions in the modes of both production and reception.

Carmen Tafolla's "Los Corts (5 voices)" provides an excellent example of this tension as it seeks to echo different voices living in the projects of San Antonio, Texas. The poem is comprised of five monologues spoken by La Madre, El Chamaquito, La Pachuquita, The Dropout, and La Viejita. The use of the diminutive to describe the little kid, the little Pachuca, and the little old lady indicates the gentle tone of the poem. This is an attempt to present in poetic form the human faces living in the poverty of the Southwest. The structure of the poem manifests the notion of political or demographic representation (*Vertreten*) in addition to the sense of artistic representation (*Darstellen*). Each voice is meant to represent a different facet of "Los Corts."

The first section speaks from the point of view of a mother who daydreams about her younger life. She remembers that she used to love the hot afternoons "Porque podía ir a buscar los gatos del barrio dormiditos en sus rincones." Now, it is her daughter instead of she who goes out looking for the neighborhood tomcats "asleep in their corners." She herself feels trapped in this afternoon heat, suffocating "de tanto calor que hace en este cuartito." The heat in her "little room" closes in on the speaker. The poem ends with the mother thinking about how her body "se me va desbaratando cada día" – is falling apart on her – and that she is made up of nothing but sweat and suffering. The baby wakens her out of her reverie and reminds her that she must get to welfare the following day. This first section does not explicitly employ the caló of the pachuco. It does, however, attempt to capture the flavor of the local idiom through its repeated use of diminutives. The language also reflects a generational difference. Either the mother speaking has, with her responsibilities and age, grown away from the street culture in which caló is spoken, or she may have immigrated to San Antonio later in life when the use of caló would have been foreign to her. In either case, the use of the language helps underscore the generational distance between this speaker and those that follow.

El Chamaquito begins his monologue with the exuberant "¡Jiiiii-jo! ¡Me jayé un daime! / ¡Ta hueno eso!" His excitement at finding a dime becomes entangled in a socioeconomic dynamic. His excitement over his good luck is due mainly to the fact he can show "esa vieja mala a la tiendita / que siempre me ta regañando" that he does have money. When the old lady in the store sees his dime, she will stop scolding him for eyeing all the cheap toys instead of buying one. The use of caló that opens this section – "¡Me jayé un daime!" means "I found a dime" – indicates that linguistic codes are linked to particular socioeconomic standings.[12] The use of caló also indicates the processes of linguistic deterritorialization and reterritorialization: caló constructs linguistic codes that claim English words like "dime" but exclude non-caló speakers from understanding them.

This process of inclusion–exclusion is brought home by the third section of the poem, in which La Pachuquita talks about la Silvia, who is after el Larry, who, in turn, is after the speaker of the poem, la Dot. Dot describes the object of her desire, who the other day was dressed to the nines: "traíba esa camisa azulita, con el collar p'arriba así, / y se veía su medallón en el chest, / y como siempre los zapatos shainados y el white hanky – / ¡ta bien pacito!" The poem attempts to reflect the specificity of these speech acts through the regional use of "traíba" for "traía," the dialect-inflected "p'arriba," the code-switching to English for "chest" and "white," the use of the caló adjective "shainados" for shined, the expression "pacito" which derives from "padrecito," a colloquial adjective of affirmation.

The use of inflection occurs in the fourth section, a monologue by a boy who tries to explain why he is dropping out of school. He argues that he won't return to school because he is made to feel stupid, he feels persecuted, he feels unjustly accused. All these excuses give way in the final parenthetical sentence "(And I *wasn't* spikking Spenish. / I *wasn't!!*)" The poem attempts to reproduce the regional accents of the community. It also conveys the significance and resistant quality of language – and its representation. The boy insists upon his innocence, that he wasn't speaking Spanish at school, an offense punishable by expulsion.

The final section closes with the monologue of La Viejita, who reminisces about her family. She points out a picture of her grandson "cuando fue su gradu-ey-chón de jaiskul." The transliteration serves as a translation of the English phrase "high school graduation." This section of the poem, however, is a monologue given primarily in Spanish. The near-monolingual quality of this portion resonates with the sense of generational difference that opens the poem. The different uses of language, the linguistic textures Tafolla attempts to convey through her text, reentrench these various linguistic codes into specific historical and cultural contexts. The generational differences, the socioeconomic realities, the discrimination against ethnic and linguistic identification, are all conveyed through the deployment of the different linguistic systems within the poem. The representation of these languages serves as a form of valorization, as an articulation of identity inextricably tied to history.

Tafolla's text, as a representative voicing of numerous linguistic codes, foregrounds its role as aesthetic representation. The conjoining of cultural representation (*Darstellen*) and political representation (*Vertreten*) forms a type of resistant response on the aesthetic level to repressive conditions that seek to silence or marginalize those linguistic codes. Tafolla's representation of regional vernaculars underscores the tension between oral and written expression. This in turn underscores the tensions inherent in the historical condition of the community "Los Corts" attempts to represent.

Where the use of vernacular formed an affirmative act of self-definition by early Chicano poets, its inclusion by later poets links language to socioeconomic and political systems that oppress and disempower the communities from which those vernaculars arise. This historicizing serves a counterdiscursive function as it writes through and against dominant and dominating discourses. The appropriations of "dime" to "daime" or "shined" to "shainada" serve as examples whose use does not imply simply finding an "authentic" or "original" voice of complete alterity. These terms represent – as do caló and other regionalisms – the incorporation and deconstruction of dominant discourses. As they are incorporated into the poetic text, they serve a representative function. In this sense their presence is similar to that of those found in "El Louie." However, in "Los Corts" their presence is aggressively textualized. The multiplicity of voices present in the poem underscores its aesthetic and textual qualities. The contrasting voices, the generational differences, the qualities of speech complicate the uses of vernacular, make them more overtly a part of an aesthetic strategy rather than a reflection *qua* validation. This foregrounds the disjuncture between the multivocalic literary text represented by the poem and the multiplicitous oral text represented by the community. Not that this alienates the poem from the community it ostensibly represents. The poem may very well reflect a quality of life in the projects. And it may speak to the constituency it seeks to represent. However, it does foreground a rupture, creating a tension between its own materiality as a text and the community so cruelly bound by the poetically thematized socioeconomic necessity.

This rupture at an aesthetic level between the speakers of the poem and the composing hand conveys the disjuncture evident in the uses of vernaculars. The languages placed in the five speakers' mouths are themselves linked to the socioeconomic impoverishment and exploitation of the community from which they speak. Their words convey something of the bravado conveyed by the speaker of "El Louie." But the sense of affirmation and valorization – however misguided – the speaker feels toward El Louie is missing in Tafolla's poetry. The sense of heroism and grandiose statement are gone. Instead, these later poems reveal the disadvantages these characters suffer and the minor sense of empowerment and affirmation they find in small acts of resistance. Be that as it may, the use of caló and other vernacular forms becomes linked in the poem with the processes of discrimination and disempowerment the poem makes evident.

Language in Tafolla's poem is thus not innocent. It is implicated in a process of systemic discrimination. Their use of language marks the speakers as much as the color of their skin or the clothes on their back. This connection between language and power is made even more explicit in Jimmy Santiago Baca's collection *Martín & Meditations on the South Valley* (1987). Section IX of the *Meditations* becomes an elegy for Eddie who, playing a form of Russian roulette, kills himself. Eddie is described by the speaker of the poem in laudatory terms as "bad little Eddie / [who] treated everybody with respect and honor" (64). The central conflict in Eddie's life was the impossibility of setting himself free, "to know what was beyond the boundaries" he was born into (64). In fights with "other locotes" or "la jura" – the police – Eddie sought a form of transcendence beyond the "boundaries" in which his illiteracy and his "brown skin / and tongue that could not properly pronounce English words" trapped him (66). Eddie, "caught like a seed unable to plant itself" tries through language to move beyond the limitations he feels. Thus the walls of the corner store where he takes his grandmother to buy groceries "were scribbled with black paint / your handwriting and initials, your boundary marker, deadly symbol to other chavos" (65). This graffiti forms "the severe, dark stitches of letters / on the walls / [which] healed your wound at being illiterate" (65).

Language as the thing that keeps Eddie bound also serves to heal his fractured sense of self. The language of the barrio positions Eddie in a place of dispossession and disempowerment. The terms Eddie hears on the street and carefully recorded in the poem – "chale / simón / wacha bro / me importa madre / ni miedo de la muerta / ni de la pinta / ni de la placa" – convey a bravado that belies the helplessness against which Eddie reacts. These words form a language that proves the only defense Eddie has against the limitations imposed on his life. Textualized within the poem, they serve as markers similar to the words Eddie scrawls on the grocery store wall. They are markers, however, that the poetic voice must interpret rather than reflect. The aesthetic representation of these linguistic codes is brought most clearly to the fore as the poem closes with a description of Eddie's voice whispering "in the dust and weeds, / a terrible silence, / not to forget your death" (66).

The speaker assumes three points of view within the poem. As with the above passage, the speaker addresses Eddie directly. In addition to the second person, the poetic voice also speaks about Eddie as a third person. And, briefly, the voice assumes the first person, speaking as Eddie pleading to his community to "Quit giving the wind our grief stricken voices / at cemeteries, / quit letting the sun soak up our blood" (66). This shifting perspective, as with Tafolla's poem, underscores the poem's distance from the constituency it represents. It does not assume one voice, does not work toward the type of simple representation evident in Montoya's poem. It moves more toward the complicated forms of representation manifested by Tafolla's aesthetic text.

The poem makes evident the impossibility of language, represents a language of silence manifested in disempowered quarters. The whispering voice present at the close of the poem, a voice paradoxically speaking the "terrible silence" not to forget Eddie's death, makes manifest the complex and contradictory position of language for both artist and community. Language within the community serves as a boundary that precludes a becoming-other and a form of resistance that heals something of the rancor due to oppression and exclusion. Language simultaneously destroys and recuperates. The representation of this process within the poetic texts suggests that poetic language likewise destroys and recuperates. The poem serves to represent a disempowered constituency, to give voice (like Montoya's "El Louie") to experiences made marginal by dominant social discourse. It does so only by distancing itself from that constituency. Like Tafolla's poem, the text is not from the community – as an oral form like a corrido or a public recital might be – but speaks through the alienated form of written expression to convey a sense of the community. The poem thus precludes its own illusory processes of becoming-other, of being the voice of the community. Instead, it positions itself outside, manifests its own constructed quality, makes manifest its own materiality as a written text, not a form of oral expression.

The inclusion of caló and other vernacular forms in Chicano poetic texts has come to represent a very complex and intricate strategy. The use of the vernacular in Chicano poetry has clearly been an attempt to make present a silenced voice. At this level, the inclusion of vernacular speech valorizes that speech through its representation. The inclusion of the vernacular – the spoken form of expression, the "authentic" voice of the barrio – places Chicano poetic expression in a contradictory position. While it attempts to move toward the community by replicating the speech of the community, it simultaneously distances itself by textualizing the spoken word. The tension between these modes of expression serve, in turn, to underscore tensions evident in other realms associated with language. The rupture inherent in oral/written expression marks a tension evident in vernacular/socioeconomic conditions. The use of vernacular expressions marks processes of discrimination and disempowerment on a social level – Eddie's illiteracy, the drop-out's use of Spanish – that plagues the communities that use these vernaculars.

The recuperation of the vernacular within poetic texts comes to represent not simply the "reality" of the community. The poem becomes no more nor less "authentically Chicano" by attempting to accurately reflect actual speech-acts.[13] Instead of authenticity, the poem evokes the social and political situations in which language forms a marker. The incorporation of these vernaculars does not merely serve to "represent" (politically/aesthetically) a community. It serves to scrutinize the processes of discrimination and dispossession the community suffers. The language manifests at an aesthetic level tensions and ruptures, becomes a part of a culturally resistant strategy, deterritorializes processes of social order. The language itself becomes a counterdiscourse.

Interstitial/Interlingual: Anzaldúa, Vigil, Rodriguez

The most aggressive form of dismantling social order can be found in the interlingualism employed by numerous Chicana poets. Certainly, as has been pointed out many times, the work of Alurista works toward a radical type of interlingualism in which the blending and punning between English and Spanish represents a profound linguistic deterritorialization. The experimentation of his poetry represents a formal interest in breaking down linguistic codes as an aesthetic challenge. Alurista himself suggests that this linguistic deterritorialization serves to delimit the audience for his poetry. The interlingualism of his poetry makes it accessible to very specific communities: "my responsibility is to communicate with my people; that is what interests me the most, what is most important to me. . . . I am interested in communicating first with our people, second with our Central and Latin American brothers and sisters, and third, and last of all, with the North American crowd, with the English-speaking crowd" (Bruce-Novoa 1980: 281). Alurista's statement suggests that his poetry speaks somehow more directly to Chicanas (presuming their proficiency in Spanish is equal to that in English), only secondarily to Latin Americans, and least to English-speaking North Americans.

This comment does not adequately reflect the interlingual nature of his poetry. Alurista's poetry requires a fairly elaborate knowledge of both English and Spanish to be comprehensible. It certainly delimits its audience and expands one's "horizon of expectation" (to invoke reader response theory), so that the repertoire of the reader required by the text expands exponentially. Readers must be functionally literate in two linguistic systems in order to make sense of Alurista's work. That it requires this literacy does not mean that it speaks directly to any one constituency, however. There are many Chicanas who do not know enough Spanish to make Alurista's poetry intelligible. And these numbers will grow. However, the type of interlingualism invoked by Alurista's poetry works well to construct a deterritorialized written expression. The poetry constructs another expression, a third expression made up of interpenetrating and fluid linguistic codes playing off and against one another.

The type of interlingualism deployed by Alurista's poetry resonates throughout contemporary Chicano poetry. This fact serves, of course, to yet delimit the audiences of this poetry. Nevertheless, the persistent use of interlingualism constructs a radical scrutiny of aesthetic representation and cultural identification. In varying degrees and to various ends, the use of interlingualism remains present in contemporary Chicano poetry. At times, its use is modified by the inclusion of a glossary to help monolingual readers understand the content of the poetry – Jimmy Santiago Baca's collections with New Directions and Luis Rodríguez's work for Curbstone Press both employ glossaries to facilitate the poetry. In both cases, the use of interlingual techniques is minimal and the poems can be adequately glossed. Other writers work primarily in Spanish with the inclusion of an occasional English word – some of the work by Tino Villanueva and Elias Elizondo represent this current. The use of a glossary cannot provide an adequate "explanation" of the poetry.

Producing poetic texts predominantly in either Spanish or English, Gloria Anzaldúa maintains certain linguistic divisions in her aesthetic texts. Her predeliction in poetry for one language over another proves interesting given the extensive code-switching Anzaldúa's prose employs.[14] In her book *Borderlands/La Frontera,* Anzaldúa does compose one poem that uses code-switching as a means of marking a socioeconomic realm. *"Sus plumas el viento,"* dedicated to Anzaldúa's mother, Amalia, describes the hard physical conditions that have served to bind the subject of the poem. The mother figure in the poem suffers the physical torment of labor in the agricultural fields of Texas. The use of Spanish, italicized in the poem, signals the hardship of these conditions: the *"matas de maíz,"* the *"manos hinchadas, quebradas,"* the *"sudor de sobacos chorriando."* These terms, inmixed with a primarily English discourse, serve to demarcate the world of the cornfield comprised of swollen and broken hands, made up of beating sun and dripping sweat. English is also used to describe this world of exploitation:

> *Ayer entre las matas de maíz*
> she had stumbled upon them:
> Pepita on her back
> grimacing to the sky,
> the anglo buzzing around her like a mosquito,
> landing on her, digging in, sucking.

The use of English moves the narrative forward while the Spanish marks the specificity of locality: "yesterday between the stalks of corn." The locale described by the Spanish phrase is one of hardship and manual labor. The world of agricultural labor becomes disrupted by the use of English, which makes the vision of violation manifest.

Marking the delimiting world of physical labor, Spanish also marks those points where the dream of something better makes itself apparent. The mother figure in the poem "listens to Chula singing *corridos* / making up *los versos* as she / plants down the rows / hoes down the rows / picks down the rows." The evocation of song that makes the day pass more quickly forms one space which helps alleviate the brutality of the fieldwork. However, the aural repetition of "*corridos . . . versos* . . . rows . . . hoes . . . rows . . . rows" represents an incessant repetition on an aesthetic level reflecting the repetition of actual physical labor.

A more extensive form of code-switching marks an escape from this drudgery and points to a greater source of hope:

> *Que le de sus plumas el viento.*
> The sound of hummingbird wings
> in her ears, *pico de chuparrosas.*
> She looks up into the sun's glare,
> *las chuparrosas de los jardines*
> *¿en dónde están de su mamagrande?*
> but all she sees is the obsidian wind
> cut tassels of blood
> from the hummingbird's throat.

The mention of hummingbirds in both English and Spanish (even more than the heavy pre-Cortesian symbolism we have seen these birds bear in Alurista's poetry) conveys a sense of hope for escape and transcendence. The mother dreams that the wind would give her its wings. She hears the buzzing sound of hummingbirds and remembers the hummingbirds of her grandmother's garden. The mother thus connects herself to her female ancestors just as Anzaldúa does with the evocation of her own mother in the poem.

The imagery of hummingbirds not only suggests a matrilineal descent, but also a counterdiscursive stance against male domination. According to Nahua history, the Toltecs under the benign guidance of Quetzalcoatl would sacrifice – rather than humans – hummingbirds and other small animals. This practice gave way before the incursion of the Mexica and their imposition of male deities such as the god of war, Huitzilopochtli. The evocation of the hummingbird cut by the "obsidian wind" thus suggests the historical movements in pre-Cortesian Mexican societies that shifted power away from women toward the militarism and brutality of men.

The significance of this evocation becomes clear in the following stanzas as the mother continues to work:

> White heat no water no place to pee
> the men staring at her ass.
> *Como una mula,*
> she shifts 150 pounds of cotton onto her back.

It's either *las labores*
or feet soaking in cold puddles *en bodegas.*

The choice for women in these conditions, the poem suggests, is between fieldwork or prostitution. The speaker makes clear that the brutality of her mother's condition – and the domination of women by men within the social world evoked by the poem – proves complete.

Although the mother dreams that the wind might give her wings, although she dreams that better work might come for her children ("*Ay m'ijos, ojalá que hallen trabajo* / in air-conditioned offices") although she dreams of getting out of her miserable conditions – the hope seems illusory:

She vows to get out
of the numbing chill, the 110 degree heat.
If the wind would give her feathers for fingers
she would string words and images together.
Pero el viento sur le tiró su saliva
pa' trás en la cara.

The hope she has for escape, for expression through poetry and writing, seems futile. The brutality of her condition slaps her in the face, just like her spit that the south wind blows back into her face. The dream the mother has is for a more cultured and nurturing world, a creative world where the flights of her imagination could take wing. The Spanish – which has provided the specifics about her condition – again here marks that place where her dreams fade beneath the harsh reality of her misery.

The poem concludes with a revision of the sacrifice evoked earlier. Again "She sees the obsidian wind / cut tassels of blood / from the hummingbird's throat." The situation is not as hopeless as before, however. Now "As it falls / the hummingbird shadow / becomes the navel of the Earth." Out of the sacrifice and brutality comes the promise of hope, the potential for centering and rebirth. The evocation of the navel connects, so to speak, the poet with her mother. For the poem does string together the words and images the mother desires. The dream becomes complete in the transmission of hope from mother to daughter.

The use of interlingualism serves to evoke both the brutality of the mother's condition and the dream for some escape from it. Code-switching marks shifts between hope and despair, dream and reality. The tension evident in the poem finds an aesthetic resonance in the deployment of an interlingualism that bespeaks both the particular character of specific socioeconomic and cultural conditions as well as the images and dreams that offer hope for a world beyond those conditions. Thus at the end of the poem the transformation in imagery from sacrifice to reconnection and rebirth represents a resolution that emerges from a revision and rewriting. The poem indicates that the search for matrilineal ancestors forms one such connection. For the image of the mother struggling and dreaming provides the speaker with the words and languages necessary to articulate the dream of hope, the dream of rebirth.

The interlingualism of Anzaldua's poem moves toward a resolution of the tensions evoked in the poem. This interlingualism – conveying the specific condition of oppression, indicating the dream for potential hope – represents a type of limited code-switching that can be explained through a glossary at the end of the poem. Effective though it is, this type of limited interlingualism represents only one possible use of code-switching. Other poets create texts more fully interlingual. Because of the fluidity with which these poets interweave linguistic codes, a glossary would prove hopelessly complicated and incomplete as a way of communicating across linguistic lines.

A prime example of this is Evangelina Vigil's 1985 poem "me caes sura, ese, descuéntate."[15] The title marks the linguistic fluidity that will run through the poem. The use of caló as a third language in the title reflects the interpenetration of "standard" English, slang English, Spanish, caló, and interlingual expression. The poem is addressed to a bullying man, a fighter whose bravado and bluster are part of an abusive and egoistic character. The use of interlingual word play devastatingly denounces the character, calls him to task and – expressing the speaker's disdain for the addressee – moves toward a linguistic and thematic resolution.

The poem opens with the type of polyglossia that marks much Chicana code-switching:

> eres el tipo
> de motherfucker
> bien chingón
> who likes to throw the weight around
> y aventar empujones
> y tirar chingazos
> and break through doors
> bien sangrón
> saying con el hocico
> "that's tough shit!"
> bien pesao
> el cabrón[16]

The opening of Vigil's poem represents a classic interlingualism. The speaker switches in the first four lines from Spanish to profanity in English back to Spanish and to English again. The rhymes – chingón, sangrón, cabrón – are all made in Spanish slang. The use of profanity and slang dominates the tone of this first stanza, indicating the anger and disdain the speaker feels for the auditor. More to the point, the vocabulary of the poem mimics the aggressive nature of the bully. The language becomes the verbal response to the physical violence the poem criticizes. The incessant code-switching creates a sense of disequilibrium, as if the speaker's attack were coming from all sides. Thus the use of interlingualism constructs a third way out: neither capitulation nor confrontation with violence.

The sense of escape becomes clearer in the second stanza. The tone of the poem shifts, and the vocabulary moves from profanity to curt irony:

> y precisamente por esa razón
> whereas ordinarily
> out of common courtesy or stubbornness
> the ground I'd stand and argue principles –
> esta vez que no
> porque esa clase de pendejadas
> mi tiempo fino no merece
> y mucho menos mi energía
> sólo que ahí se acaba el pinche pedo[17]

The lines lengthen, the words grow more complex, the profanity diminishes (at least until late in the stanza). The contrast between the two stanzas forms another type of interlingual communication. The shift is sudden, unsettling, a strategic change that proves as destablilizing as the incessant code-switching that opens the poem. The use of Spanish in the second stanza marks a break, serves to underscore the disjuncture between what would happen "ordinarily" and the reality of this present situation.

The use of Spanish in the final stanza resonates with the destabilization conveyed by the first two stanzas. Where in the first stanza the movement was between language systems, and in the second it was between different tones, the oscillation in the third stanza moves between the speaker and the addressee: "y no creas tú que es que yo a tí te tengo miedo / si el complejo ese es el tuyo." This line is impossible to translate adequately into English: "and don't you think it's that I am scared of you / when that hangup, buddy, is yours." Although the translation sounds stilted (and misses completely the echo heard in "ese es el" which highlights "tuyo"), in Spanish the phrasing forms a common emphatic construction. This construction serves to distance the bully and any possible effect he may have on the speaker from the speaker. The sense of protective distance is underscored in the remainder of the poem:

> ¿porque sabes qué, ese?
> out of pure self-interest
> I like to wear only shoes that fit
> me gusta andar comfortable.[18]

The oscillation resolves into a type of interlinguistic union that ends the speaker's conflict with the auditor – she dismisses him completely – and which creates a resolution between the linguistic polarities caused by the code-switching. The last two lines "I like to wear only shoes that fit / me gusta andar comfortable" turns on the use of the word "me." In English it forms the objective case of "I": "I like to wear only shoes that fit me." In Spanish, it forms an indirect object pronoun: "me gusta andar comfortable." The interlingual performance of the poem pivots on this moment of resolution in which linguistic systems resolve into each other and in which the thematic concerns resolve in the final word, "comfortable." The use of the word is a case of borrowing from English – the Spanish word should be "confortable" or "cómoda." "Comfortable" draws together the two dominant linguistic codes to create a third. The presence of the word could signal a switch back into English. It could signal the misuse of a false cognate. It could be the expression of a Chicanismo.

The poem deterritorializes the various linguistic codes at work within the text, sets them momentarily in flux. This deterritorialization functions in the same way that the poem deterritorializes the identity of the bully in relation to the speaker. The dismissal of his assertiveness creates a space for the speaker's sense of self to emerge. The poem thus works to create space, thematically and formally. Situated between two dominant linguistic codes, it creates meaning by playing the one off the other. Similarly, the speaker positions herself between the aggressive identity of the bully and the aggressive tone of her language so that she can construct an affirmation of identity and self-worth.

The interstitial quality evident in the poems by Vigil and Anzaldúa form a dominant theme in classic Chicano poetry. On a linguistic level, the type of code-switching these poems employ makes manifest an interstitiality. The movement between languages in Vigil's poem results in an interlingualism in which the poem points toward another language, a third language that derives from the interplay between English and Spanish. In Anzaldúa's poem, the use of code-switching serves to underscore the hard world of physical labor and exploitation that the mother figure dreams of escaping. These types of code-switching indicate two different forms of interlingualism. Vigil's poem suggests a significance that hangs between languages. Anzaldúa's poem employs interlingualism to hint at a possibility beyond the harshness of a life circumscribed by economic necessity.

Interlingualism is not always confined to the oscillation between distinct language systems. The disjuncture of meaning even within a dominant linguistic system can mark a type of interstitiality marking the borderlands of Chicano cultural identity. "The Coldest Day" (1991) by Luis Rodríguez conveys a type of double consciousness many ethnic and racial "minorities" feel in the United States. The expression of this double consciousness is interesting in this poem because it centers on the double uses of a single linguistic system. The poem describes from the point of view of a young boy the distress and desolation that arises from poverty. Opening in shadows and darkness, the boy describes how

> To me, it was the coldest day in the world,
> there in sunny LA,
> the day the gas and the lights
> were shut off because bills
> went unpaid.

The lack of agency implicit in the passive construction of the last lines conveys a sense of impotence and helplessness.

The speaker finds himself awash in this helplessness. While his mother seeks to stave off some of the harshness of their condition – "Candles lit the corner of rooms / and fired-up bricks glowed with warmth" – the inevitability and instability of their position asserts itself like the iciness that "broke through / the splintered walls." The dissolution and embattlement is brought painfully home to the speaker, who is forced to take baths in frigid waters. While he "wanted to jump out and run away," he is contained by his mother who kept "sticking me in, / rubbing me hard with soap / and saying a shiver of words." These words reinforce the disempowerment and helplessness of their condition of poverty: "This is the only way, she'd say, / the only way. . . ."

The narrative turns with the speaker's statement: "It was the coldest day in the world. / It could not be the only way!" The simple affirmation, the desire for another condition, makes itself present in the speaker's response to a sign he and his mother encounter after they search for a place to eat. Searching for a restaurant that could provide them with a hot meal, the speaker looks in the window and refuses to enter: "I pointed to a sign on the restaurant door. / It read: 'Come In, Cold Inside.'" The refusal marks a small resistance to the conditions of impoverishment and disempowerment in which the speaker feels literally submerged. The refusal also arises from the doubly encoded word "cold." Within the symbolic system of exchange – imbedded within an economic system of exchange – the restaurant sign signifies comfort and luxury. From the perspective of the speaker, however, overwhelmed by poverty and physical empoverishment, the sign incongruously boasts of the very condition he seeks so desperately to escape.

The poem's narrative describes a situation verging on the bathetic. However, this does not deter from the interesting linguistic condition evoked by the poem. The term "cold" helps locate the rupture between two signifying systems. The word marks where a disjuncture – circumscribed by socioeconomic circumstance – exists. That point marks the interstitial position of Chicano expression, the condition in which Chicano culture and society find themselves between different worlds. The interlingualism described by Bruce-Novoa as that tension between languages which produces a third, an 'inter' possibility of language, thus does not function solely between the various linguistic systems normally associated with the Chicano: Spanish, English, perhaps caló. Even within a single linguistic system, the slippage and rupture that interlingualism seeks to evoke is made evident. And this disjuncture, as with the case of Rodriguez's poem, occurs at that site where linguistic systems bound by economic exchange intersect.

Within Chicano aesthetic texts, the use of these linguistic codes marks an affirmation. The Chicana/o identity that comes to the fore makes apparent its checkered history. The mestizaje valued within Mexican nationalist ideology returns with a vengeance in a contemporary Chicano/a context. Not only do different cultures (indigenous, Mexican, American, colonial Spanish, gypsy, African, pre-Cortesian), not only do different languages ("standard" forms of English and Spanish, mexicanismos, slang and working class English, caló, regional Mexican Spanish, chicanismos, regional Chicano Spanish, indianismos), but also different social, economic, political conditions (impoverishment contrasted against luxury, disempowerment against the powerful, the voiced against the voiceless) come together to form the Chicana/o.

The point of rupture, the line of disjuncture, the other way: These mark the terrain the Chicano constructs, Chicano culture composes, Chicano poetry in its mestizaje speaks.

III

Confluences

8

Between Worlds

> Borders don't apply now.
> East L.A. is everywhere.
> – Gronk

THIRD WORLD, FIRST WORLD, FIFTH WORLD – each mythical constellation offers a prime way to consider Chicano literature. Each promises an insight into the workings of this conflicted literary product. By imposing a matrix, each delimits the potential significance of an obviously complex aesthetic expression. The present study has examined some critical frameworks by which to consider Chicano poetry as an active participant in contemporary American culture. Critical approaches to this border culture – comprised as it is of numerous sites and intense tensions – here crystallize around discussions of postcoloniality and postmodernity. Whereas I have sought to explore the benefits the conceptualizations "postcolonial" and "postmodern" bring to the study of Chicano literature – a project undertaken without apology, as I said – I must admit that I remain suspicious of an easy schematization. It bears emphasizing that neither Chicano poetry, postcolonial discourse, nor postmodernism are coterminous. They are cultural formations at play within a highly contentious historical field marked and marred by the exploitation confronting Mexican people in the United States. The name of the field, of course, is the borderlands.

The borderlands remain a site of rupture: economic disempowerment, racial categorization, sexual stratification, cultural marginalization. Against these ruptures Chicana culture constructs strategies of empowerment and affirmation. Consequently, the tensions explored in this book between the terms "postcolonial," "postmodern," and "Chicana" result in part from the fact that the Chicana maintains both the colonial and the modern within its cultural configurations. As I mentioned in Chapter 2, many Chicana/o writers and critics find their training within North American educational systems and – in addition to exposure to Latin American literary history – experience a strong grounding in the canon of Anglo-American literature. Simultaneously, poets from Alurista to Baca to Castillo – some trained within, some without educational institutions – look to the great American and European modernists as models and inspiration.[1] As Chicana/o artists deploy numerous aesthetic forms in a critical strategy of pastiche, the colonizer lives, so to speak, within the poetic products of Chicana culture.

As several critics have noted, the terms "postmodern" and "postcolonial" both inscribe the very thing they seek to distance. There is, in the critical discussions of these terms, a simultaneous destruction and return of the colonial and modern. The model we should bear in mind is not teleological or progressive – a moving beyond – but rather one that allows for transgression and movement back and forth. The model is one of crossing borders.

Coyotes at the Border

I have argued that postmodernism helps make apparent to an academic culture the critical moves Chicano poetry makes. This emphasis on the postmodern might suggest that Chicana/o poets have sprung full force into the postmodern whirlwind. This is not the case. The relationship these poets have to tradition is complex. This relationship indicates a sense of empowerment that allows them to name and define their own experiences. This means accepting, questioning, accommodating, and refusing particular traits within various Chicano traditions. Simultaneously, there is a process of reclamation that acknowledges and assumes modern and premodern (in addition to postmodern) aesthetic positions. The Chicano cannibalizes the various worlds from which cultural production emerges. The poet becomes a border crosser, but of a particular type: a coyote, a smuggler, a pollero moving people and goods back and forth across aesthetic and cultural as well as geopolitical borders.

Although the Chicano poet moves among various traditions, the relationship between premodernism, modernism, and postmodernism remains a contested issue. Postmodernism bears both a diachronic and synchronic relationship to the sociocultural configurations that precede it. As Andreas Huyssen notes:

> Postmodernism is far from making modernism obsolete. On the contrary, it casts a new light on it and appropriates many of its aesthetic strategies and techniques, inserting them and making them work in new constellations. What has become obsolete, however, are those codifications of modernism in critical discourse which, however subliminally, are based on a teleological view of progress and modernization. (1984: 49)

Modernism becomes another aesthetic landscape across which resistant cultural practices move. It no longer stands as a sacred ground of privileged discourse. The informing myth of modernism, a faith in a progression leading to a transformed and transforming future, gives way to a seeming "undecidability."

In the aesthetic realm, this instability, often ascribed as the dominant characteristic of postmodernism, manifests itself most clearly in the undermining of the relationship between signifier and signified. Marjorie Perloff sees this undermining as a primary characteristic of modernism. Although limited, Perloff's analysis does help in distinguishing the uneven terrain of modernism. She thinks of modernism as "a time of tension between rival strains, the Symbolist or 'High Modern' and the 'Other Tradition'" that highlights the irreducible ambiguity of language. The major visual artistic movements of the twentieth-century avant-garde were expressions in which surface is preferred to depth, process to structure, form to content. These preferences reflect "an oscillation between representational reference and compositional game . . . the multiple layers of meaning words have in poetry (and, by analogy, images in painting) – give way to what we might call an 'irreducible ambiguity' – the creation of labyrinths that have no exit" (1981: 33). Lost in the labyrinth, art no longer need – indeed cannot – concern itself with the quotidian concerns such as economic exploitation, persecution, injustice. The aesthetic can only dance with itself.

Postmodernism, in Perloff's articulation, then becomes the culmination of an ever-tightening circle where the border between world and word grows more menacing and impenetrable. Postmodernism represents an endpoint in which "the concern for the 'meanings below the surface' has given way to increasing interest in the play of the surface itself" (1981: 30). The aesthetic is no longer a work of cultural identification, but rather a work of enigma: "Such a 'work of enigma' is 'poised between sense and nonsense';

it is 'a revelation which is equally a re-veiling'" (1981: 30). This argument is, of course, undergirded by a faith in the progress of poetry. The "indeterminacy" of the "Other tradition" in Perloff's conceptualization becomes the culmination of an aesthetic trajectory that finds its recent embodiment – she argues – in the New Poetry her study champions.

Perloff's analysis quite astutely locates the processes that characterize modernism: the denaturalization of language, the break with language as a window onto or a mirror of reality, the interrogation of the authorial role and narrative authority. As Raymond Williams argues, under modernism, "The self-reflexive text assumes the centre of the public and aesthetic stage, and in doing so declaratively repudiates the fixed forms, the settled cultural authority of the academies and the bourgeois taste, and the very necessity of market popularity" (1989: 33). These repudiations play themselves out within a sociopolitical arena. Thus, although language may indeed be unstable, as Perloff highlights, it is never innocent, not even in its instability. Modernism's rejection of the fixed forms represents a rejection along a socioeconomic vector entrenched in history. Modernism repudiates bourgeois values and market economies. The refusal to participate within the art institutional confines of the early twentieth century is a refusal to participate in a society ruled by standards of decorum hypocritically bolstered by an exploitative economy. What we find missing from Perloff's assessment of modernism – and consequently of postmodernism – is an account of the relationship between aesthetic textuality and social functionality. No modernist or postmodernist cultural object can be understood to stand outside its sociopolitical context.

Thus though consistently antibourgeois, modernism is marked by a discontinuity that runs along political as well as aesthetic lines: "In remaining anti-bourgeois, its representatives either choose the formerly aristocratic valuation of art as a sacred realm above money and commerce, or the revolutionary doctrines, promulgated since 1848, of art as the liberating vanguard of popular consciousness" (Williams 1989: 34). The conflicts within modernism arise not so significantly from the rift between deep symbolism and nonreferentiality. Instead, the tension emerges from the way the work of art fits into its sociopolitical world. Although the avant-garde struggled against hegemonic power, the means of this struggle highlights the problematic position of art in the western world.

Either art remains in the world, struggling for social transformation as a "liberating vanguard," or it remains beyond the world, occupying a hermetic space that stands "above money and commerce." Russell Berman locates these strategies in two influential realms, the Brechtian Epic Theater and the Frankfurt School:

> The revolutionary optimism of Benjamin and Brecht hoped to harness the avant-garde immediately to political progress, while Horkheimer and Adorno viewed authentic art as the place holder of a potential opposition to monopoly capitalism and the culture industry, i.e. in both cases, the contemporary aesthetic revolution was located within the terms of a profound social reorganization. (1984/85: 34)

Berman goes on to call this aspect of modernism a "crucial particularity of the historical avant-garde."[2] These two modernist strategies place art in a privileged position: as either political vanguard or utopian vision. We can see that the development of Chicano poetic production in the face of Chicano political activism raises the similar vexed question posed by modernism: How does art transform the social world? Does it intervene directly – thus the Brechtian work of the early Teatro Campesino – or does it form a separate cultural realm of resistance which – in a mediated way – offers a vision of utopian social transformation, a *promesse de bonheur,* and so the evocation of Aztlán? This is not to imply that Chicano poetry remains anachronistically reciting questions posed nearly a century ago. Rather, the purpose here is to underscore Huyssen's observation that postmodernism does not make modernism obsolete. But the purpose here is also to emphasize that this modernism, in order not to be obsolete, must be understood against rather than outside its historical contexts.

The "crucial particularity" of the avant-garde and its interest in the role of art is a notion not yet bankrupt. However, the incessant revision of aesthetic form – a codification of teleological progress – is. As Raymond Williams notes, the techniques of modernism – instead of lifting daily life out of the market economy – have fallen into the marketplace:

> What has quite rapidly happened is that Modernism quickly lost its anti-bourgeois stance, and achieved comfortable integration into the new international capitalism. Its attempt at a universal market, transfrontier and transclass, turned out to be spurious. Its forms lent themselves to cultural competition and the commercial interplay of obsolescence, with its shifts of schools, styles and fashion so essential to the market. The painfully acquired techniques of significant *dis*connection are relocated, with the help of the special insensitivity of the trained and assured technicists, as the merely technical modes of advertising and the commercial cin-

> ema. . . . These heartless formulae sharply remind us that the innovations of what is called Modernism have become the new but fixed forms of our present moment. (1989: 36)

Modernist forms no longer shock but simply titillate. Modernist techniques serve to stimulate the market economy and simulate alienation in a move calculated to exploit genuine dissatisfaction.[3] That dissatisfaction becomes channeled into the market, and its anxiety produces not social transformation, but renewed consumption.

Williams thus incisively defines the problem of the avant-garde: Its collapse into the marketplace helps form a repressive regime of reactionary postmodernism. The drive of the historical avant-garde to "make it new" makes it a prime target for capitalist cooptation. The same mechanism that drives capitalism drives modernism: a belief in the necessity for perpetual transformation and expansion. If there is to be a break away from what Williams calls the "non-historical fixity of *post*-modernism," the hope lies in a realm outside the easily exploitable codifications of modernism based on a teleological view of progress and modernization. The hope lies in counterpoising alternative traditions against the current dominant culture. This tradition "may address itself not to this by now exploitable because quite inhuman rewriting of the past but, for all our sakes, to a modern *future* in which community may be imagined again" (1989: 36). Williams calls, finally, for a form of resistant postmodernism.

Chicano culture is not the only means by which to configure a resistant postmodernism. Nor does it necessarily represent a salvation for the modernist project. As a cultural formation, it is much more complex and contradictory than to serve simply as a deus ex machina descending onto the world historical stage of European culture. It does represent, however, a historically inflected construction in which notions of tradition and community are imagined again. These imaginings take into account the quite conflicted position of the exploited within the modern world. Chicano culture smuggles back and forth across the borders between the modern and the postmodern, between the marginal and the market place, a critical consciousness of placelessness. It works, in other words, to articulate a position for itself simultaneously within and without dominant cultural formations. So it carries across the border between modernism and postmodernism a sense of the purpose and hope for art. It invigorates the postmodern moment with a means by which the difficult relationships between history, subjectivity, domination, and resistance can be reimagined.

Ephebes, Anxiety, and Modernism: Limón and Paredes

One issue Chicano culture imagines from late in the nineteenth century onward is its relationship to modernity. Although Chicano culture certainly has remained critical of the capitalist and technological world that viewed Chicanos as a renewable (and expendable) source of cheap labor, there has historically been an ambiguous attitude toward the United States and the technology that represents it within the Chicano imaginary. Though Rodolfo Gonzales presents the participation in technological America as a "sterilization of the soul" (1967: 7), others have viewed this participation in a more positive light.

In her article "Early Mexican-American Responses to Negative Stereotyping," Doris Meyer touches upon the refusal by Congress to grant New Mexico admittance as a state. This refusal, Meyer notes, was marked by racist anti-Mexican attitudes. The hostilities toward Mexicans and people of Mexican descent influenced many issues related to their sense of cultural and national identity. New Mexicans were profoundly aware of the prejudices they faced and how those prejudices impacted negatively upon their rights as citizens of the United States. The refusal to grant statehood was met, Meyer notes, with two reactions: by a sense of outrage, exasperation, and puzzlement, or by meeting the problem "head-on by discussing the existence of negative stereotyping, the reasons for it and the injustices which it represented" (1978: 79). This last reaction often led New Mexicans to note the advances their region had experienced as a U.S. territory. Meyer points toward an article in the Albuquerque newspaper *El Nuevo Mundo* dated May 29, 1897, as an example. The article argues that train travel has allowed New Mexico to come "in contact with the great centers of civilization." The result is that in the

> formerly arid deserts are rising beautiful and modern towns which have all the comforts and advantages that in their laboratories our most illustrious inventors have known how to cull from the mysteries of progress. The marvels of Franklin, Tesla and Edison are familiar today to the native who lives in the capitals of New Mexico, who, like his countrymen, knows how to applaud and admire them. (quoted in Meyer 1978: 81)

Progress comes to the wilderness and culls, from the formerly arid deserts, "beautiful and modern towns." The newspaper article – addressed to a Spanish-speaking audience – equates technological progress with civilization. The cultural identification with technology signals something of the complicity and complexity by which Chicanos have dreamed of themselves.

The turn-of-the-century border region represents a fascinating site in which the modern world confronts the premodern. In the midst of this struggle, the Mexicano stands – negotiating positions of outrage and empowerment, dreaming of a self in a better world. However, sometimes those dreams have placed Chicanos squarely within an ideological framework that has – in the historical long run – proved limiting, detrimental, and exploitative. After all, the "marvels" of Franklin, Tesla, and Edison, which directly fed the consumerist desires of America, are nowhere more immediately present than in the maquiladora system of today. The imaginative investment in technology and modernity made evident by the discourse of the article cited by Meyers bespeaks a conflicted position for Chicanos/as at the turn of the century. At once insisting upon the modernization taking place in the borderlands of the late nineteenth century, the article from *El Nuevo Mundo* also insists that the inhabitants of the borderlands know very well how precisely to appreciate that modernization. The celebration of the new, the embrace of technology, the triumph of industrialization represent moves toward those elements of identity most strongly associated with the United States.

Octavio Paz focuses on this connection between the United States and its commitment to technological advances. Noting a strong rupture between Latin America and the United States that runs along the lines of science, he argues: "Americans were born with the Reformation and the Enlightenment – that is, with the modern world; we were born with the Counter-Reformation and Neo-Scholasticism – that is, against the modern world" (1985: 163). These historical periods, Paz argues, form the defining principles about which the northern and southern regions of America organize themselves. Essentializing as his position may be, his argument points out another source of tension within the space of the borderlands. An alliance to the Latino means an engagement with a tradition that at some level stands opposed to the modern world. The emphasis upon the rural and the agrarian – as well as the indigenous and pre-Cortesian – within Chicano poetry marks such an engagement. Conversely, the draw to the modern and the technological signals an alliance with the Anglo-American world.

On an aesthetic plane, José Limón interrogates this peculiar tension in his book *Mexican Ballads, Chicano Poems*. He examines the relationship between the corrido as a "master poem" and later Chicano poetic production as it comes to terms with its anxiety of influence.[4] From this rather limited literary critical stance, Limón constructs a compelling argument about Chicano poetry as the manifestation of a "modernism of critical difference" (1992:164). As Chicano poetry comes to terms with the paternal corrido as a strong – but irrecoverable – literary antecedent, it comes to incorporate maternal voices as an equal folkloric cultural endowment. Thus Chicano poetry can use these folkloric inheritances to "make relevant a carefully and critically appropriated Anglo-American modernism to produce socially engaged and culturally instructive . . . poems that explicitly speak of class – and race – poems of *our* climate" (1992: 164). The poetry, in Limón's argument, negotiates its way through historical social and cultural configurations in order to come to terms with the crisis of the present. Drawing on the work of Frank Lentricchia, Limón suggests that this historical crisis is represented on the cultural front by the emasculation of modernist culture: "If Lentricchia is correct [about the social irrelevance of modern poetry], Western, bourgeois, chiefly Anglo-American culture has rendered paternity, the feminine-maternal, and modernism in such a divisive hegemonic way as to place the latter two as one and in a position of sociopolitical irrelevancy" (1992: 163). Rather than succumb fully to the anxiety of influence and attempt to "masculinize" culture (as Lentricchia suggests in *Ariel and the Police*), Limón argues that we "radically alter this bourgeois definition and use of the maternal feminine" (1992: 163).

Chicana poetry thus moves toward a mature, cognizant, and critical relationship among three discontinuous sites: modernism, the paternal represented by the corrido, and the maternal represented by traditional symbols of power like la Virgen de Guadalupe. This movement, according to Limón, allows for a reinvigoration of modernism, does away with what is from an Anglo-American hegemonic position the irrelevancy of modernist culture. It does not "masculinize" poetry so much as empower the "maternal feminine" and thus reempower a critical modernism. The poetry does this by seriously engaging with its antecedents:

> Strong vernacular traditions – folklore – return to deeply inform and produce a new modernism, one redefining the "best" that has been written in terms of the best that has been said, sung, and signified. The result, it has been suggested, is the reinvigoration of a traditional modernism, now viewed as exhausted in its ability to generate social change. Once bracketed as "ethnic" or "third world," these new emerging literatures seem instead to represent a strong continuation of a critical modernism. (1992: 165)

Limón's concern with the diachronic development of Chicana poetry as a critically resistant modernism signals a productive engagement with the borderlands of cultural criticism. Just as the seminal work of Houston Baker, Jr., and Henry Louis Gates, Jr., have done in an African American framework, Limón argues that Chicana cultural production represents a deeply inflected and inflecting form of modernism. The margins – by calling upon their precursors and drawing upon hitherto devalued cultural traditions – reinvest the culture of the center with vitality and direction. The cultural production of hitherto silent constituencies imbues the moment with a moral imperative.

This is all to the good, and Limón's study culminates by positing Juan Gómez-Quiñones's 1973 poem "The Ballad of Billy Rivera" as an example of "poetry that responds to the [precursor's] patriarchal epic poetics by bringing to it the poetics of woman as well as a fine but critical sense of modernism" (1992: 131). Gómez-Quiñones's work conjoins modernism with the framework of the corrido tradition. It politicizes an ambiguous modernist aesthetic, evokes the historical connections between language and power, celebrates the communal political action of the community, marks the passing of the "exclusively male-centered world at the core of the corrido tradition," and replaces this world with the possibility of an androgynous – which is to say inclusive – vision in which men and women together can be considered heroic (1992: 149). The promise of modernism as a transformative cultural project flowers where it meets the promise of the corrido as a socially transformative cultural product. The analysis allows for a way beyond the endgame of modernism at its moment of exhaustion and the decline of the corrido at the moment of its extinction. The two cultural formations – one dominant, the other residual – interact through a poem like "The Ballad of Billy Rivera" in a mutually beneficial and life-giving way.

Limón traces Chicano anxieties of influence, arguing that certain poems, like Gómez-Quiñones's, "successfully" negotiate the two (or three) worlds of modernism and folklore. His critical judgment is astute in this regard. His study does, however, limit itself singularly to tracing lines of descent by which the corrido tradition makes itself powerfully manifest in the present and through which modernism yet remains in the world as a viable critical project. Which is to say, his study formulates a schema by which a genealogy is constructed, modernism saved, and the contribution of women within a Chicano cultural sphere can manifest itself through an empowered maternal presence.

His study focuses on contiguity, suggesting a teleological development to Chicano poetry – from tentative first (mis)steps to "historically sensitive, formally capacious" poems (1992: 153). I would add only an acknowledgment of the discontinuous and mutually exclusive elements suggested by the confluence of the premodern world of the corrido and the postmodern world of micropolitical action. The vexing question that has so haunted both modernist and Chicano artistic production remains unanswered: What precisely is the role of art in transforming a delimited and debilitating social world? Limón's work suggests that the successful incorporation of modernist poetic practices within a framework of traditional cultural production leads to some revivification of both the artistic space and the social realm into which the artistic interjects itself. *Mexican Ballads, Chicano Poems* does quite incisively trace the means by which a residual border culture becomes an emergent borderlands culture. It does not wholly interrogate the significance of those moments where the residual fails to become emergent. As an example, I turn to Limón's discussion of Américo Paredes's poetry, which represents, Limón argues, an unsuccessful melding of modernism and the corrido tradition.

In 1991, Américo Paredes published the poetry he had written sporadically over the course of his lifetime. Paredes chose those poems that he modestly claims were "menos pior" – less worse – culled with the editing help of Ramón Saldívar. The collection, *Between Two Worlds,* draws together poems written between 1934 and 1970. Which is to say, they fall mainly outside the historical scope of this volume. The poems are significant, however, in that they cross a clearly modernist style with attempts to acknowledge the border culture of the early century.

José Limón focuses on the poem "Guitarreros" as Paredes's "best poetic effort to date" (1992: 45). In many ways, the poem, written in 1935, is compelling for the problems it presents. Limón argues that the poem relies upon a modernist mode of expression. His analysis quite successfully indicates the moral quality and moral conundrum of the poem. The poem deals with the singing of a corrido, "El Hijo Desobediente," which is about a son who, in the middle of a dispute with another, curses his father, who has tried to break up the fight. For his disrespect, the son must be killed. In a final act of bravura, the son directs that he be buried in unconsecrated ground and his worldly goods dispersed.[5] The corrido ends with an evocation of a roundup in which a herd of cattle is brought down from grazing. Along with the cattle comes a black bull that has never been brought down from the mountain before. The lines describing this action – *"Bajaron el toro prieto, / que nunca lo habían bajado . . ."* – forms the epigraph to Paredes's poem. Limón argues that the restoration of moral order is quite clear in the corrido on two levels: The young son accepts his fate and affirms the "natural order of things" by distributing his goods; and "the corrido ends with the other vaqueros establishing control over the renegade bull. Like the miscreant vaquero, the black bull is strong but potentially dangerous, perhaps even evil, and he must be brought down, brought under social and moral control" (Limón 1992: 53–4). The problem presented by Paredes's poem is that the moral world evoked by the corrido was once ordered, but that world no longer exists.

This moral dilemma finds its aesthetic correlative in Paredes's poetic form: "the conventional diction of folk song is replaced by a constellation of modernist imagery – 'black against twisted black'; a mesquite like a stallion; fingers also like stallions, which drive along a bull like a song. These formal choices . . . implicitly and initially 'say' that [t]his poem is a wholly different, and perhaps better, way to craft" (Limón 1992: 51). The modernist poem "swerves" away from the traditional poetic evocation and replaces it with another quite distinct. In this case, a residual (Mexican) cultural formation is replaced by a dominant (Euramerican) aesthetic form. The movement from corrido to modern poem marks a significant move away from the heroic world suggested by the corrido: "For all its moral power, the normative impact of the past has been blunted by time and change, and only the moral desire of the young poet cast into poetry can give us limited imaginative access to it" (Limón 1992: 54). Thus the poem marks a moment of impotence. The world it evokes is lost, the poem itself pales in moral power by comparison. It signals a loss of moral certainty and rectitude. All that remains within the poetic evocation is the image of an old man affirming that "'In the old days it was so'" (Paredes 1935: 29). The old man, Limón notes, represents an image of tradition as well as the poetic voice (1992: 55), indicating the limitation of both traditional and modernist worlds. For tradition can affirm only that the past was indeed one of moral order, whereas the poetic voice can affirm only its inability to construct a new moral order.

The poem thus marks a profound inability to bring together the past and the present, to bridge the impassable gap between traditional and dominant cultural formations. Limón argues that although Paredes's poem creatively draws on the past, it cannot move successfully into the present. The poet is

> unable to come to full poetic terms with the precursor, he cannot move beyond his admiring contemplation of the past to gradually and creatively transform it into a poetic and politically critical meditation on the present. In these terms, the truncated achievement of "Guitarreros" relative to the precursory tradition also limits its capacity to address the poet's contemporary world of political discourse. (1992: 56)

In this, the poem marks a great failure within the parameters of Limón's critical framework. The political resistance of residual border culture cannot be brought into the present moment of political crisis. The poem cannot mark a contemporary critical engagement and so it fails to make the political-poetic tradition it evokes relevant to the present.

The poem's formal achievement – its deployment of a modernist poetics – signals a complete dissociation with traditional corrido aesthetics. This move thus allows the poem

> into the coterie of formal modernism at a historical moment when modernism is performing its own critical ideological service *contra* capitalism in a wider social sphere. At the same time, however, at the level of local politics, the modernist form isolates this poem too severely from its immediate context. In its aesthetics, and relative to the struggle immediately at hand, the poem's form too quickly anticipates the future and is closed off from the immediate contextual present. (Limón 1992: 58)

At one level, the poem does engage in the struggle against capitalism and its general exploitation of the border region that form, for Paredes's poem, the "immediate contextual present." At another level, however, Limón argues that the poem disengages itself from that present by employing a nonregional, nonlocal mode of artistic expression. It does not, in other words, look to the corrido on a formal as well as a thematic level.

What Limón's critique signals is that Paredes's poem belongs neither within a traditional cultural formation nor within a modernist configuration. That is, the poem helps articulate what recent Chicano poetry has come to explore more fully: the impossibility of occupying one cultural, social, or political world. "Guitarreros" fails to engage the local political conflicts that comprise the borderlands. Limón is quite correct in pointing out the difficulty of that disengagement. This does not serve to suggest that the poem is lost amid a constellation of modernism, that it fails as a Chicano poem. Rather, it indicates the highly complex and conflicted project of developing a contemporary border culture. In 1935, the type of political activism that surrounded the formation in 1973 of Gómez-Quiñones's "Ballad" could not be an influential trajectory in the articulation of Paredes's poetic voice. The type of local politics missing in "Guitarreros" – and present in "The Ballad of Billy Rivera" – marks an engagement with the micropolitical that does not characterize the modernist project. After all, modernism (whether advocated by Benjamin, Adorno, Eliot, or Stein) worked hard to integrate the various components of the world – the aesthetic, political, cultural – into a cohesive and directed whole. Or at the very least it marked the inability to undertake such a project. In any case, there is a universalizing impetus that drives modernism.

Chicana culture, by contrast, emphasizes (as Limón does) the local. Chicana culture, growing out of a profoundly decentered social experience, focuses on the decentralization of aesthetic expression. It does so in order to recapture from the center the right to speak, the power to name its marginal self and its marginal experiences. But it does away with the center's notions of the universal so that it may reconsider and retitle the universal along other lines and for other concerns. In this way, it does not make sense to talk about a Chicana modernism, just as it does not make sense to talk about a Chicana postmodernism. In both cases, those terms can help provide critical frameworks by which to consider Chicana culture. At the same time, in so naming it, borders are placed around the culture that limit its movements. Chicana culture can be better understood and valued within a critical world that takes into account the margin, as I argue postmodernism does. However, Chicana culture also highlights the gaps within that critical world, as Chapter 5 has sought to indicate. Paredes's poetry brings into sharp focus the gaps inherent in modernism, reveals the limitations of a totalizing project as it speaks from the margins where totalities dissolve. His poetry indicates the lacks evident in a unversalizing project when the category "universal" comes under so much scrutiny at the limits, at the border.

Paredes articulates a sensibility of gaps in his later poem "Canto de la muerte joven" (Song of the Young Dead), written in 1970 and dedicated to Rubén Salazar "y a todos lo demás."[6] The poem, written entirely in Spanish, opens with two questions: "And then? . . . / After that, what? . . ." questions that repeat between each stanza (ellipses in the original). The poem asks: After the demonstrations and marches, the discussions, debates, committees, after the purging of personal feelings, after the cursing of the world – then what?[7] What makes the poem compelling is not its poetic form nor its rhetorical stylings. The poem represents in its aesthetic form the type of blunt, prosaic statement characteristic of the Movimiento poetry current in 1970. Rather, the interest of the poem lies in the questions it raises: "And then? . . . / After that, what? . . ." These questions suggest a sense of futility and pointless interrogation. After the sacrifices, the deaths, the suffering – what represents the next step? And clearly, there are no answers forthcoming. Indeed, the results of the historical events that comprise the Movimiento were plagued by the very question Paredes's verse raises. There were no answers on a political level to the type of interrogation which "Canto de la muerte joven" places in the mouth of the young dead. The poem is, after all, a song of (not for) the dead. The poetic voice takes it upon itself to speak for the dead, just as we have seen other Movimiento poetry take it upon itself to speak for the Chicano, the community, the pueblo. The poem thus takes it upon itself to speak for an absolutely inarticulate constituency. And, significantly, by this point among the heroic pantheon of the dead, only questions can be asked rather than direction offered.

All this goes by way of suggesting that Paredes's poem provides a sense of what it means to occupy only one world – the political – among the great ferment of Chicano life evident in the turmoil of the Movimiento. Along the political axis, one must ask what can the next step be after sacrifice, death, injustice. Along the political axis, a sense of incoherence must emerge after the vague demands for rights and land and equality are made. The sense of unified direction indeed gives way to a series of micropolitical concerns that more fully imbue the local with political significance. Paredes's poem helps prefigure the key questions that face the Movimiento after the "revolution" – and, within the revolutionary rhetoric of the Movement, they cannot be answered. For what emerges as answers to these questions are the affirmation of Chicana identities, an interrogation of sexual roles and gender stratification, a questioning of the means by which Chicano identity is constructed, a reinvestment in the local politics that focus on environmental conservation, health care, better working conditions. "Canto" helps begin to articulate the dissolution of revolution, the endgame of a modernist concern with unity and the recuperation of a lost wholeness. These are certainly laudable concerns, but Paredes's poem indicates that the age of individual heroism is past. Although "Guitarreros" suggests a longing for a heroic age – and suggests its impossible recuperation – "Canto" clearly marks the gap between that age and this.

The Domestic Heroic: Victor Martinez

Rather than consider this gap a defeat, contemporary critics can search for ways in which political and cultural forms of resistance yet manifest themselves. Although the traditional manifestations of a heroic age may no longer be appropriate models by which to guide present cultural constructions, this does not mean that a sense of justice or morality cannot be made present. Nor does it mean that these terms are fully under the sway of hegemonic control. If the stories of the disempowered teach us nothing, at least they indicate that human communities can transcend the barbarity of civilizational violence as they seek dignified and empowering forms of social organization. What has been made problematic is the relation of art to these new configurations. Jean-François Lyotard observes:

> You cannot consider what has been happening in painting, music or sculpture for almost a century without having the feeling that the function of art has overturned. Art no longer plays the role it used to, for it once had a religious function, it created good forms, some sort of a myth, of a ritual, of a rhythm, a medium other than language through which the members of society would communicate by participating in a same music, in a common substratum of meaning. . . . And this generally went on in churches. Daily life was the realm of discourse, but the sacred was that of form, i.e. that of art. This has now become impossible. Why? Because we are in a system that doesn't give a rap about sacredness. (1968: 27)

This classic articulation of late sixties' poststructuralism indicates an overwhelming desire to name universal experience. The "system" controls the potentiality (and imposes the impossibility) of aesthetic creation connected to the sacred. The problem here lies in what Lyotard means by "sacredness." For it could be argued that within dominant social formations, the only thing sacred is the procurement and duplication of capital. However, in the margins and against the grain, a sense of the sacred yet manifests itself, even if an ultimate authority – a God or a State or a Revolution – is absent from the system of valuation upon which that sacred object rests.[8]

Chicano poetry often evokes a longing for "good forms, some sort of a myth, of a ritual, of a rhythm, a medium other than language" as a locus of present social discontent. The sacred within traditional discourses becomes a tool by which to articulate a counterdiscourse. In addition, the "good forms" within the poetry also suggest the dialectical relationship between modernism and postmodernism. Chicano poetry, as the present discussion has sought to point out, focuses on the project of construction. This process of cultural construction does not wholly devalue modernism. It does, however, insert the discourse of transcendent salvation into a much more limited field of play.

A poetic example more recent than that of Paredes yet still in dialogue with modernist forms is the work of Victor Martinez. His collection of poems *Caring For a House* (1992) gestures toward modernism by investing in a hope for transcendence while also critically recognizing that discontinuity can serve as a potential locus of resistance and renewal. The poem "Shoes," for example, recalls the work of the same title by the artist Vincent van Gogh. *Shoes* represents one of van Gogh's masterful early pieces, a moving representation of the clumsy and well-worn footwear of the peasants among whom he was living during the early part of his career. *Shoes* represents, according to Fredric Jameson, one of the canonical works of high modernism "which draws the whole absent world and earth into revelation around itself" (Jameson 1984b: 59). The shoes serve to invoke the hard and merciless life of the poor who have worn (out) the subject of van Gogh's sketch. The modernist work thus suggests that there exists a moral axis to which art must hearken. Van Gogh's work positions itself as a symbolic representation – albeit dissociated and fragmentary – of some more vast reality.

For this reason, David Antin can criticize T. S. Eliot and other high modernists for a "persistent tendency to project any feature from any plane of human experience onto a single moral axis" (1972: 118). Both Antin and Jameson suggest that high modernism invokes a vast symbolic network of meaning by which the artistic work serves as a map. Or, as Marjorie Perloff notes about Eliot's "The Wasteland," its specific geographic and historical references help to create a thickly textured poem comprised of symbolic threads "woven and designed so intricately that the whole becomes a reverberating echo chamber of meanings" (1981: 16). However, it must be noted that whereas Jameson values modernism for its allusiveness, Antin and Perloff value modernism only insofar as it is elusive, nonreferential, indeterminate.

Victor Martinez's poem, alluding to van Gogh's work, moves in two ways. On the one hand, the poem offers shoes as symbols of community, friendship, support – an image suggesting class unity:

> Out of all our enemies, all the catastrophes of nations
> scattered to rubble, plowed over with salt, we still have
> the warm friendliness, the unrelenting spirit
> of our shoes to console us.

The opening posits a sense of locality and familiarity upon which to rely in the face of the epic disaster represented by the allusion to the sack of Carthage. Shoes point toward the solidity of community and the comfort of the familiar. The shoes portrayed in the first lines of the poem relay an image of connection and, ultimately, worker unity despite disaster, despite poverty. As van Gogh's *Shoes* represent a testament to the heroism of the worker, shoes in Martinez's poem stand as an objective correlative for the power of unity and community.

The opening lines, suggesting the Roman destruction of Carthage, evoke a world historical perspective which, in the second stanza, is reversed by an allusion to the construction of the aesthetic text:

> Two bubbles chopped square out of shapeless emptiness
> how this invention hisses in a hurry to correct time
> pumping little sneezes of sympathy for our tardiness.

A diminution occurs. The move from a world historical stage to "little sneezes of sympathy" marks the ambiguous condition of art in a contemporary social configuration. The shoes, rather than actual physical objects or loci of symbolic connection, become simply "two bubbles" marking "shapeless emptiness." Martinez's poem positions its subject within a traditional high modernist framework as a symbolic object, but simultaneously foregrounds the emptiness of such an aesthetic creation. From this point, the shoes can take on a fanciful dimension, walking "in many of our dreams, conjuring music," or returning from "every tropic, every desert / to take up their jobs as stealth for the burglar, / spring under the killer's crouch, courage / for the guerrilla."

Finally, the poem offers the shoes as practical objects: "They guard us / against thistles and thorns, protect us from stone / and unseen disasters of glass." Though they stand as guards against disasters, the personification does little to elevate the condition of shoes. Rather than assume the heroic dimension of van Gogh's portrait as emblems of worker solidarity, the shoes here finally serve only as guardians against thistles, thorns, and glass. Where van Gogh's portrait uses the shoes to point toward the peasant, here the shoes "are the first / of peasants." The lowest of the low, so to speak, the shoes are nothing but shoes. Although personified by the poetic voice, they nevertheless represent nothing. As a result, they

> would never think to kneel
> before any god, or suck up to whatever tablet of the Law.
> Ravenous for distance, they supply whole lives
> with the loss of a mere heel
> yet wear death, only once.

The shoes stand for themselves, paying no obeisance to some higher moral order. That is, the poetic voice personifies them only insofar as they desire movement. These shoes were made for walking. They serve no other system or project. The ironic and playful diminishment that marks the poem serves to position the shoes in a relationship slightly noble – they "supply whole lives / with the loss of a mere heel" – but they certainly do not represent a heroic order.

Martinez's poem distances itself from the type of modernism that Paredes and Limón seem to find simultaneously attractive and repulsive. This ambiguous response is indeed the appropriate response to modernism's own ambiguity. As Alan Wilde notes: "Modernism, spurred by an anxiety to recuperate a lost wholeness in self-sustaining orders of art . . . reaches toward the heroic in the intensity of its desire and of its disillusion" (1980: 9). The desire and disillusion could well characterize the intensity of both Paredes's and Limón's literary and critical expressions. By contrast, Wilde goes on to note, postmodernism is skeptical of efforts to recuperate a lost wholeness and so "presents itself as deliberately, consciously antiheroic. Confronted with the world's randomness and diversity, it enacts an attitude . . . of a fundamental uncertainly about the meanings and relations of things in the world and in the universe" (1980: 9). This is not to argue that Martinez's poem fits snugly within a postmodern paradigm as articulated by Anglo-American criticism. But I do mean to suggest that Martinez's text problematizes the evocation of modernism within Chicano texts. The poem deploys that most potent force of the disempowered – humor – in order to reconsider the position of artistic and concrete objects. The poem, in other words, moves between modernist and postmodernist positions.

Reclaiming the Word: Castillo and Soto

The oscillation between worlds functions at the level of poetic genre as well. For Chicana poets do not form a dialogue only with an Other tradition in order to construct a poetic practice. At issue in the cultural migrations of Chicana poetry is the question of appropriation. Whereas the poetry examined in the present study has been primarily narrative or dramatic, there is – as Victor Martinez's text indicates – an active engagement with the lyric form. Why – if, indeed, as its critics claim, the lyric is dead – are Chicana poets now turning to this mode of expression? Is this an example of "minority" artists rummaging through the postmodern ruins of Euramerican aesthetic forms, kicking at a clay shard here, piecing together a bit of mosaic there, imagining the muses' whisper ghostly and hoarse?

The lyric represents a genre that is most clearly based upon a central subjectivity. The speaker meditates upon his or her position within a wider world. The expression is as personal as the emotions evoked. "The subjective being that makes itself heard in lyric poetry," Theodor Adorno notes in his essay on the lyric, "is one which defines and expresses itself as something opposed to the collective and the realm of objectivity" (1957: 59). This contrary position within the realm of subjectivity allows the speaker to express an individual identity in opposition to the outside. The negativity of the lyric – as an expression of the break or rupture between the individual and the social world – becomes in Adorno's conceptualization a "philosophical sundial of history" marking the time and tenor of a historical moment by indicating how the outside world fails the speaker, showing where the present fails to match its promise. The aesthetic text serves dialectially to point toward a wholeness where only rupture exists. The lyric poem helps to create a vision of wholeness as a promise that stands against the reality of fragmentation and dissociation.

Although the Chicana lyric does not stand to disprove Adorno's modernist vision of the lyric, it does complicate the position of art in relation to the world. The Chicana self, when it speaks in opposition through the lyric, is itself divided and multiplicitous. Thus, the Chicana lyric represents an aesthetic form in tension with itself. Moreover, the personal expression of the lyric stands in contradistinction to the function of poetry manifested by the great tradition of the corrido. As was previously noted, José David Saldívar argues, "The corrido's function is to reconcile individual experience into a collective identity" (1986: 12). The tenor of the lyric as personal expression of personal experience runs counter to this tradition. Finally, the lyric by Chicana poets is often an expression aware of its position in the borderlands, in worlds between worlds. The Chicana lyric questions the complex relationship between the subject's desire for affirmative flight – even if in the imagination – and the realization that there is no escape from the world in which that subject finds itself. The Chicana lyric therefore manifests an incessant movement of capture and escape, of always being in the moment of betweenness. This sense of being between as an affirmative position of difference is central to both Gary Soto's 1985 collection *Black Hair* – especially the aptly titled "Between Words" – and Ana Castillo's previously discussed *My Father Was a Toltec* published in 1988.

Deploying the lyric form, Castillo's poem "Cold" maps out the complicated conditions at the borderlands that make the lyric in the hands of Chicano poets not merely the reproduction of already established Euramerican aesthetic forms. The lyric opens with negative statements evoking images of what the word "cold" is not:

> Cold
> is not once
> or twice in a life
> not from a window of a fleeting train
> . . . not
> a picture postcard with rose
> cheeked children on sleds

. . . not
a crystal paperweight turned
upside down

The evocation of winter in this stanza circles around issues of leisure and luxury. What cold is not forms a picturesque backdrop to other pleasurable activities. These images convey the cold as a force that can be isolated, framed, contained – and left behind. It is on the other side of a window, portrayed in a card, contained inside a crystal bubble. This is not, the speaker emphasizes, what cold is. These images of what cold "is not" offer either a picture of nature through the aesthetic – a picture postcard, a crystal paperweight – or something to be traversed – seen from the window of a fleeting train, enjoyed on "a sleigh ride to a distant / house with smoking chimney." In either case, these positionings of nature that the speaker rejects suggest a subject wholly independent of nature, who in a sense controls nature and therefore has the luxury to encounter cold "once or twice in a life."

Against this conception of cold, the poetic voice argues for an understanding of cold as an agent that traverses the subject rather than as an object through which the subject is able to cross. Metonymically, of course, cold is meant to evoke poverty, just as the hegemonic images of sleigh rides and train rides are meant to suggest wealth. Cold, the voice states in the next stanza, "is cold / in the city surrounded by / flatland, nothing but silos / to stave off the wind." The voice speaks from an urban experience "surrounded" by farmland – an inversion, if you will, of the containment of nature in the previous stanza. The city itself is bordered, surrounded, isolated and yet traversed by the cold: "Windows rattle and call out / demons." These demons torment the individual as "joints stiffen, backs create new places to ache. A constant / quiver inhabits the body." The cold thus traverses the urban-dwelling subject, defines and determines how that subject will live.

With Castillo's poem, nature is neither a source of comfort, nor inspiration, nor empathy. Nor, most importantly, does it form a realm of objectivity against which the subjective speaker stands opposed. Instead, individuals are wholly comprised of and limited by their encounter with their environment. The speaker as a subjective being, rather than stand as "something opposed to the collective and the realm of objectivity" (Adorno 1957: 59), becomes in this lyric wholly traversed by the objectivity of the outside world. The poetic voice states flatly: "Cold / is not nostalgic / Winter emits no fond memories." There can be, the speaker thus suggests, no reimaginative engagement with the cold. It is wholly a physical torment to the point where one can laugh – that great activity of hope and defiance found in a good deal of Chicano poetry – "only to find teeth ring / sharply with pain." As the poem closes with this bitter evocation of pain, one is made aware of the contradictory position the text evokes. Although the central reality of the poem – cold – refuses containment, although it resists aesthetitization, and although it eludes the imaginative engagement integral to nostalgia and memory, the poet has yet contained, has yet aestheticized, has indeed engaged imaginatively with the cold. The poem moves but never rests between stating the impossible and accomplishing it, forming a dichotomy that echoes the poetic speaker's own problematic condition as a voice meditating upon, engaging with and simultaneously resisting the conditions in which it finds itself.

The poem thus evokes a dialectic that allows for a critical perspective on both its own form as a meditative lyric and on its thematization of subjectivity. The speaking subject is never free from the agency of cold. The "subject" in the poem becomes wholly subject to physical pain and the "constant quiver" that inhabits the body. The speaking voice creates a space for itself that moves outside that condition and yet always back to it. The anger expressed by the speaker is a moment of resistance – resistant like anger's other face, the laughter evoked in the last few lines of the poem. But, like the subject that laughs at this lyric's close, the speaking voice also suggests that its efforts are marked by a sharply ringing pain: the lack of escape.

The city is surrounded by those farmlands that have brought the Chicano to Chicago, and one is trapped by those same farmlands in the city "surrounded by / flatland, nothing but silos." The poetic voice indicates that the Chicano subject traverses the rural landscape – like the migrant worker crossing the land in search of work – and, seeking to escape it, is surrounded by that landscape in the cold labyrinth of poverty within the city. The thematized and speaking subjects of this poem are thus both agents and objects in relationship to the landscape that surrounds them: They are always between escaping and never being able to escape.

A similar sense of subjectivity and agency is evident in Gary Soto's "Between Words," the closing poem of *Black Hair.* There the speaker poses a question implicit in Castillo's work: "Just what is there to do?" The answers he proposes are simple and elemental: "Eat / Is one, sleep is another." These animal needs form, ultimately, the essential basis of existence since, as the poetic voice soon makes clear, all life ends in the gaping smile of death. The poem thus seems to rely on a very traditional theme of lyric poetry: *carpe diem.*

Against the animal needs named in the opening lines, the poetic voice posits speaking "before the night ends" as a constructive and constituting act. Immediately an inversion is suggested: Here life is equated with night rather than day, and it is before this night is finished that speech must be accomplished. The act of speaking, however, proves to be trivial and ultimately impossible:

> But before the night ends
> We could walk under
> These camphors, hand in hand
> If you like, namedropping
> The great cities of the past,
> And if a dog should join
> Us with his happy tail,
> The three of us could talk,
> Politics perhaps . . .

Where Castillo's reflections on the ambivalent act of speaking are evident through the form of her aesthetic object, Soto thematizes speech and reduces it to "namedropping" and talking politics between the speaker, the lover, and – amusingly – a dog. The lofty thoughts that would carry them away from the world are undercut by a humorous trivialization. Although the tone of Soto's lyric stands in contradistinction to the sense of anger and bitterness – the impossibility of laughter without pain – in Castillo's poem, both examine speech as an activity that oscillates between a desire away from and an inevitable return to the world. We are offered an image of the speaker and his lover walking between the camphor trees – suggestive of healing, of growth, of a positive transformation away from the earth – and across the ground, which comes to evoke an earthward-bound death by the close of the poem.

The passing and traversing here are distinct from the sense of being traversed explored in Castillo's "Cold." In Soto's poem, the passing through becomes a journey with no goal:

> Love,
> The moon is between clouds,
> And we're between words
> That could deepen
> But never arrive.
> Like this walk. We could go
> Under trees and moons,
> With the stars tearing
> Like mouths in the night sky,

And we'll never arrive.
That's the point.

The sentiment explored here, of moving between but never arriving, most marks this text as emerging from a Chicano context. One cannot help but hear the echo in these lines of Tomás Rivera's "When We Arrive" in *y no se lo tragó la tierra.* The multivocalic expression in that story creates a tension between the characters' desire "to arrive" and their realization that they will never arrive. The poem before us transforms this sense of hopelessness into an affirmation of the idea of movement and transience. There is with Soto a transformation of both Rivera's and Castillo's idea of the subject being surrounded and contained by her environment. In Soto's poem, the subject does not need to escape from his passage. Which is to say, a walk in the park is not the same kind of activity as shivering in the coldness of poverty or riding in the back of a truck on the way to another day of stoop labor. There is in Soto's poem a clear economic privilege. Nevertheless, Soto's poem too examines the liminal condition of difference.

Rather than regret the fact of being always between, the speaker notes that "To go / Hand in hand . . . / is what it's about." A sense of union, communion, and community while being between is a condition based upon difference: being neither one thing nor the other, being neither here nor there, being always between, meaning "we'll never arrive." And as the speaker suggests, "That's the point." This celebration of passage thus allows for the speaker to invoke the words of a friend who says

. . . be happy. Desire.
. . . because in the end
Not even the ants
Will care who we were
When they climb our faces
To undo the smiles. (1985: 78)

The imperative to seize the day that closes the poem seems to resolve, as is often typical of the traditional lyric, its problematic. The movement "through" is ultimately a movement between birth and death.

Certainly this sense of movement between birth and death fits thematically with Soto's collection as a whole. *Black Hair* opens, after all, with the title poem, a celebration of identity and community that has at its center the recollection by a child of his father's death. That first poem places death at the center of life. This final poem places the passage through life at the center of death. A sense of inversion and closure is therefore achieved in Soto's closing lyric expression.

Yet the language and images of "Between Words" suggest conflict. There is a tension evoked as this crossing between, which suggests a linear movement of never arriving, is described as being "the point." Just as a line indicates continuity and a point fixity, so the act of "never arriving" becomes a form of arriving. The only "arriving" evoked in the poem, however, is that moment at which the ants "Climb our faces / to undo the smiles." So Soto's work probes the border between placement and placelessness, both evoking and undoing an endlessly transient notion of arrival.

Although there seems to be a resolution toward a simple Horatian formula of *carpe diem*, the poem questions the meaning and applicability of that traditional resolution to the lyric. If life is "night," as is suggested in the third line, then what type of "day" is it that one is encouraged to seize? Beyond this sense of inversion – night for day – life here is portrayed as a continual process of becoming with an emphasis upon movement, change, lines of flight. What is there that is fixed enough to be seized? Only those emotions and those thoughts that are "between words" passed between lovers walking hand in hand. The language of the poem celebrates silence and so, too, is caught between the desire to express and the consciousness that it is unable to do so.

Similarly, though the friend of the poet commands the speaking subject and his lover to be happy – to "seize" the day – the friend also commands them to "desire." This imperative demands that the lovers engage in an activity wholly marked by being between: the need for something that can never be attained, the emotion that is fulfilled and consumed at the selfsame moment. The lyric mode here allows for an exploration of that point at which the speaking subject, the object of desire, and the mode of expression are all found in transition, never arriving. That liminal moment, as the speaker succinctly and suggestively notes, is the point.

By assuming a quintessentially European genre – a genre that at once seems most alien to and yet offers great ground for the Chicano poet to traverse, scrutinize, and mark (a mode of poetic expression that may indeed be "dead" to the world that first mapped and circumscribed it) – Chicano lyric poetry negotiates the difficult terrain between the voice, the subject, and the world. It also calls into question the traditional generic boundaries of the lyric form. The mutual interpenetration of subject and object explored by Chicano lyric poetry stands in contradistinction to the traditional lyric as a meditation premised upon the very separation between self and other. The mutually traversing agents and objects suggest a radical reconfiguration of subjectivity, a subjectivity whose artistic expression lives vigorously and productively crossing the border between genres, between languages, between cultures. The terrain marked by the terms modernism and postmodernism, colonial and postcolonial, represent only part of the cultural landscape across which Chicano poetry migrates.

Clawing the Precipice

The Mexica thought of themselves as pressing against the wind, clinging to a steep precipice, threatened at every step by a thrashing storm threatening to blow them into an abyss. The sense of embattlement experienced by the Mexica finds a correlative in the sense of embattlement experienced by Chicanos and Mexicanos in the United States. The struggles are made all the more bitter for the incessant articulation of "race" relations in this country as yet divided along black and white lines. Nevertheless, Chicano culture is characterized by its incessant clinging above the abyss. In varying ways, it has sought to posit an identity that takes into account the various influences – good and bad and ugly – that comprise the discontinuous position called the Chicano. At some level, these influences can be understood as representing five different critical worlds: the postcolonial, the postnational, the premodern, the postmodern, and the multicultural.

Certainly, as the invocation of five worlds suggests, Chicano culture moves across a complex contemporary landscape. However, it continually smuggles cultural goods across that landscape, painfully and joyfully creating another terrain that stands as a testament to the power of human endurance and creativity. Rather than discard, it recasts. Rather than reject, it affirms the reality that things do not coalesce in neat packages of personal identity, national identity, cultural identity. Terms like "national" and "marginal" and "minority" fall apart. The power of the imagination – on a communal as well as a personal level – moves readily beyond what it has already considered. But in considering, the strategies of the dispossessed are seldom to discard. Chicano culture is not in the business of adding to the trash heap of Euramerican culture. There is a luxury implicit in a model of consumption and waste – the drive to "make it new" – that the disempowered might think of as sinful. Rather, there is reclamation. And in reclaiming, one finds another voice that adds nuance and urgency to contemporary critical considerations. All in all, Chicano culture demonstrates that the creation of culture is no luxury, the play of language no innocent game. To lift pen, brush, pencil – this is an act of survival.

Américo Paredes, at the suggestion of Rolando Hinojosa, draws as the epigraph to *Between Two Worlds* a quote from Matthew Arnold: "Wandering between two worlds, one dead, / The other powerless to be born. . . ." The futility suggested by Arnold's poem, and invoked by Paredes's quote, fades when the despair over two inert worlds gives way to a sense of wonder in the very act of movement. Wandering two worlds, Paredes's poetry marks how Chicano culture could begin to move among four, perhaps five. Positioning itself against the margins of history, against the mystifications of prejudice, Chicano culture also positions itself in relation to marginality and mythology as it migrates through a difficult terrain. It moves across worlds, carrying a contraband of hope from one to another. In motion, the culture can cast a glance along the far horizons of those worlds, guess at what lies just beyond them. The wonder made evident in Chicano culture is not the getting beyond those horizons. The wonder is the movement between.

Notes

Chapter 1

1. Raymund Paredes argues this point in "The Promise of Chicano Literature" (1977).
2. For example, *Do the Americas Have a Common Literature?* edited by Gustavo Pérez Firmat (1990), *Chicano Narrative* by Ramón Saldívar (1990), *The Dialectics of Our America* by José David Saldívar (1991), *Criticism in the Borderlands*, edited by Hectór Calderón and José David Saldívar (1991), and *Border Writing* by Emily Hicks (1991). See also Héctor Calderón, "At the Crossroads of History, on the Borders of Change" (1990). For earlier discussions of literary critical trends in Chicano culture, see Carmen Salazar Parr, "Current Trends in Chicano Literary Criticism" (1979), and Joseph Sommers, "Critical Approaches to Chicano Literature" (1979).
3. See also Leo R. Chavez, "Settlers and Sojourners" (1988), for a discussion of binational families and their effect in problematizing the notion of "resident."
4. Of particular use are *Literatura Chicana: Texto y Contexto/Chicano Literature: Text and Context*, edited by Antonia Castañeda Shular, Tomás Ybarra-Frausto, and Joseph Sommers (1972); *Modern Chicano Writers: A Collection of Critical Essays*, edited by Joseph Sommers and Tomás Ybarra-Frausto (1979); *The Identification and Analysis of Chicano Literature*, edited by Francisco Jiménez (1979). For a criti-

cal collection on the Chicano novel, see *Contemporary Chicano Fiction*, edited by Vernon E. Lattin (1986).

5. See especially Cordelia Candelaria's excellent *Chicano Poetry: A Critical Introduction* (1986). Candelaria divides Chicano poetry through the early 1980s into three phases: the first produced the polemical poetry of El Movimiento, the second moved toward defining a Chicano poetics, the third saw a flowering of Chicano poetry in "a sophistication of style and technique, an individuality in treatment of subject and theme, and a mature skill and control that signal an inevitably developed form" (1986: 137). This schema is useful. However, I prefer to use the terms "early" to cover both first and second phase poetry and "contemporary" or "recent" to signify poetry written from the late 1970s through the 1980s. Other books that provide useful though more schematic overviews of Chicano poetry are *Chicano Literature* by Charles M. Tatum (1982) and *Understanding Chicano Literature* by Carl R. Shirley and Paula W. Shirley (1988).
6. Other studies that might prove enlightening are *The Third Woman: Minority Women Writers of the United States*, edited by Dexter Fisher (1980); *Beyond Stereotypes: The Critical Analysis of Chicana Literature*, edited by María Herrera-Sobek (1985); *Chicana Voices*, edited by Teresa Córdova et al. (1986); *Woman of Her Word: Hispanic Women Write*, edited by Evangelina Vigil (1987); *Chicana Creativity and Criticism: Charting New Frontiers in American Literature*, edited by María Hererra-Sobek and Helena María Viramontes (1988); *European Perspectives on Hispanic Literature of the United States*, edited by Genvieve Fabre (1988); *Breaking Boundaries: Latina Writing and Critical Readings*, edited by Asunción Horno-Delgado et al. (1989); *Mexican Ballads, Chicano Poems* by José Limón (1992).
7. See Gayatri Spivak, "Theory in the Margin" (1991: 156), for a discussion of unexamined nativism.
8. For some discussion of Tijerina's actions and effects, see Juan Gómez-Quiñones, *Chicano Politics* (1990: 115–18), John R. Chávez, *The Lost Land* (1984: 139–41), Patricia Bell Blawis, *Tijerina and the Land Grants* (1971), and Peter Nabokov, *Tijerina and the Courthouse Raid* (1969).
9. Tino Villanueva traces the etymologies and connotations of "Chicano" in "Sobre el término 'Chicano'" (1978). The word "Chicano" may be a shortened slang version of *Mexicano*, though no one is sure of its origin. Whatever its source, it had been used primarily as a pejorative term before La Causa in the 1960s. For information about the term "Chicano," and other associated terms like pocho, pachuco, cholo, I am indebted to Rafael Pérez Sandoval for the use of his (as yet) unpublished manuscript *Diccionario etimológico de chicanismos y mexicanismos en el español chicano*. With all these terms, the pejorative is implicit within the affective, as Pérez Sandoval notes. Much of the information I include about the etymology of these terms I gratefully draw from his manuscript.

10. In addition, the aural elision between pre-Cartesian and pre-Cortesian marks a critique of the Englightenment project implicit to Chicano culture.
11. I follow the schema layed out in the introduction to Inga Clendinnen's study *Aztecs* (1991).

Chapter 2

1. The move to define and redefine this cultural space proves not to be an uncontroversial position. Reacting to Bruce-Novoa's delimitation of the "space" for Chicano letters a decade later, Francisco Lomelí argues: "To establish a priori guidelines, to define the literary space in which Chicanos should write is to impose preconceptions and curtail creativity. Literature requires a free spirit if it is to nurture the idea of liberation. Moreover, writing according to restricted subjects harms Chicanos' ability to produce literature. Then the myth that our scope is confined to narrow horizons is really fulfilled" (1984:106). Lomelí's criticism proves something of an overstatement. Because Bruce-Novoa wants to situate Chicano literature in the realm of all literature, to demonstrate that its interests coincide with those of other world literatures, he does not seek so much to delimit as to open the space Chicano literature can occupy. However, one probably does want to remain suspicious of Bruce-Novoa's universalizing tendency.
2. Angie Chabram notes that both Bruce-Novoa and Saldívar form part of a Chicano literary critical presence to emerge from Yale. She is careful to note, however: "While these institutional affiliations do not signify that the circles of Chicano critical thought necessarily replicate the predominant theoretical perspectives associated with specific educational settings, they do illustrate the literary-institutional forces which are affecting the conceptual development of this emerging critical practice" (1991: 130). Which is to say, most Chicano literary criticism does not emerge "organically."
3. Unless otherwise noted, all italics are in the original texts.
4. See César Chávez, "Peregrinación, Penitencia, Revolución" (1973) and "To Be a Man is To Suffer for Others" (1973), for examples of the religious dynamic in Chicano social movement. See also Américo Paredes, "Folklore, Lo Mexicano and Proverbs" (1982), for a discussion of the folkloric in the development of Chicano culture.
5. Héctor Calderón makes a different critique of Paredes's essay, arguing against the suggestion that Chicano literature follows a simple line of descent: "How many Chicano writers, for example, can trace their writing directly back to the Spanish chroniclers?" (1990: 225). Calderón puts his finger on another vexing issue for Chicano letters: How much does it represent descent from a tradition and a heritage, and how much is that tradition and heritage constructed?
6. The term "Renaissance" to describe Chicano literary production in the 1960s

and 1970s was first applied by Felipe de Ortego y Gasca in his article "The Chicano Renaissance." For a lucid discussion of the cultural and political exclusion Chicanas experienced during the Movement and their responses, see Angie Chabram-Dernersesian, "I Throw Punches for My Race, but I Don't Want to Be a Man" (1992).

7. Although it is dangerous to graft one theoretical matrix, like the one proposed by Deleuze and Guattari in their discussion of Franz Kafka, onto another body of literature, it seems appropriate to evoke their discussion. (The contributors to *The Nature and Context of Minority Discourse* edited by JanMohamed and Lloyd have certainly and productively made a similar move.) Deleuze and Guattari deploy Franz Kafka's description of minor literature as one that highlights its social and political function, fosters collective rather than individual utterances, and deterritorializes language (1975: 16–18). The clumsy term "deterritorialization" implies not simply an alienation or estrangement – such as the historical condition of Chicanos displaced by invasion or economic necessity – but also a dissolution of system, stratification, order. Deterritorialization is thus marked by an expression that "must break forms, encourage ruptures and new sproutings. When a form is broken, one must reconstruct the content that will necessarily be part of a rupture in the order of things" (1975: 28). The rupture of form in Chicano poetry is treated more specifically in Chapter 7 of this volume. See Ronald Bogue, *Deleuze and Guattari* (1989), especially pp. 116–21, for a discussion of deleuzeguattarian linguistic deterritorialization.
8. Although 1 million people still speak Nahuatl, the image of Aztec culture that haunts Chicano artists belongs to an age long gone. Felipe de Ortego y Gasca in his article "An Introduction to Chicano Poetry" associates the pre-Cortesian Aztec with the Hellenic Golden Age (1979: 112). The invocation of five worlds is – in keeping with my topic – an allusion to the Aztec belief that we are living in the fifth world of creation. Miguel León-Portilla's often cited *Aztec Thought and Culture* provides the most comprehensive discussion of a Mexican pre-Cortesian concept of the universe. See also Inga Clendinnen's study of the Mexica, *Aztecs*.
9. As Edward Said notes in his preface to *Selected Subaltern Studies*, edited by Ranajit Guha and Gayatri Spivak, "if subaltern history is construed to be only a separatist enterprise . . . then it runs the risk of just being a mirror opposite the writing whose tyranny it disputes. It is also likely to be as exclusivist, as limited, provincial, and discriminatory in its suppressions and repressions as the master discourses of colonialism and elitism" (1988: viii).
10. "Querámoslo o no, hemos incorporado – unos más, otros menos – la visión del mundo de las clases dominantes, y . . . concomitantemente nuestra acción en la historia – inclusive en la creación literaria – estará mediatizada por esta circunstancia." Rodríguez goes on to argue that since all Chicano literature emerges from its relationship with the dominant culture, an inevitable chasm

between the Chicano writer and the community will result. This view posits the Chicano community as an agent of pure alterity. Chicano culture itself is already hybridized, and I would argue that ultimately at some level the Chicano writer provides a model by which issues of agency and identity confront and engage – rather than capitulate to – powers of dominant culture and society.

11. See Ricardo Romo, *East Los Angeles: History of a Barrio*; David Montejano, *Anglos and Mexicans in the Making of Texas, 1836–1986;* and, of course, Rodolfo Acuña, *Occupied America: A History of Chicanos*, for other versions of these events.
12. Here I echo Rodolfo Acuña's preface to the second edition of *Occupied America:* "The first edition of *Occupied America* followed the current of the times, adopting the internal colonial model which was popular during the 1960s and early 1970s. . . . I have reevaluated the internal colonial model and set it aside as a useful paradigm relevant to the nineteenth century but not to the twentieth" (1981: vii).
13. Wald suggests that the model of internal colonialism helps one understand the dynamics and specificity of racial "otherness" in the United States. He notes that internal colonial theorists suggest six areas that distinguish colonized people of color from other U.S. immigrants: 1) kidnapping, conquest, and genocide, not immigration, form the means by which they were originally incorporated into U.S. society; 2) the occupations they held – as slaves, field laborers, domestics – set them apart; 3) an American apartheid maintains a segregation in which they continue to live under worse conditions than European ethnics; 4) their religious beliefs keep them apart from European ethnics; 5) their cultures do not traditionally rely upon Greek and Roman classical civilization as a model; 6) experiences of racism and cultural Eurocentrism result in a need to reconstitute their sense of cultural identity. (This last point, in fact, forms the central focus of my study: ways in which Chicano communities and individuals use poetic forms to construct and/or express a sense of self-identity.)
14. García and de la Garza elaborate: 1) the colonized group has entered the dominant society involuntarily, through a forced process (as did the first Chicanos as the result of the Treaty of Guadalupe Hidalgo; 2) the colonizing power carries out policies to constrain, transform, or destroy native culture by devaluing or forbidding traditional ways of life and language; 3) representatives of the dominant group manage and administer the colonized group, preventing political self-representation or determination; 4) the dominant group views the colonized group as distinctively different and inferior (1977: 8–9).
15. The article "Hispanic Politicians Seek a Recipe for Raw Numbers" by Roberto Suro details the bid by Latinos for increased national political representation through the redistricting process following the 1990 census.

This move "represents the largest effort at political empowerment under way by an American minority group," according to Suro (1991: 1). (Even with this growth in potential political power, the forces of racism and prejudice that yet exist in our society forms one point where García and de la Garza cannot be critiqued.)

16. A small example: More Latinos, including Chicanos, are finding employment, more are earning at least $50,000 a year, and more are completing high school. At the same time, more Latinos find themselves living in poverty. The diversity among Latinos, on a socioeconomic level alone, is extensive and dynamic (Barringer 1991: 7).
17. For a clear overview and engaging discussion of these issues, see Helen Tiffin, "Post-Colonial Literatures and Counter-Discourse." See also Stephon Slemon, "Monuments of Empire," in which he argues that postcolonial (that is, "multicultural") criticism can learn to read not just thematic resistance to colonialism, but also "the counter-discursive investments of post-colonial figuration on the level of genre and mode" (1987: 14).
18. The "Plan Espíritual de Aztlán" was drafted at the Chicano Liberation Youth Conference in March 1969 by, among others, Alberto Urista, known better as the poet Alurista. For a brief discussion of the three traditions of Aztlán (pre-Mexica, Mexica, and Chicano) see Alurista's "Myth, Identity and Struggle in Three Chicano Novels." Here, as elsewhere, he discusses the metaphorical uses of Aztlán as a means of unifying "various delegations . . . into one nationalist body" (1988: 84). Chapter 3 of the present study elaborates on the issue of "Aztlán" and its influences in the various movements of Chicano poetry.
19. For an example of how borders serve in this capacity, one need look no further than the maquiladora system, in which U.S. companies have set up factories across the border in Mexico to profit from an eminently exploitable labor force, lax environmental laws, and corrupt enforcement agencies. Chapter 4 examines some of the effects and political repercussions of the maquiladora system.
20. Cognizant of this, Raymund Paredes, for example, notes: "The great divide in Chicano history is the year 1848 when the Treaty of Guadalupe Hidalgo ended twenty-one months of warfare between Mexico and the United States" (1982: 36). Luís Leal and Pepe Barrón argue that the period between 1848 and 1910 "was the time during which Chicano literature laid the basis on which it was later to develop" (1982: 18).
21. This is particularly true of the Southwest. However, the controversies over Chicano Studies at U.C.L.A. and the question of whether to change its status from program to department exemplifies the dynamic and still problematic position of Chicano Studies within academic institutions. Moreover, many Chicano scholars continue to be treated like second-class citizens within their departments and universities. Nevertheless, Chicano Studies is a strong and

increasingly powerful presence on campuses across the country. See Marita Hernández "Chicano Studies Find Favor on Campus" (1989) for a more complete discussion.

22. These phrases come from Ted Hamerow's rather pedestrian article, "Do we need 'cafeteria-style' education?" The article, precisely because of its pedestrianism, reveals the superficiality of the stale neoconservative argument that the "altering" of the "curricular menu" by racial, ethnic, cultural, and gender-based groups means that the "old order had to go, lock, stock and barrel" (6). The article appears in *L & S Magazine*, College of Letters and Science, University of Wisconsin–Madison (Fall 1990): 5–8.
23. As early as 1979, the late Joseph Sommers constructed a similar argument: "What legitimation has been accorded to Chicano literature and to related teaching and research in this field has been limited and ambiguous. The tendency has been to favor either the assimilation of the literature into an engulfing Anglo-American literary mainstream, or the dilution of critical perspective by means of newly validated formulae such as 'cultural pluralism' or 'ethnopoetics'" (1979: 31–2).
24. As Gayatri Spivak notes about her own position as a (non-self-identified) postcolonial critic: "A hundred years ago it was impossible for me to speak, for the precise reason that makes it only too possible for me to speak in certain circles now. I see in that a kind of reversal, which is again a little suspicious" (1990: 60).
25. "Llamo poetas de 'La Nueva Trayectoria' a aquellos que conscientemente buscan, dentro de las formas poéticas tradicionales, nuevos modelos, nuevas creaciones de metáforas personales usando la expresión chicana para crear imágenes dentro de una realidad artísticamente chicana que fije nuestra sensibilidad dentro del mosaico artistico universal." These poets, Pino goes on to note, do not express the spontaneity of a political movement or the popular sentiment of the moment. Instead, they are poets who have read and studied international poetry, from classical poets like Homer to Beat poets like Ginsberg.
26. "Los que tratan de alcanzar universalidad sin dejar de pisar sus raíces."
27. See, for example, *Multiethnic Literature of the United States: Critical Introductions and Classroom Resources*, edited by Cordelia Candelaria; *Imagining America: Stories from the Promised Land*, edited by Wesley Brown and Amy Ling; *Braided Lives: An Anthology of Multicultural American Writing*, edited by the Minnesota Council of Teachers of English; and *The Graywolf Annual Seven: Stories From the American Mosaic*, edited by Scott Walker.
28. The work of feminist critics like Christine Di Stefano and Sandra Harding provides excellent models with which Chicano and other multicultural critics can dialogue to articulate the problems of reliance upon reified accounts of race and rationality. These accounts, bequeathed by modern rationalist philosophy in constructing cultural critiques, inevitably limit the critical

potential of discourses constructed around such essentialized notions as "race" and "reason."

29. I quote here from the English translation from the well-circulated anthology edited by Valdez and Steiner, *Aztlán* (1972).
30. See in particular Chapter 5 of *Plotting Women*, in which Franco analyzes Vasconcelos's efforts to maintain a patriarchal front.
31. Here I find myself disagreeing somewhat with Ramón Saldívar in his analysis of Rudolfo Anaya's work. Saldívar argues: "Unlike other Chicano narratives . . . *Bless Me, Ultima* cancels out 'realism,' attempting to cross it out and lift it up to a higher realm of truth, as in some Hegelian dialectic. The facticity of this precritical idealist venture is nowhere more evident nor more dissatisfying than in Anaya's writings, which impose upon us the burden of restoring the whole socially concrete subtext of nineteenth- and twentieth-century Southwestern history, mythified and reified on so many levels of utopian compensation" (1990: 126). Although Anaya's narrative may signal a form of compensation, it also signals an aesthetic practice that crosses archaic modes of expression with a modern narrative form. In this aspect, his work reveals a central discontinuity that can serve as a focus for political critique.
32. "*Corrido,* the Mexicans call their narrative folk songs, especially those of epic themes, taking the name from *correr,* which means 'to run' or 'to flow,' for the *corrido* tells a story simply and swiftly without embellishments" (Paredes 1958: xi). In addition to Paredes, José Limón, María Herrera-Sobek, Ramón Saldívar, and José David Saldívar, among others, name the corrido the defining dimension of a Chicano poetics. José David Saldívar goes so far as to suggest "that the *corrido* is the central sociopoetic Chicano paradigm" (1986: 13), and José Limón argues that "the Mexican corrido is not a mere 'antecendent' or 'background' literature but rather, in [Harold] Bloom's terms, a master poem that, as key symbolic aciton, powerfully dominates and conditions the later written poetry" (1992: 2). I engage more fully with Limón's argument in Chapter 8.
33. Again, I use "1848" as a cultural icon here. Américo Paredes notes that the period from 1836 to the late 1930s – the time of greatest border conflict – is the actual historical period that forms the life span of the corrido. Corridos remained a popular form, however, and many were composed during El Movimiento to narrate the accomplishments of such figures as César Chávez and Reies López Tijerina. For a sample of corridos both traditional and new see Rumel Fuentes's "Corridos de Rumel."
34. In this respect it is useful to think of Ketu Katrak's theorizing about postcolonial women's texts: "post-colonial women writers participate actively in the ongoing process of decolonizing culture. Fanon's concept that 'decolonization is always a violent phenomenon' is useful for an analysis of how the English language is 'violated' from its standard usage and how literary forms are transformed from their definitions within the Western tradition. In

terms of language, it is as if a version of the cultural and economic violence perpetrated by the colonizer is now appropriated by writers in order to 'violate' the English language in its standard use" (1989: 169). Chapter 7 of the present study examines some of the ways Chicano poets violate standard English in a complex process of identity construction and deconstruction.

35. The term "community" is, of course, a shorthand for a series of social groupings and the qualities of shared relationships and values. There are Chicano communities that share a specific geographic locality (with an emphasis on community as a unit of social interaction), and Chicano communities that share specific systems of belief and traditions (with an emphasis on community as a relational network of shared values). Sometimes these communities coincide, sometimes they do not. When discussing "community," I more often than not refer to the second meaning. These distinctions rely on Raymond Williams's *Keywords* (1983).

36. His analysis also links the decline of interest since 1981 in forms of Mexican indigenous philosophy with the growing conservatism in the Age of Reagan: "It was *only* when dramatic transformations in ideology seemed desirable and possible that many Chicanos countered Anglo ethics, metaphysics, and logic with Mexican indigenous philosophy" (Klor de Alva 1986: 19).

37. Juan Armando Epple is representative of those critics whose enthusiasm for this project at times seems to minimize its conflicted, perhaps impossible, condition. He describes Chicano literature as "an interaction between image and imagination. The image is to see oneself existing, as if before a mirror. It describes the palpable experience of seeing oneself exist. Imagination is to project the known and the lived in a dream of the future. And literature is this (Aristotle already notes): it does not only describe what we have been – like history – but also what we can or could be" (1983: 168, my translation).

38. For a literary example of this image of women, see Rodolfo Gonzales's *Yo Soy Joaquín*: "I am / the black shawled / faithful women" and "I am the eyes of woman." For a discussion of androcentrism in pre-Cortesian Mexican culture, see June Nash, "The Aztecs and the Ideology of Male Dominance" (1978).

39. See Jean Franco's *Plotting Women* for a discussion of this phenomenon in Latin American nationalist movements. See as well Ketu Katrak's discussion of Indian liberation under Ghandi. She observes that the traditions most oppressive for women "are specifically located within the arena of female sexuality: fertility/infertility, motherhood, the sexual division of labor. The key issue of the control of female sexuality is legitimized, even effectively mystified, under the name of 'tradition'" (1989: 168).

40. See, for example, *Beyond Stereotypes: The Critical Analysis of Chicana Literature*, edited by María Herrera-Sobek (1985); *Contemporary Chicana Poetry: A Critical Approach to an Emerging Literature*, by Marta Ester Sánchez (1985); *Chicana Voices: Intersections of Class, Race, and Gender*, edited by Teresa Córdova et al. (1986); *Woman of Her Word: Hispanic Women Write*, edited by Evangelina Vigil

(1987); *Chicana Creativity and Criticism: Charting New Frontiers in American Literature*, edited by María Herrera-Sobek and Helena María Viramontes (1988); *Breaking Boundaries: Latina Writing and Critical Readings*, edited by Asunción Horno-Delgado et al. (1989); *Third Woman: The Sexuality of Latinas*, edited by Norma Alarcón, Ana Castillo, and Cherríe Moraga (1989); and *Between Borders: Essays on Mexicana/Chicana History*, edited by Adelaida R. Del Castillo (1990). For an excellent bibliography of Chicana writers and critics, refer to Norma Alarcón's "Chicana Writers and Critics in a Social Context" (1989c).

41. See also her discussion, "The Sardonic Powers of the Erotic in the Work of Ana Castillo" (1989b).
42. Of particular interest in relation to this issue are *The Dialectics of Our America: Genealogy, Cultural Critique, and Literary History* by José David Saldívar and *Do the Americas Have a Common Literature?* edited by Gustavo Pérez Firmat.

Chapter 3

1. Héctor Calderón notes that "it was the Delano strike that seized the public's imagination and mobilized many sectors of the Mexican-American community. Many students rallied and joined forces with farm workers on the picket lines. This turned out to be a decisive moment, for it was the youth, high school, and university students who were to give these regional events the sense of a broad social movement" (1990: 218). The re-creation of the Delano march in 1994 to commemorate the death of César Chávez underscores the strong political and cultural significance assigned to the Delano strike.
2. June Nash's article "The Aztecs and the Ideology of Male Dominance" provides a good overview of early Mexica "history." As she notes, "In the Aztec oral and pictographic tradition, myth and history are intertwined" (1978: 350).
3. See Juan Gómez-Quiñones, *Chicano Politics*, for an overview of the political effect of the United Farm Workers (1990: 105–7). For an early discussion of governmental blindness to Chicano issues, see Jerry Rankin, "Mexican Americans and National Policy-Making" (1973).
4. See "A Report From Aztlán" by Antonio Camejo for a discussion of La Raza Unida's successes (1970).
5. Here one finds another dichotomy. As Juan Gómez-Quiñones notes, Chicano leaders of the sixties were impeded by the contradictions between their assertive, often separatist, rhetoric and their conventional reformist demands and programs involving educational reform and voter-registration drives (1990: 141–6).
6. Alurista argues that "much of the literature that had flowed from the pens of

Anglo-American novelists, social comentators, journalists, and academicians since 1848 had rendered the Mexican in the United States as lazy, ignorant, criminally prone, and definitely not worthy of trust" (1981: 22–3). More mild in his critique and more limited in his focus, Cecil Robinson notes with bland understatement: "However naive and ethnocentric, the early accounts of Mexico written by Americans mark the opening phase of a lasting cultural involvement. . . . They vivify the emotional environment surrounding events which have had important consequences. An attitude toward Mexico frequently expressed by these writers and one with which we are still familiar in America's response to alien cultures was one of contempt for Mexico's ineptness with machinery and indifference to technological progress" (1973: 33).

7. Claims for Chicano nationalism were not sounded for the first time in 1969. In 1915, "The Plan de San Diego" was discovered by U.S. authorities in the Lower Rio Grande Valley of Texas. The Plan was an insurrectionary manifesto calling for the establishment of an independent republic made up of the states bordering Mexico. See Mario Barrera, *Beyond Aztlán,* for an overview of the various interpretations of the Plan, including its possible role as a Carranzista plot to stir up a fifth column of Chicanos in the United States during the Mexican Revolution (1988: 18–20).
8. Not only was Alurista one of the Plan's drafters, he was apparently one of its masterminds. "In Search of Aztlán" by Luis Leal notes that "before March, 1969, the date of the Denver Conference, no one talked about Aztlán. In fact, the first time that it was mentioned in a Chicano document was in 'El Plan Espiritual de Aztlán,' which was presented in Denver at that time. Apparently, it owes its creation to the poet Alurista who already, during the Autumn of 1968, had spoken about Aztlán in a class for Chicanos held at San Diego State University" (1981: 20).
9. See Acuña, *Occupied America* (1972: 130–43) as well as Ralph Guzmán, "The Function of Anglo-American Racism in the Political Development of Chicanos" (1971: 21–4), for examples of Euramerican reactions and ensuent legislation to "stem the tide" of Mexican immigration.
10. As Daniel Levy and Gabriel Székely note: "The revolution weakened the explicitly European orientation of the Díaz regime and focused on Mexico's indigenous roots. The Indian was increasingly depicted not as an exotic savage, but as a mature person – even the source of all that was good in Mexico" (1983: 34).
11. And of course the work of Paz himself has been extraordinarily influential. Of Mexico, Paz argues: "Ever since World War II we have been aware that the self-creation demanded of us by our national realities is no different from that which similar realities are demanding of others. The past has left us orphans, as it has the rest of the planet, and we must join together in inventing our common future. World history has become everyone's task and our own

labyrinth is the labyrinth of all mankind" (1950: 173). The universalism that so interests Paz forms a strong trajectory in the movement of Chicana cultural construction.

12. In a similar vein, Salvador Rodríguez del Pino reflects upon a 1977 television interview of a panel of Chicano writers: "All the participants agreed that there does exist a national Chicano literature that could be compared to a Mexican literature, a Russian, a French, etc. These national literatures express the experiences of their cultures, heritages and national values, and they demonstrate distinct characteristics that distinguish them from the other literatures" (1979b: 155, my translation). Alurista's assertions are not made in isolation.
13. Gómez-Quiñones indicates that, although its effects were politically limited, the Plan "was to substantiate the initial thrust for much of the subsequent ideological and political developments of 'cultural nationalism' among young Mexican people in the United States" (1990: 124).
14. There were movements afoot to regain land lost in the years of dispossession following 1848. Reies López Tijerina, for example, organized the Alianza Federal de Pueblos Libres in order to press claims for land rights and guarantees under the Treaty of Guadalupe Hidalgo.
15. The poem was written in 1967 and published by Bantam in 1972. In the early 1970s, several big publishing houses published works by Chicano writers. Sadly, this is no longer the case today. Although change seems to be afoot, most Chicano writers find themselves publishing with "specialty" publishers like Arte Público or small presses. For a discussion of the politics behind book publication and the failure of Chicano writers to crack "establishment" houses, see José David Saldívar, "The Hybridity of Culture in Arturo Islas's The Raid God," in his book *The Dialectics of Our America* (1991: 106–12).
16. Cordelia Candelaria discusses the various manifestations of *Yo Soy Joaquín*, as well as its position within the first phase of Chicano poetry (1986: 42–3).
17. José Limón notes that Bruce-Novoa "repeats a common mistake – that oral tradition 'simplifies' – and he limits the familial resemblances between Gonzales's self-styled epic poem and the precursory corrido tradition to superficial stylistic similarities" (1992: 116). Limón goes on to argue that the corrido exists as a negative influence within a poem that is itself an example of poetic and political adolescence (1992: 128–9).
18. See, for example, Leal and Barrón (1982: 22), Alurista (1981: 27), Carl and Paula Shirley (1988: 16), González (1977: 129).
19. Page numbers refer to the Bantam edition, which is the most widely available version of the poem.
20. No one can miss the incessant equation of Chicano identity with the male. See Cordelia Candelaria's brief discussion of the poem's androcentrism (1986: 43).
21. It should be noted that Gonzales organized the 1969 Chicano Youth

Conference in Denver where the "Plan Espiritual de Aztlán" was adopted. Moreover, he – along with Alurista – argued vehemently for the notion of Chicano cultural nationalism as a viable political strategy.

22. Fredric Jameson dwells on these issues in *Postmodernism*. He argues that the opposition between viewing new "agents of history" like Chicanos and other groups of resistance as working either fully against or for capitalism is a false one that precludes "the simultaneous possibility of active political commitment along with disabused systemic realism and contemplation" (1991: 330).
23. Abelardo Delgado's much anthologized poem "Stupid America" stands as a quintessential example of Movimiento poetry that accuses "stupid America" of misunderstanding and destroying the creative powers of the Chicano.
24. Baca does not call himself a Chicano but a detribalized Apache, foregrounding the holocaust of indigenous people by Euramericans in their territorialization of Aztlán.
25. John R. Chávez offers a concise history of the U.S. southwest from the pre-Cortesian era to the eighteenth century in Chapter 1 of *The Lost Land* (1984).
26. For a discussion of the atrocities commited by the Rangers against Mexicans and Chicanos see Américo Paredes (1958: 23–32) and Rodolfo Acuña (1972).
27. The term "line of flight" from Deleuze and Guattari is meant to suggest escape from binary choices. The line of flight is formed by ruptures within particular systems or orders. It allows for third possibilities – neither capitulation to regimes nor unconditional freedom from them. The line of flight is a way out, a means of changing the situation to something other. See *Kafka* (1975) and *Anti-Oedipus* (1972) as well as Ronald Bogue, *Deleuze and Guattari* (1989: 110–23).

Chapter 4

1. Cordelia Candelaria notes that Salinas's "Los Caudillos" "may be read as a verse summary of the Chicano Movement's actors and activities during the late 1960s and early 1970s" (1986: 112). The poem runs through the list of names and events that will, according to the poem, stoke the "conflagrating flames / of socio-political awareness." It concludes with the familiar affirmations and exhortations: "Ubiquitous? We're everywhere! / Arise! Bronze people, / the wagon-wheels gather momentum." Conflating pioneering images with the fiery rhetoric of revolution, the poem celebrates and exhorts its audience to greater activity and unity.
2. The disastrous tenure of the former Secretary of Education Lauro F. Cavazos, who blamed Latino teachers, parents, business communities, and elected officials for a 40 percent Latino school dropout rate, should demonstrate that every racial/ethnic group has a Clarence Thomas ready to embrace the

agendas of a ruling class and turn his or her back on the very constituencies that both enabled their rise to power and remain most in need of it.

3. For analyses of various expressions of a Chicano political unconscious, see Ramón Saldívar, *Chicano Narrative* (1990), and "A Dialectic of Difference" (1979), José David Saldívar, "Towards a Chicano Poetics" (1986), and "The Ideological and the Utopian in Tomás Rivera's *y no se lo tragó la tierra* and Ron Arias's *The Road to Tamazunchale*" (1985), and Héctor Calderón, "To Read Chicano Narrative" (1983). See also George Lipsitz, *Time Passages*, esp. Chapter 11, "Buscando America (Looking for America)" (1991).
4. Tomás Ybarra-Frausto, "The Chicano Movement and the Emergence of a Chicano Poetic Consciousness" (1977), provides a particularly cogent discussion of the interrelationship between the development of Chicano poetry and political activism.
5. This is not to say that the effort is not made. Cecil Robinson has traced the stereotype of Mexicans in American literature as lazy, savage, and immoral in *With the Ears of Strangers* (1973). Octavio Romano-V. in "The Anthology and Sociology of the Mexican American" (1973a) notes the characterization of Mexicans and Chicanos as passive and fatalistic within "scholarly" discourses. Carl Allsup sketches the perpetuation of these stereotypical views in the realm of contemporary advertising and television in his essay "Who Done It? The Theft of Mexican-American History" (1983).
6. The church-based groups seeking social change in Los Angeles serve as useful examples. Operating since 1977, United Neighborhoods Organization (UNO) in East L.A. and the newer South Central Organizing Committee (SCOC) and East Valleys Organization (EVO) campaign for economic and community causes. They all draw their agenda and strategies from Saul Alinsky, the social reformer of the 1930s who rallied Chicago's Irish slums into a power bloc. See Scott Harris, "Community Crusaders" (1987), for a portrait of these groups.
7. UNO, for example, lowered Eastside auto insurance in Los Angeles, established a home-improvement loan program, and helped found a gang-intervention agency. In 1987 they successfully rallied several corporate and independent grocery stores to increase the minimum wage from $3.53 to $5.01 an hour.
8. There are two positions on the effect of maquiladoras on migration. One suggests that employment along the northern Mexican border reduces undocumented immigration into the United States. The other argues that increased levels of employment along the border leads to a heavy internal migration that spills over into the United States when migrants are unable to find full-time employment. Davila and Saenz conclude that "employment activity in the maquiladoras has generally had a negative impact on undocumented immigration to the United States" (1990: 105).
9. In the words of Catalina Denman, a public health specialist at the research institute Colegio de Sonora: "In the course of just a few years the maquiladoras brought the industrial revolution and all that goes with it to a region that was

completely unprepared for it" (quoted in Suro 1991: 15). The $8 billion that companies save by manufacturing in Mexico is seldom invested to make this transition any easier.

10. Tolan quotes Kenneth O. Lillie, head of the Nogales Maquiladora Association: "It's not our job to put U.S. standards into Mexico. I'm all for seeing Mexico improve, but it's not my job to make it happen" (1990: 19).
11. See also María Patricia Fernández-Kelly's study of the maquiladora system in *For We are Sold, I and My People* (1983).
12. Gómez-Quiñones argues this point: "Crucial to this development is the need for generalized national political consciousness, agreed-upon priorities, and principled leadership" (1990: 214). His argument, premised on a coming to terms with the political process and social reality of the United States, seems compelling as one way of propelling Chicano issues onto a national stage.
13. Paredes, *With His Pistol in His Hand* (1958), studies the oral tradition that emerged as a celebration of one such act of resistance. Chapter 3 of John R. Chávez's *The Lost Land* (1984) traces some other forms of resistance. Of the Chicano history of dispossession, he notes: "Next to the heavy invasion of Anglo settlers, the most serious attack to Mexican culture in the Southwest during the nineteenth century was the assault on native landowners, an attack that almost uprooted Mexicans from the region. Though the loss of an exploitive elite's huge estates may seem deserved, the loss was also experienced by the common man because the native upper class was replaced by an even more oppressive foreign elite, more oppressive because it had little respect for the culture of the ordinary Mexican who would continue to do much of the heavy labor throughout the Southwest" (1984: 62). See also David J. Weber, *Foreigners in Their Native Land* (1973).
14. The word "jornada" is also used to mean a day of work. So the line here carries some irony – the migrants are impelled by their free spirit that controls the day's labor. I thank Katharita Lamoza for pointing out this other second reading.
15. "gente buena, / gente honesta, / gente víctima de su necesidad de migrar, / la lechuga o la justica es lo que van a sembrar."
16. See Acuña, *Occupied America* (1972: 202–3), for an overview. On 4 October 1944 the guilty verdicts were overturned by the Second District Court of Appeals.
17. In a *New York Times* editorial Peter Passell provides a review of the reports indicating the miniscule negative effect new immigrants have on the U.S. economy. His article concludes that "the conventional economic wisdom pitting American poor against the immigrant poor is crumbling. So too, perhaps, will the conventional political wisdom pitting labor against the outsider" (1990: E4).
18. Chávez, in *The Lost Land*, discusses the cultural and political benefits of

continued Mexican migration into the United States. Cultural ties are maintained, linguistic fluency is required, and a shared sense of heritage, culture, and oppression bind Chicano to Mexican (1984: 125–7, 151–5).

19. In "The Streets of Gary Soto," Julian Olivares reads the poem in a less positive light, arguing that the speaker, "in comic desperation, tries to convince [the inhabitants of middle class America] that he, too, is American by saluting America" (1990: 45). Whereas Olivares reads the poem as "a metaphor of the speaker's search for a place in American society" (1990: 45), I see it as an affirmation of the multiple identities that demarcate the Chicano experience.
20. See Yves-Charles Grandjeat, "Ricardo Sánchez," for an insightful but overly lauditory analysis of his work. He calls Sánchez "the foremost representative of 'pinto' poetry" who "epitomizes the condition of a Chicano caught in a hostile society" (1988: 33). His response is to find a voice, to project a type of writing "clearly meant to materialize into a medium" (1988: 39). Juan Bruce-Novoa, by contrast, sees in the grand gesture of Sánchez's poetic voice a compensatory gesture that masks a fear of silence: "It is as if he were filling an empty wall with graffiti, and any empty place is a lack of existence, a dangerous silence" (1982: 158). Bruce-Novoa's perception seems to more closely correspond to the experience of the poetry. I would add that Sánchez's effusive tone and style represent as well the response of a creative individual attempting to find a voice that can contest an overwhelmingly oppressive experience.
21. The term "awiry" could also indicate the use of English by Baca as a writer creating "minor" literature with a high coefficient of deterritorialization. See Deleuze and Guattari, *Kafka* (1975: 16–19).
22. In his first collection, *Crazy Gypsy*, Salinas does include a few "political" poems, which Soto notes are "often simplistic in their utterances, banal in their vision, and dependent upon 'pat' lines to move the reader" (1982: 75).
23. In *Chicano Poetry*, Bruce-Novoa points out that Romano's use of the term "movement" "creates the impression of a unified program, with purpose and ideology. There is no justification for the usage" (1982: 219, n. 2).
24. Rafael Jesús Gonzáles sketches the debate over the term pachuco, whether it derives from the word Pachoa-can of Nahuatl origin meaning "residence of the Chief," from the Nahuatl words "pachtli" and "ca" meaning "grassy place," or from a corruption of the Spanish "pachucho" meaning overripe. See "Pachuco: The Birth of a Creole Language" (1967).
25. Rosaura Sánchez in *Chicano Discourse* notes that the origins of caló "have been traced back to Spain where the gypsy language (of Indic origin) had become heavily hispanicized and mingled and greatly blended with *germanía*, the speech of Spanish delinquents. In Spain *caló* generally means 'language of the Gypsies' but is now used by the Gypsies to refer to themselves" (1983: 84–5). From its inception, the term "caló" has been associated with marginal constituencies.

26. As Juan Gómez-Quiñones notes, anger over "this act of discrimination led to the establishment by Dr. Hector García, attorney Gus García, and a group of Mexican veterans of the G.I. Forum, a well-structured and well-led organization, with formal membership initially offered to veterans. Mexican Americans had been members of veteran groups since the nineteenth century, but Anglo veteran groups displayed no specific interest in them. . . . The G.I. Forum was dedicated to assisting Mexican veterans, providing services and leadership, ending discrimination, and maximizing Mexican influence in government" (1990: 60). The G.I. Forum proved highly influential and made significant contributions in the areas of education and business for Chicanos.
27. The most extensive formal discussions remain Ignacio Orlando Trujillo "Linguistic Structures in José Montoya's 'El Louie'" (1979) and Juan Bruce-Novoa, *Chicano Poetry* (1982: 14–25). See also Cordelia Candelaria, *Chicano Poetry* (1986), and Teresa McKenna, "On Chicano Poetry and the Political Age" (1991).
28. McKenna argues that the corrido tradition diffuses itself both throughout Chicana poetic production and in the continued creation of traditional corridos. In these later corridos, McKenna argues, mythic signification like that evident in the classic corrido of Gregorio Cortez disappears. The political nature of the events celebrated in later corridos and contemporary poetry becomes subsumed by the rhetorical presentation itself (1991: 194). Formulating a similar argument, Rafael Grajeda says of the pachuco in José Montoya's "Los Vatos" "walking out of his house, past his sister and his mother, to meet his assassins, hardly compares with the dignified manner in which another legendary figure, Gregorio Cortez, is described surrendering to the sheriff upon hearing that his people are being punished because of him" (1980: 57). Although these analyses reflect astute readings of particular Chicana poems, the nostalgia for traditional heroes they evince posits a portrait of some more heroic past that the present cannot approach.
29. Although several contemporary Chicana poets draw on the corrido tradition, the folk-based production of corridos continues unabated as well. See Arturo Ramírez, "Views of the Corrido Hero" (1990), for an overview of developments in the modern production of corridos.
30. Because caló is primarily spoken, and because in Spanish a "b" or "v" beginning a word sounds the same, there is no "standard" spelling for words like bato or vato. The same is true with the caló word "watcha" and "guacha." They both mean to look or observe and are pronounced the same.
31. For a discussion of Romero's pastoral subjects and themes, see Cordelia Candelaria, *Chicano Poetry* (1986: 118–22).
32. Interestingly, Mora indicates that she has not read much Chicano poetry: "I feel that I am not as well versed as I'd like to be about Chicano literature, and the problem there is time. Like most of us I did not grow up reading it" (Alarcón 1986: 124).

33. See Miguel León-Portilla, *Aztec Thought and Culture*, for a discussion of *flor y canto* as an example of *difrasismo* – "a procedure in which a single idea is expressed by two words" – commonly used in Nahuatl (1963: 75).

Chapter 5

1. Suleiman refers to the crossing of feminism with postmodernism in this quote. She notes that the same argument can be made "for the alliance between postmodernism and Third World minorities or Afro-American writers, male and female" (1991: 127).
2. Hal Foster's introduction to *The Anti-Aesthetic* (1983) argues for a critical postmodernism that stands in contradistinction to a neoconservative antimodernism. Jürgen Habermas, in his well known "Modernity – An Incomplete Project," like Foster argues that postmodernism can represent a neoconservative reaction against modernism, but implies that any critical postmodernism is really another turn in the modernist project. Andreas Huyssen in "Mapping the Postmodern" (1984) seeks to articulate those modalities where postmodernism finds its most powerful critical focus: among green, women's, and minority movements.
3. There are, of course, notable and growing exceptions to this observation. I engage with several of these critics in the present chapter.
4. See Craig Owens's "The Discourse of Others: Feminists and Postmodernism" (1983), Elspeth Probyn's "Travels in the Postmodern: Making Sense of the Local" (1990), and Iris Marion Young's "The Ideal Community and the Politics of Difference" (1990) for discussions of the politics of locality; George Lipsitz's "Rocking Around the Historical Bloc" (1991) and Fredric Jameson's "Periodizing the 60s" (1984a) for discussions of pastiche as the aesthetic form of choice in postmodernism; C. Barry Chabot's "The Problem of the Postmodern" (1991) and Andreas Huyssen's "Mapping the Postmodern" (1984) for discussions of postmodernism as a critical cultural practice; Gianni Vattimo's "The End of (Hi)story" (1991) and Rosalind E. Krauss's "The Originality of the Avant-Garde" (1991) and "Sculpture in the Expanded Field" (1983) for discussions of postmodernism, history, and tradition.
5. "The 60s was, then, the period in which all these 'natives' [minorities, women, etc.] became human beings, and this internally as well as externally: those inner colonized of the first world – 'minorities,' marginals, and women – fully as much as its external subjects and official 'natives.' All these 'natives' of gender, race, etc. – new social and political categories – are related to a crisis in the more universal category of social class, the institutions through which a real class politics expressed itself" (Jameson 1984a: 181). As a descriptive statement, Jameson is correct. However, later in this chapter I critique his all too easy conflation of race and class politics.
6. Rivera has written on the relations between the Chicano town and gown in his

article "The Role of the Chicano Academic and the Chicano Non-Academic Community" (1986). While noting that the community's view of the academic may range from opportunistic *pendejo* to valued intellectual, Rivera concludes that the Chicano academic must become a respected member of the academy in order to work for the community from a positition of power.

7. In "Opponents, Audiences, Constituencies and Community," Edward Said suggests that academic publishers function upon the same market principles as publishers of cookbooks, exercise manuals, and others in "a very long series of unnecessary books" (1982: 3). He goes on to argue for interference across academic and other disciplines as a means of intervening in the safe reproduction of specialized knowledge. I would argue that this is an articulation of a resistant postmodern and multicultural strategy.
8. Edward Said's argument in "Opponents, Audiences, Constituencies and Community" resonates with Habermas's view. However, it is clear that Said argues for a greater sense of contingency, improvisation, immediacy. His concerns are, in short, local.
9. See, for example, Tony Tanner's *City of Words* (1971), Jerome Klinkowitz's *Literary Disruptions* (1975), Robert Scholes's *Fabulation and Metafiction* (1979), or Larry McCaffery's *The Metafictional Muse* (1982). All of these works, in distinct and original ways, posit the postmodern as primarily an aesthetic condition.
10. This argument echoes Fredric Jameson's view that postmodernism is the cultural manifestation of, response to, and engagement with postmodernity – postmodernity being the modes of production in late capitalist societies. Although I disagree with Jameson on a number of points, it must be said that his critical project is certainly an allied one. Moreover, his descriptions of (reactionary) postmodern culture are terribly astute and insightful. His overall vision of postmodernism as the logic of late capitalism seems to preclude, however, any (genuinely, would be the term Jameson would be drawn to) resistant postmodern politics. For a clear and concise discussion of Jameson's views on postmodernism, see Anders Stephanson's interview in *Social Text* (1987).
11. Gayatri Spivak's comment on her position as a multicultural critic foregrounds the ironies inherent to this condition: "A hundred years ago it was impossible for me to speak, for the precise reason that makes it only too possible for me to speak in certain circles now. I see in that a kind of reversal, which is again a little suspicious" (1990: 60).
12. See, for example, Michael Soldatenko-Gutiérrez's "Socrates, Curriculum and the Chicano/Chicana" (1990) for a discussion of the reactionary principles masked as curricular concerns for quality and their effects upon the Chicano/a scholar.
13. One thinks in this regard of Octavio Paz's discussion of Mexican identity in *Labyrinth of Solitude*: "The history of Mexico is the history of a man seeking

his parentage, his origins. . . . He wants to go back beyond the catastrophe he suffered: he wants to be a sun again, to return to the center of that life from which he was separated one day. (Was that day the Conquest? Independence?) Our solitude has the same roots as religious feelings. It is a form of orphanhood, an obscure awareness that we have been torn from the All, and an ardent search: a flight and a return, an effort to re-establish the bonds that unite us with the universe" (1950: 20). The history of dispossession is a long and insistent one in the formation of Mexican identity.

14. Helen Tiffin has talked about postcolonial cultures in a similar way: "Post-colonial cultures are inevitably hybridised, involving a dialectical relationship between European ontology and epistemology and the impulse to create or re-create independent local identity. Decolonization is process, not arrival" (1987: 17).
15. Visible as well, only after works like Henry Louis Gates's collection *"Race," Writing and Difference* (1986) and Werner Sollors's *Beyond Ethnicity* (1986) and edited collection *The Invention of Ethnicity* (1989), which represent the type of intellectual work that seeks to deconstruct social categories like "race" and "ethnicity." Ironically, in these texts, the Chicano and Chicano issues are, as Hector Calderón has observed, notably absent (1990: 228).
16. The conceptualization of the multicultural as a discontinuous space raises a slew of interesting questions. Do we want to include gay literature under the banner, or women's writing? Do we want to focus on the discourse of race as the marking that distinguishes the multicultural? Or do we want to focus on immigrant literature? Is multicultural literature a thematized or formalized condition? All of these issues present problems that, if answered, would give voice to some and silence others. For political and historical reasons tied to the development of the United States, I would make the case that the present discussion should maintain ethnic and racial markers as those that determine the boundaries of the multicultural.
17. For a fascinating discussion of an example of this dynamic process of identity construction, see Roger Rouse's "Mexican Migration and the Social Space of Postmodernism." His article studies the migration patterns of residents from Aguililla, Mexico, who, while maintaining ties in Aguililla, take up simultaneous residence in Redwood City, California: "The resulting contradictions have not come simply from persistence of past forms amid contemporary adjustments or from involvement in distinct lifeworlds within the United States. Rather, they reflect the fact that Aguilillans see their current lives and future possibilities as involving simultaneous engagements in places associated with markedly different forms of experience" (1991: 14).
18. Here Elizabeth Fox-Genovese's much cited observation proves apt: "From the perspective of those previously excluded from the cultural elite, the death of the subject or the death of the author seems somewhat premature. Surely it is no coincidence that the Western white male elite proclaimed the death of the

subject at precisely the moment at which it might have had to share that status with the women and peoples of other races and classes who were beginning to challenge its supremacy" (1986: 134).

19. Critics like Fred Pfeil in *Another Tale to Tell* (1990), Steve Connor in *Postmodernist Culture* (1989) and Michelle Wallace in *Invisibility Blues* (1990) offer counterbalance to the rather bleak function of subjectivity suggested by Jameson. These writers admit the ideological bases inherent to the construction of subjectivity, yet also posit the emancipatory potential of subject-construction when undertaken by members of devalued genders, sexualities, classes, and races. As Paul Smith has it: "the interpellation of the 'subject' into oppressed positions is not complete and monolithic; rather, interpellation also produces contradiction and negativity. The necessary existence of various and different subject-positions in the interpellated 'subject' produces resistance to the logic of domination while still being in a sense part of, or a by-product of, that logic" (1988: 152). I argue that the different cultural subject-positions available to a multicultural 'subject' establish a privileged position of resistance.
20. I use the metaphors of depth and surface as an echo of a vulgar Marxist base–super-structure model. I do not think this model is adequate or that it provides a conceptualization of the dynamic interpenetration between culture and social order. But, since I'm talking about Jameson, I'll let it stand.
21. Such critics as Héctor Calderón, José David Saldívar, Ramón Saldívar, and Richard Flores all cite Jameson's influence. The 1988 Modern Language Association Convention even included a panel on the intersection of the work of Fredric Jameson and the analysis of Chicano literature.
22. See Richard Rorty's *Philosophy and the Mirror of Nature* (1980).
23. Although I critique her for her poststructuralist essentialization of difference, Hutcheon's observations about the contradictory and simultaneous positions engendered by postmodernism and the multicultural are of value. She posits these positions, however, as "the contradictions inherent in any transitional moment" (Hutcheon 1989: 158). Why we should feel compelled to view this as a "transition" rather than a "stage of becoming" she leaves unclear.

Chapter 6

1. See Jacques Lafaye's *Quetzalcóatl and Guadalupe* (1976) for a discussion of the conflation of the Virgin Mary and the Aztec goddess Tonantzin.
2. In keeping with practices by Inga Clendinnen and Miguel León-Portilla, I use the term "Aztec" only to refer to the empire formed by the alliance between Tenóchtitlan and Tlatelolco. Nahua refers to the culture, Nahuatl to the language. The people who migrated from Aztlán and settled in the twin cities Tenóchtitlan and Tlatelolco called themselves Mexica.
3. Stephen Slemon argues that counterdiscursivity functions not only at the level

of thematic declaration of resistance, but also at the level of figuration. He argues that "it is through the refigurative, counter-discursive articulations of representational mode and generic structure, as much as through the textual manipulation of plot and character or theme and voice, that post-colonial writing reclaims its text from the dead hand of received tradition and enjoins the project of cognitive liberation; it is *within* the space of historical prefiguration that a differential, contestatory, and genuinely *post*-colonial semiotics actuates through literature in pursuit of political change" (1987: 14). The construction of mythic "memory" in Chicano cultural thought forms part of a strategy that reclaims "from the dead hand of received tradition" a project of liberation.

4. Poems by other writers, all published between 1971 and 1975, that resemble Alurista's work in these respects include Luís Omar Salinas's "Aztec Angel" in *Crazy Gypsy,* Leonardo Elias's "Aztec Mother" in *Voices of Aztlan*, edited by Dorothy Harth and Lewis Baldwin, and Nephtalí De León's "Of Bronze and Sacrifice" in *We Are Chicanos*, edited by Philip D. Ortego. As I've noted before, Alurista's name was actually Alberto Urista. Raúl R. Salinas, clearly taking a cue from Alurista, began publishing his poetry under the name raúlrsalinas.
5. Candelaria's study provides a useful description of Movement or Phase I poetry and its stylistic peculiarities (1986: 39–42).
6. Of his role as poet, Alurista states: "I'm convinced that my poetry reflects, or at least I try deliberately to reflect the experience of our people. I am not the author of my poetry. . . . The people are the authors of the language; the people are the authors of the imagery, of the symbols" (Bruce-Novoa 1980: 273). His position as a "mirror" of reality seems a little disengenuous, especially since Alurista of his own accord introduced the idea of Aztlán into Chicano discourse. The "people" in this case were consumers, not producers, of "their" symbols. See Luís Leal, "In Search of Aztlán" (1981), and Elyette Labarthe, "The Vicissitudes of Aztlán" (1990), for a discussion of Alurista's role in "discovering" Aztlán.
7. See Miguel León-Portilla's classic *Aztec Thought and Culture* (1963) for discussions of the various manifestations of Quetzalcoatl. See also Inga Clendinnen's study, *Aztecs* (1991). For a concise sketch of the significance of Quetzalcoatl and his legends, see the introduction by David Johnson to *Lord of the Dawn* (1987), Rudolfo Anaya's fictional re-creation of the Quetzalcoatl myth.
8. "huitzilopochtli empuña / machetes / pa' rajar grietas paredes / en salvajes tardes / lacera orgullos / aliviadoras mariposas papalotean."
9. More forcefully and dramatically, Ricardo Sánchez rails against "those who chant their cant about a quasi-historical phantasy, coining concepts about nahuatl dialectics and civilizations (were the Aztecs civil?), negate the fact that few of us – if any – came from a lineage of kings . . . and expect the people to identify with fantasies, distortions, beseeching them to appreciate neo-aztecan

apparitions divorced from the humanity and history of our people, as if myth were but a disneyland configuration that glorifies fantasy" (1973: 17).

10. Rosa Linda Fregoso and Angie Chabram discuss the complexity of Chicana cultural identification in "Chicana/o Cultural Representations: Reframing Alternative Critical Discourses." Their article is based on Stuart Hall's observaton that "cultural identity is neither continuous nor constantly interrupted but constantly framed between the simultaneous operation of the vectors of similarity, continuity, and difference" (quoted in Fregoso and Chabram 1990: 206).
11. Writing in the early 1980s, Saldívar goes on to note: "The task of the Chicano novel over the coming decade will not be simply to illustrate, represent, or translate a particular exotic reality nor even a certain conception of reality – this epistemological theory of reflection is theoretically sterile. Instead, it will serve to realize the *agency* of thematic figures in the process of demystifying the old world and producing a new world" (1981: 36). This critically astute observation applies equally well, I would argue, to Chicano poetry of the past decade.
12. The image is from Theodor Adorno's "Lyric Poetry and Society" (1957). Adorno argues that the aesthetic work marks the contradictions inherent to social order in history and is the manifestation of an anticipated time beyond history. This transcendent function of art resides, Adorno suggests, in the hermetic and resistant aesthetics associated with a complex and ambiguous modernism or in the authentically longing voice of folk literature. Chicano literature, speaking from a position that crosses these matrices of cultural production, stands outside Adorno's conceptualization of negative critique. I return to this issue in the concluding chapter.
13. Castillo has published two chapbooks – *Otro Canto* (1977) and *The Invitation* (1979) – as well as two collections of poetry – *Women are not Roses* (1984), which includes some of her earlier as well as new work, and *My Father Was a Toltec* (1988).
14. The poem appeared originally in *Revista Chicano-Riqueña,* 4.4 (Autumn 1976). It is reprinted in Dexter Fisher's *Third Woman* (1980: 390–2).
15. Octavio Paz discusses the sense of violation inherent to Mexican self-identity in *The Labyrinth of Solitude* (1950). He writes: "The *Chingada* is the Mother forcibly opened, violated or deceived. The *hijo de la Chingada* is the offspring of violation, of abduction or deceit. If we compare this expression with the Spanish *hijo de puta* (son of a whore), the difference is immediately obvious. To the Spaniard, dishonor consists in being the son of a woman who voluntarily surrenders herself: a prostitute. To the Mexican it consists in being the fruit of violation" (1950: 79–80). See also María Herrera-Sobek's "The Politics of Rape" (1988) and Norma Alarcón's "Traddutora, Traditora" (1989a) for a discussion of rape as a trope in the articulation of Chicano (and particularly Chicana) cultural identity.

16. Although Mexica society was highly stratified and class-bound, it was also dynamic, transforming itself over the course of its imperial expansion between 1248 A.D., when the Mexica first arrived in the central plateau of Mexico, and 1440, when Motecuhzoma I ruled the empire. See Jacques Soustelle, *The Daily Life of the Aztecs* (1955); Eric Wolf, *Sons of the Shaking Earth* (1963); and Miguel Léon-Portilla, *The Aztec Image of Self and Society* (1992).
17. Inga Clendinnen notes that women could achieve "fair independence and substantial mobility in Mexica society, despite their exclusion from the spectacular careers open to males" (1991: 157–8) and that although women had no public role, they functioned within their society exercising a degree of individual autonomy perhaps denied even men (1991: 206). These small liberties for women were, previous to the establishment of empire, more expansive and central to social organization. As June Nash notes in "The Aztecs and the Ideology of Male Dominance," the transformation from "a kinship-based society with a minimum of status differentiation to a class-structured empire" led steadily to the exclusion of lines of authority that included women. Women possessed at one time equal rights in the law and in the economy. Moreover, Toltec and early Mexica societies most likely passed on power and property matrilineally (1978: 350–3).
18. In this respect I take exception to the claims argued by Raymund Paredes in "Mexican American Authors and the American Dream" (1981). Paredes argues that Chicano writers invariably resist the ideology of possession that consumes American society. Chicano authors – speaking for and about the "labor pool" necessary to capitalism – often scrutinize economic relations in the United States. As I argue in Chapter 2, their work seems more to function within and against rather than outside the false consciousness represented by "the American Dream."
19. Although we might question Irigaray's essentialized version of the sexuality of "Woman," her analysis of the male gaze is particularly compelling.
20. I thank Ann Farnsworth-Alvear, Rosa Linda Fregoso, and Norma Cantú for their help with the present interpretation of this section.
21. At the same time, it is clear that Lucha Corpi, a self-identified Chicana, is very interested in Chicano causes. She was director of the Chicano Writers' Center and a director of the center's magazine, *Humanizarte*, and dedicates her novel *Delia's Song* to "all the Chicano students who participated in the Third World Srike, at the University of California at Berkeley, with my deepest gratitude."
22. The poems, written in Spanish, were translated by Catherine Rodríguez-Nieto.
23. I refer to the English translation of the poem. Where it seems appropriate, I have suggested alternate English phrasing in my analysis of the poem.
24. Tlazotéotl was the Mexica goddess of carnal love, sin, and confession. Through the mediation of a priest, one could once in one's life confess and

be purged of one's sins. Thus the goddess was called *tlaelquani*, the eater of filth. See Jacques Soustelle, *Daily Lives of the Aztecs*, for a discussion of Tlazoltéotl and her role in rites of purification (1955: 104, 193, 199).

25. As we have seen Michel Foucault articulate it, these forms of "micro-knowledge" work against the claims of "a unitary body of theory which would filter, hierarchise and order them in the name of some true knowledge and some arbitrary idea of what constitutes a science and its objects" (1980: 83). Thus micro-knowledge, working toward a resistance of dominant modes of thought, forms an alternate body of knowledge that – in the case of Chicano culture – derives from a variety of sources, including the mythic and folkloric.
26. For convenience, I have translated the Spanish quotes into English.

Chapter 7

1. He goes on to note that the variety of languages arises from the complex history of the Chicano. Chicanos form a population that is partly indigenous and partly immigrant. Moreover, as the development of linguistic codes like caló indicate, the variety of languages changes and modifies over time. The language used by one wave of Mexican immigrants takes hold and undergoes transformations within its new social setting. Later waves similarly add and modify their influences. This, in addition to regional differences, suggests how highly textured Chicano speech can be.
2. See Fernando Peñalosa (1980: 56ff.)
3. See Rosaura Sánchez, *Chicano Discourse* (1983), in addition to the works by L. A. Timm and Fernando Peñalosa already cited.
4. For treatments of interlingualism within Chicano literary fields, see Guadalupe Valdés Fallis, "Code-Switching in Bi-Lingual Chicano Poetry" (1976), Cordelia Candelaria, "Code-Switching as Metaphor in Chicano Poetry" (1988), and Carol W. Pfaff and Laura Chávez, "Spanish/English Code-Switching" (1986). For an excellent overview of the linguistic variations and different discursive patterns to be found in Chicano speech – from regionalist Spanish to caló to code-switching – see Rosaura Sánchez, "Spanish Codes in the Southwest" (1979).
5. Calvin Veltman concludes that, although continued immigration will increase the size of the Spanish language group in the United States, language shift to English by Spanish speakers "is both rapid and extensive" (1990: 122), such that by the year 2001, 8.5 million out of a total Latino population of 25 million will not speak Spanish at all.
6. "Pastiche is, like parody, the imitation of a peculiar mask, speech in a dead language: but it is a neutral practice of such mimicry, without any of parody's ulterior motives, amputated of the satiric impulse, devoid of laughter and of any conviction that alongside the abnormal tongue you have momentarily

borrowed, some healthy linguistic normality still exists. Pastiche is thus blank parody, a statue with blind eyeballs: it is to parody what that other interesting and historically original modern thing, the practice of a kind of blank irony, is to what Wayne Booth calls the 'stable ironies' of the 18th century." (Jameson 1984b: 65).

7. See also Ronald Bogue, *Deleuze and Guattari* (1989: 116–21).
8. *Kafka* explains the position of Kafka in relation to language: "the impossibility of writing other than in German is for the Prague Jews the feeling of an irreducible distance from their primitive Czech territoriality. And the impossibility of writing in German is the deterritorialization of the German population itself, an oppressive minority that speaks a langauge cut off from the masses, like a 'paper language' or an artificial language; this is all the more true for the Jews who are simultaneously a part of this minority and excluded from it" (Deleuze and Guattari 1975: 16–17).
9. *Kafka* suggests that the Prague German of Kafka that forms a deterritorialized language "can be compared in another context to what blacks in America today are able to do with the English language" (Deleuze and Guattari 1975: 17). Perhaps the comparison can be made, but neat parallels cannot be sustained.
10. Candelaria's essay goes on to argue that, among other things, the use of code-switching enriches the linguistic repetoire, alludes to culture (the politics of representation), reflects the social matrix (scrutinizes the discursive practices encoded in language), and asserts an ethnocultural autonomy.
11. The interlingualism thus resists rigid symbolic order, eliding meanings, foregrounding the disconnections between utterances and meaning.
12. "¡Ta hueno eso!" is not caló but a transliteration of regional dialect for "Está bueno eso," meaning "that is good." Tafolla's poem works to represent the numerous lingustic codes – Spanish, regional dialect, caló – that make up the richness of expression found in Chicano communities.
13. For example, Carol Pfaff and Laura Chávez study code-switching in five Chicano plays for their mirroring of natural discourse. They find, not surprisingly, that code-switching in the aesthetic texts is used in a much more limited way than in natural discourse. Nevertheless, they conclude, "the use of code-switching in Chicano drama supports . . . that 'code-switching' is a speech variety in its own right. Further, that it is the variety which covertly, if not yet overtly represents the true Chicano identity – drawing on both Anglo and Mexican culture – but a distinctive blend of its own" (1986: 252). Their study functions under two misconceptions: that aesthetic texts are meant to "reflect reality" and that such a thing as "the true Chicano identity" can be reflected in particular speech patterns.
14. Anzaldúa identifies at least eight languages spoken by Chicanos: standard English, working class and slang English, standard Spanish, standard Mexican Spanish, north Mexican Spanish dialect, Chicano Spanish, Tex-Mex, caló.

This list proves as good as any to indicate the polyglossia of Chicano speech. See "How to Tame a Wild Tongue" (1987: 55–8).

15. The title is impossible to translate adequately, losing the bite and dismissive tone evident in the caló. Though the title does not use profanity, roughly it could mean "you're worthless to me, fuck off."
16. "You're the type / of motherfucker / real tough / who likes to throw the weight around / and push people around / and throw punches / and break through doors / real bad / saying with your snout / 'that's tough shit!' / a real pain, / the bastard."
17. "and precisely for that reason / whereas ordinarly / out of common courtesy or stubbornness / the ground I'd stand and argue principles – / not this time / because that type of bullshit / doesn't merit my valuable time / and much less my energy / only that the bullshit stops there."
18. "because you know what? / out of pure self-interest / I like to wear only shoes that fit / I like to go about comfortable."

Chapter 8

1. Tino Villanueva, for example, has noted that his strong stylistic influences include William Carlos Williams and Dylan Thomas (presentation given at Phillips Academy, Andover, Mass., on July 26, 1993).
2. The term "historical avant-garde" finds its correlative in Latin American spaces where what in Anglo-American criticism is called "modernism" is called "vanguardismo." "Modernismo" in Latin America refers most generally to Parnassianism.
3. As Jean Baudrillard argues, the present age is one dominated by simulation: "Simulation is no longer that of a territory, a referential being or a substance. It is the generation of models of a real without origin or reality: a hyperreal" (1983: 2). The hyperreal is the sphere where signifiers evoke only their own selves and cannot point to any other reality. In fact, the category of the real disappears altogether: "No more mirror of being and appearances, of the real and its concept. No more imaginary coextensivity . . .. [The real] no longer enveloped by an imaginary . . . is no longer real at all. It is a hyperreal, the product of an irradiating synthesis of combinatory models in a hyperspace without atmosphere" (1983: 3). Hyperreality is formed by the ceaseless quotation of already quoted texts. Thus modernism becomes, in the market, another of innumerable commodities available for exploitation. The market employs a simulacra of alienation – one need think only of the extensive marketing aimed at "alienated youth," for example – in order to sell products that help form a simulated community.
4. As should be clear, Limón constructs his critical framework by relying upon and modifying Harold Bloom's critical framework about the anxiety of influence.

5. The corrido, in Spanish and English, as well as Paredes's poem "Guitarreros," are reproduced in Limón's book (1992: 46–9).
6. Salazar was a Chicano newspaperman with the Los Angeles Times who ended up as manager of KMEX, the local Spanish-language television station. As one of the only reporters with a say in the Anglo-dominated media, Salazar was an enormously popular individual among the Chicano community in Los Angeles and an enormously important individual, since he could bring the concerns of the community to a larger (and largely ignorant) audience. During the police-induced riots that followed the 1970 Vietnam Moratorium – a large protest in East Los Angeles against the war – Salazar had his head torn in half by a police tear-gas projectile while drinking a beer in the Silver Dollar Bar. "All the rest" who share the dedication may represent other Chicanos who suffered less public and publicized deaths at the hands of a repressive state apparatus.
7. "¿Y luego? . . . / ¿De allí a dónde? . . . / / Después de decirle al mundo / que chingue su santa madre, / pues no tengo el pico chueco / ni hay perro que a mí me ladre . . . / / ¿De allí a dónde? / / Después de que me desbuche / diciéndoles lo que siento, / lo que han hecho con nosotros / por tan largo, largo tiempo / / ¿Y luego? . . . / / Después de todas la marchas / y toda la discusión, / los discursos, los disparos / los comités en sesión . . . / / ¿Y luego? . . . / Carnales . . . / ¿De allí a dónde?" (Paredes, 1970; ellipses in the original). Nothing poetic is lost by paraphrasing the poem within the body of the text.
8. The 1992 uprisings in Los Angeles, for example, reflected a profound belief – and disillusionment – in the judicial system of this country. Beyond the riots as a "critique" of American justice, the looting and violence recognized an essential economic and social inequality at the heart of U.S. society. The cry "no justice, no peace" perfectly reflects this point.

Works Cited

Acuña, Rodolfo. *Occupied America: A History of Chicanos.* New York: Harper & Row, 1972.

Occupied America: A History of Chicanos, 2nd ed. New York: Harper & Row, 1981.

Adorno, Theodor W. "Lyric Poetry and Society." Bruce Mayo, trans. *Telos* 20 (Summer 1974 [1957]): 56–71.

Ahmad, Aijaz. "Jameson's Rhetoric of Otherness and the 'National Allegory.'" *Social Text* 17 (Fall 1987): 3–25.

Alarcón, Francisco. "Mestizo." In *Snake Poems: An Aztec Invocation.* San Francisco: Chronicle Books, 1992, pp. 14–15.

Alarcón, Norma. "Interview with Pat Mora." *Third Woman* 3 (1986): 121–6.

"Making *Familia* From Scratch: Split Subjectivities in the Work of Helena María Veramontes and Cherríe Moraga." In *Chicana Creativity and Criticism: Charting New Frontiers in American Literature,* María Herrera-Sobek and Helena María Viramontes, eds. Houston: Arte Público Press, 1988, pp. 147–59.

"Traddutora, Traditora: A Paradigmatic Figure of Chicana Feminism." *Cultural Critique* 13 (Fall 1989a): 57–87.

"The Sardonic Powers of the Erotic in the Work of Ana Castillo." In *Breaking Boundaries: Latina Writing and Critical Readings,* Asunción Horno-Delgado, Eliana Ortega, Nina M. Scott, and Nancy Saporta Sternbach, eds. Amherst: University of Massachusetts Press, 1989b, pp. 94–107.

"Chicana Writers and Critics in a Social Context." *Third Woman 4 (1989c): 169–78.*

"Chicana Feminism: In the Tracks of 'The' Native Woman." Cultural Studies, 4 (1990): 248–56.

Ana Castillo and Cherríe Moraga, eds. *Third Woman 4 (1989).*

Alinsky, Saul. *Rules for Radicals: A Practical Primer for Realistic Radicals.* New York: Random House, 1971.

Allsup, Carl. "Who Done It? The Theft of Mexican-American History." *Journal of Popular Culture* 17 (Winter 1983): 150–5.

Alurista. "libertad sin lágrimas." In *Floricanto en Aztlán,* 2nd ed. Los Angeles: Chicano Studies Center, 1976 [1971], np.

"address." In *Floricanto en Aztlán,* 2nd ed. Los Angeles: Chicano Studies Center, 1976 [1971], np.

"wild butterflies." In *Timespace Huracán: Poems 1972–1975.* Albuquerque: Pajarito Publications, 1976, p. 75.

"Cultural Nationalism and Xicano Literature During the Decade 1965–1975." *MELUS* 8 (Summer 1981): 22–34.

"Myth, Identity and Struggle in Three Chicano Novels: Aztlán . . . Anaya, Méndez and Acosta." In *European Perspectives on Hispanic Literature of the United States,* Genvieve Fabre, ed. Houston: Arte Público Press, 1988, pp. 82–90.

Anaya, Rudolfo A. *The Lord of the Dawn: The Legend of Quetzalcóatl.* Introduction by David Johnson. Albuquerque: University of New Mexico Press, 1987.

"Autobiography." In *Rudolfo A. Anaya: Focus on Criticism,* César A. González-T., ed. La Jolla, CA: Lalo Press, 1990 [1986], pp. 359–89.

and Francisco Lomelí, eds. *Aztlán: Essays on the Chicano Homeland.* Albuquerque: Academia/El Norte Publications, 1989.

Antin, David. "Modernism and Postmodernism: Approaching the Present in American Poetry." *Boundary 2* (Fall 1972) 1: 98–133.

Anzaldúa, Gloria. "La Prieta." In *This Bridge Called My Back: Writings by Radical Women of Color,* 2nd ed., Cherríe Moraga and Gloria Anzaldúa, eds. New York: Kitchen Table, 1981, pp. 198–209.

"Antigua, mi diosa." In *Borderlands/La Frontera: The New Mestiza.* San Francisco: Spinsters/Aunt Lute, 1987, pp. 188–9.

"*La conciencia de la mestiza*: Towards a New Consciousness." In *Borderlands/La Frontera: The New Mestiza.* San Francisco: Spinsters/Aunt Lute, 1987, pp. 77–91.

"The Homeland, Aztlán: *El otro México.*" In *Borderlands/La Frontera: The New Mestiza.* San Francisco: Spinsters/Aunt Lute, 1987, pp. 1–13.

"*La herencia de Coatlicue* / The Coatlicue State." In *Borderlands/La Frontera: The New Mestiza.* San Francisco: Spinsters/Aunt Lute, 1987, pp. 41–51.

"How to Tame a Wild Tongue." In *Borderlands/La Frontera: The New Mestiza.* San Francisco: Spinsters/Aunt Lute, 1987, pp. 53–64.

"sus plumas el viento." In *Borderlands/La Frontera: The New Mestiza.* San Francisco: Spinsters/Aunt Lute, 1987, pp. 116–9.

"*Tlilli, Tlapalli*: The Path of the Red and Black Ink." In *Borderlands/La Frontera: The New Mestiza.* San Francisco: Spinsters/Aunt Lute, 1987, pp. 65–75.

"To live in the Borderlands means you." In *Borderlands/La Frontera: The New Mestiza.* San Francisco: Spinsters/Aunt Lute, 1987, pp. 194–5.

Appiah, Kwame Anthony. "Is the Post- in Postmodernism the Post- in Postcolonial?" *Critical Inquiry* 17 (Winter 1991): 336–57.

Baca, Jimmy Santiago. "I Applied For the Board." In *What's Happening.* Willimantic, CT: Curbstone Press, 1982, p. 17.

Martín & Meditations on the South Valley. Introduction by Denise Levertov. New York: New Directions, 1987.

"A Better Life." In *Black Mesa Poems.* New York: New Directions, 1989, p. 115.

"Dream Instructions." In *Black Mesa Poems.* New York: New Directions, 1989, pp. 13–15.

"From Violence to Peace." In *Black Mesa Poems.* New York: New Directions, 1989, pp. 5–10.

"Invasions." In *Black Mesa Poems.* New York: New Directions, 1989, pp. 70–2.

"Mi Tío Baca el Poeta de Socorro." In *Black Mesa Poems.* New York: New Directions, 1989, pp. 73–5.

Baker, George Carpenter. *Pachuco: An American-Spanish Argot and Its Social Functions in Tucson, Arizona.* Tucson: University of Arizona Press, 1974 [1950].

Baker, Houston. *Blues, Ideology and Afro-American Literature.* Chicago: University of Chicago Press, 1984.

Barringer, Felicity. "Jobs and Poverty Increase for Hispanic Americans." *New York Times.* 8 Nov. 1991, natl. ed., p. A7.

Barrera, Mario. *Race and Class in the Southwest: A Theory of Racial Inequality.* Notre Dame, IN: University of Notre Dame Press, 1979.

Beyond Aztlán: Ethnic Autonomy in Comparative Perspective. Notre Dame, IN: University of Notre Dame Press, 1988.

Baudrillard, Jean. *Simulations.* Trans. Paul Foss, Paul Patton, and Philip Beitchman. New York: Semiotext(e), 1983.

Berman, Russell A. "Modern Art and Desublimation." *Telos* 62 (Winter 1984/85): 31–58.

Benjamin, Walter. "Theses on the Philosophy of History." In *Illuminations,* Hannah Arendt, ed., and Harry Zohn, trans. New York: Schocken Books, 1969 [1940], pp. 253–64.

Bhabha, Homi K. "DissemiNation: time, narrative, and the margins of the modern nation." In *Nation and Narration,* Homi K. Bhabha, ed. New York: Routledge, 1990, pp. 291–322.

Blawis, Patricia Bell. *Tijerina and the Land Grants: Mexican Americans in Struggle for Their Heritage.* New York: International Publishers, 1971.

Bogue, Ronald. *Deleuze and Guattari.* New York: Routledge, 1989.

Brown, Wesley, and Amy Ling, eds. *Imagining America: Stories from the Promised Land.* New York: Persea Books, 1991.

Bruce-Novoa, Juan. "The Space of Chicano Literature." *De Colores* 1 (1975): 22–42.

"The Other Voice of Silence: Tino Villanueva." In *Modern Chicano Writers: A Collection of Critical Essays,* Joseph Sommers and Tomás Ybarra-Frausto, eds. Englewood Cliffs, NJ: Prentice Hall, 1979, pp. 133–40.

Chicano Authors: Inquiry by Interview. Austin: University of Texas Press, 1980.

Chicano Poetry: A Response to Chaos. Austin: University of Texas Press, 1982.

"Homosexuality and the Chicano Novel." In *European Perspectives on Hispanic Literature of the United States,* Genvieve Fabre, ed. Houston: Arte Público Press, 1988, pp. 98–106.

Calderón, Héctor. "To Read Chicano Narrative: Commentary and Metacommentary." *MESTER* 11 (May 1983): 3–14.

"At the Crossroads of History, on the Borders of Change: Chicano Literary Studies Past, Present, and Future." In *Left Politics and the Literary Profession,* Lennard J. Davis and M. Bella Mirabella, eds. New York: Columbia University Press, 1990, pp. 211–35.

and José David Saldívar, eds. *Criticism in the Borderlands: Studies in Chicano Literature, Culture, and Ideology.* Durham, NC: Duke University Press, 1991.

Camejo, Antonio. "A Report From Aztlán: Texas Chicanos Forge Own Political Power." In *La Causa Política: A Chicano Politics Reader,* Chris F. García, ed. Notre Dame, IN: University of Notre Dame Press, 1974 [1970], pp. 234–40.

Candelaria, Cordelia. *Chicano Poetry: A Critical Introduction.* Westport, CT: Greenwood Press, 1986.

"Code-Switching as Metaphor in Chicano Poetry." In *European Perspectives on Hispanic Literature of the United States,* Genvieve Fabre, ed. Houston: Arte Público Press, 1988, pp. 91–7.

ed. *Multiethnic Literature of the United States: Critical Introductions and Classroom Resources.* Boulder: University of Colorado Press, 1989.

Cárdenas de Dwyer, Carlota. "Cultural Nationalism and Chicano Literature in the Eighties." *MELUS* 8 (Summer 1981): 40–7.

Carr, C. "Columbus at the Checkpoint: Guillermo Gómez-Peña Rediscovers 'America.'" *The Village Voice.* 22 Oct. 1991: pp. 43–4.

Castillo, Ana. *Otro Canto.* Chicago: Alternativa Publications, 1977.

The Invitation. n.p.: A. Castillo, 1979.

"Our Tongue Was Nahuatl." In *The Third Woman: Minority Women Writers of the United States,* Dexter Fisher, ed. Boston: Houghton Mifflin, 1980 [1976], pp. 390–2.

Women Are Not Roses. Houston: Arte Público Press, 1984.

"Cold." In *My Father Was a Toltec.* Novato, CA: West End Press, 1988, pp. 62–3.

"In My Country." In *My Father Was a Toltec*. Novato, CA: West End Press, 1988, pp. 73–5.

"Ixtacihuatl Died in Vain." In *My Father Was a Toltec*. Novato, CA: West End Press, 1988, pp. 34–5.

"The Toltec." In *My Father Was a Toltec*. Novato, CA: West End Press, 1988, p. 3.

Cervantes, Lorna Dee. "Poem for the Young White Man Who Asked Me How I, an Intelligent, Well-Read Person Could Believe in the War Between Races." In *Emplumada*. Pittsburgh: University of Pittsburgh Press, 1981, pp. 35–7.

"Astro-no-mía." In *Chicana Creativity: Charting New Frontiers in American Literature*, María Herrera-Sobek and Helena María Viramontes, eds. Houston: Arte Público Press, 1988, p. 44.

Chabot, C. Barry. "The Problem of the Postmodern." In *Zeitgeist in Babel: The Post-Modernist Controversy*, Ingeborg Hoesterey, ed. Indianapolis and Bloomington: Indiana University Press, 1991, pp. 32–41.

Chabram, Angie. "Chicana/o Studies as Oppositional Ethnography." *Cultural Studies* 4 (1990): 228–47.

"Conceptualizing Chicano Critical Discourse." In *Criticism in the Borderlands: Studies in Chicano Literature, Culture, and Ideology*, Héctor Calderón and José David Saldívar, eds. Durham, NC: Duke University Press, 1991, pp. 127–48.

Chabram-Dernersesian, Angie. "I Throw Punches for My Race, but I Don't Want to Be a Man: Writing Us – Chica-nos (Girl, Us)/ Chican*as* – into the Movement Script." In *Cultural Studies*, Lawrence Grossberg, Cary Nelson, and Paula Treichler, eds. New York: Routledge, 1992, pp. 81–95.

Chávez, César. "Peregrinación, Penitencia, Revolución." In *Aztlan: An Anthology of Mexican American Literature*, Luis Valdez and Stan Steiner, eds. New York: Knopf, 1973, pp. 385–6.

"To Be a Man Is to Suffer for Others: God Help us to be Men!" In *Aztlan: An Anthology of Mexican American Literature*, Luis Valdez and Stan Steiner, eds. New York: Knopf, 1973, pp. 386–7.

Chávez, John R. *The Lost Land: The Chicano Image of the Southwest*. Albuquerque: University of New Mexico Press, 1984.

Chavez, Leo R. "Settlers and Sojourners: The Case of Mexicans in the United States." *Human Organization* 47 (1988): 95–107.

Christian, Barbara. "The Race for Theory." In *The Nature and Context of Minority Discourse*, Abdul R. JanMohamed and David Lloyd, eds. New York: Oxford University Press, 1990, pp. 37–49.

Cisneros, Sandra. "New Year's Eve." In *My Wicked Wicked Ways*. Bloomington, IN: Third Woman Press, 1987, pp. 90–1.

"You Bring out the Mexican in Me." In *Loose Woman*. New York: Knopf, 1994, pp. 4–6.

Clendinnen, Inga. *Aztecs*. Cambridge University Press, 1991.

Connor, Steve. *Postmodernist Culture: An Introduction to Theories of the Contemporary.* New York: Basil Blackwell, 1989.

Córdova, Teresa, et al., eds. *Chicana Voices: Intersections of Class, Race, and Gender.* Austin: CMAS Publications, 1986.

Corpi, Lucha. "Lluvia/Rain." In *Palabras de Mediodía/Noon Words,* Catherine Rodríguez-Nieto, English trans. Berkeley: El Fuego de Aztlán Publications, 1980, pp. 10–11.

"Underground Mariachi." In *Palabras de Mediodia/Noon Words,* Catherine Rodríguez-Nieto, English trans. Berkeley: El Fuego de Aztlán Publications, 1980, p. 76.

"Entrevista con Lucha Corpi: Poeta Chicana." Mireya Pérez-Erdélyi. *The Americas Review* 17 (Spring 1989): 72–82.

Delia's Song. Houston: Arte Público Press, 1989.

Cuesta, Jorge. *Antología de la poesía mexicana moderna.* Mexico, D.F.: Contemporáneos, 1928.

Dasenbrock, Reed Way. "Intelligibility and Meaningfulness in Multicultural Literature in English." *PMLA* 102 (January 1987): 10–19.

Davidson, Miriam. "The Mexican Border War: Immigrant Bashing." *The Nation,* 12 Nov. 1990, pp. 557–60.

Davi!a, Alberto, and Rogelio Saenz. "The Effect of Maquiladora Employment on the Monthly Flow of Mexican Undocumented Immigration to the U.S., 1978–1982." *International Migration Review* 24 (Spring 1990): 96–107.

DeParle, Jason. "New Rows to Hoe in the 'Harvest of Shame.'" *New York Times,* 28 July 1991, natl. ed., p. E3.

de la Garza, Rudolph O., and Rowena Rivera. "The Socio-Political World of the Chicano: A Comparative Analysis of Social Scientific and Literary Perspectives." In *Minority Language and Literature: Retrospective and Perspective,* Dexter Fisher, ed. New York: Modern Language Association, 1977, pp. 42–64.

Del Castillo, Adelaida R., ed. *Between Borders: Essays on Mexicana/Chicana History.* Encino, CA: Floricanto Press, 1990.

Deleuze, Gilles, and Félix Guattari. *Anti-Oedipus: Capitalism and Schizophrenia,* Robert Hurley, Mark See, and Helen R. Lane, trans. Preface by Michel Foucault. Minneapolis: University of Minnesota Press, 1983 [1972].

Kafka: For a Minor Literature, Dana Polan, trans. Foreword by Réda Bensmaïa. Minneapolis: University of Minnesota Press, 1986 [1975].

Delgado, Abelardo. "Stupid America." In *Chicano: 25 Pieces of a Chicano Mind.* El Paso, TX: Barrio Publications, 1972, p. 32.

"El Imigrante." In *Literatura Chicana: Texto y Contexto/Chicano Literature: Text and Context,* Antonia Castañeda Shular, Tomás Ybarra-Frausto, and Joseph Sommers, eds. Englewood Cliffs, NJ: Prentice Hall, 1972, pp. 249–50.

Di Stefano, Christine. "Dilemmas of Difference: Feminism, Modernity, and Postmodernism." In *Feminism/Postmodernism,* Linda J. Nicholson, ed. New York: Routledge, 1990, pp. 63–82.

Diesenhouse, Susan. "Hispanic Parents Mobilize in Boston." *New York Times,* 11 Dec. 1988, p. 72.

Elizondo, Sergio D. "ABC: Aztlán, the Borderlands, and Chicago." In *Missions in Conflict: Essays on U.S.–Mexican Relations and Chicano Culture,* Renate von Bardeleben, ed. Tübingen: Gunter Narr Verlag, 1986, pp. 13–23.

Epple, Juan Armando. "Literatura Chicana y Crítica Literaria." *Ideologies and Literature: A Journal of Hispanic and Luso-Brazilian Studies* 4 (1983): 149–71.

Fabre, Genvieve, ed. *European Perspectives on Hispanic Literature of the United States.* Houston: Arte Público Press, 1988.

Fanon, Frantz. *The Wretched of the Earth,* Constance Farrington, trans. Preface by Jean-Paul Sartre. New York: Grove Press, 1968 [1961].

Fernández-Kelly, María Patricia. *For We Are Sold, I and My People: Women and Industry in Mexico's Frontier.* Albany: State University of New York Press, 1983.

Fisher, Dexter, ed. *The Third Woman: Minority Women Writers of the United States.* Boston: Houghton Mifflin, 1980.

Foster, Hal, ed. *The Anti-Aesthetic: Essay on Postmodern Culture.* Port Townsend, WA: Bay Press, 1983.

"Against Pluralism." In *Recodings: Art, Spectacle, Cultural Politics,* Hal Foster, ed. Port Townsend, WA: Bay Press, 1985, pp. 13–32.

Foucault, Michel. *Power/Knowledge: Selected Interviews and Other Writings, 1972–1977,* Colin Gordon, ed. New York: Pantheon Press, 1980.

Fox-Genovese, Elizabeth. "The Claims of a Common Culture: Gender, Race, Class, and the Canon." *Salmagundi* 72 (Fall 1986): 131–43.

Franco, Jean. *Plotting Women: Gender and Representation in Mexico.* New York: Columbia University Press, 1989.

Fregoso, Rosa Linda, and Angie Chabram. "Chicana/o Cultural Representations: Reframing Alternative Critical Discourses." *Cultural Studies* 4 (1990): 203–12.

Fuentes, Rumel. "Corridos de Rumel." *El Grito* 6 (Spring 1973): 4–40.

García, Chris F., and Rudolph O. de la Garza. *The Chicano Political Experience: Three Perspectives.* North Scituate, MA: Duxbury Press, 1977.

García, Eugene E., Francisco A. Lomelí, Isidro D. Ortiz, eds. *Chicano Studies: A Multidisciplinary Approach.* New York: Teachers College Press, 1984.

García, Mario T. "Internal Colonialism: A Critical Essay." *Revista Chicano-Riqueña* 6 (1978): 37–41.

Gates, Henry Louis, Jr., ed. *"Race," Writing, and Difference.* Chicago: University of Chicago Press, 1986.

Gómez-Peña, Guillermo. "Documented/Undocumented," Rubén Martínez, trans. In *The Graywolf Annual Five: Multi-Cultural Literacy,* Rick Simonson and Scott Walker, eds. Saint Paul, MN.: Graywolf Press, 1988, pp. 127–34.

Gómez-Quiñones, Juan. *Chicano Politics: Reality and Promise, 1940–1990.* Albuquerque: University of New Mexico Press, 1990.

Gonzales, Rodolfo. *Yo Soy Joaquín/I am Joaquín.* New York: Bantam, 1972 [1967].

Gonzales, Sylvia. "National Character vs. Universality in Chicano Poetry." *De Colores* 1 (1975): 10–21.

González, Rafael Jesús. "Pachuco: The Birth of a Creole Language." *Arizona Quarterly* 23 (Winter 1967): 343–56.

"Chicano Poetry/Smoking Mirror." *New Scholar* 6 (1977): 127–37.

González-T. César A., ed. *Rudolfo A. Anaya: Focus on Criticism.* La Jolla, CA: Lalo Press, 1990.

Grajeda, Rafael. "The Pachuco in Chicano Poetry: The Process of Legend-Creation." *Revista Chicano-Riqueña* 8 (Fall 1980): 45–59.

Grandjeat, Yves-Charles. "Ricardo Sánchez: The Poetics of Liberation." In *European Perspectives on Hispanic Literature of the United States,* Genvieve Fabre, ed. Houston: Arte Público Press, 1988, pp. 33–43.

Guha, Ranajit, and Gayatri Chakravorty Spivak, eds. *Selected Subaltern Studies.* New York: Oxford University Press, 1988.

Guzmán, Ralph. "The Function of Anglo-American Racism in the Political Development of Chicanos." In *La Causa Política: A Chicano Politics Reader,* Chris F. García, ed. Notre Dame, IN: University of Notre Dame Press, 1974, pp. 19–35.

Habermas, Jürgen. "Modernity – An Incomplete Project." In *The Anti-Aesthetic: Essays on Postmodern Culture,* Hal Foster, ed. Port Townsend, WA: Bay Press, 1983, pp. 3–15.

Harding, Sandra. *The Science Question in Feminism.* Ithaca, NY: Cornell University Press, 1986.

"Feminism, Science, and the Anti-Enlightenment Critiques." In *Feminism/ Postmodernism,* Linda J. Nicholson, ed. New York: Routledge, 1990, pp. 83–106.

Harris, Scott. "Community Crusaders: 3 Groups Wage Hard-Nosed Struggle for Social Change." *Los Angeles Times,* 29 Nov. 1987, Sect. II, pp. 1, 4–5.

Harlow, Barbara. "Sites of Struggle: Immigration, Deportation, Prison, and Exile." In *Criticism in the Borderlands: Studies in Chicano Literature, Culture, and Ideology,* Héctor Calderón and José David Saldívar, eds. Durham, NC: Duke University Press, 1991, pp. 149–63.

Harth, Dorothy E., and Lewis M. Baldwin, eds. *Voices of Aztlan: Chicano Literature of Today.* New York: New American Library, 1974.

Harvey, David. *The Condition of Postmodernity.* Cambridge, Eng.: Blackwell, 1990.

Hendrix, Kathleen. "Standing Together: In East L.A., Women Answer a Call to Feed the Needy, Disarm the Gangs." *Los Angeles Times,* 24 Dec. 1991, pp. E1, E6.

Hernández, Marita. "Chicano Studies Find Favor on Campus." *Los Angeles Times,* 10 Apr. 1989, p. F33.

Herrera-Sobek, María, ed. *Beyond Stereotypes: The Critical Analysis of Chicana Literature.* Binghamton, NY: Bilingual Press/Editorial Bilingüe, 1985.

"The Politics of Rape: Sexual Transgression in Chicana Fiction." In *Chicana Creativity and Criticism: Charting New Frontiers in American Literature,* María Herrera-

Sobek and Helena María Viramontes, eds. Houston: Arte Público Press, 1988, pp. 171–81.

and Helena María Viramontes, eds. *Chicana Creativity and Criticism: Charting New Frontiers in American Literature*. Houston: Arte Público Press, 1988.

Hicks, Emily. *Border Writing: The Multidimensional Text*. Minneapolis: University of Minnesota Press, 1991.

hooks, bell. "Postmodern Blackness." In *Yearning: Race, Gender, and Cultural Politics*. Boston: South End Press, 1990, pp. 23–31.

"Choosing the Margin as a Space of Radical Opening." In *Yearning: Race, Gender, and Cultural Politics*. Boston: South End Press, 1990, pp. 145–53.

Horno-Delgado, Asunción, Eliana Ortega, Nina M. Scott, and Nancy Saporta Sternbach, eds. *Breaking Boundaries: Latina Writing and Critical Readings*. Amherst: University of Massachusetts Press, 1989.

Hutcheon, Linda. "The Post-modern Ex-centric: The Center That Will Not Hold." In *Feminism and Institutions: Dialogues on Feminist Theory*, Linda Kaufman, ed. Cambridge, Eng.: Basil Blackwell, 1989, pp. 141–65.

Huyssen, Andreas. "Mapping the Postmodern." *New German Critique* 33 (Fall 1984): 5–52.

Irigaray, Luce. *This Sex Which is Not One*. Ithaca, NY: Cornell University Press, 1985.

Jameson, Fredric. "Periodizing the 60s." In *The 60s Without Apology*, Sohnya Sayres, Anders Stephanson, Stanley Aronowitz, and Fredric Jameson, eds. Minneapolis: University of Minnesota Press, 1984a, pp. 178–209.

"Postmodernism, or The Cultural Logic of Late Capitalism." *New Left Review* 146 (July/August 1984b): 53–93.

"Third-World Literature in the Era of Multinational Capitalism." *Social Text* 15 (Fall 1986): 65–88.

"A Brief Response." *Social Text* 17 (Fall 1987): 26–7.

Postmodernism, or, The Cultural Logic of Late Capitalism. Durham, NC: Duke University Press, 1991.

JanMohamed, Abdul R., and David Lloyd. *The Nature and Context of Minority Discourse*. New York: Oxford University Press, 1990.

Jiménez, Francisco, ed. *The Identification and Analysis of Chicano Literature*. New York: Bilingual Press/Editorial Binlingüe, 1979.

Katrak, Ketu H. "Decolonizing Culture: Toward a Theory for Postcolonial Women's Texts." *Modern Fiction Studies* 35 (Spring 1989): 157–79.

Kimball, Roger. *Tenured Radicals: How Politics has Corrupted our Higher Education*. New York: Harper and Row, 1990.

Klinkowitz, Jerome. *Literary Disruptions: The Makings of a Post-Contemporary American Fiction*. Urbana: University of Illinois Press, 1975.

Klor de Alva, J. Jorge. "California Chicano Literature and Pre-Columbian Motifs: Foil and Fetish." *Confluencia* 1 (Spring 1986): 18–26.

"Aztlán, Borinquen and Hispanic Nationalism in the United States." In *Aztlán:*

Essays on the Chicano Homeland, Rudolfo Anaya and Francisco Lomelí, eds. Albuquerque: Academia/El Norte Publications, 1989, pp. 135–71.

Krauss, Rosalind. "Sculpture in the Expanded Field." In *The Anti-Aesthetic: Essay on Postmodern Culture,* Hal Foster, ed. Port Townsend, WA: Bay Press, 1983, pp. 32–42.

"The Originality of the Avant-Garde: A Postmodernist Repetition." In *Zeitgeist in Babel: The Post-Modernist Controversy,* Ingeborg Hoesterey, ed. Indianapolis and Bloomington: Indiana University Press, 1991, pp. 66–79.

Krier, Beth Ann. "Baca: A Poet Emerges From Prison of His Past." *Los Angeles Times,* 15 Feb. 1989, pp. V1, V6–7.

Krupat, Arnold. *The Voice in the Margin: Native American Literature and the Canon.* Berkeley: University of California Press, 1989.

Labarthe, Elyette Andouard. "The Vicissitudes of Aztlán." *Confluencia* 5 (Spring 1990): 79–84.

Lafaye, Jacques. *Quetzalcóatl and Guadalupe: The Formation of Mexican National Consciousness 1531–1813,* Benjamin Keen, trans. Chicago: University of Chicago Press, 1976.

Lattin, Vernon E., ed. *Contemporary Chicano Fiction: A Critical Survey.* Binghamton, NY: Bilingual Press/Editorial Bilingüe, 1986.

Leal, Luis. "The Problem of Identifying Chicano Literature." In *The Identification and Analysis of Chicano Literature,* Francisco Jiménez, ed. New York: Bilingual Press/Editorial Bilingüe, 1979, pp. 2–6.

"In Search of Aztlán." Gladys Leal, trans. *Denver Quarterly* 16 (Fall 1981): 16–22.

and Pepe Barrón. "Chicano Literature: An Overview." In *Three American Literatures,* Houston A. Baker, Jr., ed. Introduction by Walter J. Ong. New York: Modern Language Association, 1982, pp. 9–32.

León-Portilla, Miguel. *Aztec Thought and Culture,* Jack Emory Davis, trans. Norman: University of Oklahoma Press, 1963.

The Aztec Image of Self and Society, edited with an introduction by J. Jorge Klor de Alva. Salt Lake City: University of Utah Press, 1992.

Levy, Daniel, and Gabriel Székely. *Mexico: Paradoxes of Stability and Change.* Boulder, CO: Westview Press, 1983.

Limón, José E. *Mexican Ballads, Chicano Poems: History and Influence in Mexican-American Social Poetry.* Berkeley: University of California Press, 1992.

Lipsitz, George. "Rocking Around the Historical Bloc." In *Time Passages: Collective Memory and American Popular Culture.* Minneapolis: University of Minnesota Press, 1991, pp. 133–60.

"Buscando America (Looking for America): Collective Memory in an Age of Amnesia." In *Time Passages: Collective Memory and American Popular Culture.* Minneapolis: University of Minnesota Press, 1991, pp. 257–71.

Lomelí, Francisco A. "An Overview of Chicano Letters: From Origins to Resurgence." In *Chicano Studies: A Multidisciplinary Approach,* Eugene E. García, Francisco A. Lomelí, and Isidro D. Ortiz, eds. New York: Teachers College Press, 1984, pp. 103–19.

"Internal Exile in the Chicano Novel: Structure and Paradigms." In *European Perspectives on Hispanic Literature of the United States,* Genvieve Fabre, ed. Houston: Arte Público Press, 1988, pp. 107–17.

López, Sonia A. "The Role of the Chicana Within the Student Movement." In *Essays on La Mujer,* Rosaura Sánchez and Rosa Martinez Cruz, eds. Los Angeles: Chicano Studies Center–Publications, 1977, pp. 16–29.

Lowe, Lisa. "Heterogeneity, Hybridity, Multiplicity: Marking Asian American Differences." *Diaspora* 1 (Spring 1991): 24–44.

Lubiano, Wahneema. "Shuckin' Off the African-American Native Other: What's 'Po-Mo' Got to do with It?" *Cultural Critique* 19 (Spring 1991): 149–86.

Lucero, Judy. "Jail-Life Walk." In *The Third Woman: Minority Women Writers of the United States,* Dexter Fisher, ed. Boston: Houghton Mifflin, 1980, p. 395.

Lyotard, Jean-François. *Driftworks.* New York: Semiotext(e), 1984 [1968].

The Postmodern Condition: A Report on Knowledge, Geoff Bennington and Brian Massumi, trans. Introduction by Fredric Jameson. *Theory and History of Literature,* vol. 10. Minneapolis: University of Minnesota, 1984.

Martínez, Elizabeth, and Ed McCaughan. "Chicanas and Mexicanas Within a Transnational Working Class." In *Between Borders: Essays on Mexicana/Chicana History,* Adelaida R. Del Castillo, ed. Encino, CA: Floricanto Press, 1990, pp. 31–60.

Martinez, Victor. "Shoes." In *Caring For a House.* San Jose, CA: Chusma House, 1992, p. 12.

Massey, Douglas S. "The Settlement Process among Mexican Migrants to the United States." *American Sociological Review* 51 (Oct. 1986): 670–84.

"Understanding Mexican Migration to the United States." *American Journal of Sociology* 92 (May 1987): 1372–1403.

McCaffery, Larry. *The Metafictional Muse.* Pittsburgh: University of Pittsburgh Press, 1982.

McKenna, Teresa. "On Chicano Poetry and the Political Age: *Corridos* as Social Drama." In *Criticism in the Borderlands: Studies in Chicano Literature, Culture, and Ideology,* Héctor Calderón and José David Saldívar, eds. Durham, NC: Duke University Press, 1991, pp. 181–202.

McWilliams, Carey. *North From Mexico.* Westport, CT: Greenwood, 1968 [1948].

Meese, Elizabeth, and Alice Parker, eds. *The Difference Within: Feminism and Critical Theory.* Philadelphia: John Benjamins, 1989.

Menchú, Rigoberta. *I, Rigoberta Menchú,* Elisabeth Burgos-Debray, ed., Ann Wright, trans. New York: Verso, 1984.

Meyer, Doris L. "Early Mexican-American Responses to Negative Stereotyping." *New Mexico Historical Review* 53 (January 1978): 75–91.

Minnesota Council of Teachers of English. *Braided Lives: An Anthology of Multicultural American Writing.* St. Paul: Minnesota Humanities Commission, 1991.

Mirandé, Alfredo. *The Chicano Experience: An Alternative Perspective.* Notre Dame, IN: University of Notre Dame, 1985.

and Evangelina Enríquez. *La Chicana: The Mexican-American Woman*. Chicago: University of Chicago Press, 1979.

Mohanty, Chandra Talpade. "On Race and Voice: Challenges for Liberal Education in the 1990s." *Cultural Critique* 14 (Winter 1989/90): 174–208.

Monleón, José. "Mesa redonda con Alurista, R. Anaya, M. Herrera-Sobek, A. Morales y H. Viramontes." In *Rudolfo A. Anaya: Focus on Criticism*, César A. González-T., ed. La Jolla, CA: Lalo Press: 1990 [1981], pp. 439–58.

Montejano, David. *Anglos and Mexicans in the Making of Texas, 1836–1986*. Austin: University of Texas Press, 1987.

Montoya, José. "El Louie." In *Literatura Chicana: Texto y Contexto/Chicano Literature: Text and Context*, Antonia Castañeda Shular, Tomás Ybarra-Frausto, and Joseph Sommers, eds. Englewood Cliffs, NJ: Prentice Hall, 1972 [1970], pp. 173–6.

"Chicano Art: Resistance in Isolation 'Aquí Estamos y no Nos Vamos.'" In *Missions in Conflict: Essays on U.S.–Mexican Relations and Chicano Culture*, Renate von Bardeleben, ed. Tübingen: Gunter Narr Verlag, 1986, pp. 25–30.

Mora, Pat. "Now and Then, America." In *Borders*. Houston: Arte Público Press, 1986, p. 33.

Moraga, Cherríe, and Gloria Anzaldúa, eds. *This Bridge Called My Back: Writings by Radical Women of Color*, 2nd ed. New York: Kitchen Table, 1981.

Mydans, Seth. "Border Near San Diego is Home to More Violence." *New York Times*, 9 April 1991, natl. ed., p. A9.

Nabokov, Peter. *Tijerina and the Couthouse Raid*. Albuquerque: University of New Mexico Press, 1969.

Nash, June. "The Aztecs and the Ideology of Male Dominance." *Signs* 4 (Winter 1978): 349–62.

Olivares, Julian. "The Streets of Gary Soto." *Latin American Literary Review* 18 (1990): 32–49.

Omi, Michael. "In Living Color: Race and American Culture." In *Cultural Politics in Contemporary America*, Ian Angus and Sut Jhally, eds. New York: Routledge, 1989, pp. 111–22.

Ortego, Philip D., ed. *We Are Chicanos: An Anthology of Mexican-American Literature*. New York: Washington Square Press, 1973.

Ortego y Gasca, Felipe de. "The Chicano Renaissance." *Social Casework* 52 (May 1971): 294–307.

"An Introduction to Chicano Poetry." In *Modern Chicano Writers: A Collection of Critical Essays*, Joseph Sommers and Tomás Ybarra-Frausto, eds. Englewood Cliffs, NJ: Prentice Hall, 1979, pp. 108–16.

"The Quetzal and the Phoenix." *Denver Quarterly* 16 (Fall 1981): 3–15.

Owens, Craig. "The Discourse of Others: Feminists and Postmodernism." In *The Anti-Aesthetic: Essay on Postmodern Culture*, Hal Foster, ed. Port Townsend, WA: Bay Press, 1983, pp. 57–82.

Padilla, Genaro. "The Recovery of Nineteenth Century Chicano Autobiography."

In *European Perspectives on Hispanic Literature of the United States,* Genvieve Fabre, ed. Houston: Arte Público Press, 1988, pp. 44–54.

"Myth and Comparative Cultural Nationalism: The Ideological Uses of Aztlán." In *Aztlán: Essays on the Chicano Homeland,* Rudolfo Anaya and Francisco Lomelí, eds. Albuquerque: Academia/El Norte Publications, 1989, pp. 111–34.

Paredes, Américo. *With His Pistol in His Hand: A Border Ballad and its Hero.* Austin: University of Texas Press, 1958.

"Guitarreros." In *Between Two Worlds.* Houston: Arte Público Press, 1991 [1935], p. 29.

"Canto de la muerte joven." In *Between Two Worlds.* Houston: Arte Público Press, 1991 [1970], p. 137.

"Folklore, Lo Mexicano and Proverbs." *Aztlán* 3 (1982): 1.

Paredes, Raymund A. "The Promise of Chicano Literature." In *Minority Language and Literature: Retrospective and Perspective,* Dexter Fisher, ed. New York: Modern Language Association, 1977, pp. 29–41.

"Mexican American Authors and the American Dream." *MELUS* 8 (Winter 1981): 71–80.

"The Evolution of Chicano Literature." In *Three American Literatures,* Houston A. Baker, Jr., ed., Introduction by Walter J. Ong. New York: Modern Language Association, 1982, pp. 33–79.

Parr, Carmen Salazar. "Current Trends in Chicano Literary Criticism." In *The Identification and Analysis of Chicano Literature,* Francisco Jiménez, ed. New York: Bilingual Press/Editorial Bilingüe, 1979, pp. 134–42.

Passell, Peter. "So Much for Assumptions About Immigrants and Jobs." *New York Times,* 15 April 1990, p. E4.

Paz, Octavio. *Labyrinth of Solitude,* Lysander Kemp, Yara Milos, and Rachel Phillips Belash, trans. New York: Grove Press, 1985 [1950/1959].

"Latin America and Democracy." In *One Earth, Four or Five Worlds: Reflections on Contemporary History,* Helen R. Lane, trans. New York: Harcourt, Brace, 1985, pp. 158–88.

Peña, Devon. "Between the Lines: A New Perspective on the Industrial Sociology of Women Workers in Transnational Labor Processes." In *Chicana Voices: Intersections of Class, Race, and Gender,* Teresa Córdova et al., eds. Austin: CMAS Publications, 1986, pp. 77–95.

Peñalosa, Fernando. *Chicano Sociolinguistics: A Brief Introduction.* Rowley, MA: Newbury House Publishers, 1980.

Pérez Firmat, Gustavo, ed. *Do the Americas Have a Common Literature?* Durham, NC: Duke University Press, 1990.

Pérez Sandoval, Rafael. *Diccionario etimológico de chicanismos y mexicanismos en el español chicano.* Unpublished manuscript.

Perloff, Marjorie. *The Poetics of Indeterminacy: Rimbaud to Cage.* Princeton: Princeton University Press, 1981.

Pfaff, Carol W., and Laura Chávez. "Spanish/English Code-Switching: Literary Reflections of Natural Discourse." In *Missions in Conflict: Essays on U.S.–Mexican Relations and Chicano Culture,* Renate von Bardeleben, ed. Tübingen: Gunter Narr Verlag, 1986, pp. 229–54.

Pfeil, Fred. *Another Tale to Tell: Politics and Narrative in Postmodern Culture.* New York: Verso, 1990.

Pina, Michael. "The Archaic, Historical and Mythicized Dimensions of Aztlán." In *Aztlán: Essays on the Chicano Homeland,* Rudolfo Anaya and Francisco Lomelí, eds. Albuquerque: Academia/El Norte Publications, 1989, pp. 14–48.

"Plan de Delano." In *Aztlan: An Anthology of Mexican American Literature,* Luis Valdez and Stan Steiner, eds. New York: Knopf, 1973 [1965], pp. 197–201.

"Plan de la Raza Unida." In *Chicano Manifesto,* Armando B. Rendón, ed. New York: Macmillan, 1971 [1967], pp. 331–2.

"Plan de Santa Barbara: manifesto." In *Literatura Chicana: Texto y Contexto/Chicano Literature: Text and Context,* Antonia Castañeda Shular, Tomás Ybarra-Frausto, and Joseph Sommers, eds. Englewood Cliffs, NJ: Prentice Hall, 1972 [1969], pp. 85–7.

"Plan Espiritual de Aztlán." In *Aztlan: An Anthology of Mexican American Literature,* Luis Valdez and Stan Steiner, eds. New York: Knopf, 1973 [1969], pp. 402–6.

Probyn, Elspeth. "Travels in the Postmodern: Making Sense of the Local." In *Feminism/Postmodernism,* Linda J. Nicholson, ed. New York: Routledge, 1990, pp. 176–89.

Radhakrishnan, R. "Culture as Common Ground: Ethnicity and Beyond." *MELUS* 14 (Summer 1987): 5–19.

"Feminist Historiography and Post-structuralist Thought: Intersections and Departures." In *The Difference Within: Feminism and Critical Theory,* Elizabeth Meese and Alice Parker, eds. Philadelphia: John Benjamins, 1989, pp. 189–205.

Ramírez, Arturo. "Views of the Corrido Hero: Paradigm and Development." *The Americas Review* 18 (Summer 1990): 71–9.

Ramos, Samuel. *Profile of Man and Culture in Mexico.* Austin: University of Texas Press, 1962 [1934].

Rankin, Jerry. "Mexican Americans and National Policy-Making: An Aborted Relationship." In *Chicanos and Native Americans: The Territorial Minorities,* Rudolph O. de la Garza, Z. Anthony Kruszewski, and Tomás A. Arciniega, eds. Englewood Cliffs, NJ: Prentice Hall, 1973, pp. 145–52.

Rebolledo, Tey Diana. "Abuelitas: Mythology and Integration in Chicana Literature." In *Woman of Her Word: Hispanic Women Write,* 2nd ed., Evangelina Vigil, ed. Houston: Arte Público Press, 1987, pp. 148–58.

"The Politics of Poetics: Or, What am I, a Critic, Doing in This Text Anyhow?" In *Chicana Creativity and Criticism: Charting New Frontiers in American Literature,* María Herrera-Sobek and Helena María Viramontes, eds. Houston: Arte Público Press, 1988, pp. 129–38.

"Narrative Strategies of Resistance in Hispana Writing." *The Journal of Narrative Technique* 22 (Spring 1990): 134–46.

Rechy, John. "El Paso del Norte." *Evergreen Review* 2 (1958): 127–40.

City of Night. New York: Grove Press, 1963.

Rivera, Tomás. *y no se lo tragó la tierra/And the Earth Did Not Part.* Berkeley: Publicaciones Quinto Sol, S. Z./Quinto Sol Publications, 1971.

"The Role of the Chicano Academic and the Chicano Non-Academic Community." In *International Studies in Honor of Tomás Rivera,* Julian Olivares, ed. Houston: Arte Público Press, 1986, pp. 34–44.

Robinson, Cecil. *With the Ears of Strangers: The Mexican in American Literature.* Tucson: University of Arizona Press, 1973.

Mexico and the Hispanic Southwest in American Literature. Tucson: University of Arizona Press, 1977.

Rocard, Marcienne. "The Chicano: A Minority in Search of a Proper Literary Medium for Self-affirmation." In *Missions in Conflict: Essays on U.S.–Mexican Relations and Chicano Culture,* Renate von Bardeleben, ed. Tübingen: Gunter Narr Verlag, 1986, pp. 31–40.

"The Chicana: A Marginal Woman." In *European Perspectives on Hispanic Literature of the United States,* Genvieve Fabre, ed. Houston: Arte Público Press, 1988, pp. 130–9.

Rodríguez, Juan. "La búsqueda de identidad y sus motivos en la literatura Chicana." In *The Identification and Analysis of Chicano Literature,* Francisco Jiménez, ed. New York: Bilingual Press/Editorial Bilingüe, 1979, pp. 170–8.

Rodríguez, Luis. J. "The Coldest Day." In *The Concrete River.* Willimantic, CT: Curbstone Press, 1991, pp. 15–16.

Rodríguez del Pino, Salvador. "La poesía chicana: una nueva trayectoria." In *The Identification and Analysis of Chicano Literature,* Francisco Jiménez, ed. New York: Bilingual Press/Editorial Bilingüe, 1979a, pp. 68–89.

"La novela chicana de los setenta comentada por sus escritores y criticos." In *The Identification and Analysis of Chicano Literature,* Francisco Jiménez, ed. New York: Bilingual Press/Editorial Bilingüe, 1979b, pp. 153–60.

Romano-V., Octavio. "The Anthology and Sociology of the Mexican American." In *Voices: Readings from El Grito, 1967–1971.* Berkeley: Quinto Sol, 1973a, pp. 43–56.

"The Historical and Intellectual Presence of Mexican-Americans." In *Voices: Readings from El Grito, 1967–1971.* Berkeley: Quinto Sol, 1973b, pp. 164–78.

Romero, Leo. "I Too, America." In *We Are Chicanos: An Anthology of Mexican-American Literature,* Philip D. Ortego, ed. New York: Washington Square Press, 1973, pp. 175–8.

During the Growing Season. Tucson: Magey Press, 1978.

Agua Negra. Boise, ID: Ahsahta Press, 1981.

Romo, Ricardo. *East Los Angeles: History of a Barrio.* Austin: University of Texas Press, 1983.

Rorty, Richard. *Philosophy and the Mirror of Nature*. Princeton: Princeton University Press, 1980.

Rothenberg, Jerome. *Shaking the Pumpkin: Traditional Poetry of the Indian North Americas*. New York: Doubleday, 1972.

Pre-Faces & Other Writings. New York: New Directions, 1981.

Rouse, Roger. "Mexican Migration and the Social Space of Postmodernism." *Diaspora* 1 (Spring 1991): 8–23.

Said, Edward. "Opponents, Audiences, Constituencies and Community." *Critical Inquiry* 9 (September 1982): 1–26.

"Traveling Theory." In *The World, the Text, and the Critic*. Cambridge: Harvard University Press, 1983, pp. 226–47.

Foreward to *Selected Subaltern Studies,* Ranajit Guha and Gayatri Spivak, eds. New York: Oxford University Press, 1988, pp. v–x.

Saldívar, José David. "The Ideological and the Utopian in Tomás Rivera's *y no se lo tragó la tierra* and Ron Arias' *The Road to Tamazunchale*." *Crítica* 1 (Spring 1985): 100–14.

"Towards a Chicano Poetics: The Making of the Chicano Subject, 1969–1982." *Confluencia* 1 (Spring 1986): 10–17.

The Dialectics of Our America: Genealogy, Cultural Critique, and Literary History. Durham, NC: Duke University Press, 1991.

Saldívar, Ramón. "A Dialectic of Difference: Towards a Theory of the Chicano Novel." *MELUS* 6 (Fall 1979): 73–92.

"Chicano Literature and Ideology: Prospectus for the '80s." *MELUS* 8 (Summer 1981): 35–9.

Chicano Narrative: The Dialectics of Difference. Madison: University of Wisconsin Press, 1990.

Salinas, Luis Omar. *Crazy Gypsy*. Santa Barbara, CA: Orígenes Publications, 1970.

"On a Visit to a Halfway House after a Long Absence." In *The Sadness of Days: Selected and New Poems*. Houston: Arte Público Press, 1987, p. 159.

Salinas, Raúl. "Los Caudillos." In *Un Trip Through the Mind Jail y Otras Excursions*. San Francisco: Editorial Pocho-Che, 1980, pp. 69–70.

Sánchez, Marta Ester. *Contemporary Chicana Poetry: A Critical Approach to an Emerging Literature*. Berkeley: University of California Press, 1985.

Sánchez, Ricardo. "migrant lament. . . ." In *Canto y Grito mi Liberación*. New York: Anchor Books, 1973, pp. 91–2.

"reo eterno." In *Canto y Grito mi Liberación*. New York: Anchor Books, 1973, pp. 43–5.

"Out/parole." *Hechízospells*. Creative Series No. 4. Los Angeles: Chicano Studies Center–Publications, 1973, p. 80.

Hechízospells. Creative Series No. 4. Los Angeles: Chicano Studies Center–Publications, 1973.

Eagle-Visioned/Feathered Adobes. El Paso, TX: Cinco Puntos Press, 1990.

Sánchez, Rosaura. "The Chicana Labor Force." In *Essays on La Mujer,* Rosaura Sánchez and Rosa Martinez Cruz, eds. Los Angeles: Chicano Studies Center–Publications, 1977, pp. 3–15.

"Spanish Codes in the Southwest." In *Modern Chicano Writers: A Collection of Critical Essays,* Joseph Sommers and Tomás Ybarra-Frausto, eds. Englewood Cliffs, NJ: Prentice Hall, 1979, pp. 41–53.

Chicano Discourse: Socio-Historic Perspectives. Rowley, MA: Newbury House Publishers, 1983.

and Rosa Martinez Cruz, eds. *Essays on La Mujer.* Los Angeles: Chicano Studies Center–Publications, 1977.

Sayres, Sohnya, Anders Stephanson, Stanley Aronowitz, and Fredric Jameson, eds. *The 60s Without Apology.* Minneapolis: University of Minnesota Press, 1984.

Scholes, Robert. *Fabulation and Metafiction.* Chicago: University of Illinois Press, 1979.

Sheehan, Edward R. F. "The Open Border." *The New York Review,* 15 March 1990: 34–8.

Shirley, Carl R., and Paula W. Shirley. *Understanding Chicano Literature.* Columbia: University of South Carolina Press, 1988.

Shular, Antonia Castañeda, Tomás Ybarra-Frausto, and Joseph Sommers, eds. *Literatura Chicana: Texto y Contexto/Chicano Literature: Text and Context.* Englewood Cliffs, NJ: Prentice Hall, 1972.

Slemon, Stephen. "Monuments of Empire: Allegory/Counter-Discourse/Post-Colonial Writing." *Kunapipi* 9 (1987): 1–16.

Smith, Paul. *Discerning the Subject,* Foreward by John Mowitt. *Theory and History of Literature,* vol. 55. Minneapolis: University of Minnesota Press, 1988.

Snyder, Gary. *Myths and Texts.* New York: New Directions, 1978 [1960].

Soldatenko-Gutiérrez, Michael. "Socrates, Curriculum and the Chicano/Chicana." *Cultural Studies* 4 (1990): 303–20.

Sollors, Werner. *Beyond Ethnicity: Consent and Descent in American Culture.* New York: Oxford University Press, 1986.

ed. *The Invention of Ethnicity.* New York: Oxford University Press, 1989.

Sommers, Joseph. "Critical Approaches to Chicano Literature." In *Modern Chicano Writers: A Collection of Critical Essays,* Joseph Sommers and Tomás Ybarra-Frausto, eds. Englewood Cliffs, NJ: Prentice Hall, 1979, pp. 31–40.

and Tomás Ybarra-Frausto, eds. *Modern Chicano Writers: A Collection of Critical Essays.* Englewood Cliffs, NJ: Prentice Hall, 1979.

Soto, Gary. "Mexicans Begin Jogging." In *Where Sparrows Work Hard.* Pittsburgh: University of Pittsburgh Press, 1981, p. 24.

"Luis Omar Salinas: Chicano Poet." *MELUS* 9 (Summer 1982): 47–82.

"Between Words." In *Black Hair.* Pittsburgh: University of Pittsburgh Press, 1985, pp. 77–8.

Sousa Santos, Boaventura de. "The Postmodern Transition: Law and Politics." In *The Fate of Law,* Austin Sarat and Thomas R. Kearns, eds. Ann Arbor: University of Michigan Press, 1991, pp. 79–118.

Soustelle, Jacques. *The Daily Life of the Aztecs on the Eve of the Spanish Conquest.* New York: Macmillan, 1962 [1955].

Spivak, Gayatri Chakravorty. "Subaltern Studies: Deconstructing Historiography." In *In Other Worlds: Essays in Cultural Politics.* New York: Routledge, 1988, pp. 197–221

"Who Claims Alterity?" In *Remaking History,* Barbara Kruger and Phil Mariani, eds. Dia Art Foundation Discussions in Contemporary Culture, no. 4. Seattle: Bay Press, 1989, pp. 269–92.

The Post-Colonial Critic: Interviews, Strategies, Dialogues, Sarah Harasym, ed. New York: Routledge, 1990.

"Theory in the Margin." In *Consequences of Theory,* Jonathan Arac and Barbara Johnson, eds. Baltimore: The Johns Hopkins Press, 1991, pp. 154–80.

Stephanson, Anders. "Regarding Postmodernism – A Conversation With Fredric Jameson." *Social Text* 17 (Fall 1987): 29–54.

Suleiman, Susan Rubin. "Feminism and Postmodernism: A Question of Politics." In *Zeitgeist in Babel: The Postmodernist Controversy,* Ingeborg Hoesterey, ed. Indianapolis: Indiana University Press, 1991, pp. 111–30.

Suro, Roberto. "Border Boom's Dirty Residue Imperils U.S.–Mexico Trade." *New York Times,* 31 March 1991 natl. ed., pp. A1, A15.

"Hispanic Politicians Seek a Recipe for Raw Numbers." *New York Times,* 12 Apr. 1992, natl. ed., p. E5.

Tafolla, Carmen. "La Isabela de Guadalupe y el Apache Mío Cid." In *Five Poets of Aztlán,* Santiago Daydí-Tolson, ed. Binghamton, NY: Bilingual Press/Editorial Bilingüe, 1985, pp. 170–2.

"Los Corts (5 voices)." *Five Poets of Aztlán,* Santiago Daydí-Tolson, ed. Binghamton, NY: Bilingual Press/Editorial Bilingüe, 1985, pp. 176–9.

Tanner, Tony. *City of Words: American Fiction, 1950–1970.* New York: Harper & Row, 1971.

Tatum, Charles M. *Chicano Literature.* Twayne's United States Authors Ser. 433. Boston: Twayne, 1982.

Tiffin, Helen. "Post-Colonial Literatures and Counter-Discourse." *Kunapipi* 9 (1987): 17–34.

Timm, L. A. "Spanish–English Code Switching: el porqué y how-not-to." *Romance Philology* 28 (1975): 473–82.

Tolan, Sandy. "Maquiladora." *New York Times Magazine,* 1 July 1990, natl. ed., pp. 16–21, 31, 40.

Trujillo, Ignacio Orlando. "Linguistic Structures in José Montoya's 'El Louie.'" In *Modern Chicano Writers: A Collection of Critical Essays,* Joseph Sommers and Tomás Ybarra-Frausto, eds. Englewood Cliffs, NJ: Prentice Hall, 1979, pp. 150–9.

Turner, Victor. "Process, System, and Symbol: A New Anthropological Synthesis." *Daedalus* 106 (Summer 1977): 61–80.

Valdés Fallis, Guadalupe. "Code-Switching in Bi-Lingual Chicano Poetry." *Hispania* 59 (Dec 1976): 877–86.

Vasconcelos, José. "The Emergence of the New Chicano." In *Aztlán: An Anthology of Mexican American Literature,* Luis Valdez and Stan Steiner, eds. New York: Random House: 1972, pp. 282–5.

Vattimo, Gianni. "The End of (Hi)story." In *Zeitgeist in Babel: The Post-Modernist Controversy,* Ingeborg Hoesterey, ed. Indianapolis: Indiana University Press, 1991, pp. 132–41.

Veltman, Calvin. "The Status of the Spanish Language in the United States at the Beginning of the 21st Century." *International Migration Review* 24 (Spring 1990): 108–23.

Vigil, Evangelina. "to the personalities in the works by José Montoya and the chucos of the future." In *Thirty an' Seen a Lot.* Houston: Arte Público Press, 1985, p. 55.

"me caes sura, ese, decuéntate." In *Thirty an' Seen a Lot.* Houston: Arte Público Press, 1985, p. 46.

ed. *Woman of Her Word: Hispanic Women Write,* 2nd ed. Houston: Arte Público Press, 1987.

Villanueva, Tino. "Que hay otra voz." In *Que Hay Otra Voz Poems.* New York: Editorial Mensaje, 1972, pp. 35–7.

"Sobre el término 'Chicano.'" *Cuadernos Hispanoamericanos* 336 (June 1978): 387–410.

Villaseñor, Victor. *Rain of Gold.* Houston: Arte Público Press, 1991.

Wald, Alan. "Theorizing Cultural Difference: A Critique of the 'Ethnicity School'" *MELUS* 14 (Summer 1987): 21–33.

Walker, Scott, ed. *The Graywolf Annual Seven: Stories From the American Mosaic.* Saint Paul, MN: Graywolf Press, 1990.

Wallace, Michelle. *Invisibility Blues: From Pop to Theory.* New York: Verso, 1990.

Weber, David J. *Foreigners in Their Native Land: Historical Roots of the Mexican Americans.* Foreword by Ramón Eduardo Ruiz. Albuquerque: University of New Mexico Press, 1973.

West, Cornell. "Minority Discourse and the Pitfalls of Canon Formation." *The Yale Journal of Criticism* 1 (Fall 1987): 193–201.

"Black Culture and Postmodernism." In *Remaking History,* Barbara Kruger and Phil Mariani, eds. Seattle: Bay Press, 1989, pp. 87–96.

Wilde, Alan. "Irony in the Postmodern Age: Toward a Map of Suspensiveness." *Boundary 2* (Fall 1980): 5–46.

Williams, Raymond. *Keywords: A Vocabulary of Culture and Society,* 2nd ed. New York: Oxford University Press, 1983.

"When Was Modernism?" In *The Politics of Modernism: Against the New Conformists.* Edited and introduced by Tony Pinkney. London: Verso, 1989, pp. 31–5.

Wolf, Eric R. "The Virgin of Guadalupe: A Mexican National Symbol." *Journal of American Folklore* 71 (January–March 1958): 34–40.

Sons of the Shaking Earth. Chicago: University of Chicago Press, 1963.

Yarbro-Bejarano, Yvonne. "Chicana Literature From a Chicana Feminist Perspective." In *Chicana Creativity and Criticism: Charting New Frontiers in American Literature,* María Herrera-Sobek and Helena María Viramontes, eds. Houston: Arte Público Press, 1988, pp. 139–45.

Ybarra-Frausto, Tomás. "The Chicano Movement and the Emergence of a Chicano Poetic Consciousness." *New Scholar* 6 (1977): 81–109.

"Alurista's Poetics: The Oral, the Bilingual, the Pre-Columbian." In *Modern Chicano Writers: A Collection of Critical Essays,* Joseph Sommers and Tomás Ybarra-Frausto, eds. Englewood Cliffs, NJ: Prentice Hall, 1979, pp. 117–32.

Young, Marion Iris. "The Ideal Community and the Politics of Difference." In *Feminism/Postmodernism,* Linda J. Nicholson, ed. New York: Routledge, 1990, pp. 300–23.

Yúdice, George. "Marginality and the Ethics of Survival." *Social Text* 21 (1989): 214–36.

Zamora, Bernice. *Restless Serpents.* Menlo Park, CA: Diseños Literarios, 1976.

Index

CAMBRIDGE STUDIES IN AMERICAN LITERATURE AND CULTURE

Continued from the front of the book

65. Thomas Strychacz, *Modernism, Mass Culture, and Professionalism*
64. Elisa New, *The Regenerate Lyric: Theology and Innovation in American Poetry*
63. Edwin S. Redkey, *A Grand Army of Black Men: Letters from African-American Soldiers in the Union Army, 1861–1865*
62. Victoria Harrison, *Elizabeth Bishop's Poetics of Intimacy*
61. Edwin Sill Fussell, *The Catholic Side of Henry James*
60. Thomas Gustafson, *Representative Words: Politics, Literature, and the American Language, 1776–1865*
59. Peter Quartermain, *Disjunctive Poetics: From Gertrude Stein and Louis Zukovsky to Susan Howe*
58. Paul Giles, *American Catholic Arts and Fictions: Culture, Ideology, Aesthetics*
57. Ann-Janine Morey, *Religion and Sexuality in American Literature*
56. Philip M. Weinstein, *Faulkner's Subject: A Cosmos No One Owns*
55. Stephen Fender, *Sea Changes: British Emigration and American Literature*
54. Peter Stoneley, *Mark Twain and the Feminine Aesthetic*
53. Joel Porte, *In Respect to Egotism: Studies in American Romantic Writing*
52. Charles Swann, *Nathaniel Hawthorne: Tradition and Revolution*
51. Ronald Bush (ed.), *T. S. Eliot: The Modernist in History*
50. Russell Goodman, *American Philosophy and the Romantic Tradition*
49. Eric J. Sundquist (ed.), *Frederick Douglass: New Literary and Historical Essays*
48. Susan Stanford Friedman, *Penelope's Web: Gender, Modernity, H.D.'s Fiction*
47. Timothy Redman, *Ezra Pound and Italian Fascism*
46. Ezra Greenspan, *Walt Whitman and the American Reader*
45. Michael Oriard, *Sporting with the Gods: The Rhetoric of Play and Game in American Culture*
44. Stephen Fredman, *Poet's Prose: The Crisis in American Verse, Second Edition*
43. David C. Miller, *Dark Eden: The Swamp in Nineteenth-Century American Culture*
42. Susan K. Harris, *Nineteenth-Century American Women's Novels: Interpretive Strategies*
41. Susan Manning, *The Puritan-Provincial Vision: Scottish and American Literature in the Nineteenth Century*
40. Richard Godden, *Fictions of Capital: Essays on the American Novel from James to Mailer*
39. John Limon, *The Place of Fiction in the Time of Science: A Disciplinary History of American Writing*
38. Douglas Anderson, *A House Undivided: Domesticity and Community in American Literature*
37. Charles Altieri, *Painterly Abstraction in Modernist American Poetry*
36. John P. McWilliams, Jr., *The American Epic: Transforming a Genre, 1770–1860*
35. Michael Davidson, *The San Francisco Renaissance: Poetics and Community at Mid-Century*
34. Eric Sigg, *The American T. S. Eliot: A Study of the Early Writings*
33. Robert S. Levine, *Conspiracy and Romance: Studies in Brockden Brown, Cooper, Hawthorne, and Melville*
32. Alfred Habegger, *Henry James and the "Woman Business"*
31. Tony Tanner, *Scenes of Nature, Signs of Man*
30. David Halliburton, *The Color of the Sky: A Study of Stephen Crane*
29. Steven Gould Axelrod and Helen Deese (eds.), *Rovert Lowell: Essays on the Poetry*

28. Robert Lawson-Peebles, *Landscape and Written Expression in Revolutionary America: The World Turned Upside Down*
27. Warren Motley, *The American Abraham: James Fenimore Cooper and the Frontier Patriarch*
26. Lyn Keller, *Re-Making it New: Contemporary American Poetry and the Modernist Tradition*
25. Margaret Holley, *The Poetry of Marianne Moore: A Study in Voice and Value*
24. Lothar Hönnighausen, *William Faulkner: The Art of Stylization in His Early Graphic and Literary Work*
23. George Dekker, *The American Historical Romance*
22. Brenda Murphy, *American Realism and American Drama, 1880–1940*
21. Brook Thomas, *Cross-examinations of Law and Literature: Cooper, Hawthorne and Melville*
20. Jerome Loving, *Emily Dickinson: The Poet on the Second Story*
19. Richard Gray, *Writing the South: Ideas of an American Region*
18. Karen E. Rowe, *Saint and Singer: Edward Taylor's Typology and the Poetics of Meditation*
17. Ann Kibbey, *The Interpretation of Material Shapes in Puritanism: A Study of Rhetoric, Prejudice, and Violence*
16. Sacvan Bercovitch and Myra Jehlen (eds.), *Ideology and Classic American Literature*
15. Lawrence Buell, *New England Literary Culture: From Revolution through Renaissance*
14. Paul Giles, *Hart Crane: The Contexts of "The Bridge"*
13. Albert Gelpi (ed.), *Wallace Stevens: The Poetics of Modernism*
12. Albert J. von Frank, *The Sacred Game: Provincialism and Frontier Consciousness in American Literature, 1630–1860*
11. David Wyatt, *The Fall into Eden: Landscape and Imagination in California*
10. Elizabeth McKinsey, *Niagara Falls: Icon of the American Sublime*
9. Barton Levi St. Armand, *Emily Dickinson and Her Culture: The Soul's Society*
8. Mitchell Breitwieser, *Cotton Mather and Benjamin Franklin: The Price of Representative Personality*
7. Peter Conn, *The Divided Mind: Ideology and Imagination in America, 1898–1917*
6. Marjorie Perloff, *The Dance of the Intellect: Studies in Poetry of the Pound Tradition*

The following titles are out of print:

5. Stephen Fredman, *Poet's Prose: The Crisis in American Verse*, first edition
4. Patricia Caldwell, *The Puritan Conversion Narrative: The Beginnings of American Expression*
3. John McWilliams, Jr., *Hawthorne, Melville, and the American Character: A Looking-Glass Business*
2. Charles Altieri, *Self and Sensibility in Contemporary American Poetry*
1. Robert Zaller, *The Cliffs of Solitude: A Reading of Robinson Jeffers*

Printed in the United States
19114LVS00003B/151-216

9 780521 478038